THE NATIONAL
GEOGRAPHIC TRAVELER

THE
CARIBBEAN

THE NATIONAL
GEOGRAPHIC TRAVELER

THE
CARIBBEAN

Nick Hanna & Emma Stanford

Contents

**Page 1: Conch shell
Pages 2–3: Walking on the
sand, Bonaire
Page 4: Girl dancing,
Antigua**

How to use this guide

See back flap for keys to text and map symbols.

The *National Geographic Traveler* brings you the best of the Caribbean in text, pictures, and maps. Divided into three main sections, the guide begins with an overview of history and culture. Following are 12 regional chapters with sites selected by the authors for their particular interest; each is treated in depth. Each chapter opens with its own contents list for easy reference.

The islands or island groups, and sites within them, are arranged geographically. Some island groups are further divided into two or three smaller areas. A map introduces each region, highlighting the

featured sites. Walks and drives, all plotted on their own maps, suggest routes for discovering an area. Features and sidebars offer detail on history, culture, or contemporary life. A More Places to Visit page rounds off some regional chapters.

The final section, Travelwise, lists essential information for the traveler—pre-trip planning, getting around, useful websites, and what to do in emergencies—plus a selection of hotels, restaurants, and shops.

To the best of our knowledge, site information is accurate as of the press date. However, it's always advisable to call ahead.

Color coding

62

Each region is color coded for easy reference. Find the region you want on the map on the front flap, and look for the color flash at the top of the pages of the relevant chapter. Information in **Travelwise** is also color coded to each region.

Visitor information

Bob Marley Museum

🅰 26 B3

✉ 56 Hope Rd.

☎ 876/927-9152

🕐 Closed Sun.

💲 $$$

Practical information is given in the side column by each major site (see key to symbols on back flap). The map reference gives the page number where the site is shown on a map, followed by the grid reference.

Further details include the site's address, telephone number, days closed, and entrance charge in a range from $ (under $4) to $$$$$ (over $25). Other sites have visitor information in italics and parentheses in the text.

TRAVELWISE

Color-coded region name

Town name

Hotel name, price range

Address, telephone & fax numbers

Brief description of hotel

Hotel facilities and credit card details

Restaurant name & price range

Address & telephone number

Brief description of restaurant

Restaurant facilities and credit card details

Hotel and restaurant prices

An explanation of the price ranges used in entries is given in the Hotels & Restaurants section (beginning on p. 353).

REGIONAL MAPS

- A locator map accompanies each regional map and shows the location of that region in the Caribbean.

WALKING TOURS

- An information box gives the starting and finishing points, time and length of walk, and places not to be missed along the route.

DRIVING TOURS

- An information box provides details that include starting and finishing points, places not to be missed along the route, the time and length of drive, or tips on terrain.

THE NATIONAL
GEOGRAPHIC TRAVELER

THE CARIBBEAN

About the authors

Nick Hanna is a graduate in Social Anthropology from Sussex University and has been a professional travel writer and photographer for 15 years. He has worked as a freelance writer for numerous national and international newspapers and magazines and has written nine guidebooks, including one that covered more than 200 tropical beaches around the world. He has also co-authored a book on the conservation of coral reefs and written extensively on the marine environment and scuba diving.

Being a seasoned island-hopper and experienced travel writer ensures that Emma Stanford is frequently drawn toward the Caribbean. She has, however, also written and edited several other works covering destinations including Hawaii, Florida, and Los Angeles, as well as Mediterranean port guides for the U.S. Navy.

History & culture

Churchgoers in Christchurch, St. Kitts

The Caribbean today

"A CARIBBEAN VACATION" IS ONE OF THE MOST EVOCATIVE PHRASES IN THE English language. The merest suggestion can unleash a stream of dreamy images featuring golden beaches, coconut palms, limpid azure seas, and hibiscus blooms accompanied by a sound track of tinkling steel-pan music or the rhythmic beat of reggae. The extended Caribbean show reel might incorporate coral-reef diving and rain forest trails, exploring colonial relics, and sailing through the Virgin Islands archipelago or the Grenadines. But however satisfying this momentary daydream may be, it cannot beat the reality, the feel of powder-soft coral sand between your toes, the squawk and colorful flash of a rare parrot in the rain forest, the taste of a fresh mango plucked straight from the tree.

The Caribbean is the quintessential escape from the grim, gray northern winter, an island paradise with guaranteed blue skies, sun-soaked lazy days and the option of a lively, reggae-fueled nightlife. If your idea of a perfect vacation involves succumbing body and soul to the languor of the tropics, relaxing by the pool or on a crescent of manicured sand with a frosted glass of planter's punch in hand, the Caribbean can deliver, no problem. Fortunately for more adventurous visitors, there is plenty more to the region than two-dimensional travel-poster imagery. To get a real feel for the islands and experience their third dimension—the varied landscapes, exotic flora and fauna, bustling waterfront towns, and friendly laid-back people—venture beyond the limited confines of the beach, resort, or cruise ship and dig a little deeper. In no time at all it will become apparent that there is no such thing as a homogeneous Caribbean entity. Each island has its own particular style shaped by a unique combination of geology, historical influences, and attitudes that can vary dramatically between neighbors separated by a few nautical miles.

CHOOSING AN ISLAND

Selecting the right combination of ingredients for a perfect Caribbean vacation needs a little research. Accommodations are a prime consideration: Should it be a romantic plantation hotel in St. Kitts and Nevis, or a family-friendly beach resort offering a wide range of activities and water sports? As a rule of thumb, the better the beaches the more developed the island, so expect a greater choice of accommodations and easy access to top beach destinations. Favorites with beach lovers include Aruba in the Netherlands Antilles; the Leeward Islands of Antigua and Anguilla; Barbados; the U.S. Virgin Islands; and Jamaica and the Dominican Republic, which both score highly on beaches and fabulous mountain scenery, as does Puerto Rico.

Caribbean activity holidays have taken off in a big way, with diving representing a major attraction for many visitors. The Cayman Islands are famously positioned on the brink of the Cayman Trench, offering dramatic wall diving. In the Netherlands Antilles, Bonaire, Saba, and Sint Eustatius forgo beaches for spectacular dive sites; or head to the Windward Islands for St. Lucia and up-and-coming Dominica.

The Windwards, which include Grenada and St. Vincent, are also celebrated for their lush rain forest highlands, which offer terrific hiking, while Trinidad and Tobago at the tail end of the island chain are an ornithologist's paradise. Interspersed with the Windwards are the French Caribbean islands of Guadeloupe and Martinique: These share many of the same physical characteristics and are the crucible for the eastern Caribbean's vibrant Creole culture. True Francophiles, on the other hand, might find themselves gravitating towards tiny St. Barthélemy, a distinctly European-style jet-set haunt reminiscent of the French Riviera.

Perfect Caribbean vacations come in all shapes and sizes, and this brief overview can only hint at the wealth of options available.

Snorkelers explore the translucent waters below a trimaran in the Netherlands Antilles.

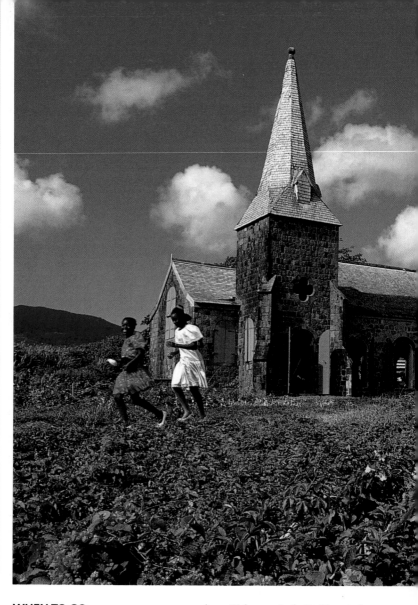

WHEN TO GO

The Caribbean region lies in the tropics, so temperatures are fairly consistent all year. Temperatures on the coast average 78–86°F (26–30°C) in the day and 59–64°F (15–18°C) at night, often tempered by cooling trade winds. At higher elevations, around 1,000 feet (300 m) above sea level or more, the temperature will drop a few degrees and may warrant packing a sweater for the evening or a light waterproof jacket for hikers heading into the mountains.

High season in the Caribbean is the generally cooler and drier period between December and April, when hotels charge their top rates. The humidity increases in the build-up to the rainy season, which lasts from June to November, though showers occur throughout the year and on a daily basis in the rain-forest highlands. After years as a winter-only destination, the early part of the wet season is becoming increasingly popular with visitors who want to sample a Caribbean vacation at more affordable prices. However, expect high humidity, as well as short, sharp downpours and a fair amount of cloudiness.

Though the Caribbean experiences few climatic extremes, the region is in the hurricane zone. These violent tropical storms rise off the coast of West Africa and gather strength as they cross the Atlantic, smashing into the islands with devastating force. In recent years, Hurricanes Luis and Marilyn in 1995 and Hurricane George in 1998 caused widespread

Churches such as this one in Christchurch, St. Kitts, are part of the fabric of Caribbean society.

destruction across the north of the region, while islands at the southern end of the island chain, such as Grenada and Trinidad, or Aruba, Bonaire, and Curaçao off the coast of Venezuela, are rarely troubled. The official hurricane season runs from June to November, though a traditional rhyme advises

View of Carriacou, one of the Grenadines. It lies about 23 miles (37 km) north of Grenada.

"June, too soon; July, stand by; September, remember; October, all over." Statistically, mid-September is the most likely time for a hurricane to pass through.

LAND & LANDSCAPES

The Caribbean islands form a 2,500-mile (4,000-km) arc from Cuba, which lies 90 miles (145 km) south of Key West on the southern tip of Florida, to Trinidad, just off the coast of Venezuela. The 50-plus islands, which do not include the Bahamas or far-flung Bermuda to the north of the region, and several thousand uninhabited cays, rocks, and reefs, encircle the million-square-mile (2.6-million-sq-km) Caribbean Sea. They are buffeted on their windward sides by the Atlantic Ocean, and the more sheltered leeward sides of the islands face the gentle Caribbean.

Early explorers christened the entire archi-pelago the Antilles, but today the islands are grouped into the Greater Antilles, or western Caribbean, consisting of Cuba (not included in this guide), the Cayman Islands, Jamaica, the Dominican Republic, Puerto Rico, and the Virgin Islands; and the Lesser Antilles, or eastern Caribbean.

The Lesser Antilles chain is further divided into the Leeward Islands and Windward Islands, interspersed with the French Antilles, the Dutch Windwards group of the Netherlands Antilles islands (Saba, Sint Eustatius, Sint Maarten/St. Martin), and Trinidad and Tobago. Barbados stands off on its own to the east of the Windward Islands. The Dutch Leewards, or ABCs (Aruba, Curaçao, and Bonaire), lie west of Trinidad along the Venezuelan coast.

GEOLOGY

The islands are poised on the brink of the Caribbean and Atlantic tectonic plates. The majority are volcanic in origin, though there are a few low-lying coral atolls such as the Cayman Islands and Anguilla, and the arid, desertlike Dutch Leewards. The oldest islands in the region lie to the north, where Jamaica, Hispaniola (Dominican Republic/Haiti), and Puerto Rico were formed around 70 million years ago.

In the eastern Caribbean, Montserrat, Guadeloupe, Martinique, Dominica, St. Lucia, St. Vincent, and Grenada remain volcanically active with bubbling mud pools and oozing, foul-smelling sulfur pits. Off the coast of Grenada, the submarine volcano Kick 'em Jenny is currently around 500 feet (150 m) below the surface and rising.

Giant philodendrons blanket the floor of the rain forests in St. Kitts.

FLORA & FAUNA

The Caribbean's mountain ranges are cloaked in dense rain forest, which grows with explosive rapidity in the fertile volcanic soil. True rain forest is the richest natural habitat on the planet and requires an annual rainfall in excess of 70 inches (178 cm), which the Caribbean islands receive courtesy of the Atlantic trade winds. In the hothouse atmosphere beneath the rain forest canopy, dozens of ferns, creepers, and bamboo flourish at the feet of giant buttress-trunked santinay trees, mahogany, gommier, and mahoe.

At higher elevations, in the montane or cloud forest, tree branches play host to a variety of bromeliads (which gain nutrients from the air) and orchids, while higher still the lichen-encrusted elfin forest opens onto grasslands frequently visited by cool, hazy drizzle and wisps of cloud.

Few mammals live in the rain forest, and indigenous species such as armadillos, opossums, and agoutis are rarely spotted. Reptiles, including tree frogs, iguanas, and dozens of species of small lizards, are a constant presence, as are winged insects such as butterflies and predatory mosquitoes. Though there are occasional sightings of non-venomous tree snakes, the sole poisonous snake is the fer de lance, found only on Martinique and St. Lucia.

Bird lovers are in for a treat in the Caribbean. Several species of rare indigenous parrot live in the Windward Islands, and the woodlands are also home to numerous varieties of hummingbirds, honeycreepers, tanagers, and cheeky bananaquits, which frequently leave the rain forest to feed on the brilliant tropical blooms in gardens.

Many species of herons, waders, ducks, and other wetland birds gather in the coastal mangrove swamps of Jamaica and Trinidad, while flamingo colonies can be found in Bonaire and Lago Enriquillo in the Dominican Republic. Seabirds, including boobies, magnificent frigatebirds, pelicans, and elegant scissortailed tropic birds, colonize rocky outcrops visible from the shore.

Just as the rain forest flourishes, so does the myriad variety of other plants and trees. While many islanders cultivate colorful flower gardens, botanical gardens are the best place to see a whole range of eye-catching heliconias and gingers, spice trees such as nutmeg and cinnamon, and flowering trees such as the yellow- or pink-blossomed poui, scarlet poinciana, and spreading immortelle, which flowers in January and February. ■

History & culture

CHRISTOPHER COLUMBUS FIRST SIGHTED THE ISLAND OF SAN SALVADOR IN the Bahamas on October 12, 1492, and sailed on into the Caribbean Sea intent on discovering a westward passage to the East Indian spice islands. The arrival of the European explorers opened the book on the recorded history of the region, and the islands were named the Antilles after the legendary island of Antillia, once thought to lie between Europe and the Americas. However, the Caribbean's first settlers had arrived several thousand years earlier—Amerindian tribes who paddled their canoes to the islands from Central America, or possibly Florida.

PRE-COLUMBIAN CARIBBEAN

The Stone Age Ciboney people (or Archaic Indians) were the earliest inhabitants of the Greater Antilles islands. Archaeological digs in Cuba have uncovered Ciboney sites about 6,000 years old, while relics in Hispaniola are reckoned to be about 4,000 years old. These nomadic hunter-gatherers lived off a nourishing and varied diet of fish and shellfish, birds, iguanas, and snakes, supplemented by roots and wild fruits, and they crafted tools and utensils from stone, wood, bone, and shells.

About 300 B.C. the first Arawak migrated to the islands. They are thought to have originated in the Amazon Basin, and then they pushed north to make the sea crossing from northeastern South America (present-day Venezuela and Guyana) to the southernmost of the Lesser Antilles. Gradually they moved up the island chain, and by the time Columbus appeared on the scene, the three major Arawak groups were populating the Greater Antilles islands and Bahamas: the Taino (Cuba, Jamaica, and Hispaniola), the Borequio or Borinquen (Puerto Rico), and the Lucayan (Bahamas).

The Arawak were more sophisticated than the Ciboney. They were farmers, cultivating cassava (for flour), yams, corn, beans, cocoa, peanuts, tobacco, and cotton. Skilled hunters and fishermen, they were also potters capable of producing earthenware for domestic and religious purposes.

Arawak society was well organized. Villages were generally built close to the shore, and each community was presided over by a cacique, or village chieftain, who was responsible for both the temporal and religious life of the village. At the center of the village was a large open-sided *carbet* (thatched shelter) where the cacique and men held council: It was out-of-bounds to women and children except by invitation to attend special ceremonies. Unmarried men could sleep here or in a separate carbet, stringing maybe a hundred hammocks from the roof. Religion played an important part in Arawak daily life. There were gods associated with food crops, fertility, and weather, and benevolent spirits that inhabited plants and animals. Religious ceremonies included snorting trance-inducing narcotics and dancing, as well as the worship of *zemi*, simple shapes or human and animal figures made of wood, bone, or stone. Arawak believed in the afterlife and took great care with burial rituals. The dead were placed in a squatting position and were equipped with personal belongings (the wives of important chieftains were buried alive), and food for the journey to Coyaba, a plentiful land of nonstop dancing and feasting.

ARRIVAL OF THE CARIB

After a thousand years, the Arawak's peaceful existence came to an abrupt end with the arrival of the Carib. Also from South America, the warlike Carib progressed northward through the Lesser Antilles, slaughtering Arawak men and assimilating women and children into their tribes. Though the proof is somewhat sketchy, the Carib had a reputation for cannibalism and were said to barbecue (a Carib word) their male victims, which included Europeans as they began to explore the region. The Carib were excellent marksmen with bows and arrows and fearlessly attacked

The mountainous island of Dominica was given its name by Christopher Columbus, who made landfall on a Sunday.

Spanish sailing ships from their wooden war canoes, or piragua (from which the simple pirogue fishing boats still used in the Windward Islands take their name). The Europeans pushed the Carib back into the rugged terrain of the Windward Islands, where they managed to hold out for more than 200 years, and a few mixed-blood survivors still live on Dominica and St. Vincent.

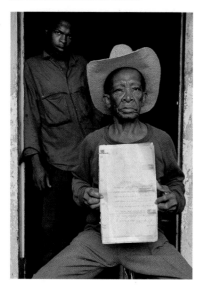

A resident of Jamaica's Cockpit Country holds a copy of the original constitution, dating back to the British colonial era.

EUROPEAN INVASION

Columbus made five voyages to the Caribbean in his attempt to discover a western route to the East Indies, stubbornly naming his finds the West Indies despite all the evidence to the contrary. On his fourth voyage, in 1502, he located the South American mainland and secured its vast mineral wealth for the Catholic kings of Spain.

During the early 16th century, Spanish settlements sprang up in Greater Antilles, first in Hispaniola, then Cuba, Jamaica, and Puerto Rico. The Arawak were enslaved, and within 50 years the indigenous population of these northern islands had been eradicated through warfare, disease, and transportation to work the mainland gold mines.

The Spanish treasure fleets making their way home to Europe acted as a magnet for pirates and privateers. Throughout the 16th and 17th centuries, French, English, and Dutch vessels preyed mercilessly on heavily laden armadas, lurking in the isolated cays of the Virgin Islands. The next logical step for the interlopers was to claim colonies of their own in the region, which became easier as Spanish influence declined in Europe during the 17th century. The British and French moved in on the Lesser Antilles, commencing a 250-year struggle for dominance in the eastern Caribbean, and the Dutch cannily selected islands with a view to their strategic importance on the trading routes used by their rivals.

COLONIAL ERA

Sugarcane was introduced to the Caribbean by Dutch planters from Brazil in the 1630s (see p. 308). From small-scale beginnings in Barbados, the enormously profitable trade in "white gold" triggered the rapid expansion of European colonialism in the region, and its labor-intensive cultivation brought an immediate demand for a cheap and inexhaustible workforce. Spanish settlers had imported small numbers of West African slaves to work their Caribbean plantations since the early days, but the sugar trade boosted numbers to unprecedented levels. Untold millions of Africans were sold into slavery and shipped across the Atlantic to work the plantations; many thousands died en route (see p. 248).

By the start of the 19th century, the importance of the Caribbean sugar trade dwindled as sugar beet production in Europe rose to satisfy local demand. The planters' profits decreased, and in 1808, the antislavery movement in Britain succeeded in banning the slave trade to the colonies. This was followed in 1834 by the Emancipation Act, which outlawed the ownership of slaves. The other European nations followed suit, and the former sugar colonies fell into a decline.

As the freed slaves abandoned the plantations, major producers such as Jamaica and Trinidad imported East Indian indentured laborers, but most islands slipped quietly into the doldrums, largely forgotten by their erstwhile colonial masters.

THE 20TH CENTURY

The Spanish-American War of 1898 introduced U.S. influence to the region. The U.S. claimed its first territory with the capture of Puerto Rico from Spain. It followed up this belated foray into Caribbean empire-building with the purchase of the U.S. Virgin Islands from Denmark in 1917.

The Caribbean islands experienced the

and oil in Trinidad all contribute to individual national economies.

COLONIAL LEGACY

As European colonists staked their claims to the Caribbean islands, each nation attempted in some degree to re-create a miniature home away from home in the sun. Thus, the Spanish Catholic heritage is readily apparent in the

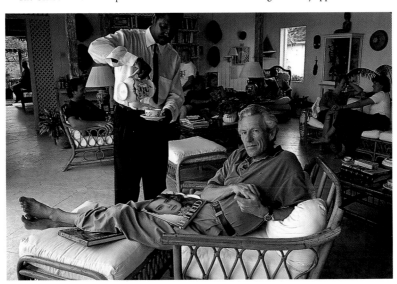

Lord Patrick Lichfield in his villa on the island of Mustique, in the Grenadines

trickle-down effect of the 1930s Great Depression, which deepened the region's economic problems and heralded the rise of grassroots labor movements. These in turn spearheaded the transition toward greater independence from Europe.

In 1962, Jamaica was the first British colony to achieve full independence, and Britain divested most of its colonies during the 1970s and 1980s. Several smaller islands opted to remain Crown Colonies, while others have joined the British Commonwealth as independent states. The Dutch and French retain closer ties with their colonies.

The region has 24 separate political entities and a stable though deeply fragmented political scene. Tourism is the economic mainstay, although sugar production in Barbados and Jamaica, bananas in the Windward Islands,

historic cities and churches of the Dominican Republic and Puerto Rico; the ex-British colonies in the Leeward and Windward Islands are rich in four-square stone Georgian architecture; the French islands retain an inimitable savoir faire combined with gastronomic flair; and in the Dutch Leewards, Curaçao's elegantly gabled buildings have been designated a World Heritage site.

Language is another legacy from colonial days. English is spoken in Jamaica, the Cayman Islands, the Virgin Islands, the Leeward and Windward Islands (Dominica and St. Lucia islanders traditionally speak a form of French patois among themselves), and Trinidad and Tobago. The Netherlands Antilles are bilingual in Dutch and English, while visitors to the French Antilles should be aware that little English is spoken outside more expensive hotels. Most Spanish-speaking Puerto Ricans also speak English, though a Spanish phrase book will prove essential in the Dominican Republic.

The great majority of Caribbean people are of African origin, and although African culture was subjugated by European customs during the colonial era, it did not disappear altogether. Freed from Old World dominance, the African heritage is now the strongest element of pan-Caribbean cultural trends. Its influence is unmistakable in music, traditional cooking, and the common animist superstitions that operate alongside traditional European religions in a very typically Caribbean compromise.

MUSIC

Music is, so they say, the heartbeat of the Caribbean, and it is certainly hard to ignore. The strains of calypso, reggae, soca (soul-calypso), and steel pan, throbbing bass dub

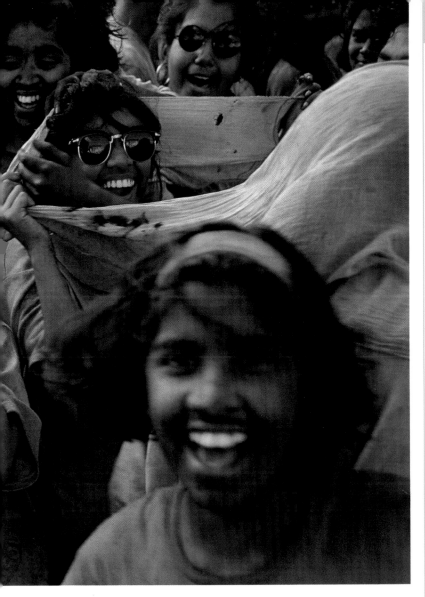

music booming out from dollar buses, and the dance rhythms of Puerto Rican salsa, merengue from the Dominican Republic, and zouk from the French Antilles, provide a catchy backdrop to the Caribbean experience.

Calypso is the grandfather of the music scene, with its origins buried way back in West African slave traditions. Forbidden to speak their native languages, slaves were, however, permitted to sing; the planters believed it helped them work faster. Yet unbeknownst to

Residents of multicultural Trinidad celebrate the Hindu festival of Phagwa in the San Juan district.

their employers, the slaves used song to keep alive the West African storytelling tradition and to pass along information and messages of protest concealed in allegorical terms. Today's calypsonians (calypso singers) are still judged not only on the music but also on the message they put across.

Trinidad is the home of calypso and steel-pan music, which originated in the dockyards of Port of Spain during World War II when oil drums were recycled for makeshift drums. Reggae emerged from the Kingston ghetto of Trenchtown with its most famous exponent, Bob Marley, in the 1970s.

Live music performances in clubs and bars are easy to find throughout the islands. Music festivals are also well worth tracking down. The most famous events include Jamaica's Reggae Sunsplash (Feb.), the St. Lucia International Jazz Festival (May), and the St. Kitts Music Festival (June).

CARNIVAL

Carnival is a magnificent explosion of elaborate costumes, music, singing, and dance that captures the creativity and natural exuberance of the Caribbean people. The date varies from island to island, but most carnivals take place in the run-up to Lent (Feb.–March), while others celebrate the end of the sugar harvest (July–Aug.) or the anniversary of emancipation.

Europeans introduced carnival to the Caribbean, marking the approach of Lent, a traditional period of Christian abstinence ("carnival" is derived from the Italian *carnevale*, meaning the removal of meat), with a hectic round of feasting and parties. After emancipation, former slaves hijacked the party season by introducing their own processions featuring folkloric characters, dancing, and African drumming, which, once banned by the authorities, became the core of the new Caribbean-style carnival.

The buildup to Lenten carnivals, such as the famous one in Trinidad (see p. 321), begins soon after Christmas, when musicians take part in the hotly contested qualifying heats, and band members and dancers participating in the main carnival processions put the final touches to their costumes.

Carnival begins in earnest on the Friday before Lent, and competitions held over the weekend decide the winners of the various calypso, steel-pan, and costume prizes. The main processions begin before dawn on Monday with a wild jump-up known as Jouvert (*jour ouvert* or daybreak in French Creole), followed by Tuesday's dazzling Mardi Gras parade.

FOOD & DRINK

Traditional Caribbean cooking is simple, nutritious, and filling, using plentiful local ingredients from fresh fish and seafood to a wide variety of tropical fruits and vegetables supplemented with chicken and a little red meat. Staple foods such as rice 'n' peas (the "peas" are red kidney beans), fried plantains (a variety of banana that is inedible raw), spinachlike callaloo, starchy breadfruit, and root vegetables (yam, eddoe, cassava) known as "ground provision" are found throughout the islands. Adventurous visitors should sample soursop, sugar and golden apples, tart tamarinds, and tiny plums. Markets are the best place to find and taste what is in season.

Guadeloupe and Martinique are renowned for Creole cuisine (see p. 238), while Puerto Rican specialties such as *lechón asao* (roast suckling pig), and *locrio* (a variation on paella) served in the Dominican Republic, show a distinctive Spanish influence. The Indian influence is unmistakable in Trinidad's curries and rotis (chapati envelopes filled with curried meat, seafood, or vegetables) that have now become a popular snack food in neighboring islands. Jamaican jerk is said to have been invented by runaway slaves who cooked in earth pits covered with branches.

RUM & BEER

Rum has been produced in the Caribbean since the 17th century, when sugar planters first distilled a spirit from molasses. Still made throughout the region, the best quality rums traditionally come from Barbados, Jamaica, Guadeloupe, and Martinique. While most islanders prefer their rum neat, visitors are more attracted to the long list of rum cocktails available, including piña coladas (flavored with pineapple and coconut), cuba libre (with cola), fruit daiquiris, and planter's punch (the original only has lime and cane juice, but added fruit juices are popular today). There are also delicious nonalcoholic fruit punches.

Wine is not produced in the Caribbean, so it is expensive. Local breweries, on the other hand, turn out some good lager-type beers. Particularly good are Banks from Barbados, Carib from Trinidad and franchises on several islands, Presidente from the Dominican Republic, and Red Stripe from Jamaica. ∎

The third largest island in the Caribbean after Cuba and the Dominican Republic/ Haiti, Jamaica offers a staggering display of magnificent waterfalls and mountain landscapes, fascinating historic sites, and a vibrant cultural life.

Jamaica

A Jamaican Rastafarian

Jamaica

THE ARAWAK INDIANS WHO SETTLED JAMAICA CHRISTENED IT XAYMACA (land of wood and water). Despite the island's larger population today, the description is still largely accurate. The Spanish occupation from 1510 onward led to the decimation of the native population and the arrival of the first slaves. Most Jamaicans can trace their ancestry to those slaves, as well as those brought over under later British rule. Jamaican culture is a vibrant fusion of African and European influence.

Under British rule the slave trade boomed, providing a labor force for the sugar plantations. Jamaica also served as a haven for pirates and buccaneers, encouraged by the British to make Kingston's Port Royal their base for harassing the Spanish fleets. Slave rebellions were also a prominent feature of Jamaica's history until British emancipation in 1834, four years after the British parliament had abolished the slave trade.

The island became a British Crown Colony in 1866, and during the 1890s the first tourists arrived on banana boats from North America. The Depression of the 1930s led to bloodshed and riots as the economy faltered, giving birth to the country's first labor union and the socialistic People's National Party (P.N.P.) led by Norman Manley (1893–1969). Universal suffrage was granted in 1944, and in 1962 Jamaica won full independence.

Jamaica's culture is a potent brew of fierce national pride, reggae and Rastafarians, sassy attitudes, and snatches of the local dialect (known as Jamaica Talk). The poverty and absence of opportunity that led to the political unrest and occasional riots of the past still affect much of the island.

With about one million visitors a year, Jamaica has one of the largest tourism industries in the Caribbean—and that means it has one of the widest selections of accommodations, from luxury villas or budget cottages on the beach to private mountain retreats.

Jamaica's 4,244 square miles (10,992 sq km) embrace an enormous variety of landscapes. Like many of its neighbors, the island evolved from a broad arc of volcanoes

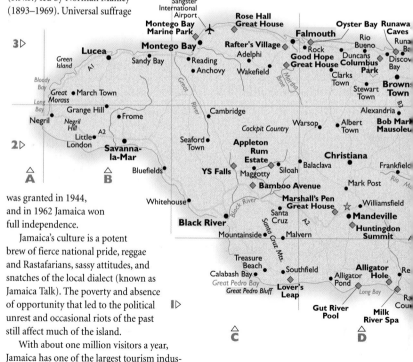

rising from the seabed billions of years ago. This igneous rock forms the Blue Mountains, which traverse the eastern third of the island and reach their summit at the 7,399-foot (2,256-m) Blue Mountain Peak. The land surrounding the Blue Mountains is capped by limestone plateaus that cover about two-thirds of the island. Over the centuries, rivers have carved sinkholes, caves, and deeply rutted gullies in the limestone—most visible in the Cockpit Country.

An offshore coral reef shields the white, sandy beaches of Jamaica's north shore, where there are many resorts. The eastern coastline, unprotected from the ocean swells, is far more rugged and dramatic. With a few exceptions, the south and west coasts are typified by volcanic black-sand beaches.

Jamaica's mist-shrouded mountains are the source of more than a hundred rivers. The longest, the 44-mile (71-km) Black River, flows out to sea on the southwest coast.

The island's lush vegetation includes more than 3,000 varieties of trees and plants. Of these, about 800 are indigenous, including 200 species of orchids, 550 types of ferns, and 60 species of bromeliads.

Almost half of Jamaica is under cultivation. Before Europeans arrived, the only native fruits were guava, pineapple, and soursop. Successive colonists introduced breadfruit, sugarcane, coconuts, and ackee, a yellow fruit that, when combined with saltfish (cod), is a national dish. Today, huge plantations cloak the landscape with sugarcane, bananas, cocoa, coffee, rice, tobacco, and citrus fruits.

Besides agriculture and tourism the other mainstay of Jamaica's economy is bauxite, which has provided towns such as Mandeville (see pp. 54–59) with considerable wealth. The "red gold" is extracted from the earth then converted into aluminum.

Jamaica has a population of about 2.5 million, just under a third of whom live in the capital, Kingston. ∎

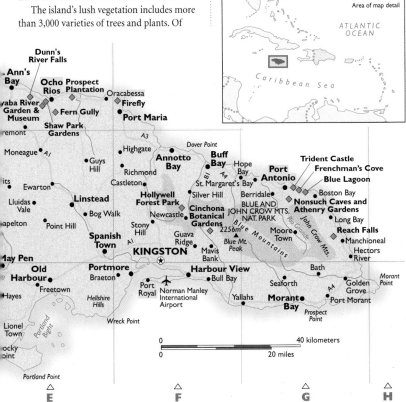

Kingston

Kingston
◪ 25 F2
Visitor information
✉ 2 St. Lucia Ave.
☎ 876/922-9200
🕐 Closed weekends

THROBBING WITH ENERGY AND SPIRIT, JAMAICA'S dynamic capital is home to almost one million people. The largest English-speaking city in the Caribbean, it is also one of the most important cultural and political hubs in the region.

Kingston owes its growth to its magnificent natural harbor, the seventh largest in the world. The British recognized its strategic importance, building no fewer than five forts on the sandspit of Port Royal (see pp. 30–31) in the 17th century. When an earthquake destroyed Port Royal on June 7, 1692, its inhabitants fled to Kingston, and the concentration of economic and political power in the city eventually led to the capital being transferred here from Spanish Town in 1872. The city kept on growing, and today it spreads into the foothills of the Blue Mountains.

The heart of Kingston is the downtown area, which embraces the waterfront, historic sites, and to the west some of the city's most notorious slums. In the center is the **Parade,** once the British army's parade ground. Today it reverberates with the sound of reggae as vendors of cane juice, cassettes, bus tickets, and baubles ply their wares. The green heart of the Parade is **Sir William Grant Park,** a

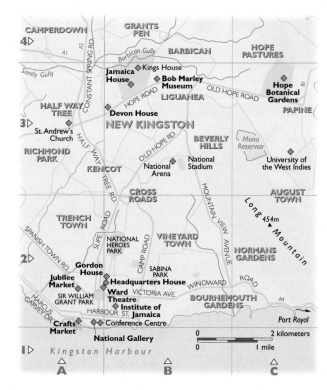

leafy square with a fountain and statues of Queen Victoria, Norman Manley (see p. 24), and Alexander Bustamante (1884–1977), founder of the country's first trade union. On the north side of the Parade is the **Ward Theatre** *(Tel 876/ 922-0453),* an elegant building, completed in 1911, which hosts performances by amateur dramatic groups as well as the National Dance Theater Company. To the west of the Parade is the colorful **Jubilee Market,** a good place to sample some of the country's exotic fruits and vegetables.

A few minutes' stroll east from here on Duke Street is **Headquarters House,** which was built in 1755 by a wealthy local merchant, Thomas Hibbert, as part of a wager with three other rich friends to see who could construct the most elegant building to win the attractions of a local beauty. Hibbert lost, but the winning house is no longer in existence. Headquarters House, with its handsome white facade and graceful fan window, has served as both a military headquarters and as home to Jamaica's legislative assembly, which met here between 1872 and 1960. Today it houses the offices of the National Heritage Trust, but you can visit the rest of the building, which includes the debating chamber and a lookout on the roof with splendid views of Kingston, the mountains, and the harbor. Next door stands **Gordon House** *(Corner of Beeston & Duke Sts., Tel 876/922-0200),* where the House of Representatives and the Senate meet. *(Entrance to the public gallery is free during debates.)*

Jubilee Market
- 26 A2
- Spanish Town Rd.
- Closed weekends

Headquarters House
- 26 B2
- 79 Duke St.
- 876/922-1287
- Closed weekends

The ornate Ward Theatre was built on the site of the former Theatre Royal.

Fronting Kingston Harbour, the waterfront was once embellished with fingerlike piers jutting into the sea, but these were swept away when the area was redeveloped in the 1960s and a new shipping port was created farther west. **Ocean Boulevard** along the waterfront is lined with high-rise office buildings, shops, hotels, and apartments. About midway you'll find the bronze sculpture "Negro Aroused," a famous work by Edna Manley (1900–1987), the former wife of politician Norman Manley. It captures the spirit of the 1930s labor movement in its depiction of a bowed worker uncoiling from the chains of bondage. The original bronze is in the **National Gallery,** the highlight of the waterfront area. Its impressive permanent collection includes numerous wood carvings (particularly noteworthy are those by Edna Manley), African-style and Rastafarian paintings, landscapes, and contemporary photography covering a variety of Jamaican themes.

Walk two blocks west to the **Crafts Market** (*Ocean Blvd., closed Sun.*), a good place to hunt for carvings, souvenirs, T-shirts, and jewelry. In the other direction on East Street is the **Institute of Jamaica,** which was founded in 1879 for the "encouragement of literature, science and art." The institute houses the **National Library,** which holds one of the largest collections of historical documents in the Caribbean, as well as the **Museum of Natural History,** which chronicles the arrival on the island of coconuts, bananas, sugarcane, and other plants that now form the backbone of Jamaica's agricultural sector.

NEW KINGSTON

Poised midway between downtown and the city's uptown area, **New Kingston,** is the **National Heroes Park,** a 75-acre (30-ha) open space that was once the city's race track. After independence the government converted part of it into a park to celebrate the country's national heroes, including Norman Manley and Alexander Bustamante (the founders of modern Jamaican politics); Sam Sharpe (1801–1832) and Paul Bogle (died 1865), both Baptist preachers involved in slave rebellions; Marcus Garvey (1887–1940), father of the Black Power movement; and Nanny, a legendary 18th-century leader of the Maroons. Norman Manley, Alexander Bustamante, and Marcus Garvey are buried here. Simón Bolívar (1783–1830) and Antoneo Maceo (1845–1896), independence leaders in South America and Cuba, are also honored in the park.

New Kingston extends from the busy crossroads of Half Way Tree Road right up into the Blue Mountains. Wealthy merchants settled this district in the 18th century when they fled the noise and squalor of downtown to build large residences surrounded by grazing land for their horses and cattle.

Today this relatively gentrified zone houses both businesses and residents, and most visitors to the capital choose to stay in hotels around here.

Many people make a pilgrimage to this part of Kingston to visit the **Bob Marley Museum,** the most popular attraction in the city. The house was a recording studio for Marley's Tuff Gong record label, as well as his home from 1975 until his death from brain cancer in 1981. A statue of Marley with his favorite guitar and soccer ball stands at the entrance. (This is the only thing that may be photographed; cameras are prohibited elsewhere in the house.) The one-hour guided tour

---

Allow an hour to explore the Bob Marley Museum.

National Gallery
- 🅰 26 A2
- ✉ Roy West Bldg.
- ☎ 876/922-8540
- 🕐 Closed weekends
- 💲 $$$

Institute of Jamaica
- 🅰 26 B2
- ✉ 12 East St.
- ☎ 876/922-0620
- 🕐 Closed weekends

National Heroes Park
- 🅰 26 B2
- ✉ Duke St.
- ☎ 876/922-0620
- 🕐 Closed Sun.

Bob Marley Museum
- 🅰 26 B3
- ✉ 56 Hope Rd.
- ☎ 876/927-9152
- 🕐 Closed Sun.
- 💲 $$$

leads you through the grounds and house, which contains memorabilia of Marley's life, including his gold and platinum records, his favorite denim stage shirt, and several unusual guitars. There's also a re-creation of Wail'n'Soul—the shack in the poor Trenchtown area that was Marley's first house in Kingston. From here he first sold his records. Two rooms are wallpapered with Marley's international press clippings, and another still has bullet holes in the wall from a failed assassination attempt in 1976. The tour ends with a film about his life, screened in the room that once housed the Tuff Gong studio. There are also a photo gallery and several souvenir shops.

The other main draw in New Kingston is **Devon House.** The house was built in 1881 by Jamaica's first black millionaire, George Stiebel (1820–1896), who made his fortune in gold mining in South America. He lived here until his death. This fine Georgian-style mansion has been refurbished with four-poster beds, chandeliers, Chippendale cabinets, and other original antiques. The courtyard,

which was formerly slaves' quarters, houses upscale craft souvenir shop, and an excellent bakery and ice cream shop. A restaurant occupies the former stables.

Also along Hope Road you can peek through the gates of **Jamaica House,** the prime minister's office, which stands amid expansive lawns, manicured shrubbery, and graceful palms.

The **Hope Botanical Gardens,** said to be the largest botanical gardens in the Caribbean, stretch along the outskirts of New Kingston. Located on the former estate of Maj. Richard Hope, who arrived in Jamaica with Oliver Cromwell's army in 1655, the 200-acre (81-ha) gardens feature pathways meandering between pond and lakes, greenhouses, and numerous flowering trees and shrubs. The grounds also contain elements to keep children amused—an aquarium, small zoo, and playground. Although neglected in recent years (and still suffering from the effects of Hurricane Gilbert), the gardens are popular with Kingstonians escaping the heat of the city on weekends. ■

The Hope Botanical Gardens offer respite from the heat of the city.

Devon House

🏛 26 B3
✉ 26 Hope Rd.
☎ 876/929-7029
🕐 Closed Sun.
💲 $

Hope Botanical Gardens

🏛 26 C3
✉ Old Hope Rd.
☎ 876/927-1257

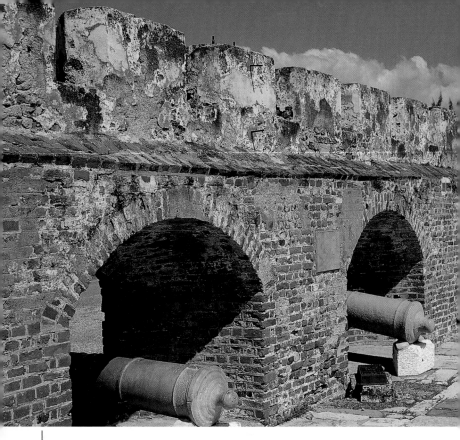

Port Royal

Originally known as Fort Cromwell, Fort Charles was renamed on the restoration of King Charles II of England in 1660.

IN THE 17TH CENTURY PORT ROYAL WAS AMONG THE wealthiest ports in the Caribbean. Built on a small island in Kingston Harbour and connected to the mainland by a causeway (the Palisadoes), it was first used by the Spanish to repair their ships. When the British captured Jamaica in 1655, they strengthened its defenses by building five forts. The combined nautical and military legacies create a powerful atmosphere in the present-day fishing village.

Port Royal

25 FI

Traders took advantage of this safe haven, and Port Royal grew to a city of some 6,000 people. The wealth from trade and pirate booty turned it into one of the richest cities in the Caribbean, with fine brick houses, piped water—and innumerable brothels, gambling dens, and taverns.

The Catholic Church condemned it as "the wickedest city in Christendom," and for many people it must have seemed like judgment day when a massive earthquake on June 7, 1692, sent most of the city to the watery depths, killing 2,000 people and sinking all the ships in the harbor. Most of the inhabitants fled to Kingston. Port Royal suffered further from a major fire in 1702 and another earthquake in 1907.

Today Port Royal is a quiet fishing village and the home base of the

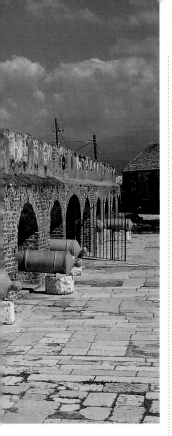

1779–1780. Between the fort and the water is Giddy House, a former ammunition store that now tilts at an alarming angle. Next to it is a massive gun emplacement, the Victoria and Albert Battery, which was also pitched earthward by the severe earthquake of 1692.

Other places of interest in Port Royal include the **Old Naval Hospital,** a stone-and-cast-iron building dating from 1819 and now in disrepair. **St. Peter's Church** is noteworthy for the tombstone in its graveyard inscribed with the tale of Frenchman Lewis Gaddy, who was swallowed up by the earthquake but was then spat out by an aftershock into the sea.

The submerged portion of Port Royal, covering 33 acres (13 ha), now lies in depths of up to 40 feet (12 m). Excavations by Texas A&M University's Institute of Nautical Archaeology have turned up a watch whose hands stopped at 11:43 a.m. on June 7, 1692, thus giving a precise time for the earthquake. Port Royal belongs to an elite group of archaeological sites that have stayed undisturbed over the centuries: Everyday items such as furniture, tableware, pots and pans, tools, and shoes remain more or less in place as they were left—except, of course, that they are now underwater.

Plans are now underway to develop the sunken city as an attraction for divers and to redevelop the entire Port Royal area as a port of call for cruise ships, with actors in period costumes interpreting life in this 17th-century pirate stronghold. The ambitious project will include a new pier, a renovated museum, and restaurants and shops. The aim is to create one of the most exciting historical and cultural attractions in the Caribbean—with a service industry to match. ■

A tombstone commemorates Lewis Gaddy, who died in the earthquake of 1692.

Fort Charles
✉ Off Elizabeth Ave.
☎ 876/967-8438
$ $$$

Jamaican Coast Guard. You can reach Port Royal by car or ferry from Kingston *(for ferry details contact Kingston visitor information, Tel 876/929-9200)*, and it is easily navigable on foot *(allow 2–3 hours).* Of the buildings that survive, one of the most impressive is **Fort Charles,** the first of the five forts built around the port. Although it is now landlocked, due to the earthquake, its embrasures still feature cannon pointing out to sea. Within the fort is the **Maritime Museum,** which depicts the history of Port Royal with artifacts dredged up from the sunken city. To one side of the fort's parade ground stands a raised wooden platform known as Nelson's Quarterdeck. The young commander kept watch here against the threat of a French invasion fleet in

Blue Mountains

Named after the hazy blue mist that can envelop the peaks, this wilderness is the most biologically diverse area in the country.

Blue & John Crow Mountains National Park

 25 G2

☎ 876/997-8044 or 876/997-8069

ONE OF THE LONGEST CONTINUOUS MOUNTAIN RANGES in the Caribbean, the majestic Blue Mountains dominate the eastern third of Jamaica, rising to a height of 7,399 feet (2,256 m) at Blue Mountain Peak. On these slopes some of the world's finest coffee is grown—sharing space with a profusion of verdant forest.

Bordering the eastern fringes of Kingston, the Blue Mountains form a cooling contrast with the sprawling metropolis below. High rainfall feeds the lush vegetation, which includes towering trees shrouded in a green veil of epiphytic lichens, mosses and bromeliads, prolific bamboo and ferns, and more than 500 species of flowering plants. The mountains are also home to the largest butterfly in the Americas (the giant swallowtail), coneys (a type of rabbit),

snakes, tree frogs, neotropical birds, and numerous rare species.

However, they are under threat from illegal logging and dumping, erosion, forest fires, and water pollution. Hurricane Gilbert also took its toll in 1988. The **Blue and John Crow Mountains National Park** was established in 1993 to protect 193,000 acres (78,100 ha) of this area.

The most accessible parts are toward the park's western end, reached via Rte. B1, which runs

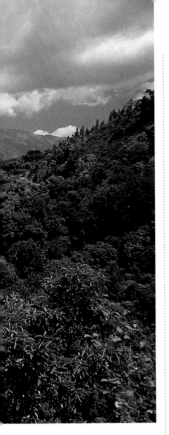

5,000 feet (1,524 m), contain a wide range of imported and endemic trees, shrubs, and flowering plants. The road is tortuous, and you will need a four-wheel-drive vehicle.

More easily accessible is the **Hollywell Forest Park** (*Tel 876/997-8044 or 876/997-8069*) 2 miles (3 km) north of Newcastle, which covers 300 acres (121 ha) of magical montane forest with pines, eucalyptus, soapwood, and dog-wood trees, often shrouded in mist and alive with birdsong.

The area is also famed for its coffee, introduced to the Blue Mountains in the 18th century. The high-quality beans grown here soon commanded top prices in Europe, but the industry suffered a setback with the abolition of slavery in 1834, and hurricanes took their toll in the following century. In the 1950s the government stepped in to save the plantations; it established guidelines ensuring that only coffee grown just below 5,000 feet (1,525 m) could use the Blue Mountain label.

At the **Mavis Bank Coffee Factory** a tour of the plant is rounded off with a cup of the country's finest brew. And if you feel like a liqueur after your coffee, visit the famous **World's End Liqueur Factory,** one of the top makers of flavored rums in the country. ∎

from Kingston to Buff Bay in the north. The **Cinchona Botanical Gardens** (*Tel 876/974-7075*) were established in 1886 to provide quinine from cinchona trees. The project failed, but the gardens then became a botanical research center. The 10-acre (4-ha) grounds, clinging to the ridge at an elevation of

Connoisseurs consider Blue Mountain coffee the finest in the world .

Mavis Bank Coffee Factory
- 🅰 25 F2
- ✉ Mavis Bank, St. Andrew
- ☎ 876/977-8013
- 🕐 Closed weekends; Mon.–Fri. by appt. only
- 💲 $$$

World's End Liqueur Factory
- 🅰 25 F2
- ✉ Guava Ridge
- ☎ 876/926-8888

Sports & activities

Hiking: The Blue and John Crow Mountains National Park features more than 30 hiking trails; many of them follow old mule tracks. The most spectacular views are from the 7-mile (11-km) track to Blue Mountain Peak, from the village of Mavis Bank. You can hike the trails in the Hollywell Forest Park by yourself, but a guide is recommended and several organizations can arrange this for you. Blue and John Crow Mountains National Park office (*Guava Ridge, St. Andrew, c/o P.O. Box 2779, Kingston 8, Tel 876/977-8044*); or the Jamaica Conservation and Development Trust (*95 Dumbarton Ave., Kingston 10, Tel 876/960-2848, www.greenjamaica.com*) ∎

Port Antonio

Port Antonio

▲ 25 G2

Visitor information

✉ City Center Plaza

☎ 876/993-3051

PORT ANTONIO'S GLORY DAYS, BOTH AS A BANANA PORT and an upscale resort, are well behind it, and this quiet backwater is now mostly frequented by independent travelers who use it as a base for exploring the natural attractions in the area.

Take in the terrific panorama of the port, sandwiched between its two harbors, from the aptly named Bonnie View Hotel *(Tel 876/993-2752)* that sits atop Richmond Hill to the south of Port Antonio. The hotel, built in 1943, also offers horseback riding on its 25-acre (10-ha) grounds and hiking trails into the Blue Mountains.

Boundbrook Wharf, on Port Antonio's western harbor, was once Jamaica's main transshipment port for bananas and the inspiration for the "banana boat" song "Day O" ("Work all night for a drink of rum, daylight come and me wanna go home"). Nowadays fruit is loaded mechanically.

The downtown area is easy to navigate, centering as it does on a central square and clock tower; alongside the square you'll find the busy Musgrave market. From here it is a short stroll up to **Titchfield Peninsula,** which bisects the two harbors, at the end of which you'll find the crumbling remains of **Fort George** *(Fort George St.),* dating back to 1791 and now part of Titchfield High School. The fort was once one of the most powerful in the region, but little remains except for a few cannon and parts

Panorama of Port Antonio, with Navy Island offshore

of its 10-foot-thick (3-m) walls. You might like to look in at the venerable **DeMontevin Lodge** (21 Fort George St., Tel 876/993-2604), an ornate colonial relic dating from 1881 that has seen better days but retains its elegant Victorian gingerbread architecture and wood-paneled interior.

Back in the town center you can turn your attention toward an unusual building on the waterfront known as **St. George's Village** (Gideon Ave.). Conceived and built by local architect Ziggy Fahmi, this striking new structure resembles a complex of town houses from different eras in history. Its interior conceals two levels of shops, one of the best art galleries in Jamaica (representing the works of well-known Jamaican artists, such as locally born Ken Adendana Spencer), a café, and an imaginatively designed restaurant upstairs

with views over the bay. Its success depends, alas, on cruise ships, which may never return.

Across from St. George's Village is the redbrick **Christ Church** (Gideon Ave.), a neo-Romanesque structure built on the site of an earlier church in the mid-19th century. It has some impressive memorials dating back to the 17th century.

Just offshore from Port Antonio (reached via a five-minute ferry ride from West Pier) is **Navy Island,** which was a barracks for the British Navy in the 18th century. Errol Flynn bought the 60-acre (24-ha) property when he arrived in Port Antonio and allegedly used it as a hideaway to court Hollywood starlets. His former home is now a hotel, the **Admiralty Club** (Tel 876/993-2667). It has a gallery dedicated to Flynn, displaying posters and stills from his movies, and offers facilities for day visitors, including tennis courts and two beaches (one is clothes optional). A nature trail winds its way through Navy Island's verdant vegetation. The island now belongs to the government, which plans to sell it for development.

Four miles (6.5 km) south of Port Antonio and easiest reached by car are the **Nonsuch Caves and Athenry Gardens.** Your guide will first take you through the caves themselves, which feature impressive formations (including shapes resembling various figures and animals that have been given names) and caverns, as well as a bat colony hanging from the ceiling in the lofty Cathedral Cavern.

Well-lit concrete paths and steps lead through the caves and out into the 3-acre (1-ha) gardens of well-tended tropical plants and flowers. The café on the promontory, 600 feet (183 m) above sea level, commands a breathtaking view of the coastline and Port Antonio. ■

Nonsuch Caves & Athenry Gardens
🄼 25 G2
✉ Nonsuch, Portland
☎ 876/993-3749
💲 $$$

The dramatic Nonsuch Caves are a popular excursion from Port Antonio.

Around Port Antonio

Frenchman's Cove

25 G2

San San Beach

$

THE COASTLINE TO THE EAST OF PORT ANTONIO embraces some of the prettiest coastal scenery in the country, with rugged headlands interspersed with golden beaches and some fine hotels in choice locations. (Day visitors usually must pay a small charge, which also includes use of the hotel facilities.)

Rafting on the Rio Grande, a popular pastime

Heading east from town on Rte. A4, the first major landmark is extraordinary **Trident Castle,** a fantasy creation that is part of the neighboring Trident Hotel *(P.O. Box 119, Port Antonio, Tel 876/993-2602).* About a mile (1.5 km) from here you come to **Frenchman's Cove,** a gorgeous little beach framed by rocky headlands and skirted by a cool mountain stream. Another 0.75 mile (1 km) along is **San San Beach,** a narrow strip fronting a broad bay with reasonable snorkeling on the reef, and it is an easy swim across to a small beach on jewel-like Pelew Island, on the east side of the bay.

Just past San San Beach is the **Blue Lagoon** (*Tel 876/993-8491*). Surrounded by forest foliage, the lagoon is a limestone sinkhole fed by underground streams. This scenic spot was indeed the setting for the Brooke Shields movie *Blue Lagoon* (1980) as well as *Club Paradise* (1986), which was filmed in the restaurant/bar hanging over the water's edge. It is a lovely spot for a swim and lunch.

Two miles (3 km) east is **Dragon Bay** (*P.O. Box 176, Port Antonio, Tel 876/993-8751*). At the hotel you can have a drink at the beach bar where Tom Cruise displayed his bartending talents in the film *Cocktail* (1988).

Continuing on, you then reach **Boston Bay,** a big public beach famous for its jerk cooking (see p. 38). This is primarily a fishing beach, but in rough weather the incoming swells can create good conditions for surfing. The main road and the beach are lined with stands selling authentic, sizzling jerk chicken, pork, or seafood.

It is 2 miles (3 km) to the next major stopping point of **Long Bay,** a broad expanse of sand that is considered to be Jamaica's top surfing spot. A few beach bars, guesthouses, and discos have sprung up along the road to cater to independent travelers, creating a laid-back atmosphere. The beach, however, is not in the same league as the surf. Unless you're a surfer, or you just like the rollers, there is little reason to linger.

One of the highlights of this part of the coast is lovely **Reach Falls,** accessible via a well-paved road from Manchioneal on the coast. The falls are part of the Driver River, which tumbles down from the John Crow Mountains into a series of cascades and crystal-clear pools where you can swim. The entrance fee includes a guided walk up to the falls. Although not as spectacular as Dunn's River (see p. 42), it has far fewer people here, and it is a lovely spot to while away an hour or two.

Extending deep into Portland behind Port Antonio is the **Rio Grande Valley,** a lush wilderness overlooked by the splendor of the Blue Mountains. The main attraction is rafting along the Rio

Frenchman's Cove is ideal for picnics.

RIO GRANDE RAFTING

You can book a trip on the Rio Grande from your resort or drive yourself to the put-in point at Berridale and buy your ticket there *(Rio Grande Attractions, Tel 876/993-2778).* Arrange for an insured driver to deliver your car to the finishing point at the Rafter's Rest restaurant in St. Margaret's Bay. Do not under any circumstances hire unofficial drivers. ■

Blue Lagoon,
Dragon Bay,
Reach Falls
Ⓜ 25 G2
Ⓢ $

Grande, one of Jamaica's largest rivers. Originally the bamboo rafts were used by local farmers to carry their bananas to Port Antonio, but when Errol Flynn arrived here, he started organizing raft races for his friends; the trip has now become one of the area's most popular attractions. The three-hour trip from Berridale to the coast passes through some delightfully unspoiled scenery—riverside villages, gorges, and shoals. The 30-foot-long (9-m) rafts are built from lengths of bamboo lashed together, with a seat for two at the back, and poled along by a raft captain standing at the front. There are stops for swimming and to buy snacks or drinks from vendors. ■

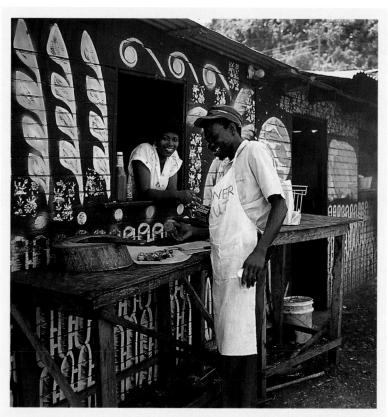

Jerk chicken makes a tasty lunchtime or evening meal.

Jerk cooking

Jerk cooking may have originated in the 17th century with the Maroons (see p. 48), who hunted wild boar in the mountains and then marinated the meat in a spicy sauce to preserve it. Today jerk cuisine is found all over the island and is one of Jamaica's most distinctive styles of cooking. The meat (usually chicken or pork) is marinated in a special blend of spices (including peppers, cinnamon, pimento, and nutmeg) and then slowly grilled over a pimento wood fire. Boston Beach is a good place to buy a few bottles of the marinade to take home. ■

Oracabessa

AS YOU PASS THROUGH THIS TRANQUIL VILLAGE, 15 MILES (24 km) east of Ocho Rios on Rte. A3, it is hard to imagine anything much happening. Oracabessa (from the Spanish for "golden head") was a busy port at the beginning of the 1900s, but since the demise of Jamaica's banana exporting industry in the late 1960s it has slumbered peacefully, with life revolving around its daily market. In its heyday Oracabessa attracted royalty, literati, and politicians.

Oracabessa

🅰 25 E3

Oracabessa has an interesting literary heritage, and it can thank two famous writers for this. The first is the English playwright Sir Noel Coward (1899–1973), who built a house in the hills midway between Oracabessa and neighboring Port Maria in the 1950s. His home until his death, **Firefly** has now been restored to look as it did when he lived here, with his paintings on easels in the studio, two grand pianos back to back in the music room, and the table set for lunch as it was on the day the Queen Mother visited on February 28, 1965. Coward's simple grave on the hillside overlooks one of the most stupendous views on the island, taking in the Blue Mountains to the south and the coastline to the north, which stretches into the Caribbean Sea.

The second writer is Ian Fleming (1908–1964), who wrote most of the James Bond novels in **Goldeneye,** the house he built on the outskirts of Oracabessa. Fleming wintered here every year from 1946 to 1964, and his guests included such notables as Graham Greene (1904–1991), Truman Capote (1924–1984), and Sir Anthony Eden (1897–1977). The house now belongs to Island Outpost, and although not open to visitors, it can be rented. On 70 acres (28 ha) of reclaimed land below Goldeneye's headland, Island Outpost is now creating an ambitious tourism project in which the local community is actively involved. The plan includes building a new beach, a low-density resort, and a series of shops, bars, and restaurants. ■

Noel Coward entertained royalty and celebrities at his home, Firefly.

Firefly

🅰 25 F3

✉ Grants Pen, St. Mary

☎ 876/997-7201

🕐 Closed Sun.

💲 $$$

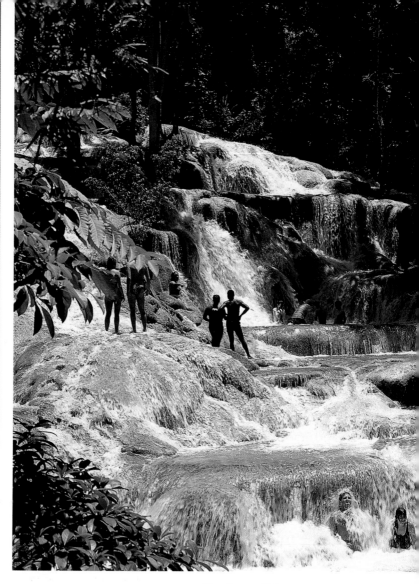

Ocho Rios

Ocho Rios
🗺 25 E3
Visitor information
✉ Ocean Village
   Shopping Centre
☎ 876/974-2570

SITUATED MIDWAY ALONG JAMAICA'S NORTH SHORE, OCHO Rios is the country's second largest resort, after Montego Bay. The town, which lies at the intersection of the main north coast route and Rte. A3 to Kingston, is a popular getaway spot for residents of the capital, just a 90-minute drive away. But far more visitors disembark from the cruise ships that moor at the dock at the western end of the bay. And, like many of Jamaica's coastal resorts, Ocho Rios has some superb hotels, such as the long-standing Jamaica Inn, tucked away in quiet coves on either side of town.

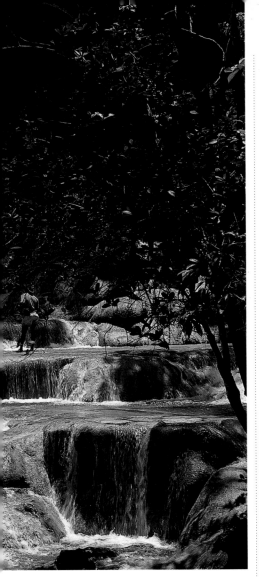

you can expect to find the real Jamaica. The town sprawls around the bay and is disfigured by the bauxite-loading terminal looming above the cruise ship dock.

In the 19th century, Ocho Rios was surrounded by plantations, principally for sugarcane and pimentos. In the 1920s an old plantation house at Shaw Park became the country's first upscale hotel, and it was soon followed by several others—but the resort's development was held back by the absence of an accessible beach. Meanwhile high levels of the valuable mineral bauxite, used to produce aluminum, were found in the local soil. By the 1960s this had led to the construction of a deepwater terminal for exporting bauxite, a neighboring cruise ship terminal, the draining of swamps behind the town, and the importation of thousands of tons of white sand to create a resort beach.

Today **Turtle Beach** buzzes with activity and water sports. Around and behind the beach, you'll find plenty of opportunities for eating out and enjoying the varied nightlife, and you can easily stroll around Ocho Rios in an hour or two. The main daytime activity is shopping, with several malls and dozens of stalls providing an outlet for all manner of handmade crafts as well as duty-free items for cruise ship passengers. The only reminders of the town's history are the remains of its fort. Built by the British in the 17th century, it is now dwarfed by the adjoining bauxite works. Two rather forlorn cannon point out to sea from the surviving stonework ramparts.

Modern industry and the potent colonial military heritage would seem to overwhelm Ocho Rios, but the surrounding natural wonders dispel any sense of

A bathing suit is essential garb for climbing the Dunn's River Falls.

The Spanish who settled here christened the area Las Chorreras, referring to the "gushing water" of Dunn's River Falls (see below). The British mistook the name as Ocho Rios, or "eight rivers," even though no such rivers existed. Today its name is usually shortened to Ochi.

Despite the wide sweep of the bay and the mountain backdrop, Ocho Rios is not the most attractive of resorts—or indeed a place where

Turtle Beach

▲ 25 E3

⑤ $

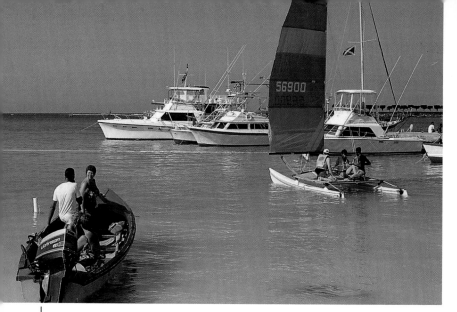

You can sail and fish, as well as snorkel in Ocho Rios.

overdevelopment. Foremost among these attractions is **Dunn's River Falls** *(Map 25 E3, off Rte. A1 between St. Ann's & Ocho Rios, Tel 876/974-2857)*. The spectacular falls cascade down 600 feet (183 m) of slippery rocks and ledges before spilling out onto the beach below. All day, long daisy chains of tourists wend their way up the falls, getting thoroughly drenched (a bathing suit is essential) in the process. The surefooted guides carry dozens of cameras around their necks as they lead the hand-holding climbers upward. The whole process is as entertaining to watch from the wooden steps running alongside the falls as it is to do. The rocks are regularly scrubbed to remove slippery algae, but this is not an activity for the frail. Although you may climb on your own, it is unwise to do so: The on-site ambulance is put to use several times each week, mostly for people not using guides. Another tip is to stay near the front of the chain because you're more certain of finding the correct footholds. With up to 20 or 30 people in a chain, those at the back can find themselves following a route quite different from that of the guide at the front. ■

Sports & activities

Diving & snorkeling: Resort Divers *(1 Carib Arcade, Ocho Rios, Tel 876/972-0905)*; Garfield Diving Station *(Shop 13, Santa Maria, Ocho Rios, Tel 876/974-5749)*.

Water sports: Ocho Rios offers a wide range of options for water sports. Among the most popular are yacht and catamaran cruises, which visit nearby Dunn's River Falls. An open bar, buffet lunch, and booming reggae are included in the price of a half-day trip. A reliable operator is Red Stripe *(Tel 876/974-2446)*.

Tours: Guided horseback tours are available through Hooves Ltd. *(Tel 876/972-0905)*; Chukka Cove Farm *(Tel 876/972-2506)*; Prospect Plantation *(Tel 876/994-1058)*. ■

The sweetly fragrant frangipani

Around Ocho Rios

SHAW PARK GARDENS

Within a few minutes' drive of Ocho Rios, in the hills high above the town, lies Shaw Park Gardens. Once the grounds of the original Shaw Park Hotel, which burned down in 1937, the 25-acre (10-ha) gardens overflow with frangipani, bougainvillea, crotons, bamboo, and many other glorious tropical plants. A lovely cascade drops almost vertically from the rock face. A magnificent 80-year-old banyan tree arches its massive branches over a large pond that was the original hotel swimming pool. The lawns where the hotel once stood command superb views of the coast from 550 feet (168 m). The site has a bar and a gift shop.

🅰 25 E3 ✉ Shaw Park Rd. ☎ 876/974-8888
💲 $

COYABA RIVER GARDEN & MUSEUM

Near Shaw Park Gardens, the wooden walkways of these landscaped gardens traverse well-tended beds, miniature waterfalls, and ponds. The site was once an Arawak settlement (*coyaba* means "heaven" in Arawak), and the small museum concentrates on pre-Columbian Jamaica as well as its more recent history.

It also has a café-bar and craft shop.

🅰 25 E3 ✉ Shaw Park Rd. ☎ 876/974-6235
💲 $

FERN GULLEY

Heading south from Ocho Rios on Milford Road (Rte. A3 to Kingston) is the famous 3-mile (5-km) stretch overhung with a canopy of dense vegetation said to include more than 500 varieties of native ferns. First planted in the late 19th century, this deep gully would be a remarkable beauty spot were it not for the heavy traffic now threatening to wipe out many of the plants with noxious fumes.

PROSPECT PLANTATION

Two miles (3 km) east of Ocho Rios, and signposted off Rte. A3, the attraction offers tours in open-top buses to a working plantation, growing crops such as cocoa, soursop, ackee, pimentos, and limes. This popular tour takes you around the farm in a tractor-drawn jitney (open trailer) and provides a commentary on the crops. You are given the chance to stop occasionally and sample them. Horseback rides are also offered.

🅰 25 E3 ✉ Prospect ☎ 876/974-2058
💲 $$$$$ ■

Around Falmouth

THE TOWN OF FALMOUTH, 23 MILES (37 KM) EAST OF
Montego Bay, was once one of the busiest ports in Jamaica, exporting
sugar from nearby plantations and importing slaves and goods.
Today, Falmouth wears a down-at-the-heel air, but the riches accumulated are reflected in the many elegant, Georgian-style town
houses erected here. Providing a contrast is the town of Nine Miles,
where Jamaican legend Bob Marley grew up. Sugar, slavery, and reggae provide a shorthand view of Jamaican history.

Falmouth
🅰 24 C3

**Good Hope Great
House grounds**
🅰 24 C3
✉ Trelawny, Falmouth
☎ 876/954-3289
💲 $$$

The town centers on **Water
Square** (so named because
Falmouth was Jamaica's first town
to provide piped water) and nearby
Market Street. Here you'll find
the old courthouse, the Baptist
Manse, Barrett House, Tharp
House, the William Knibb
Memorial Baptist Church (named
after an antislavery campaigner),
and other reminders of the glory
days, such as St. Peter's Anglican
Church (1791). Most of these
buildings are only viewed from
the outside, but you can also go
on informative walking tours
with **Jamaica Heritage Trail**
(Tel 876/954-3033).

East of Falmouth on Rte. A1 is
Oyster Bay, also known as the

Luminous Lagoon, which is said to
contain one of the world's largest
concentrations of bioluminescent
microorganisms. The water lights
up with bright green phosphores-
cence when disturbed. You can rent
a boat to take you fishing—or
indeed for a dip in these eerie
waters—through the Fisherman's
Inn *(Tel 876/954-3427).* Tours are
also available from Glistening
Waters *(Tel 876/954-3229),* a
restaurant and marina on the
lagoon's shoreline.

South of Falmouth is the **Good
Hope Great House,** one of the
most impressive of the remaining
plantation houses. Built in 1755, it
commanded a sugar estate of
10,000 acres (4,050 ha) and 3,000

slaves. Today the Georgian-style house is a luxury hotel surrounded by 2,000 acres (810 ha) of grounds where fruit is grown.

Running through the estate is the Martha Brae River, which rises in Cockpit Country and reaches the sea east of Falmouth. Rafting trips start at the **Rafter's Village,** signposted from Martha Brae *(Tel 876/952-0889)* 3 miles (5 km) inland, coasting downstream for just over an hour through dense tropical vegetation and limpid pools.

BAYSIDE SITES
The town of **Discovery Bay** is a major port for bauxite exports, and the orange-stained facilities dominate the landscape. Just outside town, on Rte. A1, is **Columbus Park,** an open-air museum with historical artifacts as well as a mural depicting Columbus's landing nearby in 1494.

Runaway Bay is a major center for all-inclusive hotels, several of which line the beachfront. **Breezes Golf & Beach Resort** has an excellent PGA-quality 18-hole golf course that is also open to people not staying at the resort.

Between Discovery Bay and Runaway Bay are the **Runaway Caves** (signposted by the side of Rte. A1), an impressive and extensive cave system once inhabited by Arawak. During the 17th century, Spanish troops fleeing the British hid here. The 45-minute tour includes a boat ride on an interesting underground lake.

Rte. B3 heading inland to Alexandria is the best road to take to reach the **Bob Marley Mausoleum** in his hometown of Nine Miles. Surrounded by high fences topped with characteristic red-gold-and-green flags, the compound is revered by Rastafarians and visited by fans from all over the world. At its center is the hut where Marley was brought up, complete with the small bed he sang of in "Is This Love." Behind the hut is the meditation stone where he rested his head to sleep or contemplate. The mausoleum itself is housed in a small chapel of Ethiopian design, which also contains his guitars, favorite football, a Bible, and other items. Sadly, a multistory building rising up behind the mausoleum now blights this revered spot. ■

The Bob Marley Mausoleum is in Nine Miles, Marley's hometown.

Columbus Park
⚠ 24 D3
💲 $

Breezes Golf & Beach Resort
⚠ 24 D3
✉ Runaway Bay
☎ 876/954-2346

Runaway Caves
⚠ 24 D3
💲 $

Bob Marley Mausoleum
⚠ 24 D2
✉ Nine Miles
💲 $$$

Montego Bay

MONTEGO BAY IS THE COUNTRY'S SECOND LARGEST CITY
(with a population nudging 125,000) and its biggest resort. It is
Jamaica's tourism capital, with a wider range of accommodations
(some three dozen hotels) and amenities than anywhere else on the
island. Although its beaches cannot compare with Negril, it has an
undeniably attractive setting in a sweeping natural harbor backed up by
a fringe of gently sloping hills. This feisty resort also hosts the Reggae
Sumfest (August), which pulls in devotees from all around the world.

Montego Bay
🅰 24 C3
Visitor information
✉ Cornwall Beach
☎ 876/952-4425
🕐 Closed Sun.

Reggae Sumfest
☎ 876/979-1720

When Columbus anchored here in
1494, he accurately christened it El
Golfo de Buen Tempo (The Bay of
Good Weather), but its present-day
name derives from the days when
the Spanish hunted wild boars in
the surrounding hills for export.
They called it Manteca Bahia, the
Bay of Lard. The English interpreted
this as Montego Bay; nowadays

most people just call it Mo'Bay.

Montego Bay became a sugar
and banana town during the 19th
century, but with the decline in
these trades its fortunes revived
only when it gained international
recognition as a spa. In the late
19th century, a local physician,
Alexander McCatty, began to extol
the virtues of swimming in salt

water at his Sanatorium Caribee. He donated the land to the community as a bathing club in 1906, and in the 1920s it was discovered by an English doctor, Sir Herbert Baker, whose articles about the mineral springs, at what had become known as Doctor's Cave Beach, marked the beginning of tourism at the resort.

Today **Doctor's Cave Beach** forms part of the tourist stretch of the town, along Gloucester Avenue, now known as the Hip Strip. The beach club has good swimming and all the necessary facilities (changing rooms, lifeguards, etc.). Next door is a rival club at **Cornwall Beach,** which has a lively bar built around a huge almond tree. Both beaches are open 9 a.m.–5 p.m. daily and cost J$30 ($0.75) for the day. Most of the other beaches along here belong to individual hotels.

Encircling these beaches is an extensive fringing reef that forms part of the **Montego Bay Marine Park,** covering some 9 square miles (23 sq km) of coral reef, sea-grass beds, and mangroves. Snorkeling, diving, and glass-bottom boat tours are readily available if you want to experience the reef at closer quarters. Other water activities include Jet-skiing, parasailing, and a 110-foot-long (33-m) water slide that ejects you into the ocean from the deck above the busy waterfront bar of Margueritaville—just the chance to make a big splash.

Around one mile (1.5 km) south of the Gloucester Avenue hotel zone is the downtown, a gaudy, lively, typically Caribbean area. Its focal point is **Sam Sharpe Square,** named after a local Baptist minister who led the Christmas Slave Rebellion in 1831. The minister and many of his 450 followers died on the gibbet in this square. On the northwest corner you can also see the **Cage,** a small building that was once used to house drunken sailors or slaves who

At Doctor's Cave Beach, a private swimming club, nonmembers can enter for a small fee.

The room in Rose Hall where Annie Palmer is said to have murdered her third husband

Rose Hall Great House

🅰 24 C3
✉ Rose Hall
☎ 876/952-5164
💲 $$$$$

were out past the Sunday curfew of 3 p.m. Nearby is a tableau of five bronze statues, the **Sam Sharpe Memorial,** which depicts him alongside fellow martyrs who shared the credit for hastening the abolition of slavery. A short walk away is the **Crafts Market** with about 200 artisan stalls *(Harbour St., daily 7 a.m.–7 p.m.).*

Also worth a look is the 18th-century parish church of

St. James, a handsome white limestone building in the shape of a Greek cross. Considered to be one of Jamaica's finest churches, it was extensively restored after an earthquake in 1957 caused considerable damage.

Eight miles (13 km) east of Mo'Bay is one of Jamaica's most famous plantation houses, **Rose Hall Great House.** Occupying a commanding position on the hillside with lawns sweeping downward toward the sea, it was built between 1770 and 1780 at the heyday of the sugar plantation era. Local legends says that this splendid Georgian house is haunted by the ghost of a wicked mistress, Annie Palmer, who ruled over it for 13 years and murdered several husbands. Supposedly a voodoo practitioner, she is said to have been strangled in her bed by one of her slave lovers: The story was fictionalized in Herbert Lisser's 1958 book, *The White Witch of Rose Hall.* The house was abandoned in the 19th century, and sympathetically restored in the 1960s; it contains beautiful original antiques and is well worth a visit. ∎

Cockpit Country

South of Montego Bay is an area known as Cockpit Country, a 500-square-mile (1,300-sq-km) region of strange limestone formations riddled with caves and sinkholes. This jungle-covered landscape, which has few towns, was one of the main refuges for runaway slaves between the 17th and 19th centuries. They became known as Maroons, and their intimate knowledge of the sometimes impenetrable terrain and guerrilla tactics meant that few missions to track them down succeeded. Also known as the District of Look Behind

(which the pursuing British soldiers were obliged to do frequently), the region is peppered with peculiar and evocative place-names such as Me No Sen You No Come, Rest and Be Thankful District, and Quick Step. For over a century the Maroons lived in this isolated area, developing their own culture and harassing the British until a peace treaty was signed in 1739.

Tours of Cockpit Country are operated by Maroon Attraction Tours *(32 Church St., Montego Bay, Tel 876/952-546, closed Tues., Thurs., and Sat.).* ∎

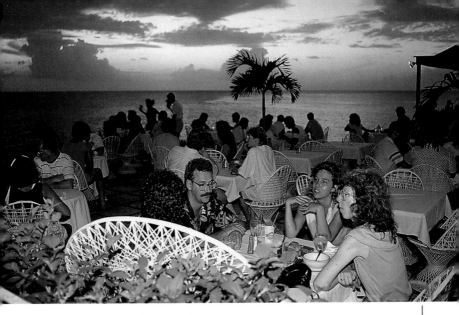

Negril

LYING AT JAMAICA'S FAR WESTERN TIP, NEGRIL IS OFTEN regarded as Jamaica's most permissive and hedonistic resort. The truth is perhaps somewhat more prosaic, but nonetheless Negril has traded on its laid-back, indulgent image for two decades or more.

Like so many others, the resort started out as a simple fishing village. Cut off from the rest of the country by swampland, it received its first trickle of visitors when the road to Montego Bay (52 miles/84 km to the east) was completed in 1965. Soon afterward its glorious 7-mile-long (11-km) beach was discovered by hippies, who descended en masse to live in simple huts beneath the coconut palms and while away their days smoking marijuana (ganja) and experiencing sunsets enhanced by readily available hallucinogenics. ("Mushroom tea" is still a specialty you can find on the beach.)

In the late 1970s one of Jamaica's first all-inclusive resorts, Hedonism II (there was no Hedonism I), opened at the eastern end of Long Bay, Negril's main beach. Tales of unlimited alcohol,

nudity, and sex soon cemented Negril's reputation as a center for uninhibited bacchanalia. A building boom that began in the 1980s marked the beginning of mass tourism, inevitably quashing the freewheeling spirit it tried so hard to emulate. Today Negril has about 50 hotels and guesthouses, several of which are all-inclusive.

The bay is a nonstop parade of Jet skis, parasail boats, day-trip catamarans, glass-bottom boats, and dive boats, and you have to be careful now where you plunge into its once pristine waters: Safe swimming is restricted to buoyed-off zones away from the boats.

For all the new elements, Negril retains a certain insouciant attitude, and the traditional ingredients—beach bars where reggae plays non-stop and the ganja and Red Stripe beer circulate freely—are still there.

Negril
△ 24 B2
Visitor information
✉ Coral Seas Plaza
☎ 876/957-4243

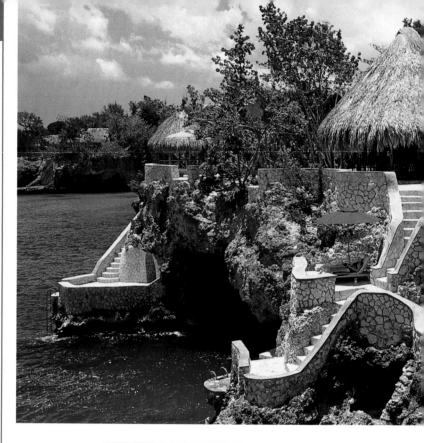

Sports & activities

Diving & snorkeling:
Negril's offshore reefs have recently been declared a marine park to help protect this fragile environment. Licensed operators include Negril Scuba Centre *(Tel 876/957-4425)*; Blue Whale *(Tel 876/957-4483)*; Sundivers *(Tel 876/957-4336)*; Scuba World *(Tel 876/957-6290)*.

Water sports:
Recommended catamaran-tour operators include Wild Thing *(Tel 876/957-5392)*; Sandals Beach Watersports *(Tel 876/957-5216)*. Parasailing is available through Ocean Tours *(Tel 876/957-4693)*. ■

It has a great reputation for live music, and big-name bands visit the resort regularly.

Most of the action takes place on Long Bay, Negril's main beach. Here you'll find the majority of hotels, beach bars, discos, and vendors offering everything from aloe massages to hair braiding. Although many hotels have cordoned off parts of the beach, you can still walk the entire shoreline; it takes around an hour. To the north of Long Bay is **Bloody Bay,** a perfect crescent-shaped beach that so far has just two all-inclusive hotels at its western end. If you want peace and quiet, this is the place to come. You can walk its shores until the mangrove boughs bending into the water at the far end prevent you from going any farther. Bloody Bay takes its name from the days when

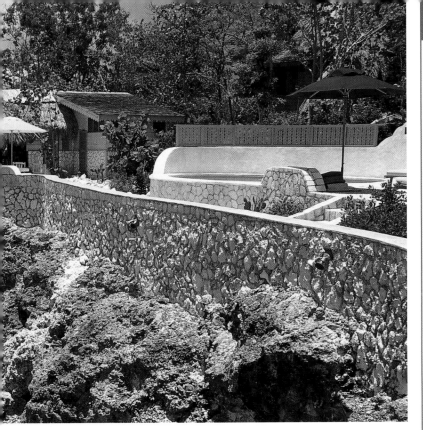

whales were once butchered here. Offshore lies a small island, **Booby Cay,** named for the booby birds (sooty terns) that nest here; it is also famous as the location used in the shooting of Jules Verne's *20,000 Leagues Under the Sea* (1954).

Behind both beaches runs Norman Manley Boulevard, a long straight road that separates the hotels from an area of swampland known as the **Great Morass.** Jamaica's second largest wetland, this 6,000-acre (2,300-ha) refuge protects crocodiles, land crabs, and numerous species of birds, including egrets, parakeets, jacanas, and Jamaican euphonias. Norman Manley Boulevard leads down into Negril town; there are a couple of shopping malls and a craft market in the small town center but little else to detain you.

Beyond the town is Negril's **West End,** a 3-mile (5-km) stretch of coastal road peppered with guesthouses and hotels. This area is now undergoing a resurgence in popularity as an alternative to the mass tourism that has taken hold on the beaches, and some of Negril's most imaginatively designed resorts (such as the Rockhouse Hotel and The Caves) can be found here, p. 354. There are no beaches, but you can reach the waters beneath the cliffs via stone steps, iron ladders, and diving boards. Cliff diving is one of the West End's hallmarks, particularly at Rick's Café. Every evening, busloads of tourists watch the sun sink beneath the horizon here. The West End terminates at **Negril Point,** where there is a historic lighthouse, built in 1894. ■

The Caves resort occupies one of the choicest stretches of the Negril waterfront.

Rastafarianism

The characteristic colors of Rastafarianism—red, black, green, and gold—are highly visible in Jamaica, adorning everything from bar fronts to bus stops and braided belts. The Rastas themselves, with their dreadlocks piled high under tall hats or knitted tams, have come to symbolize the face of Jamaica—even though for mainstream society they are still cultural rebels.

Looking to Africa

The Rastafarian movement has its roots in the teachings of the black activist Marcus Garvey (1887–1940), a national hero who prophetically advised his followers to "look to Africa, where a Black King shall be crowned." In 1930 Ras Tafari Makonnen (Ras is an honorific given to royalty, Tafari his family name) was crowned Negus of Ethiopia, taking the title Emperor Haile Selassie, King of Kings, Lord of Lords, Conquering Lion of the Tribe of Judah. The Scriptures seemed to support his claims to divinity, and Selassie was elevated to the role of the messiah who would redeem black people from suffering and white oppression.

In its early days Rastafarianism provoked considerable antagonism as it developed support in the poorer parts of Kingston, and police consistently harassed Rasta communities that they believed were drug-crazed and planning to undermine white society. In the 1970s Rastafarianism gained a degree of respectability when the politician Norman Manley visited Haile Selassie in Ethiopia and was presented with a sacred rod, which he deployed with great effect in political rallies back home. Casting himself as the people's savior, he swept to power in the 1972 elections with the support of Rastas and their allies.

Musical breakthrough

But the real turning point for Rastafarianism came in the 1970s with the huge success of Bob Marley and the Wailers, whose music spread the word about Rasta beliefs worldwide. Reggae and Rastas became Jamaica's trendiest cultural export, but inevitably a certain commercialization set in, affecting the credibility of the movement.

The Rastafarian faith is based on the belief that Rastas are one of the lost tribes of Israel, and that eventually they will be delivered from Babylon (the corrupt white world) and returned to the promised land in Ethiopia, or Zion. Rastas let their hair grow until it mats together into dreadlocks, following the directive in Leviticus (21:5): "They shall not make baldness upon their heads, neither shall they shave off the corner of their beard, nor make cuttings in the flesh." Following the injunction not to make "cuttings of the flesh," Rastas believe in herbal bush medicine, and many are also strict vegetarians following a regime of natural and unprocessed foods, known as I-tal. Salt, meat, dairy products, and alcohol are eschewed in favor of pulses and vegetables.

Rastas are renowned for their copious consumption of marijuana ("ganja" or "herb"), which was introduced to Jamaica by Indian plantation workers in the late 19th century. Smoking it is a religious sacrament, as outlined in Psalm 104:14: "He causeth the grass to grow for the cattle, and the herb for the service of man." Smoking the sacred herb is believed to provide access to a higher level of spirituality and is often accompanied by recitations of prayers or poems at "reasonings," when the communal pipe or chalice is passed round the group counterclockwise.

Many latter-day Rastas don't follow all these precepts and smoke ganja whenever they wish, eat meat, drink, and allow their dreadlocks to hang loose. The 100,000 Rastas in Jamaica today are split into numerous sects, and many have gravitated toward the more Christian-based Ethiopian Orthodox Church. The more traditional still remain in rural communes (called camps), venturing out only to secure supplies they cannot produce themselves.

Finally, what do those vibrant Rasta colors represent? Red stands for the blood spilled in Jamaica's history, black represents the skin color of the majority of the population, gold stands for the victory over oppression, and green symbolizes the fertility of both Jamaica and Ethiopia. ∎

Above: Bob Marley's music spread the word about Rasta beliefs worldwide.

The belief in letting the hair grow until it mats into dreadlocks can lead to some spectacular results (above). The Rasta faith has adherents throughout the Caribbean; this young woman (right) is from Montserrat.

Mandeville

JAMAICA'S FIFTH LARGEST TOWN, MANDEVILLE (LOCATED 2,000 feet/600 m above sea level), was established in the early 19th century and once served as a hill station for British soldiers recuperating from the heat of the coastal areas. The landscape around Mandeville has been shaped—and in places, marred—by large-scale bauxite mining. Yet the surrounding hills are scented with a heady aroma of coffee, chocolate, and spices. The town is the capital of the parish of Manchester, created in 1816.

Left: The bauxite industry is an important export earner for Jamaica.

Mandeville is the center of Jamaica's bauxite industry. As you approach, you cannot fail to notice the massive, red-stained bauxite factories and the huge scars on the landscape caused by the extraction of Jamaica's "red gold." Bauxite has been a major industry here since the 1950s, when the bauxite companies built housing suburbs for their employees on the undulating hillsides outside the town center.

The tranquil atmosphere of Mandeville, combined with the wealth created by bauxite, has turned it into one of the main centers for expatriate Jamaicans returning to their homeland from Britain. Many are snapping up the large homes built for Americans and Canadians who once managed the bauxite industry.

The oldest buildings in the town cluster around Mandeville Square (now a rather scrappy, fenced-in patch of grass), recently renamed **Cecil Charlton Park** after a former mayor.

On the south side of the square is the parish church of **St. Mark,** built in 1819. Opposite the church is the Georgian-style **courthouse,** constructed a year later. The venerable **Mandeville Hotel,** just to the east, was established as an officers' quarters and mess in 1875. It claims to be the oldest hotel in Jamaica; the entrance is shaded by three equally old sandbox trees. A more recent Mandeville landmark

Mandeville
🄼 24 D2

Mrs. Stephenson's Garden
✉ 25 New Green Rd.
Ⓢ $

is **Mrs. Stephenson's Garden.** The owner is a regular winner at the town's annual flower show, and her garden is a riot of orchids, anthuriums, and other beautiful plants.

Northwest of Mandeville is **Marshall's Pen Great House.** Built in 1795, the house was once used as a "factory" for preparing coffee beans. It has since become a home filled with artifacts, including

The tranquil rural landscapes provide a striking contrast to the bauxite mines.

The parish church of St. Mark, at the heart of Mandeville

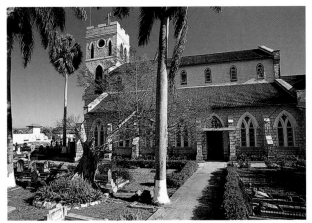

Marshall's Pen Great House
- 24 D2
- Winston Jones Hwy.
- 876/963-8569
- By appt. only
- $$$$$

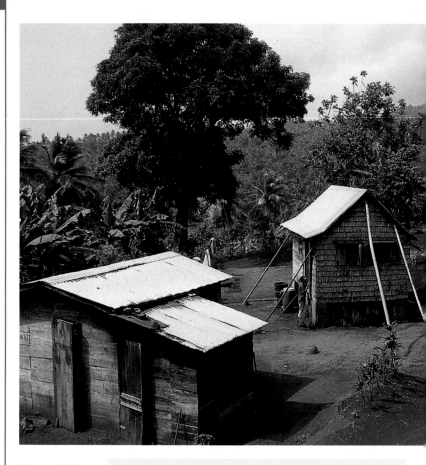

Community tours
show Jamaican
life in the
countryside.

**Huntingdon
Summit**
✉ George's Valley Rd.
☎ 876/962-0585

Kirkvine Works
☎ 876/962-3141
🕐 By appt. only.
One day's
notice required

Community tours

It is often said that tourism in the Caribbean has created a wide gulf between visitors, isolated in luxurious hotel "ghettoes," and local Jamaicans, often holding menial service jobs. This is a failing of the tourist industry and can sometimes build resentment among locals. In Mandeville a new approach known as community tourism is being pioneered to introduce tourists to the real Jamaica. Visitors can spend the night in villages where tourists would not otherwise venture; they can visit farms, schools, flower shows, and private parties. The hosts are carefully chosen to ensure that participants will be met with friendly hospitality and come away with a positive experience of the local people and villages. A pioneer in this field is Countrystyle Community Tours (*P.O. Box 60, 62 Ward Avenue, Mandeville, Tel 876/ 962-3725 or 800/JAMAICA, Fax 876/962-1461, e-mail: paulov@ infochan.com*) with contacts throughout the country. If you have a burning urge to visit a disco in downtown Kingston, for instance, they will arrange a safe escort for you. ■

One of Jamaica's excellent liqueurs

shell and stamp collections, Oriental objets d'art, and antiques. The grounds serve as a bird sanctuary and nature reserve. (Owner Arthur Sutton's son, Robert, has written the definitive guide to birds of Jamaica.)

Another mansion, to the south of town, is **Huntingdon Summit,** home of Cecil C. Charlton, a self-made millionaire who was also mayor of Mandeville for more than 20 years. The pagoda-like house is renowned for its ostentatious interior, esoteric furnishings and trophy-filled library. An indoor swimming pool is connected to another one outdoors by an underground tunnel.

If you want to see what made Mandeville so wealthy, you can tour Alcan Jamaica's **Kirkvine Works** to the northeast of town. This is the largest alumina plant in Jamaica. Alcan owns more than 30,000 acres (12,000 ha) in the surrounding area that are either not yet mined or under rehabilitation.

You can also visit the **High Mountain Coffee Factory,** Williamsfield, where producers JSP roast, grind, and package some of the finest coffee in Jamaica, including the renowned Blue Mountain brand. Nearby is the **Pioneer Chocolate Factory.** Founded in the 1920s, it is still turning out cocoa butter, drinking chocolate, and chocolate bars. Another product of Williamsfield is a well-known spicy sauce, Pickapeppa, made from a closely guarded recipe that includes tropical fruits, spices, onions, tomatoes, mangoes, and hot peppers. The **Pickapeppa Factory** has been in operation since the 1920s. ■

High Mountain Coffee Factory
✉ Williamsfield
☎ 876/963-4211
🕐 By appt. only. Closed weekends

Pioneer Chocolate Factory
☎ 876/963-4216
🕐 By appt. only. Closed weekends

Pickapeppa Factory
✉ Shooter's Field
☎ 876/962-2928
🕐 By appt. only. Closed weekends

Mandeville drive

This drive from Mandeville into the neighboring parish of St. Elizabeth passes through lovely stretches of countryside along the way. The road is in reasonably good repair, and driving conditions are relatively easy.

From Mandeville, follow signs out of town toward Christiana, and then turn left at a sign marked Kendall. After 2 miles (3 km) you'll see the massive **Alcan bauxite factory ❶**. This is the biggest mining operation in Jamaica, scouring the "red gold" from vast pits in the surrounding area and leaving a fine red film of bauxite powder over the countryside. Some of the unused pits on either side of the road are being rehabilitated as farmland.

Follow the road for about a mile (1.6 km), and turn left toward Christiana. At Shooter's Hill turn left onto Rte. B6 past the disused Orchid Sanctuary.

The stretch of road between here and **Balaclava ❷** is an idyllic farming region reminiscent of the English countryside. Sheep and cattle graze in well-tended pastures surrounded by low stone walls, presided over by towering tropical trees like the silk cotton. Occasionally these majestic specimens are found on their own in the middle of a field—shrouded sentinels with a green mantle of luxuriant bromeliads and hanging lichens.

About 21 miles (34 km) from the start, the road opens out to reveal a panorama of hills stretching into the distance to the south. To the north rise the higher peaks of Cockpit Country (see p. 48), forest-clad and almost impenetrable.

From Balaclava Rte. B6 gently drops to the valley floor, where a good, wide road bisects the massive sugarcane fields on either side, rolling off into the distance like some vast green carpet.

Two miles (3 km) beyond the ramshackle little town of Siloah is the **Appleton Rum Estate ❸** (see p. 62). After visiting the estate, drive to the town of **Maggotty** and then head south to the junction with Rte. A2 (8 miles/13 km). Turn right and soon you find yourself driving along **Bamboo Avenue ❹**, a 2-mile (3-km) stretch completely overshadowed by giant bamboo, which arches over it to create a photogenic tunnel of foliage.

One mile (1.6 km) farther west, take a right signposted to reach **YS Falls ❺** (see p. 61), which is part of a huge cattle farm. There's a shortcut from Maggotty to YS Falls, on Rte. B6, but the poor road means that it is only recommended for experienced drivers.

From YS Falls return to Rte. A2 and turn left to head back to Mandeville. This is a big busy road, but the driving conditions are good. ■

YS Falls

Appleton
Rum Est

Vauxhall

Maggotty   Maggotty
                  Falls

YS ❺
Falls   B6
B6   Black

YS

BAMBOO AVENUE   ❹   Newton

A2   Holland   West
                          Lacovia

Black   Lacovia
             Tombstone

                          East
                          Lacovia

See area map page 24
► Mandeville
⬌ 74 miles (118 km)
🕑 Allow 3–4 hours
► Mandeville

NOT TO BE MISSED
- Alcan bauxite factory
- Appleton Rum Estate
- YS Falls

Bamboo Avenue

Mandeville parish church

Mandeville courthouse

Black River was once a thriving port shipping logwood.

South coast

THOUGH JAMAICA'S SOUTH COAST IS OFF THE TOURIST track, it repays adventurous travelers with mountain scenery, busy coastal fishing villages, hidden beauty spots, and discreet resorts tucked away in tranquil coves.

Black River

24 C2

The landscapes of the southern parishes range from arid, cactus-strewn savannas to lush cattle pastures and vast swamplands. In the easternmost parish, St. Elizabeth, the main town is **Black River,** a peaceful port facing Black River Bay. Its main street has several colonnaded timber houses harking back to Black River's heyday in the mid-19th century when the town was a thriving depot for the export of logwood, which was used to produce textile dyes. Black River claims to be the first town in Jamaica to introduce electricity, telephones,

and the automobile. The invention of synthetic dyes killed off the logwood industry, and the town reverted to its earlier existence as a quiet backwater.

Most of the activity in Black River centers on the wharfside and the main street, where you'll find such faded gems as the Waterloo Guesthouse, the Invercauld Hotel, and the yellow-brick parish church of St. John's. Alongside the town's bridge is the **Hendrick's Building,** dating from 1813, which now houses the Chamber of Commerce and a Jamaica Tourist

Board office *(2 High St., Tel 876/965-2074)*.

The majority of visitors come here for a boat safari on the Black River itself, one of the few easily accessible waterways in Jamaica for spotting wildlife (see p. 62). The 44-mile (71- km) river, Jamaica's longest, is named for the inky black color of its waters (an appearance due to the peat moss lining the riverbed). The river is the main source for a vast swampland known as the Great Morass, which covers about 125 square miles (324 sq km) on either side of the lower reaches of the river as it descends from its source in Cockpit Country (see p. 48) south of Montego Bay. In the course of its relatively short route—compared with other rivers in North America, for example—the Black River empties an area of astonishingly varied landscape.

The boats travel about 6 miles (10 km) through swaths of water hyacinths and beneath the bows of venerable mangrove trees. You're likely to see flocks of roosting cattle egrets and possibly whistling ducks, herons, ospreys, and jacanas—just some of the hundred or so species of birds that live here. The main attractions, however, are the crocodiles. Once abundant around Jamaica's coastline, their numbers are now much reduced due to loss of habitat and hunting. About 300 remain in this refuge, and at least 12 of these are regularly spotted on the boat safaris. They all have names (albeit a different name depending on which boat you take!) and are used to being approached by the boats and fed scraps. Don't, however, be lulled into complacency.

YS Falls is 10 miles (16 km) to the north of Black River, signposted off Rte. A2. This scenic cascade lies at the heart of the 2,500-acre (1,000- ha) **YS Farm,** where the owners raise pedigree

Red Poll cattle and thoroughbred racehorses. The origin of the name YS has been debated for decades. One version is that it derives from the Gaelic word *wyess,* meaning "winding" or "twisting," to describe the river; another is that it comes from the original 17th-century owners, John Yates and Richard Scott, who branded their cattle with the first letter of each of their surnames.

The tour starts at the visitor center, where a tractor-drawn jitney takes you on the 10-minute ride across farmland to the falls. This is a well-maintained area, with grassy spots for picnics and shaded gazebos alongside the riverbank. A wooden stairway leads up the topmost and most spectacular waterfall, and there are caves behind some of the cascades to explore and cool pools where you can swim. ■

A refreshing sense of informality attracts visitors to some of the more out-of-the-way sights, such as Windsor Caves.

YS Falls
🗺 24 C2
✉ Off Rte. A2
☎ 876/997-6055
🕐 Closed Mon.
$ $$$

A roadside shack on the south coast

More places to visit in the south

ALLIGATOR HOLE

Just beyond Gut River Pool, near Milk River Spa, is a small nature park, Alligator Hole, which is home to rare and endangered manatees. The manatees live in a maze of reeds in the river delta and come in close to the jetty to be fed. You can rent a boat at the jetty with a guide to take you out to look for them, but don't expect too much. Manatees are reclusive creatures, and the most you might see is a shadowy form gliding past underwater near the riverbank, or telltale bubbles rising from the reeds as you silently drift by. You can also rent kayaks here.

🅰 24 D1

APPLETON RUM ESTATE

Three miles (5 km) east of YS Falls, beyond the small junction town of Maggotty, lies the Appleton Rum Estate. Set amid the rolling sugarcane fields of the Black River Valley, this 250-year-old institution is the oldest rum-producing factory in the English-speaking Caribbean, and its products are among the most popular on the island. Most of the process is now mechanized, although some of the copper distillation pots are over a century old. An aging donkey demonstrates the old-fashioned method of squeezing the juice out of the cane by turning a grinder. You can peek into the warehouse where over 8,400 barrels of maturing rum rise up in tiers to the ceiling. The tour ends in the visitor center, where you

Black River safaris

Boat journeys up the Black River, which last about 90 minutes, are available. One of the most experienced operators is St. Elizabeth Safari *(Tel 876/965-2229).* Tours are also operated by Black River Safari Boat Tours *(Tel 876/965-2513).* ■

can sample some of the 13 varieties of rum and other liquors produced here.

🅰 24 C2 ☎ 876/963-9215 🕐 Closed Sun. 💲 $$$$$

AROUND GREAT PEDRO BLUFF

At the far end of Great Pedro Bay is Great Pedro Bluff, which is one of the few places in the Caribbean where a dry savanna exists in the coastal zone; efforts are underway to give it protected status. Beyond here (signposted from Southfield) are the sheer cliffs and lighthouse *(Tel 876/965-2651)* of

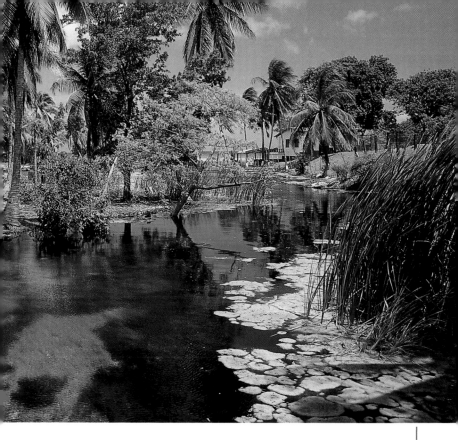

Lover's Leap, where, legend has it, two slaves who were forbidden to meet each other leaped to their deaths rather than be separated. Entrance to the clifftop is through a café-restaurant complex. The view is spectacular, with the sheer bluff of the Santa Cruz Mountains dropping 1,700 feet (518 m) almost straight down to the ocean; the panorama extends down the coastline to Rocky Point and Clarendon in one direction, and back toward Great Pedro Bluff and Treasure Beach in the other.

Ten miles (16 km) east of Treasure Beach is the fishing village of Alligator Pond. From here a scenic drive winds (18 miles/29 km) along the south coast toward Alligator Hole and Milk River Spa. This wild, unspoiled part of the country embraces dry savanna as well as the extensive swamplands of the Long Bay Morass. Midway along is an exquisite little spot known as the **Gut River Pool.** The river flows under the road and emerges in an oasis of palm trees, bulrushes, and water lilies,

The Gut River is an oasis of cool greenery on a mostly arid coastline.

with crystal-clear pools that you can jump into from the surrounding rocks: It's very popular with local lads cooling off on weekends.
🗻 24 C1

TREASURE BEACH

The main resort area on the south coast is picturesque Treasure Beach, 19 miles (30 km) east of Black River. In fact, Treasure Beach is not just one beach, but a series of connected bays including Billy's Bay, Frenchman's Bay, Calabash Bay, and Great Pedro Bay. Most of the accommodations are based in Calabash Bay, where a series of guesthouses and one large hotel provide simple lodging for those wanting to get away from it all. The pace of life follows a rural rhythm and the coming and going of the brightly colored fishing boats.
🗻 24 C1 ∎

Spanish Town

Spanish Town

⚑ 25 E2

JAMAICA'S CAPITAL FOR OVER 300 YEARS, SPANISH TOWN IS today a large industrial city with few traces of its past prominence. Called St. Jago de la Vega by the Spanish who founded the first capital here in 1523, the city was later razed by British soldiers during the invasions in 1596 and 1643. It remained the capital under the British until 1872 when Kingston took over the role. Nestled within the modern cityscape are fascinating reminders of Spanish Town's past—and of the European powers that shaped Jamaica.

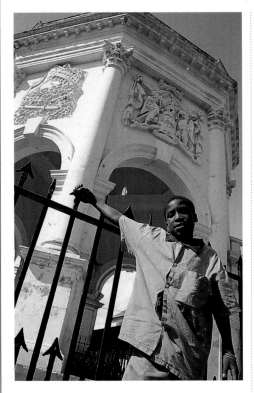

Visitor at Rodney Memorial

People's Museum of Craft & Technology

✉ King's House, Parade Sq.

☎ 876/922-0620

🕐 Closed weekends

💲 $

At the heart of the city is **Parade Square,** a park surrounded by the faded grandeur of Georgian buildings. On the north side is the **Rodney Memorial,** built to commemorate Admiral Rodney's defeat of the French fleet off Guadeloupe in 1782. Sculptured by John Bacon the marble statue depicts Rodney in classical attire and is flanked by two rare cannon captured from the

French flagship. The cupola housing the statue is adorned with friezes depicting the battle itself. The buildings that flank the memorial, linked by a porticoed walkway, house the **National Archives** *(closed weekends).*

The redbrick Georgian facade on the west side of the square is all that remains of the **King's House,** built in 1762 as the governor's residence but largely destroyed by fire in 1925. The stables now house the **People's Museum of Craft and Technology,** which features industrial and agricultural equipment (including an ancient sugar press, coffee huskers, and corn grinders) and other items relating to the country's industrial heritage. They provide a snapshot of Jamaican history. Opposite the King's House is the former House of Assembly, which now houses local government offices.

To the south of Parade Square stands the **Cathedral of St. Jago de la Vega** *(White Church St.).* The oldest Anglican cathedral outside England, it was built in 1714 on the site of a 16th-century Spanish church. The black-and-white checkered floor tiles in the aisle belonged to the original Catholic church. The elaborate interior contains many important monuments from the colonial era and elaborately carved pews and choir stalls. ∎

Exploiting a location almost in the center of the Caribbean, the Cayman Islands are one of the most prosperous nations in the region. The principal industries are offshore finance and tourism, with visitors lured to the pristine waters.

Cayman Islands

A pufferfish inflates itself when threatened.

Cayman Islands

THE CAYMAN ISLANDS ARE A GROUP OF ISLANDS SITUATED ALMOST IN THE middle of the Caribbean, 480 miles (772 km) southwest of Miami. There are three islands in this British Crown Colony, each different in character. The biggest island, Grand Cayman, is the home of the capital, George Town, as well as Seven Mile Beach, one of the most famous in the Caribbean. Tourism and offshore finance have given the island's 31,000 inhabitants one of the highest per capita incomes in the region. About 90 miles (145 km) to the northeast lie the two sister islands of Cayman Brac and Little Cayman, both comparatively undeveloped.

The three islands share a similar appearance—relatively flat, mostly covered with dry scrub. The Caymans sit on the edge of the Cayman Trench, a massive trough that drops some 25,000 feet (7,620 m) into the deepest part of the Caribbean Sea. The reef walls that surround the islands descend into the depths and attract scuba divers from all over the world. Divers call it the Underwater Capital of the Caribbean. The islands are probably one of the world's most successful sport-diving destinations, thanks largely to marine conservation policies that have evolved from a simple ban on spearfishing in the early 1980s to the creation of marine parks and a comprehensive network of mooring buoys in the 1990s.

Diving is the backbone of the islands' tourism industry, with around 80,000 divers visiting annually. The Caymans' most popular dive site, Stingray City, off **Grand Cayman,** generates about a million dollars a year. This spectacular underwater attraction is unique in the Caribbean, with around 30 or more friendly stingrays coming in to be handled and stroked in the shallow waters of the North Sound. Because this experience takes place in depths of just 3–12 feet (1–4 m), it is also accessible to snorkelers.

The first European sighting of the islands was by Columbus on May 10, 1503, when he was blown off course on his way to Hispaniola. The explorer spotted the two smaller islands, **Cayman Brac** (see p. 78) and **Little Cayman** (see pp. 71–73). Although he didn't stop to explore, Columbus noted the enormous numbers of turtles in the surrounding waters and named the islands Las Tortugas. Over the next hundred years or so they came to be known as Las Caymanas, from the Carib name for the saltwater crocodiles that were also abundant around the islands.

In the 16th century, Dutch, French, English, and Spanish sailors used the islands as places to take on water and capture sea turtles, an abundant source of fresh meat for

2▷

0 _____ 10 kilometers
0 _____ 6 miles

Little **Cayman** Snipe Point

Jacksons Crawl Bay
Bloody Bay Point
Marine Park Charles Bight Sandy Point
Spot Bay Tarpon
Lake South Hole Sound Wearis Bay

Booby Pond Nature Reserve
West End Preston South
Point Bay Town

The Bight Spot North
Tibbetts Turn Bay East
Cayman The **Peter's** Point
Brac Museum Half Way Bluff **Cave**
Stake Bay Ground **Brac Parrot** Pollard Bay
West End Banksville **Bat Cave** **Reserve**
West End *Cayman Brac*
Point Gerrard
Smith
Airport

△ △ △ △
A B C D

1▷

Area of map detail

ATLANTIC OCEAN

Caribbean Sea

the long sea voyage back to Europe. Even though Sir Francis Drake visited Grand Cayman in 1586 and reported that the caymanas were edible, the islands remained unclaimed and uninhabited.

The Cayman Islands came under English jurisdiction in 1655, when England took Jamaica and neighboring islands from the Spanish; they were formally recognized as British territory in 1670. In the mid-1660s the first settlers arrived from Jamaica, setting up semipermanent habitations on Little Cayman and Cayman Brac to trade turtles, vegetables, water, wood, and coconuts with passing ships. Grand Cayman, which offered better protection from pirate attacks, was settled beginning in 1700.

The Caymans developed a maritime economy. By the late 1800s up to one-third of the population was employed as merchant sailors, fishermen, or turtle catchers. The islanders rescued numerous mariners shipwrecked on the offshore reefs and salvaged lumber and cargo to build their houses and supply other needs. Over the course of time, however, a growing sense of self-sufficiency began to take hold among the islanders. They began to turn from salvage to construction. By the 1780s the Caymanians were building their own

schooners and becoming renowned throughout the Caribbean as master boatbuilders. Shipbuilding prospered for more than 150 years, until the final launching of a traditional Caymanian ship in January 1967.

Although the first legislative assembly was formed in 1832, the islands remained a dependency of Jamaica until 1959. Following Jamaica's independence from Britain in 1962, the Caymans chose to remain a British Crown Colony. In 1966 they introduced landmark legislation to encourage the growth of the offshore banking industry, today one of the mainstays of the economy.

The first tourists arrived on board the cruise ship *Atlantis* in 1937, and in 1953 the first airfield opened on Grand Cayman. Today the islands receive more than 300,000 visitors every year. ■

The tax-free myth

According to accepted wisdom the Cayman Islands' tax-free status is thanks to the Wreck of the Ten Sails. In 1794 a convoy of ten merchant ships from Jamaica wrecked on the reefs of Grand Cayman's east end, but thanks to the brave efforts of the local settlers, everybody was saved. Legend has it that a member of the British royal family was on board and in gratitude King George III proclaimed that the islanders should never be taxed. This is a colorful tale—but untrue. In fact, the income tax was abolished in 1971 by the Finance Ministry in order to kick-start a sluggish economy. The policy eventually paid off, and today the Caymans are the world's fifth largest offshore banking center. ■

A shipwreck lies in George Town Harbour.

Grand Cayman

THE LARGEST OF THE THREE CAYMAN ISLANDS, GRAND Cayman is 22 miles (35.4 km) long and 4 to 8 miles (6.4–12.8 km) wide. The most prosperous of the islands, Grand Cayman is home to 90 percent of the country's 31,200 residents. A busy coastal fringe gives way to an interior of gardens, lakes, and natures woodlands.

George Town
- 66 C1

Visitor information
- The Pavilion, Cricket Sq.
- 345/949-0623

National Museum
- Harbour Dr., George Town
- 345/949-8368
- Closed Sun.
- $$$

Most of the development on Grand Cayman is concentrated along **Seven Mile Beach** (which is actually just 5.5 miles/8.8 km long), a glorious stretch of powdery sand sloping into the shallow waters of West Bay. Although about 50 hotels and condominiums line the beach, none has been allowed to rise higher than the beach's trademark casuarina trees and ruin its aesthetic appeal (the land itself only rises to 12 feet/4 m). Behind the beach, however, is a strip of shopping malls, fast-food outlets, bars, and restaurants.

Grand Cayman's capital, **George Town,** is primarily a business center clustered around a protected harbor. The harbor is a popular stop for cruise ships, which disgorge their passengers by the thousands into the duty-free souvenir and jewelry shops on the surrounding streets. One of the few remaining 19th-century structures has been converted into the commendable **National Museum.**

Displays chronicle the natural and seafaring history of the islands.

To the north of Seven Mile Beach is the **Cayman Turtle Farm,** one of the island's most popular tourist attractions despite its controversial history. Many conservationists disagree with the farm's attempts to have the interna-

tional ban on farmed turtle products lifted. You'll see the various stages in a turtle's life, from the tiny hatchling (2–3 inches/5–8 cm) to the four-year-old creatures that are slaughtered for their meat, shells, and oil (used in cosmetics). You can eat turtle soup and burgers on the premises, but don't buy shells (or jewelry made from shells) because importing them is illegal in many countries. The farm also has a small area set aside for native species, such as the Caymanian parrot, bananaquit, macaw, and the agouti (otherwise known as the Caymanian rabbit).

A short distance east of the farm, however, you can go to **Hell.** In the 1930s, so the story goes, a British commissioner shot at a bird and missed. His exclamation, "Oh hell,"

Hawksbill turtles are now rarely seen around the islands.

Sports & activities

Diving & snorkeling:
Grand Cayman has more than 40 dive operations, reflecting its enormous popularity with sports divers. Many specialize in particular areas, but divers who want to sample a number of sites can sign up for a Best of Caymans dive package, which brings together three major operators to allow a variety of dives on the North Wall, East End, and South and West Sides. Contact DiveTech *(Tel 345/949-1700);* Fisheye *(Tel 345/947-4209);* Ocean Frontiers *(Tel 345/947-7500);* or Cayman Islands Watersports Operators Association *(Tel 345/949-8522, fax 345/949-0220).* ∎

Cayman Turtle Farm
🅐 66 A2
✉ West Bay
☎ 345/949-3894
💲 $$$

was adopted as a place-name. The small area of phytokarst rocks is supported by the **Hell post office** *(Tel 345/949-1087)* and souvenir shop.

The south coast features two new attractions. The first of these is **Pedro St. James,** just outside the township of Savannah. Built about 1780, this historic building is the oldest surviving structure on the island. It has had a colorful history: The solid stone house was built using slave labor and was originally referred to as St. James Castle. It was in the dining room here that judges held court and Caymanians took the decision to form an elected legislature. Recently it has been extensively restored, and the complex now includes a visitor center and audiovisual theater, oceanfront restaurant, and other amenities. But the real strength of Pedro St. James is its depiction of the lives of the early settlers, the realities of slavery, and the re-creation of times past. In the mansion's upstairs dining

room, the island's first elected assembly convened on December 10, 1831, and from the Palladian staircase here the Proclamation of Emancipation abolishing slavery was read in 1835.

Eight miles (13 km) farther east, just outside the township of Breakers on Frank Sound, is the **Queen Elizabeth Botanic Park.** This 65-acre (26-ha) park, jointly managed by the National Trust for the Cayman Islands and the government, features colorful gardens, a trail through native woodlands, and a lakeside nature reserve. Halfway around the woodland trail is an iguana enclosure with several specimens of Grand Cayman's endangered blue iguana, which can be seen basking in the sunlight. One of the park's highlights is the superb **Heritage Garden,** which has a restored Caymanian house as its focal point and features gardens and a "caboose" (outdoor cooking area). ■

Blue iguanas

The Cayman blue iguana is the most endangered rock iguana in the West Indies. Destruction of habitat and predation by dogs and cats have brought this giant lizard to the brink of extinction. The National Trust for the Cayman Islands is working on a conservation program for the iguana, with

support from the Worldwide Fund for Nature and the U.S.'s National Zoological Park. The enclosure in the Queen Elizabeth Botanic Park protects captive-bred iguanas until they are released into the wild. The iguanas live an almost natural life here, eating wild plants and berries and sunning themselves. ■

Pedro St. James

🅰 66 B1

✉ Savannah, off coast road

☎ 345/947-3329

💲 $$$

Queen Elizabeth Botanic Park

🅰 66 C2

✉ North Side

☎ 345/947-3558

💲 $$$

Despite its fierce appearance, the blue iguana is a peaceful vegetarian.

Little Cayman

A diver strokes
one of the many
stingrays at
Stingray City.

THE SMALLEST AND LEAST DEVELOPED OF THE CAYMAN
Islands, Little Cayman is a far cry from the commercial frenzy of
Grand Cayman's Seven Mile Beach. Nine miles (15 km) long and
just one mile (1.5 km) across at its widest point, the island is predominantly flat scrub in the interior and fringed with palm trees and
sea grapes along its shoreline.

Carin and Arawak peoples may
have visited the island from Cuba
and Jamaica, drawn by supplies of
fresh turtle, but its first permanent
settlers were a ragged band of
escaped slaves and shipwrecked
sailors who set up a turtling station
here in the 1660s. By 1900 there
were still only 200 people on the
island, making a living from
phosphate mining, shipbuilding,
and turtle catching. A hurricane
destroyed most of the houses in

1932, and the inhabitants migrated
to Cayman Brac or Grand Cayman
in search of work.

Isolated for many decades,
Little Cayman has remained comparatively undeveloped, and it is
these qualities—peace, quiet, and
wilderness—that now attract
tourists. Diving, bird-watching, and
fishing are the main activities.

The diving is superb. Extending
along the north shore of the island
is **Bloody Bay Marine Park,**

Little Cayman

🗺 67 AI

Booby Pond interpretive center

🏛 67 AI
✉ Outside Blossom Village
🕐 Closed Sun.

CAYMANITE

Caymanite is a rare, semiprecious rock that is found only in Cayman Brac and on the eastern end of Grand Cayman. A hard dolomite, formed during the Oligocene-Miocene epoch (between 16–25 million years ago), it has a composition similar to manganese nodules found on the ocean floor. The stone's colored layers are formed by its various metallic contents, with manganese dominating in the black layers, iron in the red layers, and nickel, titanium, and copper among the others. When polished, the stone is made into jewelry. ∎

Sports & activities

Diving & snorkeling:
There are dive centers in all the main resorts on Little Cayman. Southern Cross Club (*Tel/fax 345/948-1099, e-mail: scc@candw.ky, www.SouthernCrossClub.com*); Reef Divers (*Little Cayman Beach Resort, Tel/fax 813/323-8727, e-mail: bestdiving@aol.com, www.braclittle.com*); Pirate's Point (*Tel 345/948-1010, fax 345/948-1011*); Paradise Divers (*Paradise Villas, Tel 345/948-0001, fax 345/948-0002*). ∎

one of the Caribbean's most spectacular dive locations. The reef wall here starts in just 20 feet (6 m) of water and plunges some 6,000 feet (1,830 m) to the ocean floor. These pristine walls feature an abundance of marine life, including giant barrel and elephant ear sponges, massive elkhorn corals, lush forests of sea fans, and reef fish of all sizes and descriptions. Eagle rays and turtles flip lazily past in the deep blue, and the coral canyons and crevices harbor a mass of gobies, blennies, basslets, wrasses, and other brilliantly colored fish (see above for dive operators).

Little Cayman is also an important reserve for birdlife. **The Booby Pond Nature Reserve** (*National Trust for the Cayman Islands, Tel 345/949-8368*), just outside Blossom Village, is home to the largest colony of red-footed boobies in the Western Hemisphere. Some 20,000 of these pelagic seabirds nest here, wandering the oceans in search of food by day and returning to roost at night. The Caymans' only

breeding colony of magnificent frigatebirds also nests here, and you'll often see them engaged in aerial battles with the boobies as they return at sundown, trying to get them to disgorge their catch. The reserve has been designated a Wetland of International Importance under the 1971 RAMSAR convention. An **interpretive center** and a bird-watching tower are beside the road. The islands are also home to a significant iguana population: The lizards can often be seen sunning themselves beside the road.

Tarpon Lake, a large, brackish pond in the middle of the

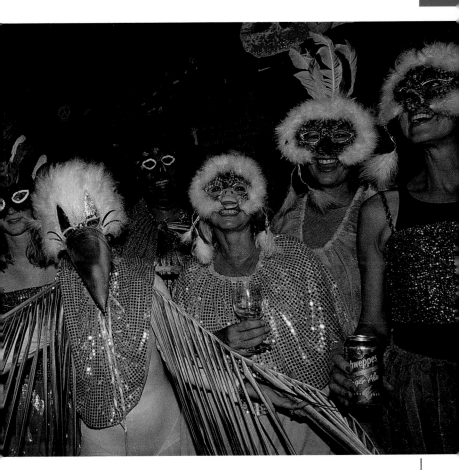

island, is a curiosity: During Hurricane Gilbert, in 1988, the lake was flooded with seawater, and the tarpon now found in the lake have since developed into a subspecies of those out in the ocean. There are nature trails around the lake, and you can fish from the jetty.

For fishing fanatics the main attractions are spectacular bone-fishing on the flats of **South Hole Sound** and deep-sea fishing for marlin, tuna, and wahoo. ■

"Booby" (with blue beak) leads revelers at a fund-raiser for the Booby Pond Nature Reserve.

How Bloody Bay got its name

Legend has it that Little Cayman was once settled by pirates and buccaneers who anchored their boats on the north shore and made forays out to attack passing ships. The British finally dispatched a squadron to deal with this problem by using the element of surprise. As the British ships came into view, the pirates raced for their ships but were cut off and attacked as they attempted to board. The subsequent massacre was how Bloody Bay gained its name. ■

Coral reefs of the Caribbean

Beneath Caribbean waters lies the complex and colorful environment of coral reefs. This mysterious, enchantingly beautiful world more than matches the terrestrial flora and fauna of the islands. It is second only to the rain forests in terms of biological diversity.

The coral reef

Coral reefs have existed for 450 million years, making them among the oldest ecosystems on the planet. These remarkable structures have been built up over the centuries by tiny coral animals, or polyps, which convert sunlight and the carbon dioxide from seawater into calcium carbonate with the help of captive partners known as zooxanthellae plants that live within their tissues. The polyps use this calcium carbonate (or limestone) to build the stony structure in which they live. This symbiotic relationship only functions in warm, clear tropical waters where there is enough sunlight for the zooxanthellae to perform. Another curious fact is that nearly all of the world's coral reefs lie off east-facing shores. Equatorial currents tend to be west-flowing, so the flow of nutrients essential for the development of

Opposite: School of blue-striped grunts
Below: Yellow tube sponge and snappers

polyps comes in from the east. So in this respect, the coral reefs of the Caribbean resemble the greatest of them all—the Great Barrier Reef along Australia's northeast coast.

The Caribbean is home to around 50 species of hard corals; each builds its own unique structure. Among the more familiar are the brain corals, which can grow up to 6 feet (1.8 m) across and resemble a human brain; staghorn corals, which branch out like deer antlers; elkhorn corals, which form dense patches in the surf zone; star corals, which are important reef builders; pillar corals, whose distinctive pillars can grow up to 10 feet (3 m) high; and boulder corals, which are found almost everywhere.

There are also about 20 species of soft corals, the most prominent of which are large sea fans or gorgonians. Others include black corals, sea whips, sea plumes, and sea rods. Colorful sponges of all descriptions—delicate azure vase sponges, blood-red barrel sponges, and bright yellow tube sponges—are another important component in the dynamic reef environment, playing host to tiny invertebrates or providing hiding places for fish.

Reef fish

The Caribbean is home to about a thousand species of fish belonging to more than 140 families. Many of them display a dazzling array of colors as they school around the reef. Among the most common are butterfly fish, particularly the four-eyed and banded butterfly fish, and angelfish, such as the magnificent queen angelfish, the yellow-and-gray French angelfish, and the black-and-yellow rock beauty. Damselfish are common on the shallow reefs, darting out from their hiding places in the coral to graze on algae; one species, the striped sergeant major, lays its eggs in round patches and defends them aggressively against all comers.

The wrasse family are prime scavengers on the reef, and their behavior is full of surprises. The males rule a harem of females, but should the dominant male get eaten, then one of the females changes sex to take his place. Closely related to the wrasses are the brightly colored

Food-catching tentacles

Mouth

Stomach

Polyp skeletons

Coral polyp

Young coral

Tropical vegetation

Volcanic cone: Layers of ash and lava

Volcanic cone continually erodes as its base sinks into the sea.

The volcanic cone vanishes beneath the sea, and coral grows over it.

Channels in the coral let nutrient-bearing water flow into the lagoon.

Sandy lagoon

Limestone formed by skeletons of polyps

Reefs are formed by accumulated limestone that has been created by the hard, outer skeletons of tiny coral polyps.

parrotfish, 14 species of which live in the Caribbean. Parrotfish feed off algae in the coral rock, grinding up surprisingly large quantities with their powerful jaws and expelling it as coral sand.

Predators often seen hovering near the reef include jacks, pompano, and scads, as well as the ubiquitous snappers, of which

there are 19 species. Snappers usually school facing into the current, maintaining the same position in the water column and grabbing anything that comes their way. Groupers, like snappers, are prime food fish and not as common as they once were. Groupers can grow up to 8 feet (2.5 m) in length and weigh more than 650 pounds (295 kg). The great

Vegetation grows on the sandy islands ringing the lagoon.

Manta

Eagle ray

Staghorn coral

Green turtle

Elkhorn coral

Nurse shark

Sargeant major fish

Four-eyed butterfly

Red tail parrot

Damsels

Banded butterfly

Barracuda

Grouper (yellow mouth)

Rainbow parrot

Snapper

Blue sponge

Scads

Tiger shark

Electric ray

Jack

Queen angel

Sand and fine material are deposited at low tide until sandy islands are formed.

Black coral

French angel

Brain coral

Rock beauty

Yellow tube sponge

barracuda usually hunts on its own, often around a chosen reef or wreck site; the three smaller species of reef barracuda are more often seen in schools.

Sharks, rays, & turtles

The Caribbean has 44 recorded species of sharks, although most of these stay away from areas with people. The most common is the harmless nurse shark, often found resting on the seabed. There are 22 species of rays, among them the southern stingray (which inhabits Grand Cayman's famous Stingray City), the majestic eagle ray, and the electric ray. Probably the most awe-inspiring ray is the Atlantic manta, also known as the devilfish or giant devil ray, but it is rare to encounter these graceful creatures underwater. Other Caribbean residents include hawksbill and green turtles, although their numbers are now much reduced because of human predation for their meat and shells. ■

Cayman Brac

Cayman Brac

67 C2

ALTHOUGH IT'S JUST 90 MILES (145 KM) TO THE NORTHEAST of Grand Cayman, Cayman Brac seems a world away from the frenetic atmosphere of the main island. Quiet, easygoing, and laid-back are some of the adjectives used to describe this little island, which is usually referred to as "the Brac."

BRAC BOAT-BUILDING

The first settlers were a random assortment of people including Jamaican planters, ship-wrecked mariners, and adventurers. In 1833 slaves from Africa arrived on Cayman Brac and quickly established the island's reputation for boat-building, which remained one of its principal activities until the 1960s, when sail was super-seded by motor yachts. Small boats used for turtle catching, known as "catboats" (because they could silently sneak up on unsuspecting turtles), were also built here. The story of the Brac's early days is related in the quaint Cayman Brac Museum *(Stake Bay, Tel 345/948-2622, closed weekends, $).* ∎

The island supports a thriving community of about a thousand people. Residents (known as Brackers) are renowned for their hospitality and friendliness.

The Brac is 12 miles (19 km) long and just a mile (1.5 km) wide. The western portion is flat, whereas the eastern half is dominated by a central bluff, which rises to dramatic cliffs some 140 feet high (42 m) at the shoreline. This bluff that gives the island its name ("brac" is Gaelic for "bluff"). The bluff supports a wide variety of plant life, most notably saguaro cactuses and century plants, and numerous species of birds, including brown boobies, frigatebirds, white tropic birds, herons, egrets, and bananaquits.

You can explore limestone caves around the bluff (most are marked as turns off the main road). **Bat Cave** houses a small bat colony, and **Peter's Cave** is famous as a hurricane shelter.

Other island inhabitants include a small population of endangered Brac parrots. The best place to look

for them is in the **Brac Parrot Reserve,** which covers 180 acres (73 ha) of rocky woodland on the bluff of the island. The reserve is reached by taking the main cross-island route, Ashton Reid Road, and turning down Major Donald Drive (also known as Lighthouse Road), which runs along the top of the bluff toward the lighthouse at North East Point.

The main attraction in the Brac is scuba diving. The island is sur-rounded by pristine reefs teeming with fish and has around 45 regis-tered dive sites. The newest of these is the spectacular wreck of a former Soviet warship sunk here in September 1996. The 330-foot-long (100-m) frigate, originally known as *Patrol Vessel no. 356,* was part of the Soviet fleet stationed in Cuba during the Cold War and was pur-chased from the Russians with the express intent of sinking it as an artificial reef. Renamed the **M.V. Captain Keith Tibbets** in honor of a local personality, it now lies in 55 to 110 feet (17.5–33.5 m) of water just off the island's north shore. ∎

Sports & activities

Diving & snorkeling:
The island's two dive operators are located at the two main hotels. Both offer a full-service facility and have professional photo/video centers.
Reef Divers (Brac Reef Beach Resort, Tel 345/948-1323 or 800/327-3835, fax 345/948-1207, e-mail: bracreef@candw.ky, www.braclittle.com); Peter Hughes's Dive Tiara (Divi Tiara Resort, Tel 345/948-1553 or 800/367-3484, fax 345/948-1316, e-mail: divtiara@ candw.ky). ∎

Scattered across nearly 250 square miles (650 sq km) of ocean to the southeast of the Bahamas, the Turks and Caicos group counts some 50 low-lying islands and cays. This remote British dependency is only now being discovered by tourists.

Turks & Caicos Islands

The pink flamingo thrives among the mangroves of Turks and Caicos.

Turks & Caicos Islands

THE TURKS & CAICOS ISLANDS LIE ABOUT 575 MILES (926 KM) SOUTHEAST of Miami and consist of two island groups separated by the 22-mile-wide (35-km) Turks Island Passage. To the west is the Caicos group: West Caicos, Providenciales, North Caicos, Grand Caicos, East Caicos, and South Caicos. To the east is the Turks group: Grand Turk and Salt Cay. The country's eight islands and 40 small cays encompass just 166 square miles (430 sq km). Tourism is only now arriving to these low-key islands.

The Turks and Caicos are more sea than land. They are located on two shallow, sand-covered limestone banks that cover nearly 13 times that of the land area. These huge banks provide important habitats for marine life. Many are covered with sea-grass meadows, where burrowing sea urchins, sea cucumbers, bivalves, and mollusks live in abundance. The banks are a rich fishing ground, particularly for conch: Huge piles of empty shells on the islands testify to the popularity of this seafood. About 1.5 million conch are eaten locally each year, and another 2.5 million are exported. Lobster from the banks is another major export.

The first inhabitants of these islands were Lucayan migrating from Haiti; they arrived in the Bahamas chain around 1,200 years ago. After making landfall on Sand Cay or the Seal Cays, the Lucayan established themselves on the northwest corner of **Grand Turk.** This site, which has been extensively excavated, is the oldest known settlement in the Bahamas chain and was occupied from around A.D. 705 to 1170. Analysis of bones at the site reveals that the inhabitants ate mostly sea turtles. Artifacts recovered include shell beads, a mother-of-pearl pendant, a nearly complete greenstone ax, and conch-shell tools. The most important find from pre-Columbian times on Grand Turk has been a wooden paddle, dating from A.D. 1100. It is now on display in the Turks & Caicos National Museum (see p. 83).

No one lived on the islands when the first Europeans arrived. Controversy surrounds the issue of whether Columbus made his first landfall here or on San Salvador in the Bahamas; the evidence points to the latter. In the 17th century, Bermudians settled Grand Turk, Salt Cay, and South Caicos, using slave labor to rake the salinas for the salt trade. They also deforested the islands in order to speed up the evaporation process.

During the American Revolution, Loyalists fleeing the conflict set up plantations here for sisal and cotton, again using slave labor. With the abolition of slavery in 1834 the plantation system collapsed, and the Loyalists left the islands. The slaves remained and relied on subsistence farming and fishing. The old plantations eventually returned to wilderness.

Area of map detail

Despite their connections with the Bermudian salt rakers, the islands were under the jurisdiction of the Bahamas from the 18th century onward. This situation was unpopular because of the high taxes being paid to Nassau, and just over a century later this system was abandoned. The islands were annexed to Jamaica from 1873 until Jamaican independence in 1962. The salt industry soon suffered a mortal blow and was closed down in 1964.

The Turks & Caicos then became a British Crown Colony. Tourism began with the development of an airstrip and a Club Med on Providenciales shortly thereafter, and although the industry has been slow to take off, visitor arrivals are now hovering around 100,000 annually. Financial services and fishing are the other mainstays of the economy. ■

Local boys hand-line fishing, Grand Turk

Whitby
Flamingo Ponds
Bottle Creek
North Caicos
Conch Bar
Bambarra
Armstrong Pond
Lorimers
Grand Caicos
Bank
Ocean Hole
East Caicos
South Caicos
Cockburn Harbour
Six Hill Cays
Long Cay
Donkey Sanctuary
Turks and Caicos National Museum
Cockburn Town
Grand Turk
Gibb's Cay
Waterloo
Long Cay
Fish Cays
Cotton Cay
East Cay
Ambergris Cays
Balfour Town
Salt Cay
Columbus Island Passage
(Turks Island Passage)
Seal Cays
Bush Cay
Big Sand Cay
H.M.S Endymion

C   D   E   F
2▷
1▷

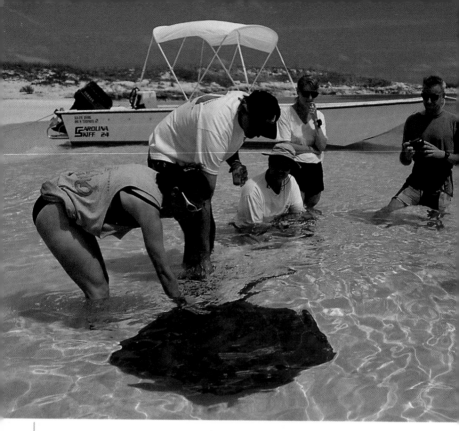

Interacting with
stingrays at Gibb's
Cay

Grand Turk

GRAND TURK COVERS ONLY 7 SQUARE MILES (18 SQ KM)
but has a population of about 4,000, largely because it is the seat of
government for the country. As with other islands in the Turks and
Caicos, the vegetation is largely scrub and cactus, interspersed with
flat expanses of disused salt pans. The occasional broken-down
windmill punctuates this landscape where wild donkeys and horses
wander freely. Like the windmills, they are sad remnants of the
defunct salt industry, which flourished until the 1960s.

Grand Turk

🗺 81 E2

Visitor information

✉ Front St.,
Cockburn Town

☎ 649/946-2321

What Grand Turk lacks on land in
natural beauty is more than made
up for by the glorious, exuberant
world of its coral reefs. Just a stone's
throw offshore on the west side of
the island, a sheer wall drops away
from about 40 to 7,000 feet
(12–2,134 m) in one fell swoop,
providing some of the most
thrilling reef diving in the
Caribbean. All diving off Grand

Turk is within 10 to 15 minutes of
the shoreline, so operators simply
pick up clients from the beach outside their hotels and whisk them
straight to the dive sites. All the
operators use small boats, carrying
around six people, and offer a
personal service.

One of the best excursions is Sea
Eye's half-day barbecue trip to
Gibb's Cay, an uninhabited island

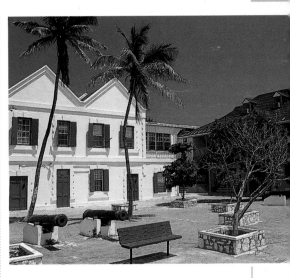

The government
complex in
Cockburn Town

where you can hand feed and snorkel with stingrays and free dive to the seabed for conch, which the crew will then use in a conch salad.

Don't come to Grand Turk if you're looking for sophistication, nightlife, entertainment, shopping, or culture. Nevertheless, many nondivers enjoy themselves enormously, especially those visitors who like quirky, out-of-the-way places. The people are friendly, the sights are few, the pace is relaxed. You can cycle the entire length of the island in a couple of hours, exploring the beaches and salt pans en route. Note that there is little natural shade.

Grand Turk's administrative center (and the capital of the islands) is **Cockburn Town.** The government offices reside in a series of brightly painted buildings (many

recently restored) surrounding a small square where old cannon still face out to sea. Slightly to the north, you'll see the blue-trimmed **Odd Fellows Lodge,** one of the oldest buildings on the island. The emancipation of the slaves was announced here in 1832.

Grand Turk's unexpected jewel is the superb **Turks & Caicos National Museum.** It is housed in one of the oldest stone buildings on the island, Guinep House, which is thought to have been built by a former shipwright who named it after the magnificent guinep tree outside its door.

The museum's centerpiece is its extensive display on the Molasses Reef Wreck, the oldest European shipwreck so far discovered in the Caribbean. The early 16th-century Spanish caravel foundered on the rim of the Caicos Bank, and numerous items from the ship are on display. Remains of the hull and rigging, as well as cannon, crossbows, tools, and the personal possessions of the crew, provide a fascinating time capsule of the daily life of early Hispanic Americans. The upper floor of the museum is

Turks & Caicos National Museum
- ✉ Guinep House, Front St.
- ☎ 649/946-2160
- ⏱ Closed Sun.
- 💲 $

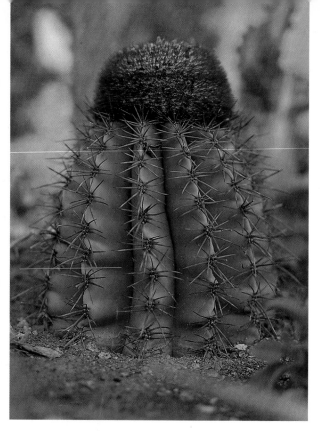

The Turks head cactus thrives in the sunbaked soils of Grand Turk island.

ISLAND DONKEYS

Grand Turk was once famous for its donkeys, which were found all over the island, roaming the scrub, foraging in gardens, standing quietly in the shade, or even holding up the traffic on the roads. They were introduced by settlers in the 17th century to haul cart-loads of salt to the waiting ships. By the 1800s more than 800 of the long-eared beasts were on the island, but after the salt trade collapsed in 1964, the donkeys came to be viewed as a nuisance rather than an asset. Some were exported to islands that needed them, such as Jamaica. Many now live in a donkey sanctuary on the north shore. About 50 animals, however, still roam free, caus-ing mischief, as they have always done. ■

devoted to natural history, the salt trade, Lucayan Taino, and other aspects of the islands' history.

The Chief Minister's office, **Waterloo** (*Front St., Tel 649/946-2309*), the Treasury, and other government offices reside in a series of wood-clad buildings to the south of Cockburn Town. Farther down

Front Street (0.3 mile/0.5 km) is **South Base,** a former Air Force missile tracking base that had its moment of fame in 1962 when the first U.S. astronaut to go into orbit around the Earth, John Glenn, was brought ashore here after his Mercury capsule splashed down just offshore. ■

Sports & activities

Diving & snorkeling:
Sea Eye Diving (Grand Turk, Tel 649/946-1407, e-mail: ci@caribsurf.com, www.interlog.com/~reefnet/ GTurk); Oasis Divers (Grand Turk, Tel 649/946-1128, e-mail: oasisdiv@tciway.tc, www.oasisdivers.com); Blue Water Divers (Salt Raker Inn,

Grand Turk, Tel 649/946-1226, e-mail: mrolling@caribsurf.com, www.microplan.com/bluerake.htm).

Sportfishing: For trips with a guide, contact Ossie Virgil (Tel 649/946-2018), or write to Sand Dollar Tours (P.O. Box 78, Grand Turk); Dutchie's (Airport Rd., Tel 649/946-2244). ■

Islands around Grand Turk

SALT CAY

The only other inhabited island in the Turks group, Salt Cay (*Tel 649/946-2321*) lies 7 miles (11 km) to the south of Grand Turk. Bermudians first landed here in 1645, and salt production began in 1673, lasting for almost 300 years until the collapse of the industry in the 1960s.

Recently declared a UNESCO World Heritage site, Salt Cay has a landscape dominated by reminders of its age-old industry. Miles of intricate low stone walls and canals (used to speed up evaporation) are still visible, as are numerous derelict windmills. Bermudian architecture predominates, most noticeably in the form of the White House in **Balfour Town,** which was built in the 1830s.

In the 19th century, Salt Cay was also a major center for whaling. Nowadays the whales are more valuable alive than dead. Visitors may be lucky enough to spot migrating humpbacks from January through March.

Like Grand Turk, Salt Cay was deforested long ago, but the lack of terrestrial flora is more than compensated for by a flourishing underwater environment. The island has numerous buoyed dive sites and offers virgin diving on its reef walls with their tunnels, undercuts, and caverns. A diving highlight is the wreck of the H.M.S. *Endymion,* a British warship dating from 1790; it was armed with 18 enormous cannon to protect British maritime trade.

Whatever your reason for being here, Salt Cay's residents (there are just 190 of them) will welcome you with open arms and—as the sign at the airport states—urge you to "return by any means."

SOUTH CAICOS

Tourists very seldom visit South Caicos (*Tel 649/946-2321*), once a major commercial center for the islands, but this was not always the case. In fact, the island had the first hotel in the Turks and Caicos Islands, the Admiral's Arms Inn; it opened in the 19th century to serve the Brazilian pilots who stopped here en route between Miami and South America. Their repeated missions were a result of the Turks and Caicos role as a drugs transship-

ment port in the 1980s. This problem climaxed in 1986 when Chief Minister Ernest Sanders was arrested on smuggling charges.

During the 19th century, South Caicos was at the center of the trade in another kind of "white gold" when the salinas of Grand Turk and Salt Cay could not meet the demand for salt from the North American market. The salinas of South Caicos were fed by a unique boiling hole, a subterranean passage that allowed salt water to naturally flow into the pans, where windmills pumped it into a series of reservoirs. The hot, dry climate, in combination with the boiling hole, allowed the island to export more salt than any of the islands and even to set up three steam-driven salt mills.

Today South Caicos still claims the best anchorage in the archipelago at **Cockburn Harbour,** a busy fishing port and the center of the export trade in queen conch, spiny lobster, and bonefish. The tourism potential of the island is as yet unrealized, even though it has some superb beaches (particularly Long Beach), excellent diving along its eastern shoreline, and beautiful, uninhabited cays nearby (Long Cay, Ambergris Cays, Fish Cays, and Bush Cay) that can be visited on day trips. Accessible only by boat, none of the cays have any accommodations. Diving and snorkeling trips from South Caicos can be organized through Club Caribe (*Tel 649/946-3444*).

EAST CAICOS

Covering some 38 square miles (98 sq km), East Caicos (*Tel 649/946-2321*) is one of the largest islands in the archipelago. **Flamingo Hill,** on its north side, is the highest point (156 feet/48 m) in the Turks and Caicos, but most of the island consists of swamps, mangroves, and tidal mudflats.

At the beginning of the 20th century, the settlement of Jacksonville administered a 50,000-acre (20,000-ha) sisal plantation and cattle farm, but the island is now uninhabited. In fact, it is the largest uninhabited island in the Caribbean. Near Jacksonville are several caves with evidence of Lucayan occupation, including petroglyphs carved on the walls. ■

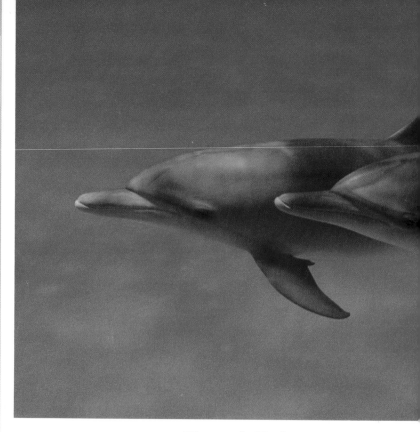

Grand Caicos

WITH AN AREA OF 48 SQUARE MILES (124 SQ KM), THIS IS THE largest island in the Turks and Caicos archipelago. Its 300 inhabitants live mainly in the three settlements of Conch Bar, Lorimers, and Bambarra and depend on fishing and small-scale tourism.

Grand Caicos
🗺 81 C3
Visitor information
✉ Front St., Cockburn Town, Grand Turk
☎ 649/946-2321

Grand Caicos was occupied by the Taino between A.D. 750 and 1500, who called it Aniyana.

Armstrong Pond, south of Bambarra, is an important Taino settlement (one of 38 on the island). It features the only ceremonial ball court in the region and an arrangement of stones that may have had astrological significance. In **Conch Bar** you can explore a series of caves with a local guide (*day trips to the caves from J&B Tours, Providenciales, Tel 649/946-5047, fax 649/946-5288*).

The island's northwest coast is characterized by dramatic limestone cliffs (unique in the archipelago) interspersed with beautiful, deserted beaches. A trail along the coastline, known as the **Crossing Place Trail,** was the main highway on the island until the King's Road was built farther inland in the 1980s to connect the three settlements. The trail's name refers to the fact that it ends up at the ferry crossing to North Caicos. Because the trail passes through some of the most memorable scenery in the Turks and Caicos, the British National Trust is developing the site for hiking and mountain biking.

Another unusual feature is the **Ocean Hole,** on the south side of the island, which is 1,200 feet (366 m) wide and about 200 feet (60 m) deep. It is thought to have been a land cave before being flooded many thousands of years ago and losing its roof. This marine sinkhole is home to bonefish, sharks, and other pelagic fish, and it can only be reached by boat. ■

Bottlenose dolphins are sometimes seen in Grand Caicos waters.

Island wildlife

Grand Caicos is one of the main nesting sites in the islands for the impressive ocean-going frigatebird, which also nests on Penniston Cay and other uninhabited islands. The uninhabited cays are important nesting areas for the sooty and roseate terns, Audubon's shearwater, and brown noddy. Four species of turtles (hawksbill, green, loggerhead, and leatherback) live in the surrounding waters, although local consumption of these endangered species is still common. The islands have a flourishing population of bottlenose dolphins, including the semitame JoJo, which frequents Grace Bay on Providenciales. In winter, humpback whales pass by on their way from cold northern seas to their breeding grounds southeast of Grand Turk. Divers often hear their haunting songs underwater. ■

North Caicos

North Caicos
▲ 81 C4
Visitor information
✉ Front St., Cockburn
    Town, Grand Turk
☎ 649/946-2321

IN CONTRAST TO THE ARIDITY OF MOST ISLANDS IN THE group, North Caicos is comparatively lush and is considered the garden center of the country. It does have a higher rainfall (for reasons not fully understood) and its fertile soil produces abundant crops of tomatoes, corn, papaya, yam, pumpkin, lime, and avocado on farms tucked away in the interior.

North Caicos is a get-away-from-it-all retreat with superb beaches.

Like its sister islands Grand and East Caicos, its southern parts consist mostly of mangrove lagoons and swamps (see p. 85). On the north coast, powdery sand beaches slope into a shimmering lagoon that leads out to a line of breakers crashing onto the offshore reef.

Most of its 1,500 inhabitants live in five settlements connected by just a few roads (some of them recently metaled, some still dirt tracks).

North Caicos is just a 10-minute flight from Providenciales, with frequent daily departures; boats take 30 minutes.

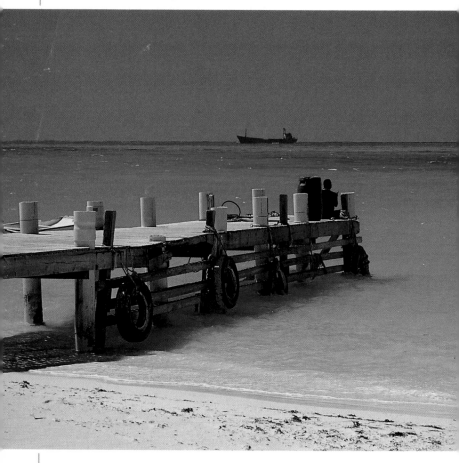

EXPLORING THE ISLAND

The Global Airways *(Tel 649/941-3222)* North Caicos Explorer includes flights, a guided tour of the island, and lunch at a beach-front hotel. J&B Tours *(Tel 649/946-5868)* operates a North Caicos Getaway package, which includes scooter rental, boat to the island, a map, and snorkel gear. ◾

Place-names echo the island's idiosyncratic history: Hungry Hole (a hidden lagoon); Ready Money (a plot of land that changed hands swiftly because the buyer had just that); Snaky Pond and Rat Cay; Mountain Pond and Pumpkin Bluff Pond; Laughland, another settlement, lies on the shore of Bottle Creek.

Just over 200 years ago Wade Stubbs, a Loyalist from Florida, was granted 860 acres (340 ha) for a plantation on North Caicos, near the present-day landing of Belleville. By the time of his death in 1821 he had nearly 400 slaves working on his plantation, **Wade's Green.** One of the best preserved ruins in the Caicos Islands from the Loyalist period, the site is currently being developed by the National Trust as a tourist attraction.

North Caicos has the second largest population of flamingos in the Caribbean, but depending on where they are on the extensive Flamingo Ponds, you may only see them as pink dots in the distance. There are plans to build a board-walk through the mangroves to allow people to get closer to these magnificent birds. Until that happens, take binoculars.

Protected under the international RAMSAR convention, the nature reserve (see below) supports substantial numbers of West Indian flamingos and other waterbirds, including West Indian whistling ducks and breeding colonies of magnificent frigatebirds. ◾

Caicos nature reserve

Stretching over 210 square miles (544 sq km), the North, Grand, and East Caicos Nature Reserve is one of the largest protected areas in the Caribbean. A wilderness of tidal sloughs, mangroves, mudflats, and saline ponds, this important wetland zone links the dry uplands of the islands with the turquoise banks. Submerged banks, creeks, and lagoons provide critical nursery habitat for flamingos (above), lobsters, conchs, turtles, and other marine species. ◾

An aerial view of Chalk Sound

Providenciales (Provo)

ABOUT 25 MILES (40 KM) LONG AND 3 MILES (5 KM) WIDE, Providenciales is the most developed of the islands in terms of tourism and commerce. Commonly called Provo, the island has wide, sandy beaches and dramatic offshore diving sites.

Providenciales

▲ 80 B3

Visitor information

✉ Turtle Cove Landing

☎ 649/946-4970

On a cloudy day you can sometimes see a green sheen on the underside of the cloud banks over Providenciales. This unique phenomenon is caused by reflections from shallow inland lagoons such as **Chalk Sound,** which is protected as a national park. Chalk Sound National Park *(Tel 649/946-4970)* is a huge shallow expanse of chalky blue-and-turquoise water dotted with green rocky islets.

Along its north shore lies **Grace Bay,** a superb sweep of fine, powdery white sand that ranks among the top beaches in the Caribbean. Most of the islands' hotels are strung out along this magnificent beach. Surrounding Grace Bay is the **Princess Alexandra Marine Park,** a vast area of offshore patch reefs, walls, and lagoons *(Tel 649/946-4970)*. The island has some excellent diving here and farther along the coast at **Northwest Point** (see p. 91).

Providenciales once had three large sisal and cotton plantations. The ruins of one of these,

Sports & activities

Diving & snorkeling:
Provo Turtle Divers *(Providenciales, Tel 649/ 946-4232, fax 649/941-5296, e-mail: ProvoTurtleDivers@Provo.net, www.provo.net/ptd);* Flamingo Divers *(Providenciales, Tel 649/946-4193 or 800/204-9282, fax 649/946-4193, e-mail: flamingo@caribsurf, www.provo.net/flamingo);* Caicos Adventures *(Turtle Cove Marina Plaza, Tel 649/941-3346 or 800/513-5822, fax 649/941-3346, e-mail: divucrzy@caribsurf.com, www.caicosadventures.tc).*

Golf: Provo Golf Club *(Tel 649/946-5991, fax 649/956-5992, e-mail: provgolf@ caribsurf.com, www. provogolfclub. com).* ■

OUT ON THE WATER
A visit to some of the surrounding uninhabited cays (particularly Little Water Cay—see p. 94) is a must during a stay on Provo. The biggest water sports operator is J&B Tours *(Tel 649/946-5047).* A fleet of 11 fast powerboats takes visitors on half- or full-day excursions to the cays, on beach cruises, on snorkel trips, and on beach barbecues. Other operators include Sand Dollar Cruising *(Tel 649/946-5238)* and Silver Deep *(Tel 649/946-5612),* as well as a local character called Bettlejuice *(Tel 649/946-5236),* who provides an entertaining beach tour. ■

Cheshire Hall, can be seen just off the Leeward Highway near the new government medical clinic. Tourism development began with the building of a jet runway and a Club Med in the 1960s, and although new condominiums and hotels are still being added, it is not yet a mass-market destination.

Of Provo's three original settlements—**Five Cays, Blue Hills,** and **The Bight** (meaning "the Bay")—the most scenic is Blue Hills, a small fishing port on the north coast. Government offices and other businesses are located in **down town,** near the airport, but in general the island lacks a focal point. Shopping malls and other

Dive boats moor up between dives at Northwest Point.

The queen conch (above and below right) has distinctive eyes.

Island conchs

The beautiful, pink-lipped shellfish known as the queen conch *(Strombus gigas)* has been a staple of the Caribbean diet since long before Columbus arrived in the New World. Today more than 40 million conchs are harvested annually in the shallow waters surrounding the Bahamas, Bermuda, Florida, and the Turks and Caicos. The waters of the Caicos Bank have supplied some four million of these but, as elsewhere in the region, the harvest is declining due to overfishing. Conchs are now listed as an endangered species. The Caicos Conch Farm, which employs more than 20 workers, is the only facility of its kind in the world. Its current target is to export a million conchs a year from their inventory of three million conchs at various stages of development. The farm has recently developed new markets in Florida and elsewhere with the introduction of live-in-the-shell conchs, which are more tender and sweeter than frozen conch. ■

facilities have sprung up haphazardly along the main road, the Leeward Highway. The closest the island has to a central focus is **Turtle Cove,** where you'll find hotels, a few restaurants, and a tourist office clustered around the yacht basin.

Provo's new 6,560-yard (6,000-m), par 72 championship golf course on the eastern end of the island was designed by Karl Litton. It is already lauded as one of the best in the Caribbean.

At the far eastern end of the island is a deep channel that separates Provo from adjacent Mangrove Cay. This natural harbor, known as **Leeward Going Through,** is currently being developed as a marina. Alongside the marina is the **Caicos Conch Farm.** The only one of its kind in the world, the farm was set up in 1984 to develop techniques for conch farming on a commercial scale. The educational tour of the farm embraces the various stages the conchs move through, from the hatchery to the subsea pasture (where they grow to maturity). The conch farm exports live conchs to Florida and also sells them to local restaurants. ■

A Provo fisherman skillfully removes the flesh from a conch shell.

Caicos Conch Farm
- ✉ At the Marina
- ☎ 649/946-5330
- 🕐 Closed Sun.
- 💲 $

The rock iguana has become one of Little Water Cay's main attractions.

Islands around Providenciales

PARROT CAY

This 1,300-acre (526-ha) island is privately owned and was once run as a plantation; the remains of the plantation house can still be seen. Its original name was Pirate Cay, thanks to the fact that between 1718 and 1720 it was supposedly home to the notorious pirate Anne Bonny and her lover, Calico Jack Rackham.

PINE CAY

Another private island, this 800-acre (324-ha) hideaway has a fine sandy beach on its north coast and several freshwater ponds populated by saltwater fish—one of the unexpected legacies of Hurricane Donna in 1960. Non-motorized water sports, tennis, bikes, and golf

Island iguanas

The rock iguana species *(Cyclura carinata)* to be seen on Little Water Cay is unique to these islands. This long-lived, territorial reptile mates but once a year, producing 7 to 12 eggs per clutch. Rock iguanas have disappeared from many inhabited islands due to predation by humans, cats, and dogs. About 50,000 rock iguanas remain in the Turks and Caicos, the largest population in the world, with about 1,000 on Little Water Cay and the rest on Ambergris Cay, at Fort George, and in other island reserves. ■

carts are available from the exclusive Meridien Club on the shore *(Tel 212/696-4566 or 800/331-9154, fax 212/689-1593).* Pine Cay is very peaceful: No cars are allowed, only bicycles and golf carts. There are nature trails through the different areas and by the freshwater ponds.

LITTLE WATER CAY

This uninhabited cay close to Provo, now a protected area under the National Trust of Turks and Caicos *(Tel 649/946-1723),* is popular with day-trippers who come to see its iguanas. Unfortunately, the increasing numbers of visitors have damaged the habitat and affected the behavior of the iguanas (which were being fed with inappropriate food such as lettuce or potato chips). Tourists must stay on a boardwalk trail and can no longer feed the iguanas. Sail Provo runs boat excursions to Little Water Cay *(Tel 649/946-4783).*

WEST CAICOS

Isolated and uninhabited, West Caicos is noted for its surrounding reefs, which are visited by day boats from Providenciales, as well as by live-aboard dive boats (see p. 91). The small sandy coves on the west coast are frequented by divers on their surface intervals, as is the inshore saltwater Lake Catherine, home to waders and ducks. The ruins of a railroad and sisal press are at **Yankee Town** *(Tel 649/946-4970).* ■

Site of the first Spanish colony in the Americas, the Dominican Republic encompasses virtually everything from colonial architecture to a lush, mountainous interior and some of the best beaches in the Caribbean.

Dominican Republic

Island color as captured by a local painter

Dominican Republic

OCCUPYING THE EASTERN TWO-THIRDS OF THE ISLAND OF HISPANIOLA (the remaining third is Haiti), the Dominican Republic holds many superlatives. It was home to the first European colony in the New World, and it has the Caribbean's highest peak, largest lake, and biggest city. But above all it is known for its extensive white sand beaches. Within the last decade it has built a substantial tourist industry on the basis of these beautiful natural assets. Beyond the beach resorts, however, tourism has had minimal impact. If you're adventurous you will be rewarded with discovering an enormously diverse country. If you travel beyond the tourist spots, you'll need to know some Spanish.

This fertile island was heavily populated by Taino Indians when Columbus first arrived on these shores in 1492. He named it Isla Española (or Hispaniola) and decided it would be an ideal place for a colony, especially since gold deposits were also discovered.

The first settlement was built on the north coast at La Isabela, but it was a bad choice—difficult to defend, hot, and disease-ridden. The present-day capital, Santo Domingo, was established on a much more promising site at the mouth of the Ozama River in 1496. During the early years of Spanish rule, the economy was fueled by gold, but by 1515 the gold had run out and the Spanish began to ignore Hispaniola in favor of the more lucrative mines of South America and the prospect of wealth in Mexico.

By the 17th century the northwestern part of the island was occupied by pirates and French buccaneers, who managed to resist attempts by the Spanish to drive them out. France took advantage of this to claim the western third of the island, which was then ceded to them under the Treaty of Ryswick in 1697. Over the next century Saint Domingue, as the French portion was known, became one of the richest colonies in the Caribbean thanks to sugarcane plantations. The eastern part of the island languished under the Spanish, whose attentions had moved elsewhere.

In the 1790s Toussaint L'Ouverture (1743–1803) led a slave uprising in Saint Domingue. The Spaniards supported Toussaint, forcing the French to abolish slavery. In 1794 Toussaint suddenly switched sides and joined forces to oust the Spanish from the island. Toussaint gained control in 1795 and held on until 1802, when Napoleon Bonaparte sent an expeditionary force to arrest him.

Meanwhile, rebels had driven the French forces out of the western part of the island, and the Republic of Haiti was declared on January 1, 1804. The Spanish recaptured the eastern part of the island in 1809, but they were driven out by settlers intent on independence, which was won in 1821. But independence was not to last. The Haitians invaded in 1822 and controlled the whole island for the next 22 years. The occupation fostered an underground opposition movement, La Trinitaria, which seized control in 1844 and declared the independence of the new country, known as the Dominican Republic.

Since independence, politics in the Dominican Republic have swung between democracy and dictatorship. The dark years under Gen. Rafael Leonidas Trujillo (1891–1961), from 1930 until 1961, are still remembered with horror by many.

The country's economy today is based on tourism, agriculture, and mineral exports.

Sugarcane is still the largest crop; most of it is harvested by workers from Haiti. The near-slave status of the Haitian cane cutters and the abuse of their civil rights by the government have become something of an international scandal. Gold and silver mining is of considerable importance, and the deposits of ferronickels are estimated at 10 percent of world reserves. Among the other export commodities are coffee, cocoa, rice, and cigars. Tourism is the largest earner of foreign exchange, generating in excess of two billion dollars from the 2.5 million or so tourists who visit every year. ■

Santo Domingo's Catedral Basilica Menor de Santa Maria

Santo Domingo

THE CAPITAL AND CHIEF PORT OF THE DOMINICAN Republic, Santo Domingo is the oldest city in the New World and can lay claim to the first university, cathedral, and hospital in the Americas. The city was founded by Christopher Columbus's brother Bartoloméo in 1498, after the Spanish abandoned their attempts to found a colony on the north coast. Santo Domingo has become the hub of life in the Dominican Republic and a magnet for commerce from neighboring islands.

Santo Domingo
🗺 97 D2
Visitor information
✉ Calle Isabel La Catolica 103, Zona Colonial
☎ 809/682-0185

Opposite: Interesting perspectives inside the Faro a Colón

Built on the east bank of the Río Ozama, the city was christened Nueva Isabel. Its name changed to Santo Domingo when the city was moved to the west bank after a hurricane in 1502. It flourished as a port, and from here the Spanish launched major expeditions to Mexico, Puerto Rico, Cuba, and the Pacific. As the riches of the Spanish Main were revealed, Santo Domingo lost its preeminent position in the Caribbean. It suffered a further blow in 1562, when an earthquake destroyed much of the city. English privateer Sir Francis Drake (circa 1540–1596) also caused considerable damage when he attacked the city in 1586.

Despite its decline, Santo Domingo continued to play a major role as the political and commercial center of the country. During the regime of Rafael Trujillo, Santo Domingo was known for 25 years as Ciudad Trujillo, but with the death of the dictator it reverted.

Today Santo Domingo is the industrial, financial, and commercial heart of the Dominican Republic and home to some 2.5 million people. The restored colonial city is a World Heritage site. The colonial zone is the most attractive part of the city, with pleasant squares, outdoor cafés, and a wealth of historic buildings.

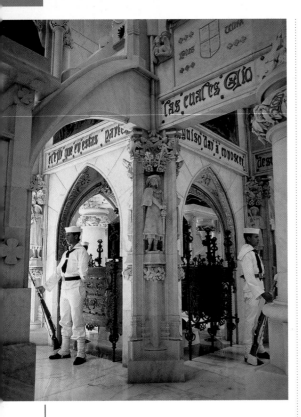

The tomb inside the **Faro a Colón** is said to hold the remains of Columbus.

of caves near the monument offer a natural counterpoint to the controversial monument.

Without doubt, the monumental Faro a Colón is a talking point both within the Dominican Republic and beyond. Despite the fact that from the exterior it resembles a shoddy, concrete apartment complex (appropriately enough, since many slum houses were bulldozed to clear the site), the interior is well worth a visit. The idea of a monument to Columbus was first proposed in the 1920s, and a design competition was won by a British architectural student, J. Cleave. The structure, in the shape of a recumbent cross, was eventually built in 1992.

The building covers an area of 107,500 square feet (10,000 sq m), its outer walls featuring plaques bearing the names of every Latin American state. At the center of the cross is the marble **tomb of Columbus,** guarded by uniformed sentries. A sarcophagus said to hold his remains was moved here from the city's cathedral on the opening day—October 6, 1992. The corridors on either side of the tail of the cross contain some rather uninspiring cultural displays contributed by 50 countries around the world. One highlight, however, is an original **Mayan almanac** (one of only four known) dating back to the 14th century. Another precious artifact is

EASTERN QUARTERS

Santo Domingo's eastern quarters are the home of one of the city's most extravagant showcases, the **Faro a Colón** (*Tel 809/592-5217*), which was built as part of the 500th anniversary of Columbus's landfall in 1492. A dramatic series

The enigma of Columbus's ashes

The Faro a Colón claims to hold the remains of Christopher Columbus, but is this true? When the explorer died in 1506, he was buried in Valladolid, Spain. Three years later his body was moved to Seville and in the 1540s sent back to Santo Domingo. His remains were then shipped to Cuba when France gained control of Santo

Domingo in 1795, and from there back to Seville in 1898. However, in 1877 renovations in the cathedral revealed a casket beneath the altar bearing the inscription "Almirante Cristobal Colón," and it is these ashes that now lie in state in the Faro a Colón. Whether the ashes are those of Columbus can probably never be proved. ∎

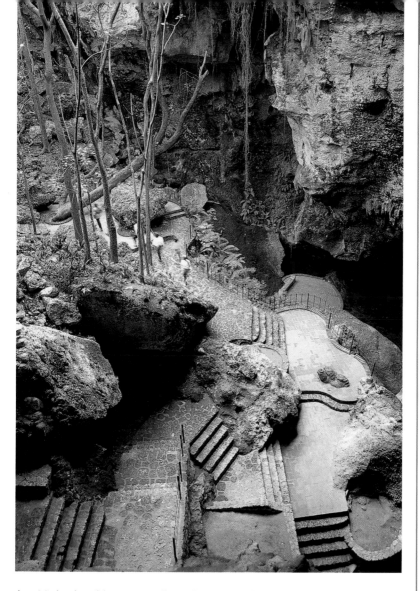

the original anchor of the *Santa Maria*, Columbus's flagship, salvaged from the north coast of Haiti, where the ship sank in 1492. The opening of the monument was marred by several explosions in the city, protesting the extravagance in a country with much poverty. Critics also point to the huge cost in electricity for the lasers that occasionally beam a cross shape into the clouds when most of the urban population is still suffering continual power cuts.

A few minutes' drive down the Avenida de las Americas from the Faro a Colón are a series of caves known as **Los Tres Ojos** (The Three Eyes). These spectacular series of collapsed caves contain dramatic formations and underground lakes, the last of which is reached via a rope-winched raft. Luxuriant tropical vegetation adds

Los Tres Ojos is an unusual sight to find in a city.

Los Tres Ojos
✉ Parque Los Tres Ojos, Ave. de las Americas
💲 $

Plaza de Cultura
✉ Ave. Cesar Nicolas Penson

Museo del Hombre Dominicano
✉ Plaza de Cultura
☎ 809/687-3622
⊕ Closed Sun.—Mon.
💲 $

A colorful version of the Washington Monument soars above the Malecón.

a lost world atmosphere to this unusual location—all the more striking because it's so close to a major city center.

THE MODERN CITY

The modern center of Santo Domingo extends north and west of the colonial zone, down to the seafront and Avenida George Washington (usually referred to simply as the Malecón). This seafront avenue is at its liveliest in the evenings, when Dominicans stroll or even dance to the sounds of merengue (see below) blasting out from portable stereos. The annual Merengue Festival takes place here.

In the heart of downtown is the **Plaza de Cultura,** a large park that includes four large museums, the **Teatro Nacional** (*Tel 809/687-4086*), and **Biblioteca Nacional** (*Tel 809/688-4086*). The best of the museums is the excellent **Museo del Hombre Dominicano,** the largest archaeological and anthropological museum in the Caribbean. It contains a wealth of material relating to pre-Columbian civilization. The museum occupies the third and fourth floors of a large building, and the best exhibits are found on the third floor. Here you'll see the fossil remains of an extinct bear, *Megatorio,* once hunted by the prehistoric Taino, as well as ceremonial axes dating from 2000 B.C. Comparative displays of South American indigenous cultures place

Merengue

Throughout the Dominican Republic you'll hear the sound of merengue, the national music. Traditionally this fast music has been played by a three-man combo performing on either a *tres* or *cuatro* (both are similar to a guitar), a *tambora* (double drum), and a *guiro* (calabash). The country's annual Merengue Festival (*Tel 809/586-3676*) is held between late July and early August. Most of the action takes place on Santo Domingo's Malecón, transformed into a vast open-air disco for the occasion. ∎

Taino history in context. Hundreds of prehistoric pieces include necklaces and jewelry, shaped stones used to grate the staple food, yucca, dozens of examples of the three-headed god of agriculture (*Trigonolito*), heart-shaped pots with phallic necks (fertility symbols), artistically decorated conch shells that were used as trumpets for communicating across a distance, and elaborately carved stone rings whose purpose is unknown. A burial display shows skeletons in a fetal position (the Taino believed in reincarnation, and therefore buried corpses in the fetal position so that they were ready for rebirth); one's jaws are open in a grimace of suffocation (Taino chiefs were polygamous, and when they died their wives were buried with them—alive). The fourth floor, which documents the influences that have shaped today's culture in the Dominican Republic, will take less of your time.

Next door is the **Museo Nacional de Historia y Geographica** (*Tel 809/689-0106*), which contains memorabilia from the Trujillo era (including the briefcase, wallet, comb, photos, and other items that belonged to the former dictator) and model ships relating to the Haiti-Dominican conflicts in the 19th century. However, the presentation of the displays is old-fashioned and rather dull.

The **Museo de Historia Natural** (*Tel 809/689-0106, closed Mon.*) contains a few stuffed birds and is equally missable. On the other hand, the **Museo de Arte Moderno** is well worth a visit, with contemporary works by both Dominican and foreign artists in the permanent collection.

Go east from the Plaza de Cultura to see the **Palacio Nacional,** an imposing neoclassic

building constructed in 1947. It once housed the congress, but it is now the home of the president.

A welcome retreat from the heat and bustle of Santo Domingo can be found on the city's northwest outskirts at the **Jardin Botanico.** Established in 1976, the gardens cover 0.75 square miles (2 sq km). You could easily pass half a day here. A "road train" takes visitors around the broad perimeter track, but a leisurely walk will give you more chance to appreciate the tropical plants and trees. There are separate areas for orchids, water plants, bromeliads, palms, cactuses and succulents, medicinal plants, and a wide variety of endemic Caribbean species. The Japanese garden, with its bamboo groves and ornamental ponds, is a particular highlight. Although labeling is haphazard,

The neoclassic Palacio Nacional, built from rose-colored marble

Museo de Arte Moderno
☎ 809/685-2153
🕐 Closed Mon.
💲 $

Palacio Nacional
✉ Calle Dr. Delgado
☎ 809/686-4771
🕐 By appt. only

Jardin Botanico
✉ Ave. República de Colombia
☎ 809/567-6211
🕐 Closed Mon.
💲 $

The 18th-century gateway to the Fortaleza Ozama recalls Spanish colonial might.

in this area is the **Fortaleza Ozama.** Built by Governor Nicolas de Ovando in 1502 on a steep bank overlooking the mouth of the Río Ozama, the fortress was Santo Domingo's principal defense from the 16th century and was occupied by the military until the 1970s. The last fort to be built by the Spanish as they moved from north to south across the island, it guarded the harbor throughout the colonial period. You enter the fort via a neoclassic gateway added in 1787.

Directly ahead is the impressive **Torre del Homenaje** (Tower of Homage), a solid structure with 7-foot-thick (2-m) walls whose clean lines and battlements give it the semblance of a medieval castle: Its design is unique in the New World. You can climb to the top of the turret to gain some idea of the strategic importance of the fort, which guarded every major Spanish flotilla as it left the harbor for the conquest of the Americas—although the historical illusion is hard to conjure up in the face of the giant cement factory looming on the opposite side of the river.

To one side of the tower is an 18th-century armory, beyond which can be seen the remnants of a temporary fort built before the tower was erected. The statue on the grounds is of Gonzalo Fernandez de Oviedo, the fort's governor from 1533 to 1557.

Another major building in the colonial zone is the **Alcázar de Colón.** Built between 1511 and 1516 by Diego de Colón (Columbus's son, who became the first viceroy of the New World), this impressive building has a beautiful Renaissance facade with graceful arcades and is a copy (on a slightly smaller scale) of a castle in Toledo, Spain. Most of the superb furnishings and artworks are genuine

these lovely gardens are a delight.

East from the botanic gardens is the **Parque Zoologiqué** (*Nacional Avenida, Los Arroyos, Tel 809/562-3149, closed Mon.*). Located in an unused limestone quarry across the road from an extensive slum area, the zoo covers 24 acres (9.5 ha). Most animals are in open enclosures, but many (including cheetahs, hyenas, and others used to roaming the African plains) are imprisoned in small cages. On a more humane note, the zoo is attempting to nurture a dwindling population of the rare solenodon, a small, insectivorous indigenous mammal that looks a bit like a rat. There are only 500 left in the country, but so far two-thirds of the captive population has died.

COLONIAL ZONE

The historic colonial zone lies on the western banks of the Río Ozama, overlooking the cruise ship terminal and bulk-grain shipment docks in the Puerto Ozama. You should certainly allow at least a day to visit its sights (see pp. 106–107).

Among the key historic buildings

Fortaleza Ozama
- Calle Las Damas
- $

Alcázar de Colón
- Plaza Espana
- $

16th-century. They were a gift from the Spanish government when the palace was restored in the 1950s and are not the originals that were once here. Note the wooden ceilings, particularly the one in the entrance hall decorated with 42 sculptured animal heads—a Spanish custom to ward off evil spirits.

For an overview of the history of the Dominican Republic, you can look into the **Museo de las Casas Reales.** The collection covers the country's history from displays on the Taino through Columbus's arrival, colonization, the plantations, and slavery. There's a highly credible reconstruction of an 18th-century pharmacy (the brightly colored ceramics are, however, reproductions), but the highlight is an extraordinary collection of ancient armaments, including a bronze Roman legionnaire's helmet dating from A.D. 1, elaborately decorated Turkish and Moroccan muskets, a Ceylonese executioner's scimitar, Japanese samurai swords, and English crossbows. Between the court rooms you'll see a carved elephant's tusk dating from 1552.

Take time to go to the **Pantéon Nacional** at the northern end of the Calle Las Damas. Originally built in the mid-18th century as a Jesuit convent, the pantheon was used as a tobacco warehouse and, later, as a theater after the Jesuits left the island. In the 1950s Trujillo converted it into a memorial to the heroes of Dominican history; the huge candelabra was a gift from the Spanish dictator Gen. Francisco Franco. Every two hours you can see the changing of the guard. ∎

Traders size up the day's selection at the central market of Santo Domingo.

Museo de las Casas Reales
✉ Calle Las Dama
$ $

Pantéon Nacional
✉ Calle las Damas
🕐 Closed Mon.

The impressive double archway of the northern portal of the Catedral Basilica Menor de Santa Maria

Colonial zone walk

The walk starts and ends in the Plaza Colón (Columbus Square), a busy meeting place surrounded by old stone buildings and arched walkways, with a statue of the explorer at its center. On the way you have a chance to savor the pride of Santo Domingo's colonial legacy, an ensemble of handsome buildings and monuments that mirror the country's sometimes turbulent history.

On the south side of the square is the **Catedral Basilica Menor de Santa Maria** ❶ *(no shorts or short skirts allowed).* Built between 1514 and 1540, it was the first cathedral in the New World—as well as the oldest church of any description in the Caribbean—and the remains of Columbus were supposedly uncovered here during restoration work in 1877 (see p. 100). The tranquil interior features a 17th-century mahogany throne as well as stained-glass windows. The cathedral was fully restored in 1992.

Palacio de Borgella ❷ flanks the east side of the square. Built during the Haitian occupation in the mid-19th century, it has a graceful, porticoed facade on two levels. It served as the seat of congress until 1947 and now houses administrative offices and a post office.

From here make your way to El Conde, a lively pedestrian street lined with shops and cafés that bisects the heart of the colonial zone. El Conde leads down toward the seafront and the Calle las Damas, a pleasant, tree-lined street where the ladies of the court would take their evening stroll in colonial days. Most of the oldest and loveliest buildings in the colonial zone are located on this street.

- 🗺 See area map page 97
- ▶ Plaza Colón
- 🔁 3 miles (5 km)
- 🕐 Allow 2–3 hours
- ▶ Plaza Colón

NOT TO BE MISSED
- Palacio de Borgella
- Casas Reales
- Monasterio de San Francisco

Turn right onto the Calle las Damas to visit the **Fortaleza Ozama** (see p. 104), then double back toward the north: On your right is the **Hospital Palacio Nicolás de Ovando** ③, built in 1502 as the residence of the governor after whom it is named. This beautiful building is now the Hotel Palacio Nicolas de Ovando (53 Calle las Damas, Tel 809/687-3101). Opposite is the **Panteón Nacional** (see p. 105).

Continue on to the end of Calle las Damas, where you'll find the imposing palace of the **Casas Reales** ④ (Corner of Calle las Mercedes and Calle las Damas), which once housed the governor's office, the royal court of justice (Real Audiencia), treasury, and military administration. Built in the early 16th century, it now houses the excellent **Museo de las Casas Reales** (see p.105). Opposite is a sundial, dating from 1753, on a site with fine views over the port.

Beyond here the street opens out into a large plaza. On the east side is the imposing **Alcázar de Colón** (see p.104). Opposite the Alcázar is **La Atarazana** ⑤, a series of eight buildings that housed the royal armory, customs house, and warehouses; today they are shops, restaurants, and bars.

From La Atarazana turn left onto Calle Isabel la Católica to see the **Casa del Cordón** ⑥ (Corner of Calle Emiliano Tejera). Built in 1509, it was one of the first stone buildings on the island; it is named after the cord the Franciscan order wore around their robes and which is carved in stone above the doorway. Today it is a branch of the Banco Popular.

Follow Calle Tejera across Calle Arzobispo Merino and then onto Calle Hostos: Here you will find the ruins of the **Monasterio de San Francisco** ⑦, the first monastery in the

New World. Built in the early 16th century, it was sacked by Sir Francis Drake and then further damaged by earthquakes in 1673 and 1751. Take Arzobispo Merino back to the Plaza Colón. ∎

Alcázar de Colón overlooks Plaza de Maria Toledo.

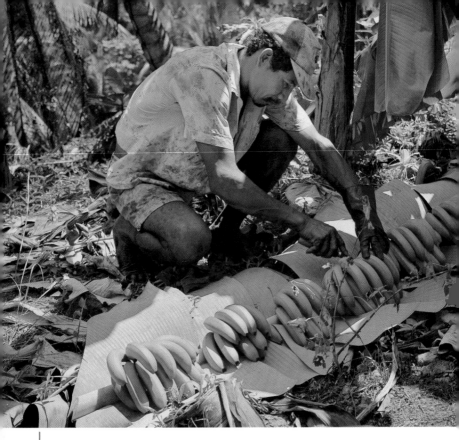

West of Santo Domingo

Bananas are divided into hands at the base of the tree at harvesttime.

THE SOUTHWESTERN CORNER OF THE REPUBLIC IS AN ARID region with some unusual coastal landscapes. This is an area scarcely touched by tourism, although the opening of a new international airport in Barahona and a new highway from the capital means that access is now getting easier.

San Cristóbal

🅰 97 C2

Casa Las Caobas & Castillo del Cerro

☎ 809/528-3553

💲 $

Some 15 miles (24 km) to the west of Santo Domingo is the town of **San Cristóbal,** where the country's first constitution was signed (on November 6, 1844), but it is better known as the birthplace of the dictator Rafael Trujillo. His main residence, **Casa Las Caobas,** sits in ruins on a hilltop just outside town; there are plans to restore it. Trujillo also built the **Castillo del Cerro,** a grandiose, six-story house on another hilltop nearby.

From San Cristóbal the main road (Rte. 2) leads to Baní, to the southwest of which is **Las Salinas** (*Contact Ceferino V. Castillo, c/o the Gobernacion Provincial, Tel 809/522-4335*). Just outside this fishing village on the Bahía Las Calderas are the largest sand dunes in the Caribbean. From Baní, **Barahona** is just over 60 miles (100 km) to the west.

Located on the Bahía de Neiba, Barahona has a population of more than 80,000. Its new airport, the

Aeropuerto Maria Montés (named after a Dominican actress who starred in Hollywood movies in the 1940s and 1950s), is intended to promote tourist development in this relatively remote part of the country. One of the main attractions is the coastal scenery south of Barahona. Here the Sierra de Baoruco reaches almost down to the Caribbean, and small fishing villages are interspersed with coves and inviting sandy beaches (although swimming is not always possible because these are surfing beaches). After the fishing village of Enriquillo, the route turns inland, toward the town of Pedernales on the border with Haiti.

NATURAL WONDERS
Parque Nacional Jaragua covers 189 square miles (500 sq km) on the southwesterly tip of the island. The park is distinguished by its dry climate, limestone formations, lagoons, and saltwater lakes. You need to be well prepared to visit this area, with its rough terrain and lack of water and decent maps. Official regulations stipulate that you should be accompanied by a guide. Contact one of the guide services listed for Isla Cabritos. The largest protected area in the Dominican Republic, the park includes two offshore islands, **Beata** and **Alto Velo.** The park is also known for its pelicans, terns, and iguanas.

Inland 36 miles (58 km) on Rte. 46 from Barahona, is **Lago Enriquillo,** a massive saltwater lake that is said to be the biggest in the Caribbean. Lying between 100 and 130 feet (30–40 m) below sea level, the lake is fed by streams from the Sierra de Neiba and the Sierra de Baoruco, but it has no outlet to the sea. Water loss is purely by evaporation, leading to a salt content in the lake three times higher than that of the Caribbean Sea. The lake is home to an abundance of wildlife, including crocodiles, iguanas, and flamingos.

Of the three islands in the lake, the biggest is the 5-mile-long (8 km) **Isla Cabritos** (Goat Island), the only one protected as a national park (see below). Home to goats, the island also holds crocodiles and many resident and migratory birds, including flamingos, clapper rails, and roseate spoonbills. The two smaller islands are known as **La Islita** and **Barbarita.** You can drive all the way around the lake, and at the western end you can cross over the border to Haiti. It is best to visit Isla Cabritos early in the morning when the animals are out foraging.

About 0.5 mile (800 m) to the east of **La Descubierta** at the western end of the lake is a series of pre-Columbian petroglyphs carved into the rock face. These are marked by signs from the Carretera Enriquillo. ■

Barahona
🗺 96 B2
Visitor information
✉ Carretera Batey
Central, Edificio
Defrimpo
☎ 809/534-3650

Parque Nacional Jaragua
🗺 96 A1

Isla Cabritos
🗺 96 A2

Visiting Isla Cabritos

To visit Goat Island, you should obtain a permit from the local office of the Dirección Nacional de Parques (DNP) in nearby La Descubierta *(Tel 809/537-5831, fax 809/566-8809),* although in practice few people bother. The boat trip takes about 20 minutes (maximum 18 people). This trip is well worth it; the best time for spotting crocs is early morning or evening. Tours are also run from Santo Domingo by Martisant *(Tel 809/585-7887)* and Ecoturisa *(Calle Santiago No. 203-B Gazcue, Santo Domingo Tel 809/221-4104).* ■

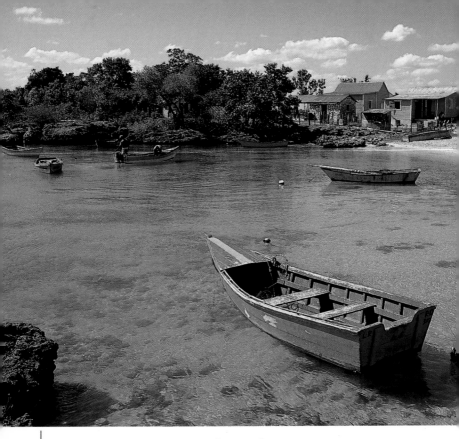

Southeast coast

THE SOUTHEAST COAST HAS SOME OF THE COUNTRY'S
white-sand beaches, lapped by the azure waters of the Caribbean
and backed up by swaying palms. In recent years large, luxurious all-
inclusive hotels have sprung up on many of the better beaches.
Wealthy Dominicans have built luxury villas here to escape the pollution and overcrowding of Santo Domingo.

**Parque Nacional
del Este**
🅰 97 E2

Boca Chica
🅰 97 D2
Visitor information
✉ Jesus Escotto, Calle
Duarte, esq. Caracol,
2da, Plaza Boca
Chica
☎ 809/523-5106

The countryside is mostly flat plains
in the center and south, carpeted by
extensive sugarcane plantations,
with a low range of mountains, the
Cordillera Oriental, to the north.
Much of the wealth of the major
towns in this region, such as San
Pedro de Macorís and La Romana,
comes from the sugar industry.

The region also has its natural
attractions, in the form of dazzling
offshore islands and the Parque
Nacional del Este (see p. 113), and
man-made ones, in the form of a
mock Italianate village, the Altos
de Chavón.

Heading east from Santo
Domingo along the Autopista de
las Américas, you pass some fine
stretches of coastline before arriving at the main international
gateway to the island, Las Américas
airport. A short distance past here
is **Boca Chica,** a beach resort on
a shallow bay never more than
5 feet (1.5 m) deep. It was one

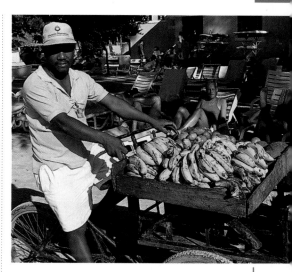

Macorís, lies at the mouth of the Río Higuama, 9 miles (14.5 km) east of Juan Dolio. This town was the center of the Dominican sugar industry at the turn of the 20th century, and remnants of its glory days can be seen in its houses, fire station, and the neoclassic church of **San Pedro Apostol** on the banks of the river. The town is unusual in that it shows a marked cultural influence from the Leeward and Windward Islands. In the 19th century skilled craftsmen and builders were brought in from the smaller British islands to help build the Victorian-style wooden houses that can still be seen on Avenida Independencia. They brought with them their own dances (called *guyolas*) and music *(cainanés).* You can see both performed during the annual **Fiestas Patronales** *(June).*

A fruit vendor plies his wares on Boca Chica beach.

LA ROMANA

The provincial capital, La Romana, is also a sugar town, and the hoot of diesel engines pulling carloads of cane to the Central Romana Corporation factory, which forms much of the skyline, is a familiar

of the first areas to be developed for tourism on the island under the Trujillo regime. Now it's a busy resort that fills up rapidly with residents from the capital on weekends; it has a genuinely local atmosphere.

The beaches at **Juan Dolio,** 25 miles (40 km) east of Santo Domingo on Rte. 3, are a better choice, although they can also be noisy and crowded on weekends. The main beaches along here are **Embassy Beach** (a small cove popular with body surfers), **Playa Guayacanes** (calmer and more extensive), and **Playa de Juan Dolio** (also a reasonable beach). There is a small mall with restaurants and shops in the village of Juan Dolio, but you'll find little else to visit in the vicinity.

One of the biggest towns on the south coast, **San Pedro de**

San Pedro de Macorís
🗺 97 D2

La Romana
🗺 97 E2
Visitor information
✉ Calle Teniente Amado Garcia (Governacion Principal)
☎ 809/550-6992

The main plaza at Altos de Chavón, an Italianate village high in the hills

Casa de Campo, Altos de Chavón, & Museo Arqueológico

🅰 97 E2

☎ 809/523-3333 or 800/877-3643

Dirección Nacional de Parques (National Parks Office)

✉ Ave. Independencia 539, esquina Cervantes, Santo Domingo

☎ 809/221-5340

Higüey

🅰 97 E2

Visitor information

✉ Calle de la Altagracia

☎ 809/554-2672

sound during the cutting season (Nov.–July). The factory's name comes from *la balanza romana*, the Roman scales once used to weigh the sugar exports. The sugar company is one of the largest cane sugar producers in the world, responsible for more than a third of the country's total output and owner of some 167 square miles (432 sq km) of canefields around the town.

A drop in sugar prices in the 1970s led to the development of the deserted area of scrub, east of La Romana, into a tourist complex that has since grown into the gigantic **Casa de Campo** (Country House).The biggest resort in the region, it boasts its own international airport, with direct flights from the United States. Its 11 square miles (28 sq km) of grounds include four golf courses, a 245-acre (100-ha) shooting center, stables with 150 riding horses and 150 polo ponies, 14 swimming pools, a private beach and marina, 13 tennis courts, 9 restaurants, and much more (see p. 360). The resort is so big that people get around it on golf carts.

Under the same ownership and on the same site as Casa de Campo is the **Altos de Chavón,** a mock Italianate village built in the 1970s and 1980s. Anyone may visit. A re-creation of a 16th-century medieval village and constructed entirely from coral rock and stone, it has attractive cobbled alleyways festooned with hibiscus and bougainvillea and a huge amphitheater, which seats 3,000 people. It was inaugurated with a concert by Frank Sinatra in 1982. The village overlooks the deep cleft that the Río Chavón has carved through the landscape and features several art galleries, a school of design, craft shops, a church, and numerous restaurants. Prices here are undeniably high, but the best reason to visit is the superb **Museo Arqueológico,** which contains an excellent collection of Taino art and ceremonial objects. Only the capital's Museo de l'Hombre Dominicano can rival it. Although the collection here is not as comprehensive, it is extremely well presented and well lit, with adequate labeling and information. The centerpiece is a rare, carved wooden idol, but the museum is also strong on artistic pieces, amulets, jewelry, ceremonial objects and axes, and household items (*closed Mon.*).

Offshore from La Romana is the uninhabited **Isla Catalina,** which has beautiful white sand beaches on the coastline facing the mainland. The interior is arid, but the reefs on the leeward shore are excellent for diving. There are some good shallow reefs and also a wall that drops 165 feet (50 m). For information on dive trips, contact Casa de Campo. Excursions are also run from dive operations at Punta Cana.

The fishing village of **Bayahibe,** popular with independent travelers, is about 15 miles (25 km) southeast of La Romana on Rte. 3, turning south at Los Cinco Caminos. A few budget hotels are dotted among the small wooden houses and cafés in the village.

Bayahibe also has a mile-long (1.6-km) sandy beach fringed with coconut palms and is a popular spot for tours hopping-off to Isla Saona offshore.

Isla Saona forms part of the **Parque Nacional del Este,** which includes the island itself and a stretch of coastline from Bayahibe to the Bahía de Yuma. The 53-square-mile (137-sq-km) Isla Saona has only two small fishing villages—Adamanay on the southwest coast and Punta Gorda on the west coast—but hundreds of people visit each day, drawn to its fantastic white sand beaches. For information contact the Dirección Nacional de Parques.

About 20 miles (32 km) inland from La Romana is the town of **Higüey,** one of the oldest on the island, founded in 1502. It holds little of interest to the visitor apart from being a major center of pilgrimage; in the heart of the town is the **Basilica de Nuestra Señora de la Merced,** a 16th-century Spanish church.

The Basilica de Nuestra Señora de Altagracia, Higüey

Bayahibe

Carnival

In the Dominican Republic the carnival tradition has become associated with the historic dates of February 27, 1844, when national leader Juan Pablo Duarte re-took Santo Domingo from the Spanish, and August 16, 1865, when the Dominican Republic became a fully independent country. Carnival is celebrated on these days irrespective of when Lent is. The days preceding these dates are animated with street dancing, parades, and parties. The highlight, however, is the carnival costumes of the *diablos cojuelos,* or lame devils, which chase people around the streets. They're known as *lechones* in Santiago, *cachuas* (horned devils) in Cabral, *toros* (bulls) in Montecristi, *papeluses* (paper devils) in Cotuí, *diablos de hojas de platano* (plantain leaf devils) in Barahona, and *mascaros* (masked devils) in Bonao. Each of these forms is represented by suitably decorated masks. Some of the best examples can be seen in the Santiago Museo Folklórico de Tomás Morel (see p. 116). ∎

The *diablos cojuelos* (lame devils) are the highlight of the carnival festivities.

Manatí Park Bávaro

- ⬛ 97 E2
- ✉ Plaza Bávaro
- ☎ 809/552-0807
- 💲 $$$$$

Just 550 yards (500 m) to the north of this is the massive **Basilica de Nuestra Señora de Altagracia,** which is dedicated to the country's patron saint. This huge concrete structure was built in the 1950s and is intended to resemble a 200-foot-high (60 m) pair of hands praying. An annual pilgrimage is made to the site each year on January 21.

COASTAL ATTRACTIONS

Due east from Higüey is the **Coconut Coast,** an uninterrupted stretch of some of the most gorgeous beaches on the island stretching from **Punta Espada** through **Punta Cana** and **Bávaro** almost all the way to **Punta Sabaneta.** Fine white sand, backed by coconut plantations, slopes off into a reef-protected lagoon that features excellent swimming and water sports. There are scuba diving and snorkeling offshore. This area has become one of the most intensively developed in the country, with a string of all-inclusive hotels, many with first-class facilities, spread out along different stretches of the beach.

Behind the beach hotels is the new **Manatí Park Bávaro.** The park features enclosures with iguanas, parrots, vultures, butterflies, storks, an aquarium with sharks and rays, plus regular performances by parrots, dancing horses, seals, and dolphins. For an extra fee, visitors can swim with the dolphins.

The park includes a re-creation of a Taino village, with a regular cultural show depicting the Taino way of life. ∎

Santiago de Los Caballeros

Horse-drawn carriages await tourists in Santiago de Los Caballeros.

THE SECOND LARGEST CITY IN THE DOMINICAN REPUBLIC (population 750,000), Santiago de Los Caballeros is the major industrial and agricultural center in the fertile Valle Cibao. Any industrial smoke, however, can probably be linked to the main crop, tobacco; Santiago is a major producer of hand-rolled cigars and mass-produced cigarettes. The city's name derives from the 30 Spanish nobles (caballeros) who founded the town on Columbus's orders in 1495.

A sprawling, prosperous metropolis, Santiago has built its fortunes on tobacco and rum. At the turn of the 20th century, it had no fewer than 26 cigar factories. Although it still produces high-quality cigars, much of the production has now switched to cigarettes. The huge Martinez factory still turns out 60,000 cigars a day—all made by hand—but its fully automated machinery also produces 18 million cigarettes in the same period. The cigarmaking process is fascinating to watch, as the skilled workers roll the leaves and bind them with a wrapper into the familiar tubular shape. More than 20 factories are still in operation, and the local tourist office can provide details about tours.

On the northeast corner of

Santiago de Los Caballeros

🅜 97 C3

Visitor information

✉ Maria I. Rodriguez, Ayuntamiento Municipal

☎ 809/582-5885

Museo del Tabaco

✉ 148 Calle 16
de Agosto

🕑 Closed Sun.

**Museo Folklórico
de Tomás Morel**

✉ 174 Restauracion St.

☎ 809/582-6787

🕑 Closed Sun.

💲 Donation

Santiago's central square, in the **Parque Duarte,** is the **Museo del Tabaco.** The museum's dusty displays, which trace the history of tobacco growing and production over the centuries, now look somewhat dated, and information panels are in Spanish only. Nevertheless, it is worth visiting for the evocative pre-World War II lithographs and other advertising graphics.

The Parque Duarte itself, whose shady confines are alive with shoeshine boys, vendors of shaved ice, and picnicking office workers, is remarkably small for a city of this size. On the west side you'll find the **Centro de Recreo,** built in 1894. Inside it houses a private billiards club. Its splendid facade is currently undergoing restoration. Next door is the privately owned

Palacio Consistorial, a more sober edifice from the same period.

A few minutes' walk from the Parque Duarte is the **Museo Folklórico de Tomás Morel.** This quaint museum is a treasure trove of curiosities, from Taino pottery to early calculators and cameras, but the main draw is a priceless collection of hundreds of carnival masks (see p. 114). Santiago is famous for carnival masks, and those presented here range from the grotesque and surreal to the humorous. Worth noting are the masks from the Hoya district of Santiago, characterized by forests of spiky protuberances on the horns. The museum plays an active part in supporting local folklore traditions.

One monument you can't miss—even if only by virtue of its commanding position above the city—is the **Monumento a los Héroes de la Restauración,** on Avenida Monumental, which rises some 220 feet (67 m) from a hilltop in the center of Santiago. Made of white marble, this huge monument was constructed during the Trujillo era and honors the heroes of 1844 who helped force the Haitians out and restore self-government to the Dominican Republic (in fact, Trujillo intended it as a monument to himself).

The interior houses displays about the creation of the republic. An elevator, often not working, and steps take you to a platform with panoramic views over Santiago, the Valle de Cibao, and the mountains. Note the frescoes at the top of the stairs, which are by the well-known contemporary Spanish painter Vela Zanetti.

The city's main thoroughfare, **Calle del Sol,** runs from the monument down to Parque Duarte, where most of the better shops in the city are found. ∎

Cigarmaking

Cigarmaking has a long tradition in the Dominican Republic and plays an important role in the culture and economy of the country.

The prime tobacco-growing area is along the Yaque Valley, which borders the Río Yaque del Norte for some 15 miles (25 km) from the outskirts of Santiago northwest to the town of Esperanza. Despite a period of decline in the 1960s, the recent upsurge in demand for premium cigars around the world has generated a welcome boom in this area.

The Dominican Republic currently exports about 140 million hand-rolled cigars to the United States annually, making it the top exporter in the region, ahead of Honduras and Cuba. Internationally known brands such as Dunhill, Partaga's, and H. Upmann are produced here. ∎

Opposite:
Tobacco is an important crop around Santiago, much of it being made into cigars.

Cordillera Central

Jarabacoa
🏔 97 C3
☎ 809/574-6890

Salto de Jimenoa
🏔 97 C3
💲 $

INHOSPITABLE AND REMOTE, THE MOUNTAINS OF THE Cordillera Central (Central Highlands) run diagonally across the western half of the Dominican Republic, culminating in the island's highest point—Pico Duarte (10,410 feet/3,175 m). There is no easy access to this wilderness area, which includes two major national parks (the Parque Nacional Armando Bermúdez and the Parque Nacional José del Carmen Ramírez) and the sources of some of the country's major rivers (such as the Río Yaque del Norte and the Río Yaque del Sur).

One of the most easily accessible of the hill stations is **Jarabacoa,** which you reach on Rte. 28 that winds up from the central highway (Rte. 1), passing through pine forests that have earned this region the title of the Dominican Alps. The alpine-style chalets in the woodlands are popular with vacationers.

Set in a broad valley and surrounded by the foothills of the Cordillera Central, Jarabacoa is a cool retreat with equable year-round temperatures. Many wealthy Santiago residents have weekend homes here, scattered around the outskirts of town amid fields of cultivated flowers, strawberries, pimentos, and manioc.

There is little to see in Jarabacoa itself, although the charming park at its center, shaded by a magnificent tree whose branches arch over the entire square, is typical of small Dominican towns. A church, which adjoins the park, contains modern frescoes by a well-known local artist, Roberto Flores.

Rafting is popular on the upper reaches of the Río Jimenoa.

Jarabacoa's appeal lies mostly in its proximity to mountainous terrain, rushing rivers, and unspoiled countryside. One of the most popular places to visit is the impressive **Salto de Jimenoa** waterfall; it is easily reached via a turnoff 2.5 miles (6.5 km) from the town center on the La Vega road and a 4-mile (6-km) drive along a dirt track to a hydroelectric station below the falls. The falls themselves are an easy 10-to-15-minute walk from here across a series of swing bridges. Set in a jungle-filled, natural amphitheater, the cascade tumbles down an 80-foot-high (24-m) rock face into a huge pool where you can swim.

The Río Jimenoa converges on the other side of the town with the Río Yaque del Norte at a spot 2 miles (3 km) from Jarabacoa known as the **Balneario La Confluencia.** This spot is popular with locals for weekend picnics and swimming.

The countryside around Jimenoa is perfect for exploration and adventure sports, with a network of paths and dirt tracks winding through remote hamlets and small farms. On the fringes of town (1 mile/1.5 km to the south) is the busy **Rancho Baiguate** (*Tel 809/574-6890*), the country's only multiactivity adventure center. The ranch offers a wide range of things to do, including horseback riding, quad biking, mountain biking, parapente (descending from hill, or mountaintops beneath a specially designed canopy), rafting, trekking, canyoning (rappelling down canyons), tubing, jeep safaris, and expeditions to the top of the Pico Duarte. Within a short distance of Rancho Baiguate are the **Baiguate Falls,** which can be reached on quad bikes from the ranch down several dirt tracks (journey time is around 20–30

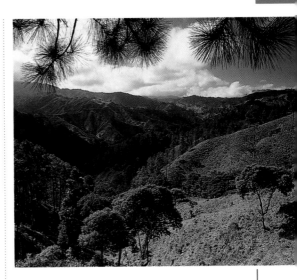

Cordillera Central is the Republic's largest mountain range.

minutes) and then a short walk. Here you'll find another natural swimming pool. Rafting takes place on the upper section of the Río Jimenoa, an 8-mile (13-km) ride downstream with Class III rapids. The ranch also provides accommodations and can arrange visits to a local coffee factory and excursions to watch the making of Indian bread *(casabe)* and view other local activities.

Continuing beyond Jarabacoa on the same badly potholed road (Rte. 28) brings you to the town of **Constanza,** set in a high valley surrounded by the peaks of the Cordillera Central. Like Jarabacoa, it is a prime growing area for soft fruit crops such as strawberries, raspberries, peaches, pears, and apples. The town itself is very peaceful, with just a handful of restaurants and hotels, and in December and January temperatures drop below freezing. The main activities are walking and visits to the 100-foot-high (30-m) **Agua Blanca** waterfalls, 6 miles (10 km) to the south. These are much less visited than the falls around Jarabacoa. ∎

CLIMBING PICO DUARTE

Climbing Pico Duarte, the highest mountain in the Caribbean, is usually undertaken as part of an organized expedition because it's a three-day round-trip from the village of La Ciénega to the peak itself. Outfitters include the Rancho Baiguate (*Tel 809/574-6890*) and Iguana Mama in Cabarete (*Tel 809/571-0908*). ∎

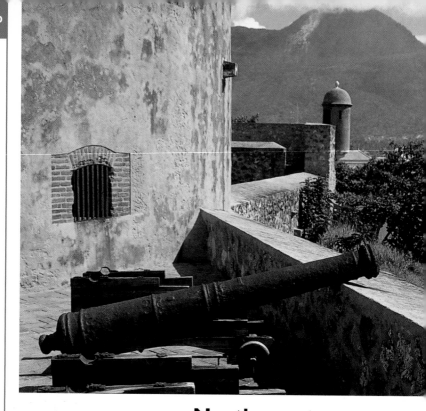

The guns of the Fortaleza de San Felipe, with the Pico Isabel de Torres in the background

North coast:
around Puerto Plata

THE ATLANTIC COAST OF THE DOMINICAN REPUBLIC extends for some 150 miles (241 km) from Monte Cristi on the Haitian border in the west to the Peninsula de Samaná in the east. In the scenic hinterland a patchwork of canefields lies beneath the rugged Cordillera Septentrional. The coast has some excellent beaches, but because they border the Atlantic, the sea can be rougher here, and some of these beaches are more suited to bodysurfing than snorkeling.

Puerto Plata
△ 97 C4
Visitor information
✉ Cesar José de
   los Santos,
   Calle Harmanas,
   Mirabel 8
☎ 809/586-3676 or
   809/586-5000

**Fortaleza de
San Felipe**
✉ End of the Malecón
$ $

The coast's main town is **Puerto Plata** (Silver Port), founded in the early 16th century. Above it towers the dramatic **Pico Isabel de Torres** (2,554 feet/779 m), which bears the scars of a landslide on its seaward slopes. Part of the mountain forms a nature reserve, the Reserva Científica Isabel de Torres. At the top of the mountain is a restaurant-café with superb views. You can either drive up or take the newly restored cable car, the only one of its kind in the Caribbean.

Puerto Plata has an attractive and very long seafront promenade, the Malecón, at the western end of which lies the **Fortaleza de San Felipe**. The fortress is one of the oldest in the Caribbean, built between 1564 and 1577 to deter pirate attacks. But in 1659 three shiploads of buccaneers captured it. The fort was partially destroyed when the pirates were eventually forced out, and then it was rebuilt on the orders of King Philip II of Spain, after whom it is now named.

Restored in the 1970s, the fortress has small lookout towers facing the sea and a massive keep at its center, where you'll find the small museum. The exhibits, mostly remnants of 16th-century armaments, are not as compelling as the interior of the keep itself.

Puerto Plata's town square, the **Parque Central,** has several turn-of-the-century wooden houses with characteristic gingerbread style fretwork on the balconies and windows. At the center of the square is a typical pavilion, known as **La Glorieta,** and on its southern side is the modern **Catedral de San Felipe,** built in imitation art deco style.

Apart from the fort, the town's star attraction is the excellent but highly commercialized **Museo de Ambar Dominicano** (Dominican Amber Museum), just a short stroll from the Parque Central. You'll find some fascinating exhibits in this well-presented museum, mostly of insects and small creatures frozen in time since they got stuck on a resinous tree some 50 million years ago. There are also examples of rare blue amber, found nowhere else in the world: Its smoky coloration is thought to derive from the impregnation of ash during volcanic eruptions.

TOWARD HAITI

Westward from Puerto Plata, Rtes. 1, 5, and 29 pass through arid, cactus-strewn landscapes toward the Haitian border. Near the colorful fishing village of **Luperón** is the site of the first European town in the New World, **La Isabela,** which is now the **Parque Nacional Histórico La Isabela.** Columbus founded the settlement on January 1, 1494, and named it in honor of the Spanish queen. Excavations have revealed the stone foundations of the church and Columbus's house.

The last town before the border is **Monte Cristi.** Faded Victorian buildings hark back to its heyday in the 19th century when it flourished as a major port for the export of timber and agricultural produce.

Of more interest is the nearby **Parque Nacional Monte Cristi,** which covers 204 square miles (528 sq km) of coastline and offshore islands, known collectively as the Cayos Siete Hermanos. This important sanctuary is home to alligators and several rare species of birds, such as the wood stork and the American oystercatcher. ■

THE AMBER COAST

The northern coastline is sometimes called the Amber Coast, thanks to the amazing discoveries in amber deposits that form the basis of Puerto Plata's amber museum. The title is something of a misnomer, though, because the amber actually comes from around 15 mines in the shale and sandstone sediments between Puerto Plata and Santiago in the interior. ■

Crane flies caught in amber

Museo de Ambar Dominicano

✉ Calle Duarte 61
☎ 809/586-2848, www.ambermuseum.com
🕐 Closed Sun.
💲 $

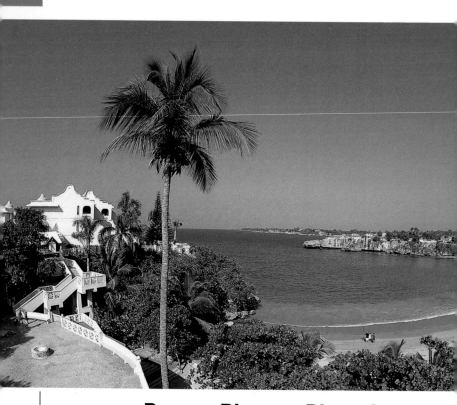

Sosúa offers a wide variety of water sports.

Puerto Plata to Playa Grande

SOME 3 MILES (5 KM) TO THE EAST OF PUERTO PLATA IS THE resort complex of Playa Dorada, which now counts 18 hotels along its sandy bay. The complex also has a first-class golf course and a commercial center with a good selection of shops, restaurants, cafés, and other facilities. Continuing east, you encounter a less built-up coastline, and the lovely lagoon by Río San Juan is a highlight for many visitors.

Sosúa
⚑ 97 C4
Visitor information
✉ Jose Martinez, Edificio Gel Brown, 2da, Planta, Autopista Luperón
☎ 809/579-2254 or 809/571-3433

Cabarete
⚑ 97 C4

Sosúa (17 miles/27 km east of Puerto Plata) has a big, lively beach and an extensive beach market. Most water sports, including scuba diving and snorkeling excursions, are available from operators at the beach. The town is divided into two sections. To the west of the beach is **Los Charamicos,** a fishing community. The district known as **El Batey,** where most of the hotels, restaurants, shops, and tourist facilities are located, flanks the eastern side. El Batey was settled by about 600 Jewish refugees fleeing from Nazi Germany in 1941. The settlers developed a thriving dairy industry, and although many moved away after the war, their legacy remains in the form of memorial plaques, a synagogue, and bakeries.

Cabarete, which is 7 miles (11 km) east of Sosúa, is one of the top windsurfing resorts in the Caribbean and frequently hosts world championship events. It's a very safe destination, thanks to the sideshore winds that bring tired windsurfers back to the beach. From December through September, the tradewinds generally blow at 15–25 knots in the afternoon, with the strongest winds from late spring through summer. Skill levels include all abilities in summer, with novice sailing from April to December in the mornings.

Because the resort attracts so many windsurfing fanatics, it has a young, international clientele and a lively atmosphere, with plenty of partying in the beachside bars. But, even if you're not a windsurfer, you can enjoy an excellent beach that stretches around the bay. The resort also boasts the highest concentration of budget guesthouses and small hotels on the island.

Cabarete is also a major center for mountain biking and hiking tours of the surrounding countryside, thanks to the presence of the **Iguana Mama Mountain Bike Center** (*Tel 809/571-0908; e-mail: iguanamama@codetel.net.do*). This innovative company offers well-organized, fully guided tours and also plows a percentage of its profits back into local environmental and educational programs.

Some 39 miles (63 km) east of Sosúa is the small fishing village of **Río San Juan,** a picturesque jumping-off point for trips on the nearby Laguna Grí Grí. Boats set off from the jetty at the end of the main street, Calle Duarte, for a two-hour trip through a mangrove-lined canal that eventually opens out to the sea. The excursion continues along the coastline and enters one or two sea caves before stopping for a swim in a natural pool (*piscina natural*).

Continuing on some 7 miles (11 km) past Río San Juan, you'll come to **Playa Grande,** an impressive ribbon of sand that curves more than 0.5 mile (1 km) around a lovely bay. But the riptides can be strong.

Just past here is the **Parque Nacional Cabo Francés Viejo,** a protected coastal rain forest with dirt tracks leading off the road to deserted beaches and bays. Finally, there is the provincial capital of **Nagau** on the Bahía Escocesa, but it has very little to offer tourists. ∎

Río San Juan
🅼 97 C4
Visitor information
✉ Miguel Falette, Calle Duarte
☎ 809/598-2831

Playa Grande
🅼 97 C4

Parco Nacional Cabo Francés Viejo
🅼 97 D4

Cabarete is the place to go for some of the best windsurfing in the Caribbean.

Sports & activities

Windsurfing: Cabarete's biggest and best equipped windsurfing center is the Carib Bic Centre, which has a full range of equipment and offers rental and tuition (*Tel 809/571-0640, fax 809/571-0649, e-mail: caribbic@ codetel.net.do*).

More than 100 windsurfing competitors from 20 or so countries descend on the resort each June for the famous Cabarete Race Week (*Tel 809/571-0567, fax 809/571-0856, e-mail: cabareterace@codetel.net.do, www.hispaniola.com/race*). ∎

Peninsula de Samaná

Samaná

🏝 97 D3

Visitor information

✉ Miguel A. Luis,
Calle Santa
Bárbara, Edificio
Gubernamental

☎ 809/538-2332

**Parque Nacional
Los Haitises**

🏝 97 D3

Las Terrenas

🏝 97 D3

**Coconut palms
and banana plants
(foreground)
thrive on the
Peninsula de
Samaná, which
covers an area
of nearly 400
square miles
(1,036 sq km).**

ONE OF THE MOST BEAUTIFUL REGIONS OF THE Dominican Republic, the Peninsula de Samaná juts out from the northeastern corner of the island. The peninsula is bisected by the Cordillera de Samaná (Samaná Highlands). The Cordillera slopes, luxuriant with coconut palms and pines, plunge into the azure waters of the Bahía de Samaná on one side and the Caribbean on the other. Fine beaches and tropical islands provide sea-level attractions.

When Columbus made landfall here in January 1493, he met with a hostile reception from the native Taino, who showered him with arrows. This prompted him to name the bay **Golfo de las Flechas** (Gulf of Arrows). White settlers arrived from the Canary Islands in 1756 and founded the town of Santa Bárbara de Samaná, usually called simply **Samaná.** Most of the town was rebuilt after a serious fire in 1946 and isn't particularly attractive. But it is the departure point for boat trips (*Tel 809/538-2588*) to view humpback whales: Up to 3,000 arrive in the bay to mate and give birth between January and March. Samaná is also one of the jumping-off points for trips to the offshore

island of **Cayo Levantado,** with its superb beaches.

You can also make day trips from Sánchez over to **Parque Nacional Los Haitises** on the south side of the bay, a protected area of coastal mangroves and small cays that is a haven for birdlife. Its inland section includes several caves filled with petroglyphs and shards of pottery. Trips to the park can be arranged by tour operators from resorts in Puerto Plata, Sosúa, and Cabarete. For more information contact the Dirección Nacional de Parques (*Tel 809/221-5340*).

On the north coast is the resort of **Las Terrenas.** It boasts some of the country's best beaches, which run for around 7.5 miles (12 km) eastward and westward. ■

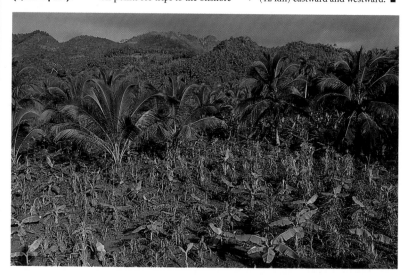

Puerto Rico has been a commonwealth territory of the status United States since 1952. This has conferred several advantages, including U.S.-style communications and highways, but beneath this veneer beats a Spanish heart.

Puerto Rico

An evocative silhouette at sunset in San Juan

Puerto Rico

THE MOST EASTERLY OF THE GREATER ANTILLES, PUERTO RICO LIES 1,000 miles (1,600 km) southeast of Miami between the Virgin Islands and the island of Hispaniola. Almost rectangular in shape, it measures 95 miles (153 km) from east to west and 36 miles (58 km) from north to south. A range of mountains, the Cordillera Central, runs across the center of the island from east to west, reaching its highest peak at the Cerro de Punta (4,387 feet/1,338 m).

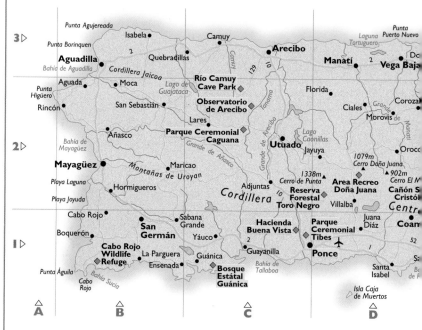

Puerto Rico is unusual in that it is the first Overseas Commonwealth Territory of the United States, and although Spanish is the island's first language, English is widely spoken and Puerto Ricans are U.S. citizens. Puerto Rican culture, music, and dance are Latin American in inspiration, but commercial life is organized with American efficiency. The island has wonderful four-lane highways, but turn off into the countryside and you can find yourself on a potholed rural road.

Puerto Rico's interior is partially clad in dense tropical rain forest, although just one percent of the island's original forest now remains. Huge clumps of bamboo grow alongside the roads and river valleys, and tree ferns, lianas, hibiscus, bougainvillea, and flame trees flourish almost everywhere.

The central mountains are ringed by coastal plains. In the northwest the landscape is shaped by the strange hillocks and caves of limestone karst formations, while in the drier southwest the land is dominated by cactus and other drought-resistant plants.

To the native Taino, the island was known as Boriquen, which meant "land of the noble lord" and referred to their belief that the god Juracan lived atop the highest mountain. From this vantage point he controlled the weather (the word "hurricane" is derived from his name). When Columbus arrived here on his second voyage to the Americas in 1493, he named it San Juan Bautista. With Columbus was Juan Ponce de Léon, who returned to settle the island in 1508; he soon renamed it Puerto Rico or "rich port."

The Spanish enslaved the island's 30,000 Taino and set them to work in the gold mines, but inevitably there was conflict and the Indians were decimated. Ponce de Léon himself was wounded in Florida in 1521 and died in Cuba; his bones were brought back to lie in San Juan's cathedral.

Once the gold was exhausted in the late 16th century, Puerto Rico was neglected by

movement grew in strength and the Spanish appointed a series of military governors (known as the Little Caesars) who ruthlessly repressed any hint of revolution. The first serious uprising took place on September 23, 1868, and the Republic of Puerto Rico was declared. The authorities acted swiftly, however, crushing the revolt at San Sebastian, which came to symbolize the island's struggle for independence.

In 1897 autonomy for Puerto Rico was finally granted, but it did not last long because

in 1898 the United States, then at war with Spain, invaded the island. Puerto Rico was ceded to the United States in December 1898, and U.S. citizenship granted to islanders in 1917. In 1952 the island became a commonwealth, but its status is a matter of constant debate. Many politicians in Puerto Rico would like to see it become the 51st state of the Union. In December 1998, however, the Puerto Rican electorate rejected a proposal to do just that.

Nearly a third of Puerto Rico's 3.5 million residents live in and around the capital, San Juan. Over the last 50 or so years the economy has shifted from a rural to industrial base, and the island now has a well-developed tourist infrastructure with first-rate hotels and good communications. ■

Spain, and the few settlers who remained fought an almost constant battle against diseases, hurricanes, and invasions from Carib, pirates, and European privateers.

In 1765 the Spanish king Carlos III sent an envoy to develop the island's sugar plantations, and trade began to pick up; coffee and tobacco were also exported. In 1809 Puerto Ricans were given Spanish citizenship, but as the century progressed, the independence

San Juan

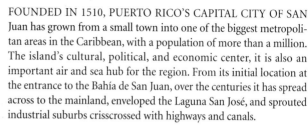

San Juan

🗺 127 E3

Visitor information

✉ Paseo de la
Princesa, Old San
Juan Station

☎ 787/721-2400

FOUNDED IN 1510, PUERTO RICO'S CAPITAL CITY OF SAN
Juan has grown from a small town into one of the biggest metropolitan areas in the Caribbean, with a population of more than a million.
The island's cultural, political, and economic center, it is also an
important air and sea hub for the region. From its initial location at
the entrance to the Bahía de San Juan, over the centuries it has spread
across to the mainland, enveloped the Laguna San José, and sprouted
industrial suburbs crisscrossed with highways and canals.

If the outskirts of San Juan appear
unappetizing, the center, by contrast, is a real delight. Old San Juan
covers just seven blocks on a long,
narrow islet at the northeast
entrance to the bay; four causeways
connect it to the mainland. An area
of considerable charm, much of
the old town has recently been
restored to its original 18th-century
character. The streets are paved
with cobblestones, originally
brought over from the mainland as
ships' ballast, and lined with pastel
houses with wrought-iron balconies
and shuttered windows.

**Turrets on the
huge Castillo de
San Felipe del
Morro in Old
San Juan**

The entire old town is surrounded by more than 6 miles
(10 km) of walls, 50 feet (15 m)
high and 20 feet (6 m) thick,
studded with small stone sentry
boxes known as *garitas*. San Juan
has two massive and formidable
forts, built to protect the city in the
days when buccaneers and pirates
were a constant threat.

**Public
transportation
information**

☎ 787/250-6064

El Capitolio

✉ Ave. Ponce de Léon

☎ 787/721-6040

🕐 By appt. only

Today the only invasion the old
town faces is by armies of cruise
ship passengers. Two piers lie at the
very foot of the town, and when
both berths are occupied it can
seem overrun with day-trippers.
Nevertheless, Old San Juan is
clearly a community with a life
that isn't solely defined by tourism,
and locals go about their business,
play dominoes in the cafés, and
promenade in the evenings, much
as they would anywhere else in
Puerto Rico.

**Opposite: Hato
Rey, the city's
main financial
district**

SAN JUAN (NEW CITY)

Unlike Old San Juan, where
everything is within walking
distance, in the city proper you'll
need to use public transportation,
taxis, or a rental car to get around.
Make the effort, though, since
the rewards range from lively
stretches of beachfront to bustling
merchant districts, and a chance to
see Puerto Rico's famous Bacardi
rum being made.

Within 550 yards (500 m) of the
confines of Old San Juan is **El
Capitolio,** a white marble building
built in the 1920s as the seat of the
island government (Senate and
House of Representatives). A guided
tour will take you inside the rotunda
where friezes depicting the country's
history decorate the elaborate dome.

On the Atlantic seafront, immediately beyond where Old San Juan
is connected to the mainland, is
Condado, a beach strip of high-
rise resort hotels behind which are
streets full of restaurants, designer
shops, fast-food outlets, and souvenir shops. This hotel strip continues along the coast as far as **Isla
Verde** (6 miles/10 km), another
major beach resort area.

Inland from Condado is the
downtown district of **Santurce**
and, beyond here, the financial
district of **Hato Rey,** where glass-
fronted skyscrapers line the street
known as the Golden Mile.

Three miles (5 km) farther
south still is the suburb of Río

Castillo de San Felipe del Morro
- ✉ Calle del Morro
- ☎ 787/729-6960
- 💲 $

Casa Blanca
- ✉ 1 Calle San Sebastian
- ☎ 787/724-4102
- 🕐 Closed Mon.
- 💲 $

Museo de las Americas de Ballajá
- ✉ Calle Borzegay
- ☎ 787/724-5052

Museo del Arte y Historia
- ✉ 150 Calle Norzagaray
- ☎ 787/724-1875
- 🕐 Closed Mon.

El Morro has been massively fortified over the centuries.

Pedras, home to the University of Puerto Rico. The **University Museum** (*Ave. Ponce de Léon, Tel 787/763-4408, closed Sun.*) features displays on Puerto Rican history and archaeology as well as contemporary art exhibitions. To the south and east of the university campus are the **Botanical Gardens** (*Corner of Rtes. 1 and 847, closed Mon.*), a tranquil retreat with numerous walks and waterways meandering among some 200 acres (80 ha) of lush tropical vegetation. The palm garden is particularly appealing.

Another attraction outside Old San Juan is the **Bacardi Rum Distillery** (*Rte. 88, Catano, Tel 787/788-1500, closed Sun.*), which you can reach by a short ferry ride from Pier Two in Old San Juan. The 45-minute conducted tour takes in the bottling plant, a museum, and the distillery itself.

OLD SAN JUAN

Old San Juan is a fascinating storehouse of the island's treasures, from colonial fortresses and civic buildings that underpinned Spanish rule

to the wealth of historical artifacts on display in its museums.

The most prominent feature of the old town—it dominates the approach by sea and is easily visible from the air—is the massive **Castillo de San Felipe del Morro,** or El Morro as it's known. Sprawling over a rocky promontory at the northwestern tip of the old town, El Morro was begun in 1540 and gradually added to over the centuries until it achieved its present form in 1783. Built on six different levels, the fort's interior is a fascinating complex of tunnels, labyrinths, dungeons, turrets, and ramps. A small museum traces the fort's history, and a reconstruction of an 18th-century military barracks evokes the soldiers' lives. The courtyard here was used in the filming of Steven Spielberg's slave epic, *Amistad* (1997).

Old San Juan's second fort is the **Fuerte San Cristóbal** (*Blvd. del Valle, Tel 787/729-6960*). Although it's not as well known as El Morro, it is much bigger, covering some 27 acres (11 ha). Completed in 1678, it was designed to protect the landward side of the town and has five separate bastions linked by underground tunnels, each of which had to fall for the fort to be overrun.

The downtown area features numerous restored historic buildings. The foremost is **La Fortaleza** (*Calle Recinto Oeste, Tel 787/721-7000, closed weekends*), built between 1533 and 1540 but later considerably modified. Today it houses the governor's residence and is believed to be the oldest executive residence in continuous use in the Western Hemisphere. Various ceremonial rooms and the gardens are open to visitors (*contact the Conservation Trust of Puerto Rico*).

Another reminder of the Spanish establishment is the

Casa Blanca, originally built as a home for Ponce de León in 1521. The explorer died before he could move in, and the original frame house was destroyed by a fire. Ponce de León's son-in-law built the present house in 1523, making it the oldest of about 800 Spanish colonial buildings in Old San Juan, and his descendants occupied it for some 250 years. It's now a historical museum, with some fine examples of colonial furniture. It also has three lovely courtyards: The Italian courtyard, with fountains and brickwork; the classical courtyard, a wild area leading down to the sea; and the Spanish courtyard, modeled on the Alhambra in Granada, Spain.

One of the most fascinating of the old town's museums is the **Museo de las Americas.** The exhibits trace the evolution of the cultures of the New World over the centuries, including pre-Columbian, and features a comprehensive collection of carnival costumes from Peru, Guatemala, Mexico, Venezuela, Cuba, and the Dominican Republic. Another interesting museum is the **Museo del Arte y Historia,** which houses exhibitions of Puerto Rican art and offers an audiovisual presentation on the history of the city. There are also fascinating exhibits at the **Museo del Indio,** which has displays on indigenous Taino culture and archaeological digs, and at the **Casa del Libro** *(225 Calle Cristo, Tel 787/723-0354, closed Sun.),* which is housed in an 18th-century building and features exhibits related to books and bookbinding. Its 5,000 volumes include many rare books. For exhibits on a lighter note, visit the enjoyable **Museo del Niño.** It contains a wide variety of exhibits relating to childhood, such as large collections of dolls and toys.

A popular exhibition in the central old town is that of **The Butterfly People,** who have created a display of mounted butterflies in the upstairs gallery of an 18th-century building. It's purely a commercial venture, with no educational value. To find out more about the flora and fauna of Puerto Rico, visit the **Conservation Trust of Puerto Rico,** which has informative displays and a short film on the island's ecology. ■

The Fuerte San Cristóbal still dominates San Juan's harbor.

Museo del Indio
- ✉ 109 Calle San Jose
- ☎ 787/721-2864
- 🕐 Closed Mon.
- 💲 $

Museo del Niño
- ✉ 150 Calle del Cristo
- ☎ 787/722-3791
- 💲 $

The Butterfly People
- ✉ 152 Calle Fortaleza
- ☎ 787/723-2432
- 🕐 Closed Sun.
- 💲 $

Conservation Trust of Puerto Rico
- ✉ Calle Tetuen 155, San Juan
- ☎ Tel 787/722-5834 or 787/722-5882

Old San Juan walk

This lovely walk through Old San Juan traces a roughly circular path, beginning and ending at the Plaza de Colón, one of the many elements of San Juan that play up the Columbus connection. Along the way you can appreciate the disparate components—fortresses, churches, museums, and monuments—that combine so harmoniously in this colonial district.

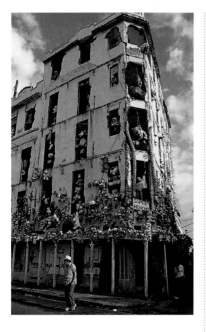

The curious La Casa de los Peluches in Old San Juan

Start in the **Plaza de Colón** at the entrance to the old city, where a statue commemorates the explorer. Follow Avenida Muñoz Rivera uphill to the **Fuerte San Cristóbal** ❶ (see p. 130). After a look at the fort, take Boulevard del Valle along the seafront. On your right you'll see a sprawling collection of closely packed houses clinging to the seashore beneath the city walls. This is the **Barrio La Perla,** originally a village that sprang up to serve the military community; it is now home to some 10,000 people who form a tight knit community. La Perla is considered to be quite distinct from other areas of the city, and for safety reasons it is not recommended to venture down here unaccompanied. After a few hundred

yards, you'll see an extraordinary house on your left, **La Casa de los Peluches** ❷ *(Blvd. del Valle)*, which is covered with thousands of stuffed toys. The work of local artist Thomas Huerta, it houses a lively bar.

As you continue toward Calle Norzagaray and the **Museo del Arte y Historia** (see p. 131), the **Convento de los Dominicos** ❸ is on your left. Built in the early 16th century, it was later used as a headquarters for the U.S. Army. It has now been fully restored and houses the Puerto Rican Institute of Culture *(Tel 787/724-0700)*, which features a chapel with an ornate altar, religious manuscripts, and an art gallery *(Closed Sun.)*. Just past here is the **Plaza del Quinto Centenario**. One of the highest points in San Juan, it was built as part of the 500th anniversary of the discovery of the New World. Its centerpiece, Totem Telúrico, is a 40-foot-high (12-m) sculpture in black granite and ceramics, referred to locally simply as "the totem" due to its tall, cylindrical shape. It's the work of Jaimé Suarez, one of the country's foremost artists. From its southern end two columns point skyward to the North Star, the guiding light for maritime explorers.

On the west side of the square stands the **Cuartel de Ballajá** ❹ *(Tel 787/724-5052)*. This handsome, three-story neoclassic building has porticoed galleries on the inside courtyard, and it used to house the military barracks. It was constructed in the mid-19th century and was the largest building erected in the Americas by Spanish engineers.

Continue on toward the broad expanse of park that leads across the headland to the impressive **Castillo de San Felipe del Morro** ❺ (see p. 130). Then return across the park and follow the road down to the **Casa Blanca** ❻ (see p. 131). From the Casa Blanca take Calle San Sebastian to the Plaza de San José, in one corner of which is the **Iglesia de San José** ❼ *(Tel 787/725-7501)*. Ponce de

León was originally laid to rest here, but his ashes were moved to the Catedral de San Juan in 1971. Note the fresco (1550) on the far left.

Outside the church is a statue of Ponce de León, made from melted-down cannon. In one corner of the Plaza San José is the **Museo de Pablo Casals** *(Tel 787/723-9185, closed Sun.)*, dedicated to the memory of this famous Spanish cellist who founded the Casals Festival, held on the island every year since 1957 at the Luis A Ferré Performing Arts Center *(Tel 787/721-7727)*. The museum is a collection of memorabilia from the cellist's career and features videotapes of all the Festival concerts.

Follow Calle del Cristo downhill, passing the archbishop's residence (No. 50) on your right, to reach the **Catedral de San Juan** ⑧, a grandiose structure topped with three cupolas. Inside, a marble tomb holds the remains of Ponce de León *(Tel 787/722-0861)*.

Turn right and walk down the Caleta de San Juan, one of the prettiest little streets in Old

San Juan, to reach the **Puerta de San Juan** ⑨, once the city's main entrance. Go through the gateway and turn left, following the attractive promenade running alongside the harbor and past **La Fortaleza** (see p. 130).

Turn east past the fountain, continuing on past **Presidio de la Princesa** (now housing the tourist board offices) down the Paseo de la Princesa back toward the docks. Follow Calle Recinto Sur back to the Plaza de Colón. ∎

- ▲ See area map pages 126–27
- ▶ Plaza de Colón
- ↔ 1.5–2 miles (2.5–3 km)
- ⏱ Allow 2–3 hours
- ▶ Plaza de Colón

NOT TO BE MISSED
- Convento de los Dominicos
- Museo de Pablo Casals
- Catedral de San Juan

The east

El Yunque
🅰 127 F2

**El Portal Tropical
Forest Center**
🅰 127 F2
☎ 787/888-1880
💲 $

EASILY ACCESSIBLE FROM SAN JUAN, THE EASTERN END OF the island is the area most frequently visited by day-trippers and features several nature reserves, including El Yunque rain forest. This 28,000-acre (11,000-ha) reserve is by far the most popular attraction in Puerto Rico, with about a million visitors each year.

The largest forested area on the island, **El Yunque** includes many spectacular waterfalls, thousand-year-old trees, brightly colored flowering plants, and a wealth of bird species. Although much can be seen from the road, the best way to experience the forest is to set off on any of the 13 hiking trails, which cover 23 miles (37 km) of varied terrain throughout the park.

The forest is located in the Sierra de Luquillo, 25 miles (40 km) east of San Juan. Take Rte. 3 from the capital, and near Luquillo turn south into the mountains on Rte. 191. About 3 miles (5 km) along this road is the **El Portal Tropical Forest Center.** Approached via an elevated walkway through the forest canopy, this excellent visitor center has more than 10,000 square feet (930 sq m) of exhibits. These relate to fauna such as the national emblem, the *coqui* frog, the different types of forest within the park (which include tabonuco, colorado, palm, and cloud), and the management of tropical forests worldwide. A film on El Yunque is shown every half hour, alternating between Spanish (9 a.m.–4 p.m.) and English (9:30 a.m.–4:30 p.m.).

Although known as El Yunque in Puerto Rico, the park's official name is the **Caribbean National Forest.** The area was sacred to the Taino Indians, hence the name Yunque, from "Yuke" or sacred lands, and petroglyphs carved on rocks within the riverbeds are evidence of the Taino

presence. In 1876 King Alfonso XII of Spain declared 12,000 acres (4,800 ha) of mountainous land in the Sierra de Luquillo as a forest reserve, making it one of the oldest forest reserves in the Western Hemisphere. After the Spanish-American War in 1898, the Spanish crown lands became U.S. property, and in 1903 the area became the Luquillo Forest Reserve, making it the only tropical rain forest in the U.S. national forest system.

El Yunque is home to the endangered Puerto Rican parrot.

From El Portal the road (Rte. 191) leads up toward **La Coca Falls** (alongside the road at 5 miles/8 km), which has an 85-foot (26-m) drop. The **Yokahu Tower** (5.5 miles/9 km), one of several observation towers within the park, affords magnificent views across the mountains. About 0.5 mile (1 km) past here you'll see signs for the **Big Tree Trail.** This lovely mile-long (1.6-km) route, which leads past some of the largest trees in the forest, also passes **La Mina Falls,** probably the most spectacular in the park. At 7 miles (11 km) is the **Sierra Palm Information Center,** which has a picnic area and ranger service, and slightly farther on is the **Palo Colorado Information Center.** Here a trail winds up to the **Mount Britton Lookout Tower** and the peak of El Yunque itself, at 3,496 feet (1,065 m). Allow two hours for the round-trip to the summit.

On the island's northeastern tip, beyond the port of Fajardo, is **Las Cabezas de San Juan Nature Reserve.** This 316-acre (128-ha) reserve is unique because of the range of different ecological communities—sandy beaches, rock escarpments, coral reefs, offshore cays, dry forest, mangroves, and lagoons. The site's most significant natural feature is the **Laguna Grande,** one of three bioluminescent lagoons on the island. At its eastern end a lighthouse, **El Faro,** built in 1880 (the second oldest on the island) houses a nature center and an observation tower. ∎

Las Cabezas de San Juan Nature Reserve & El Faro

🄰 127 G2
✉ Rte. 987
☎ 787/722-5882
🕐 By appt. only
💲 $$$

Hiking is a good way to explore El Yunque.

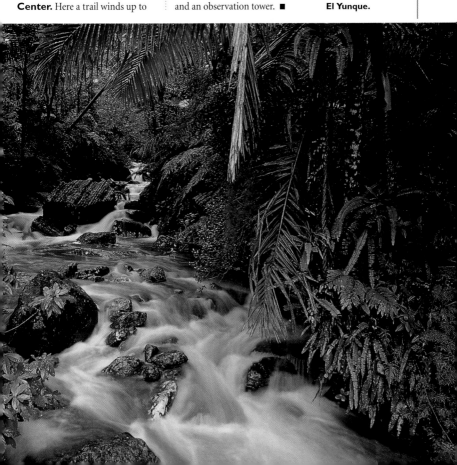

Vieques & Culebra

Isla de Vieques
△ 127 G2
Visitor information
✉ Mayoral Bldg., 449
Carlos Lebron St.
Isabel Segunda
☎ 787/741-5000

**El Fortin Conde
del Mirasol**
☎ 787/741-1717
🕐 Wed.–Sun., other
times by appt. only
$ $

**Camp Garcia &
N.A.S.D.**
☎ 787/741-0628
🕐 Closed p.m.
$ Free, with photo ID

Isla de Culebra
△ 127 H2
Visitor information
✉ Pedro Marquez St.,
Rte. 250, Dewey
☎ 787/742-3291,
www.culebra.org

**Culebra National
Wildlife Refuge**
✉ El Campamento,
Culebra
☎ 787/742-0115

LOCATED 7 MILES (11 KM) OFF THE PORT OF FAJARDO, ISLA de Vieques is the largest of Puerto Rico's offshore islands, covering about 80 square miles (207 sq km). Most of the island is owned by the U.S. Navy, so it has remained largely unspoiled. Despite attempts to develop tourism further, at present the island is very quiet and laid-back, its dry, rolling hills mostly occupied by roaming wild horses and its beaches (it has more than 50) spectacular. Snorkeling and diving around the coastline are excellent .

Most of the 9,000 residents of Vieques live in the main town of **Isabel Segunda,** where the ferries arrive from the mainland. The town has an attractive central square (with a bust of South American revolutionary, Simón Bolívar, who came here in 1816), where you'll find the tourist information center.

On the hill above the town is a restored fort, **El Fortin Conde del Mirasol,** which was one of the last forts to be built by the Spanish.

The other main settlement on the island is lively **Esperanza,** on the south coast, which has a string of bars and restaurants along its seafront.

To the south of Esperanza is **Sun Bay,** one of the island's biggest and most popular beaches, with picnic and camping areas.

Vieques's best known natural attraction, **Mosquito Bay** (also known as Phosphorescent Bay), lies just beyond Sun Bay. This large, shallow bay is surrounded by mangroves and is full of bioluminescent organisms (dinoflagellates), which glow eerily when disturbed by a boat paddle, prop, or your hand dangling in the water. Nighttime trips are organized by Blue Caribe Dive Center *(Tel 787/741-2522)* and Island Adventures *(Tel 787/741-0717).*

The U.S. Navy owns the eastern and western ends of the island, but these bases, **Camp Garcia** and

N.A.S.D. (Naval Ammunition Supply Department), are open to visitors except when maneuvers are taking place. Within the bases are some of the island's best beaches— Red Beach, Blue Beach, Green Bay, Garcia Beach, and Secret Beach.

Vieques can be reached either on the frequent ferries from Fajardo *(75-minute crossing, reservations advisable on weekends, Tel 787/863-3360)* or by flying from either San Juan or Fajardo *(contact Vieques Air Link, Tel 787/741-3266).* Once there, you can get around by *publicos* (shared public taxis), or you can rent a car from Island Car Rentals *(Tel 787/741-1666)* or Sammy's Car Rental *(Tel 787/741-0106).*

ISLA DE CULEBRA

Even more unspoiled than Vieques is the island of Culebra, measuring about 7 miles by 3 miles (11 by 5 km) and surrounded by a series of rocky cays and islets. The landscape is hilly, with tropical rain forest. This peaceful island is home to just 2,000 people, most of whom live in and around the main settlement, **Dewey** (known locally as Pueblo).

About 40 percent of the island forms part of the **Culebra National Wildlife Refuge,** which includes 23 offshore islets and four reserves on Culebra itself. The most important nesting beaches for birds such as terns and boobies are Resaca Playa and

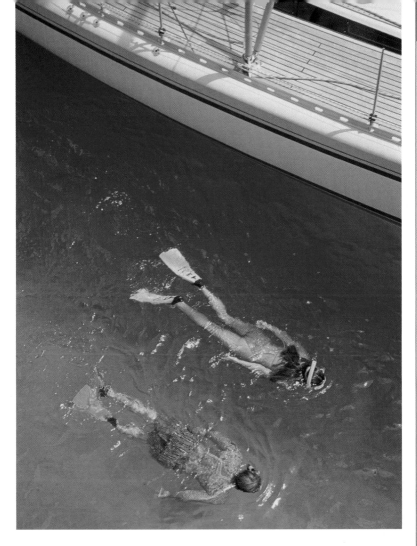

Brava Playa. Contact the refuge for information on guided nighttime walks to watch the leatherback turtles nesting.

The island's best known beach is the mile-long (1.5-km) **Flamenco Playa** on the north coast. This gorgeous stretch of white sand is best visited during the week, because on weekends it fills up with day-trippers. Other good beaches include **Playa Soni** and **Playa Resaca,** on the east coast.

You can reach Culebra from San Juan or Fajardo on Flamenco Airways *(Tel 787/723-8110 or 787/863-3366)* or by ferry from Fajardo *(90-minute crossing, reservations recommended on weekends, Tel 787/863-3360)*. You can get around the island by bicycle or rent a car from Prestige *(Tel 787/742-3242)* or Willy Solis *(Tel 787/742-3537)*. The municipal tourist office is located in the **City Hall.**

Diving can be arranged through Culebra Divers *(P.O. Box 474, Culebra, PR 00775, Tel 787/742-0803, e-mail: culebrad@aol.com)*. ■

The offshore reefs around Culebra offer fine diving and snorkeling.

Ponce

PUERTO RICO'S SECOND LARGEST CITY, PONCE, LIES MIDWAY along the island's southern coastline. Established in 1662, the city flourished during the late 19th century when it was a major exporter of sugar and rum. The architectural gems from this period benefited from extensive renovations as part of the Columbus quincentennial celebrations; more than 600 of its 1,000 historic buildings have now been restored. Ponce's turn-of-the-century charm is accentuated by the horse-drawn carriages rolling sedately down tree-lined avenues still lit by gas lamps (albeit reconstructions).

Ponce's Plaza Las Delicias (above) is also home to the gaudy Parque de Bombas (above left), the old fire station.

At the heart of the city is the aptly named **Plaza Las Delicias** (Square of Delights), where fountains and shady trees provide a cool atmosphere in which to sit and watch the world go by. At its center is the 17th-century Spanish Creole-style **Catedral de Nuestra Señora de Guadalupe** (*Tel 787/842-5695*), while immediately behind the church is Ponce's most famous monument, the red-and-black-striped **Parque de Bombas,** or fire station. Built for an agricultural fair in 1882, it only later became the city's fire station. It seems a strange juxtaposition, with the gaudy building abutting the classical cathedral. The church authorities tried to have this colorful structure moved, but the people of Ponce had become so attached to it they refused to do so. Inside, a **museum** contains antique fire-fighting tools, uniforms, and a splendid old fire engine.

The story of the city is well documented in the nearby **Museo de la Historia de Ponce.** An exhaustive but rewarding tour of the ten exhibition halls embraces the ecology, economy, architecture, politics, and daily life of Ponce over the centuries. It ends with a 35-minute documentary about the city.

After leaving the museum, note

Ponce
🗺 126 C1
Visitor information
✉ 2nd floor, Fox Delicias Mall
☎ 787/840-5695

Parque de Bombas
✉ Plaza las Delicias
☎ 787/284-4141, ext. 342
🕐 Closed Tues.

the buildings on **Calle Isabel.** You can see houses built in the four different styles for which the city is famous—classical, Creole, Ponce Creole, and art deco. Note also the chamfered pavements on each street corner. These allowed the easier passage of horse-drawn carriages so that the wheels would ride smoothly up on a turn, avoiding an uncomfortable jolt for passengers.

On the other side of Calle Isabel from the museum is the **Casa Wiechers Villaronga.** Now fully restored, this interesting building was constructed in 1911 and features many adaptations to the tropical climate—underfloor ventilation, louvered fretwork windows, stained-glass panels to filter the sunlight, and the pressed tin ceilings that are a hallmark of Ponce architecture. One of its peculiarities

is a *mirador,* an outdoor observatory on the roof, supported by columns. The dining room contains some outstanding examples of art deco furniture, ceiling lights, and glass, all of which were imported from Spain.

The city is extremely proud of its **Museo del Arte,** which was designed by Edward Durell Stone, the architect of the Museum of Modern Art in New York. Noted for its elegant interior, the museum claims to hold the largest collection of art in the Caribbean—over 850 paintings, 800 sculptures, and 500 prints spanning more than five centuries of Western art. It is particularly strong on the pre-Raphaelites, the baroque period, and contemporary Latin American works. One of its most famous paintings is "Flaming June," by the pre-Raphaelite Frederick Lord

Museo de la Historia de Ponce
- ✉ 51–53 Calle Isabel
- ☎ 787/844-7071
- 🕐 Closed Tues.
- 💲 $

Casa Wiechers Villaronga
- ✉ 106 Calle Reina & Calle Menendez
- ☎ 787/843-3363
- 🕐 Closed Mon.
- 💲 $

Museo del Arte
- ✉ Ave. las Americas
- ☎ 787/848-0505
- 💲 $

"Flaming June," Ponce Museo del Arte

Caribbean, with burials dating back to A.D. 700. Two dance grounds and seven ball courts (one in the form of a star) have been discovered here, underlining its importance as a major ceremonial center. It is assumed that there is a correlation between the positions of these constructions and solstices or equinoxes.

The largest court, measuring about 110 yards (100 m), is the longest in the Caribbean; 187 skeletons have been unearthed here, some showing evidence of human sacrifice. A re-creation of a Taino village and a small museum display Indian ceremonial objects, pottery, and jewelry. The bilingual guides give informative tours about this particular site and about the pre-Columbian Taino culture generally. They shed light on similarities between Taino culture and that of the Maya in Mexico.

HACIENDA BUENA VISTA
Farther north of town, this wonderful old coffee plantation has been restored using 19th-century techniques and tools. Built in 1833, when the country's coffee production was at its peak, the whole estate is powered by an ingenious system of hydraulics. The original owners received permission to divert the Río Canas to provide power for their machinery if all the water was returned to its source—and this is how the system still works. Not a drop is wasted as the hydraulics power the depulping, husking, and polishing machines.

The manor house has also been fully restored, with the help of old photographs and family documents, to show how the hacienda was furnished and managed. The estate is set in a subtropical environment, home to the Puerto Rican screech owl, hummingbirds, and the mangrove cuckoo—among others. ∎

Museo Castillo Serrallés
- ✉ 17 El Vigia
- ☎ 787/259-1774
- 🕐 Closed Mon.
- 💲 $

Parque Ceremonial Tibes
- ✉ Rte. 503
- ☎ 787/840-2255, http://ponce.inter. edu/tibes/tibes.html
- 🕐 Closed Mon.
- 💲 $

Hacienda Buena Vista
- ✉ Rte. 10
- ☎ 787/722-5882
- 🕐 Closed Mon.–Thurs.
- 💲 $$$

Leighton. The museum also stages frequent special exhibits.

Perched high above the town is the **Museo Castillo Serrallés.** Built in the 1930s in Spanish revival style, the mansion was originally the home of the Serrallés family, owners of the Dom Q rum distillery. This airy, multilevel house combines Spanish and Moorish elements; the interior features period furnishings and a beautiful inner courtyard.

The fascinating tour includes the history of the oldest rum-making family on the island, permanent and temporary exhibits, and a short film on the sugar and rum industries. The site also has a gift shop and an excellent café with views over Ponce.

PARQUE CEREMONIAL TIBES
This fascinating Taino site, located just outside of Ponce, is said to be the oldest cemetery in the

West of Ponce

THE SOUTHWESTERN CORNER OF THE ISLAND IS THE driest part of the country, especially in the 1,618-acre (655-ha) Bosque Estátal Guánica, just outside the port of Guánica. This dry forest is unique in Puerto Rico because it contains 700 plant species, 48 of which are endangered, and 16 of which exist nowhere else.

The **Bosque Estátal Guánica** (Guánica Forest Reserve) is also home to snakes, lizards, and endangered birds. About ten marked trails cross the arid scrub within the park, which also has a large, double bay, **Playa de Ventenas,** a popular beach with local surfers.

Guánica itself was the beachhead for 16,000 American troops during the landings in July 1898 in the Spanish-American War. On the hill above town is an old fort, currently being restored.

Between Guánica and the forest is a beach with a big hotel, the Copamarina Resort. Offshore is **Gilligan's Island,** a popular destination for day-trippers. You can also take excursions from the hotel into the coastal mangroves.

Farther west is **La Parguera,** which has grown from a fishing village into a popular resort area. It's a lively spot, particularly on weekends, and is also well known for the nearby **Phosphorescent Bay.** This lagoon amid the coastal mangrove swamps is similar to the bay on Vieques (see p. 136), although the latter seems to have more dinoflagellates in the water (*boats depart every 30 minutes from La Parguera between 7:30 a.m. and 10:30 p.m.*).

At the southwestern tip of the island is the **Cabo Rojo lighthouse** *(Tel 787/851-7070),* from where you have views back down the coast.

Five miles (8 km) inland from here is a wildfowl sanctuary, **Cabo Rojo Wildlife Refuge,** located around the Boquerón Lagoon, near the resort of Boquerón. ∎

Bosque Estátal Guánica
🗺 126 C1
✉ Dept. of Natural & Environmental Resources
☎ 787/724-8774

Cabo Rojo Wildlife Refuge
🗺 126 B1
✉ Rte. 301
☎ 787/851-7258

Boquerón, long a popular vacation spot, boasts some good beaches.

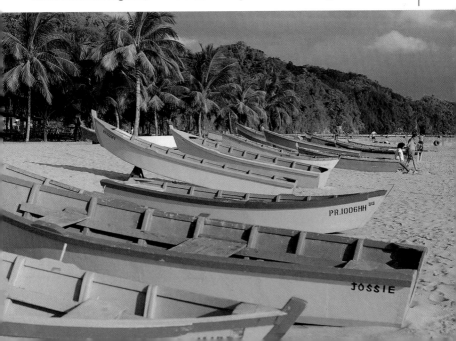

Drive: The Panoramic Route

Snaking its way through some of Puerto Rico's most fabulous scenery as it traverses the length of the island, the Panoramic Route is a classic drive, unlike any other in the Caribbean. It takes at least two days, but there are several mountain *paradors* (country inns) where you can stay. This description is from east to west. Many parts of the road are extremely narrow, so drive carefully. The route is marked at most junctions (brown signs with R.U.T.A. and symbols for mountains), but not all, so take care.

The route starts in the coastal town of **Maunabo,** heads inland to Yabucoa, and then crosses the Río Guayane before starting to climb into the foothills. Small settlements dot the ridge along which the road runs, with valleys and ravines on either side overflowing with clumps of bamboo, tree ferns, and banana plants. After about 6 miles (10 km), the road starts to climb even more steeply. At this altitude, small coffee plantations replace the cattle pastures of the lowlands.

The route then enters the **Reserva Forestal Carite ❶,** (*Tel 787/721-2400*) 6,000 acres (2,430 ha) of rain forest. The reserve is home to 50 species of birds and has several waterfalls and a blue pool known as the Charco Azul. Past here the views open up on both sides, with the sea and coastal plains visible to the south. Lagos Carite and Patillas can be seen, too.

The road continues along the ridgebacks of the Sierra de Cayey, bypassing the town of Cayey itself and rising again to a high point at the **Mirador Piedra Degetau ❷.** An observation tower, plus picnic and other

---

🅜 See area map pages 126–27
► Maunabo
⬌ 120 miles
🕑 1.5–2 days
► Mayagüez

NOT TO BE MISSED
- Reserva Forestal Carite
- Cañon San Cristóbal
- Cerro Doña Juana

Bamboo shades the road toward the end of the drive.

MAYAGÜEZ

106 Montañas de Maricao
Los Rábanos 135
105 Las Vegas
Limón 2
Uroyan
RESERVA FORESTAL MARICAO
Indiera Alta
120
105 128
128 RESERVA FORESTAL GUILARTE
131 Adjuntas
143
1338m Cerro de Punta
CENTRA
Area Rec Doña Jua
Divisoria
107
RESERVA FORESTAL TORO NEGRO
Cer Do Juan
149

CORDILLERA CENTRAL

Along the Cordillera Central

PONCE

0   20 kilometers
0   10 miles

facilities mark this summit, which is dedicated to the memory of Don Frederico Piedra Degetau y Gonzales (1862–1914), a distinguished writer and patriot who was inspired by this panorama.

Just to the north is the town of **Aibonito 3**, once a retreat for the wealthy and still retaining some of its grandiose homes. It is also the highest town in Puerto Rico. Beyond Aibonito the **Cañon San Cristóbal** (San Cristóbal Canyon) **4**, the island's deepest gorge, plunges 700 feet (210 m) into the Río Usabon. The Conservation Trust of Puerto Rico *(P.O. Box 4747, San Juan, Tel 787/722-5834)* is developing nature trails, but in the meantime only experienced hikers should attempt to descend its steep slopes.

The route twists and turns along the spine of the Cordillera Central, offering stunning panoramas across the whole island both to the north and south coasts. Beyond the Cerro El Malo (2,957 feet/902 m), the road enters another forest, the 7,000-acre (2,830-ha)

Reserva Forestal Toro Negro (Toro Negro Forest Reserve). This is a particularly scenic area, with the road shrouded by a leafy canopy of bamboo.

Six miles (10 km) northeast of here is the **Area de Recreo Doña Juana** (Doña Juana Recreation Area). It's worth stopping and taking the path opposite, which leads to a huge swimming pool in the forest. The route beyond here leads upward to the **Cerro Doña Juana 5** at 3,538 feet (1,079 m). This is an easy path with no steep gradients and takes around 90 minutes for the return trip. At the top you can climb a small tower for a panorama of the mountains and the coastline. Beyond here you pass the **Cerro de Punta** (4,387 feet/1,338 m), the island's highest point. It bristles with radio masts.

The road descends momentarily to the quiet little township of Adjuntas before climbing once more through the Cordillera Central, skirting the Montanas de Uroyan and finally ending on the west coast at **Mayagüez.** ■

View from the tower at Cerro Doña Juana

SAN JUAN

Carolina

902m
Cerro
El Malo
143
155
4 **Cañón San Cristóbal**
Aibonito 3
Cayey
14
RESERVA FORESTAL CARITE
1 52
Campamento Guavate
181
2
Mirador Piedra Degetau
Las Tetas
14
63
1
Lago Carite
184
Sierra de
Cayey
Guayane
182
Yabucoa
15
179
Lago Patillas
181
Guayama
3
Maunabo
START

The northwest

The 706-acre (286-ha) Río Camuy Cave Park contains one of the most spectacular and complex cave systems in the world.

NORTHWEST PUERTO RICO IS A LIMESTONE LABYRINTH laced with caves, underground rivers, and massive sinkholes. You can tour through the Río Camuy Cave Park, which takes in different caves and sinkholes, or visit the prehistoric Parque Ceremonial Caguana. The area also includes the fascinating Observatorio de Arecibo (see pp. 146–47).

RÍO CAMUY CAVE PARK

In the heart of the limestone karst country near Arecibo is the Río Camuy Cave Park. The caves have been carved out over the centuries by the Río Camuy as it carries the rainfall of the Cordillera Central down to the sea. Only two other rivers in the world (the Metali in Papua New Guinea and the Reha in Yugoslavia) can match this underground torrent.

Your guided exploration of this world of lofty caverns, mighty stalactites, and huge sinkholes begins at the visitor center, where there is a short audiovisual presentation on the cave system. You then board a motorized tram for the descent through a steep, winding ravine to the main cave, the **Cueva Clara de Empalme** (Clear Cave at the Crossroads). Sunlight filters through a natural entrance to the cave, and

Río Camuy Cave Park

🗺 126 C2

✉ Rte. 129, N of Lares

☎ 787/893-3100

🕐 Closed Mon.–Tues.

💲 $$$$$

from the uppermost cliffs, and water cascades down the sinkhole's moss-covered sides.

After the Cueva Clara, the tour continues to the **Sumidero Tres Pueblos** (Three Townships Sinkhole), so named because the borders of three local districts, Camuy, Hatillo, and Lares, coincide here. This measures some 400 feet (122 m) deep and 650 feet (198 m) in diameter: Its 6-acre (2.5-ha) base could hold all of San Juan's El Morro fortress. In one cave at the side of this sinkhole, artifacts have been discovered that show it was once occupied by the pre-historic Taino.

The last sinkhole on the tour is the **Espiral,** which spirals down-ward toward the underground river. A series of 200 steps and walkways leads down to it.

To avoid the weekend crowds, visit on a Wednesday, Thursday, or Friday. Tours are available in Spanish or English.

PARQUE CEREMONIAL CAGUANA

South of Río Camuy Cave Park, between Utuado and Lares, is the Parque Ceremonial Caguana. Dating from A.D. 1200, Caguana is one of the largest and most impor-tant Taino ceremonial centers in the Caribbean. In addition to the large central court there, there are ten rec-tangular courtyards, as well as a cir-cular one. Although permanently inhabited by very few people, the center attracted large crowds to religious ceremonies.

Circled by limestone hills, the setting is impressive. The grounds contain many trees and plants, such as silk cottonwood, sapodilla, palms, and cedars, which were used for food and building materials. A small interpretive center has dis-plays of ceramics, carvings, and other Taino artifacts. ∎

Parque Ceremonial Caguana

✉ 9 miles (14.5 km) W of Utuado on Rte. 111

☎ 787/894-7325

A Taino carving on display at the Parque Ceremonial Caguana

pathways lead to the wonders beyond. The main cavern reaches some 200 feet (60 m) at its highest point, dwarfing the visitors walking around its perimeter. Stalactites hang from the ceiling in various strange shapes. Almost at the cave's center, is an enormous stalagmite 17 feet (5.1 m) high and 30 feet (9 m) in diameter. Five different species of bats live in the caves, as well as crickets, guavas (a kind of tarantu-la), and microscopic shrimp that thrive in the pools of water within the caves. On one side of the Cueva Clara is a deep cleft, at the bottom of which the Río Camuy flows.

Alternatively, to the east you emerge into a vast sinkhole (a col-lapsed cave) that is more than 150 feet (45 m) in diameter and 420 feet (128 m) deep. Lianas hang down

Observatorio de Arecibo

D riving through the deeply cleft landscape of limestone karst to the south of Arecibo, the road switchbacks through deep ravines and up over ridges where cattle graze in small pastures. Eventually a slender concrete tower becomes visible, rising to an improbable height above the steep green hillsides: It is the first indication of what lies ahead, the extraordinary Observatorio de Arecibo (Arecibo Observatory)—the world's largest radio telescope.

Even if you had no idea what this telescope is capable of doing, it would be impressive. The enormous central dish, which covers more than 20 acres (8 ha), is surmounted by a cat's cradle of wires suspended from three concrete pylons—and hanging like a giant spider in the middle is the receiver itself, weighing just under a thousand tons.

In fact, when it was built in 1963, no one knew for sure that this supersensitive receiver of cosmic radio signals would work at all. It is so big that of course it cannot move: The planet itself has to move for it to change direction. But Arecibo has paid off handsomely. It can examine weather patterns in the troposphere just 2 miles (3 km) above us, as well as probe the heart of quasars some 10 billion light years away. Major discoveries made here include the existence of pulsars (most of those known were mapped here), pulsars orbited by planets, ice in Mercury's polar regions, the rotational cycles of Venus and Mercury, and other productive astronomical information.

But Arecibo has also become associated with something that has more to do with the *X-Files* than radar astronomy—the search for extraterrestrial intelligence, or SETI. The telescope is featured in the film *Contact* (1995) and Dr. José Alonso, head of the visitor center, is quick to dismiss the notion that there has been a cover-up. "People are always very curious about the fact that this facility is capable of detecting signals from extraterrestrial civilizations," he says. "Many believe that we have in fact detected such signals and are keeping it

This amazing observatory is set in a natural crater high in the mountains.

quiet. The truth is that we do monitor a number of stars with surrounding planets that we believe could develop or have developed intelligence with whom we might be able to communicate. We look at them once in a while to see if there is any signal, but none has so far been received. People want to believe that it has happened, but it hasn't happened yet." The telescope collects a huge amount of data, all of which has to be analyzed, and there are so many billions of stars that the chances of pointing it at an area where there might be life are slim. Only around 5 percent of the telescope's work is devoted to SETI.

Inside the control room, banks of computer screens monitor the telescope, and arrays of fiber-optic cables feed the data into mainframes that send it to even bigger number crunchers at Cornell University; the observatory is part of the National Astronomy and Ionosphere Center operated by Cornell University and the National Science Foundation. Outside, a large container houses the research facility of Operation Phoenix, a privately funded foundation that recently began work on a renewed search for extraterrestrial intelligence .

The observatory recently opened a wonderful new interpretive center, the Angel Ramos Foundation Visitor Center (*Tel 787/878-2612, closed Mon.–Tues.*). Located at the foot of one of the giant towers supporting the telescope, the center has some excellent and highly informative displays on science and astronomy.

Inspecting the illuminated platform above the reflector

The first floor houses exhibits on "The Earth and our Solar System, Stars, and Galaxies," and "Tools and Technologies," as well as an auditorium. The second floor concentrates on the work at Arecibo. ∎

Mona Island

Mona Island

 See inside back cover

SOMETIMES CALLED "THE GALAPAGOS OF THE CARIBBEAN" because of its remoteness and abundance of wildlife, Mona Island is located 46 miles (74 km) off the western coast of Puerto Rico. Just under 7 miles (11 km) long and around 4.5 miles (7 km) wide, the island has a dry climate and is classified as a subtropical dry region.

Lying in the middle of the Mona Passage, the island was once inhabited by Taino Indians who left behind a series of hieroglyphics and rock paintings in the caves that dot the 200-foot-high (60-m) cliffs on the island's shoreline. Pirates and buccaneers later visited the island, and it's rumored that they may have left a different kind of treasure in these same caves.

In the 1880s a German entrepreneur, Anton Mobins, was granted a license to mine phosphate on the island and about 200 people lived on the island to work in this industry. It was during this period that roads were built and the caves first explored. The mining company ceased trading in 1896 due to competition from Peru and the United States, and since then the island has been largely uninhabited.

This isolated island is renowned for its wildlife, which includes bats, seabirds, and iguanas that can be up to 3 feet (90 cm) long. It also has untouched coral reefs, particularly on its eastern and western coastlines, which are known for their prolific marine life.

Diving and ecotour operators organize tours to the island, which is accessed by private boat or airplane. Caves that can be visited to see Taino petroglyphs include **La Esperanza, El Gato,** and **La Negra.** Some of the more popular beaches frequented by visitors are **Playa Brava, Playa de la Mujeres, Playa del Uvero, Playa Sardineras,** and **Playa de Pajaros.** It's also possible to camp on Playa Sardineras with prior permission from the Department of Natural Resources, which also maintains several cabins where you can stay. There are no shops or any other kind of facility, so you have to bring all the food and water you need. ∎

Brown boobys, one of the seabirds that can be seen on Mona Island

Mona Island

Permission to visit Mona Island must be obtained from the Department of Natural Resources *(Tel 787/722-1726).* Expeditions to the island are sometimes undertaken by ecotour operators such as Aventurisla *(P.O. Box 22242, San Juan PR 00931-22242, Tel 787/790-7816)* and Eco Aventuras *(P.O. Box 22768, San Juan PR 00931-2768).* ∎

A jewel-like scattering of tiny volcanic islands, rocks, and reefs embedded in a turquoise sea, the Virgin Islands archipelago is the final link in the chain of Greater Antilles islands, and it is a magnet for sailors and sun lovers.

Virgin Islands

Soper's Hole marina, Tortola (BVI)

Virgin Islands

SPREADING OUT FROM THE VIRGIN PASSAGE, 50 MILES (80 KM) EAST OF
Puerto Rico, the 100-plus Virgin Islands lay a ragged trail across 1,000 square miles
(2,600 sq km) at the northeastern corner of the Caribbean Sea. Only a few of the greenest
islands are inhabited; the rest are Robinson Crusoe islets and secretive cays once favored by
pirates, rocky outcrops colonized by seabirds, and razor-sharp, wave-washed reefs.

At dawn and dusk, the hazy horizon of the
Virgin Islands is a magical thing broken by
layer after layer of superimposed outlines:
Unless you are a "belonger," as the local
residents are called, or possess a cartographer's
eye and a relief map, it is almost impossible to
get your bearings.

Christopher Columbus first sailed into this
nautical maze on his second voyage to the New
World in 1493. Struck by their beauty (and profusion), he named the islands Las Once Mil
Virgines, after the legend of St. Ursula and the
11,000 virgins (see below). The tiny islands held
little attraction for the major European powers
as they set about carving up the region, but
their numerous secluded harbors and safe
anchorages were a godsend for pirates, smugglers, and privateers such as Sir Francis Drake
(1540–1596), who played hide-and-seek with
the Spanish fleet and gave his name to the Sir
Francis Drake Channel, one of the most
picturesque maritime channels in the world.

The earliest European settlers were mid-
17th-century Dutch *boucaniers,* who moved
onto Tortola and raised cattle to supply

passing ships with dried meat cured in smoke-
houses called *boucans.* The British snatched
control of the island in 1672 and laid claim to
the 60 or so cays and crags at the eastern end
of the archipelago, now the British Virgin
Islands (BVI). Meanwhile, the Danes secured
the western islands of **St. Thomas** (1665)
and **St. John** (1684) and purchased **St. Croix**
from the French in 1733. St. Thomas they
transformed into a flourishing free port; St.
John and St. Croix were carpeted with sugarcane. In 1917, the Danish possessions were
sold to the United States for 25 million dollars.

The legend of St. Ursula

The obscure and highly questionable
legend of St. Ursula dates from the
Dark Ages, when the Christian daughter of
an English king sought to avoid marriage to a
barbarian chief. Agreeing to the marriage on
the condition she could undertake a visit to
Rome in the company of virgins, she selected
her retinue and sailed away. For three years
she trained the women into a fighting force,
hoping to overthrow her betrothed, but
he discovered the ruse and had all 11,001
virgins massacred in the city of Cologne
in Germany. ■

Today, together with 70 more rocks and reefs, they comprise the United States Virgin Islands (USVI).

Only 2 miles (3 km) separate the islands of St. John (USVI) and **Tortola** (BVI), but the American and the British islands are light years apart in style. St. Thomas and St. Croix are indubitably American, upbeat and among the most developed and prosperous islands in the region. The American Paradise welcomes more than 1.5 million visitors a year and has fast-food franchises, icy air-conditioning, and standards of service rarely encountered elsewhere in the Caribbean. St. John is altogether quieter and boasts an unspoiled national park, which covers two-thirds of the island.

A 40-minute ferry ride away are the relaxed British Virgin Islands, laid back to the point of horizontal. With a population of around 18,000 compared to the 113,000 on the U. S. Virgin Islands, the islands have a more traditional rural West Indian feel, and local life proceeds at a distinctly leisurely pace. Here, the tourism industry has been kept deliberately low key and pitched at an upscale but casual market. Yachting is a top attraction and many visitors simply use the islands as a jumping-off point for a sailing trip. ■

U. S. Virgin Islands

THREE DISTINCT IDENTITIES, THE ISLANDS OF ST. THOMAS, ST. JOHN, and St. Croix (pronounced Croy) are linked by their common history. During the colonial era, the islands were Denmark's only Caribbean possessions and both St. Thomas and St. Croix preserve attractive Danish colonial architecture in their main waterfront towns.

With the emancipation of slaves on the Danish islands in 1848, and the subsequent collapse of the sugar industry, the Caribbean colonies were on the wane by the 1860s when the strategic potential of the island group first attracted American interest. The need to protect the Panama Canal (opened in 1914), coupled with German naval activity in the region during World War I, finally prompted the United States to purchase the islands from Denmark and place them under the administration of the U.S. Navy. The Department of the Interior took over in 1931, and self-

government was introduced in 1936, but the islanders were not permitted to elect their own governor (previously selected by the President) until 1968. Today, Charlotte Amalie on St. Thomas is the capital of the U.S. Virgin Islands, which are unincorporated territories of the United States. The islanders are U.S. citizens and taxpayers, and their 15-member legislature is represented by a nonvoting delegate in Congress.

Cosmopolitan St. Thomas is the main gateway to the islands. It is a major cruise ship destination offering excellent duty-free

**Above: Divers circling coral in the clear
waters of the U.S. Virgin Islands
Right: Frederick Evangelical Church on
Government Hill, Charlotte Amalie**

shopping, fine dining and accommodations,
several lovely beaches, and a few sight-seeing
attractions, all combining to make it an ideal
choice for a short break. St. John is an easy day
trip away, although for visitors in search of
peace and quiet this tiny island could well be
a better option. St. Croix is the least known
of the USVI trio but well worth a visit. The
island was struck a cruel blow by Hurricane
Hugo in 1989, but 1995's Hurricane Marilyn,
which caused considerable damage to St.
Thomas and St. John, raised St. Croix's
profile. The island provides a good balance of
pretty towns, shopping bargains to match St.
Thomas, and more varied and interesting
sight seeing opportunities. ■

St. Thomas

THE FOUNDATIONS OF ST. THOMAS'S FORTUNES WERE laid back in the 1670s by the traders of the Danish West India Company. The original settlement on the site of Charlotte Amalie provided a welcome watering hole for Caribbean merchants and pirates, including Edward Teach (died 1718), better known as Blackbeard. A certain raciness lingers on bustling St. Thomas, as islanders offer cruise-ship passengers their first taste of the Caribbean.

St. Thomas

⛰ 150 A2

Visitor information

✉ P.O. Box 640,
Charlotte Amalie,
USVI 00804

☎ 340/774-8784

Above: A carved pirate recalls St. Thomas's early days.
Opposite: The Paradise Point Tramway provides a bird's-eye view of St. Thomas Harbour and Charlotte Amalie.

As the town prospered, it was renamed Charlotte Amalie in honor of the Danish queen (wife of Christian V) in 1691, and by the early 18th century its waterfront warehouses were crammed full of silks, guns, gold, and manufactured goods, which were traded for Caribbean sugar, rum, indigo, and cotton. While European conflicts were mirrored between the colonial powers of the Caribbean, St. Thomas continued to grow rich on the strength of Danish neutrality. They also supplied arms to colonists fighting the American Revolution. For a time at the height of the plantation era, St. Croix eclipsed St. Thomas as the most

important island in the group and the capital was moved to Christiansted on St. Croix in 1775; it returned to Charlotte Amalie in 1871.

Bustling Charlotte Amalie (see p. 156) is the hub of the 12-by-3-mile (19-by-5-km) island. Beaches, bays, and hotels dot the island's ragged central and eastern shorelines (the western end is largely undeveloped), and the interior rises steeply to the 1,556-foot (474-m) peak of Crown Mountain, its ridges and crags peppered with houses and vacation residence. More than 50,000 people live here, making it one of the most populous islands in the region, and numbers

Above left: Walking tall at Carnival time
Above right: Shopping for bargains in the alleys off Main Street, Charlotte Amalie

Virgin Islands Museum
✉ Waterfront Hwy., Fort Christian
☎ 340/776-4566
🕐 Closed weekends
💲 $

are boosted daily by thousands of cruise-ship passengers who are shepherded to mountaintop observation points and spectacular Magens Bay (see p. 159). In St. Thomas you can find diving and water sports, deep-sea fishing, and the magnificent Mahogany Run golf course, but the island's chief sport is undoubtedly bargain hunting in Charlotte Amalie.

CHARLOTTE AMALIE

Radiating from its charming Danish colonial origins, Charlotte Amalie skirts the outline of St. Thomas Harbor, and clambers up into the amphitheater of surrounding hills. In the bay, giant cruise ships (up to ten at a time on a busy day) lie at anchor and disgorge their human cargo onto the waterfront, where the merchants of Main Street await, their mercantile instincts as finely honed as the 18th-century traders whose warehouses they now occupy.

Make an exploratory foray down **Dronningens Gade** (as Main Street is also known) and its warren of narrow alleys to discover a commercial kaleidoscope every bit as dazzling and cutthroat as it must have been 250 years ago, although the barrels and bales have been replaced with designer labels and electronic gadgets.

Main Street is at the heart of Charlotte Amalie's historic district, which stretches from Rothschild Francis Market Square in the west to Emancipation Park in the east. The park is a good place to begin a walkabout with a visit to **Fort Christian.** The bloodred fort was built between 1672 and 1680, and it

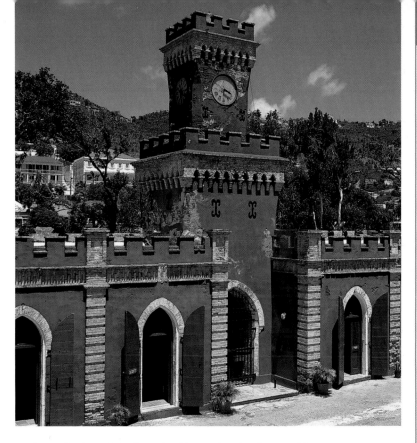

now houses the **Virgin Islands Museum** and a local art gallery laid out in the former jail cells. Alongside detailed historical displays, small exhibits cover bush medicine and colonial furnishings, and pride of place in the central courtyard goes to an antique, animal-powered cane crusher. From the battlements, there is a view down to the 19th-century **Danish barracks building** near the waterfront, which has been spruced up with a lick of peppermint green paint to accommodate the Virgin Islands Legislature. The official ceremonies that marked the transfer of ownership of the Danish Virgin Islands to the United States were held here in 1917.

Above the park is **Government Hill,** crisscrossed with a grid of narrow streets and flights of steps lined with attractive private homes, public buildings, and monumental churches. Near **Government House,** a white neoclassic edifice on Kongens Gade, the **99 Steps** (actually 103) strike up toward **Bluebeard's Castle,** a stone watchtower with tremendous views. The bricks used to construct the steps and many local buildings made their way out to the Caribbean as ballast shipped from Denmark in the holds of ships.

West from here, on Crystal Gade near the junction with Raadets Gade, is **St. Thomas Synagogue,** flanked by palms and dating from 1833. The domed interior has a sand-covered floor, which has its origins in Sephardic tradition; it symbolizes the flight of the Jewish people out of Egypt across the desert. St. Thomas's first Jewish congregation were refugees from

Fort Christian's clock tower was added in 1874 when the building became a police station, courthouse, and jail.

**Paradise Point
Tramway**
✉ Long Bay Rd.
☎ 340/774-9809
💲 $$$$$

**Atlantis
Submarine**
✉ Havensight Mall,
Bldg. 6
☎ 340/776-5650
💲 $$$$$

**ISLAND-
HOPPING BY
FERRY**

Inter-island ferries are a great (and inexpensive) way to explore the Virgin Islands. Frequent daily services link St. Thomas and St. John. The crossing takes just 20 minutes from Red Hook on the east end of St. Thomas to Cruz Bay, St. John; or 45 minutes from Charlotte Amalie. There are also ferry services from St. Thomas and St. John to the British Virgin Islands of Tortola (daily), Virgin Gorda (several times weekly), and Jost van Dyke (weekends). Proof of citizenship is needed for travel between the USVI and BVI. ■

Dutch Sint Eustatius, exiled for their involvement in the arms trade during the American Revolution. Back down on the main drag, the Jewish Pissarro family once ran a trading store at **Dronningens Gade 14,** where Impressionist artist Camille Pissarro (1830–1903) was born. Four blocks west, between Store Strade and Strand Gade, is the **covered market,** which comes alive on Saturdays when farmers from the West End venture into town to sell their homegrown fruit and vegetables.

Around the harbor in the eastern suburbs, and fronted by Havensight Mall, is the **West Indian Company Dock,** Charlotte Amalie's main cruise-ship berth. It is also the shore base for **Atlantis Submarines** (see p. 200, reservations advised). The perfect solution to reef diving without getting wet, the tours begin with a harbor cruise; then passengers are

ferried out to the Buck Island Reef and transferred to a miniature submarine. The one-hour narrated dives reach a depth of 90 feet (27 m) below the surface, where the reef is a mass of spectacular hard and soft corals regularly visited by colorful blue chromis, rock beauties, angelfish, moray eels, and sea turtles among others.

Across the street from Havensight is the **Paradise Point Tramway,** which hoists a fleet of glass-enclosed cable cars to an observation deck 700 feet (210 m) above sea level (road access also). The deck provides splendid views of the harbor, sheltered by Hassel Island in the foreground, and Water Island beyond. On a clear day it is possible to spot St. Croix on the far horizon. There is also a short nature trail, a restaurant, shops, and a bar for sunset cocktails when the city turns into a blaze of twinkling lights encircling the bay. ■

Sports & activities

Day sails: Boat trips with lunch, swimming, and snorkeling from Nightwind Charters (Tel 340/775-4110); Treasure Isle Cruises (Tel 340/775-9500); or aboard the Winifred, maximum six guests (Tel 340/775-7898). For a day trip to the BVI, contact Stormy Petrel, maximum 12 guests (Tel 340/775-7990).

Diving & snorkeling: Chris Sawyer Diving Center (Red Hook, Tel 340/775-7804 or 800/882-2965, fax 340/775-9495); Coki Dive & Snorkel Center (Coki Beach, Tel 340/775-4220); Dive In! (Sapphire Beach Resort, Tel 340/775-6100 or 800/524-2090).

Golf: Mahogany Run Golf Course (Mahogany Run Road,

north coast, Tel 340/775-7050, information 800/253-7103, tee-time reservations Tel 340/777-6006, fax 340/777-6280).

Kayaking: Nature tours with snorkeling in the Mangrove Lagoon marine sanctuary from Virgin Islands: Ecotours (Holmberg's Marina, East End, Tel 340/779-2155).

Powerboat rentals: Aqua Blue (Sapphire Beach Resort, Tel 340/775-1242); Nauti Nymph (Red Hook, Tel 340/775-5066).

Sportfishing: Several outfits operate out of the American Yacht Harbor at Red Hook, including Marlin Prince (Tel 340/779-5939) and Prowler Sportfishing Charters Inc. (Tel 340/779-2515). ■

Around St. Thomas

CORAL WORLD

An 80,000-gallon (363,000-litre) reef tank display, 21 aquariums showcasing rare marine plant and animal life, a predator tank, and stingray pool are among the attractions at this popular marine park on St. Thomas's northeast coast. But the real showstopper lies beneath the waves, where the picture windows of the underwater observatory resemble a darkened marine theater in the round opening onto a 360-degree panorama of the ocean bed. A touch pool and the rescued baby turtle exhibit are particular hits with kids, and there are daily talks by marine experts as well as feeding sessions at the baby shark pool. The park is adjacent to busy Coki Beach, which has a dive and snorkel center.

▲ 154 C2 ✉ Coki Point ☎ 340/775-1555 $ $$$$$

ESTATE ST. PETER GREAT HOUSE & BOTANICAL GARDENS

Draped across the hillside 1,000 feet (305 m) above Magens Bay, these 10-acre (4-ha) botanical gardens are a monument to triumph over adversity. In 1989 they were decimated by Hurricane Hugo; also destroyed the original great house; they were flattened by Hurricane Marilyn six years later. The recovery is impressive, and you can tour the gardens on wooden boardwalk trails shaded by banana plants and breadfruit trees, tall stands of lobster-claw heliconias, and brilliant tropical gingers. The great house has been reconstructed and furnished in contemporary style. A gallery sells Caribbean artworks and there is a riveting series of photographs taken in the wake of Hugo. Viewing decks are equipped with orientation boards that point out local landmarks and more than 20 neighboring Virgin Islands.

▲ 154 B2 ✉ St. Peter Island Rd. ☎ 340/774-4999 $ $$$

MAGENS BAY

Over the mountain ridge from Charlotte Amalie, St. Thomas's most famous beach lines the base of a huge rectangular bay carved out of the north coast. Magens Bay's idyllic mile-long (1.5 km) stretch of powder-soft sand fringed with palm trees is a prime contender in any list of the world's top beaches. It certainly gets busy, but on weekdays there is usually plenty of room for everyone. Several beach bars and restaurants cater to the crowds.

▲ 154 C2 ✉ Magens Road $ $

ST. PETER MOUNTAINTOP

The top of St. Peter Mountain is the setting for yet more superlative views over Magens Bay and off to St. John and the British Virgin Islands. This spot also claims to be the birthplace of the banana daiquiri; alcoholic and nonalcoholic versions are available at the viewing deck bar.

▲ 154 B2 ✉ Off Crown Mountain Rd. ☎ 340/774-2400 ■

The Coral World underwater observatory juts out from Coki Point above the sandy strip of Coki Beach.

Cruising

The Caribbean is the ultimate cruising destination, an idyllic combination of sun, sea, and varied landscapes, where it is possible to wake up every morning with a new island group on the bow and a different port at the foot of the gangplank. Christopher Columbus and Sir Francis Drake may have pioneered Caribbean cruising half a millennium ago, but the modern dictionary definition of cruising, "to make a trip by sea for pleasure, calling at a number of ports," reveals a leisure concept wildly at odds with those early seagoing missions of exploration and plunder.

More cruise ships ply Caribbean waters than any other place on earth. There are more than a hundred vessels to choose from, and they vary considerably in terms of size, atmosphere, facilities, and itineraries. For first-time cruise passengers, selecting the perfect cruise can be a bewildering experience, but there are ways of narrowing down the field.

One of the first rules of cruising is that size does matter. Although no indicator of price or the vessel's position on the luxury scale, size does influence the type of cruising experience available. For instance, smaller ships catering for as many as 500 passengers can visit offbeat destinations inaccessible to larger vessels; they tend to allow their guests additional time ashore and to enjoy a more relaxed, intimate atmosphere. On the downside (although several smaller vessels offer a positively sybaritic degree of luxury), space is necessarily restricted.

The most common Caribbean cruising options are the medium (500- to 1,000-passenger) and large (1,000- to 2,000-passenger) cruise ships. They fall into three main categories: luxury-class vessels appealing to a sophisticated clientele with top-notch facilities from water sports and spa treatments to gourmet cuisine and spacious accommodations; premium class cruise ships offering good food, a high standard of service, and a broad spectrum of organized activities and entertainment; and standard class vessels aimed at a more casual crowd with fewer facilities, simpler menus, and limited cabin space. In a class of their own are the mega-ships, giant floating resorts with 2,000-plus passengers and a lifestyle that revolves around a range of shipboard activities and a wild nightlife, which rather precludes much in the way of sight-seeing.

The onboard activities package is a major consideration when planning a week or two afloat. Most medium to large cruise ships offer a day-long program of activities, which might include exercise classes, shore excursions, quiz competitions, cocktails to the accompaniment of a steel band, and an elaborate Las Vegas-style evening show, followed by a session in the discothèque. Mainstream vessels are all equipped with movie theaters, casinos, game rooms, and exercise facilities (worth remembering as the average cruise passenger gains around 4 pounds/2.2 kg) during a week-long cruise). All these features and up to five meals a day (excluding alcoholic drinks) are included in the price of the cruise. Families should also check that the cruise line offers adequate children's facilities. Make sure that the supervised daytime activities programs cover the right age group(s), and ask about the availability of babysitters, kids' meals, cribs, high chairs, and other vital equipment.

The most popular cruise duration on the Caribbean run (excluding shorter trips to the Bahamas) is between one and two weeks. The majority of round-trip itineraries originate from the South Florida ports of Miami and Port Everglades in Fort Lauderdale, although some cruise lines operate out of San Juan, Puerto Rico. Most cruise itineraries feature a different port every day with two days at sea (sometimes three days on longer trips). High season (and high prices) is mid-December through April, but cruises are possible throughout the year and ships stay well clear of the Hurricane Belt from August through October. Cruises are rarely booked directly with the cruise line. For the best deals and expert advice consult a travel agent with membership of the Cruise Lines International Association (CLIA) or the National Association of Cruise-Oriented Agencies (NACOA). A wealth of cruising information is on the Internet, too. ∎

Above: Cruise passengers step ashore at Heritage Quay in St. John's, the capital of Antigua.
Right: Gourmet buffets are a major attraction on board.
Below: Sailing into Great Bay and the famous duty-free port of Philipsburg, Sint Maarten.

St. John

St. John
⚠ 151 C3

A 2-MILE (3 KM) FERRY RIDE ACROSS THE PILLSBURY SOUND from St. Thomas, St. John is the unspoiled gem of the USVI. Two-thirds of it is a national park, created with the help of Laurence Rockefeller, who donated the first chunk of land in 1956 (a cunning move to prevent anybody else building near his Caneel Bay resort), and much of the remaining third is untouched. Dense woodlands carpet the rolling hills and sandy bays punctuate the irregular coast.

Left: Fortunately the name of the restaurant doesn't reflect the nature of the Virgin Islanders. Far left: St. John's forested hinterland slopes down to the north shore and a clutch of dazzling white sand beaches nestled in quiet coves.

are believed to have leapt to their deaths at Mary Point on the north coast. Things have been very quiet since, and the population of 3,500 mainly consists of incomers from down island and American expatriates lured by the serenity.

CRUZ BAY & AROUND THE ISLAND

Most visitors arrive in St. John at the **Cruz Bay ferry dock** to be greeted by a coterie of taxi drivers chewing the fat by the bandstand and an engaging huddle of shops and restaurants set back from the waterfront. Over the hill south of town is **Great Cruz Bay,** the island's busiest resort area. But most visitors set off on their round-island tour by taking the North Shore Road out of Cruz Bay, past the attractive Mongoose Junction mall, housed in a local plantation-style stone complex, and the informative **national park visitor center** *(Tel 340/776-6201).*

St. John's best beaches rim the north coast from Honeymoon Beach on Caneel Bay, through Hawksnest Bay, famously gorgeous **Trunk Bay,** and Cinnamon Bay (backed by a campground) to Maho Bay. Beyond Maho, a side road heads off to the **Annaberg Plantation** *(Tel 340/776-7450),* where a self-guided

During the colonial era, St. John was planted with sugarcane and cotton. One of the Caribbean's most successful slave revolts was staged on the island in 1733, when slaves armed with cane machetes massacred settlers and managed to hold the Danish garrison for nine months. The uprising was eventually quashed with the help of French troops, and the last rebels

Sports & activities

Day sails: Adventurer
(Tel 340/771-6950); Hurricane
Alley *(Tel 340/776-6256)*.

Diving & snorkeling:
See opposite.

Horseback riding:
Carolina Corral *(Coral Bay,
Tel 340/693-5778)*.

Kayaking: Rentals and guided
sea kayaking trips from Arawak
Expeditions *(Tel 340/693-8312)*.

Rock climbing: Adventures
Unlimited *(Tel 340/693-5763)*.

Water sports: Cruz Bay
Watersports *(Tel 340/776-6234)*
offers snorkeling, and wreck and
reef dive trips with equipment
rental, PADI and NAUI dive
tuition, and powerboat outings
to the BVI. ■

tour leads around the foundations of
slave cabins, the old windmill, boiling room, and storehouse.

The North Shore Road then
meets Centerline Road, which
returns to Cruz Bay along a twisting
mountain route with sensational
views across to Drake's Passage. Its
eastern arm continues to the quiet
village of Coral Bay, St. John's
original settlement.

Straddling the island around
three 1,000-foot (300-m) peaks,
culminating in Bordeaux Mountain
(1,277 feet/389 m), the land-based
portion of **Virgin Islands
National Park** is a subtropical
tangle of forest greenery that has
swallowed up all but the merest
traces of the hundred-plus plantation estates that once carpeted the
landscape. The visitor center
provides a helpful introduction

with maps, historical and natural
history displays, and an activities
program. A relief model graphically
illustrates St. John's rugged terrain
and details the park's 22 trails.
These vary from short walks around
Cruz Bay to more challenging hikes
such as the Reef Bay Trail, which
descends to the south coast from
Centerline Road.

A smart way to avoid the strenuous return trip on this route is to
take the Park Service guided tour
(check schedules). Walkers are
bused to the trailhead for the
2.5-mile (4-km) downhill hike
through wet and dry forest to the
Reef Bay sugar mill ruins. The trail
detours to a petroglyph site decorated with rock carvings attributed to
Arawak Indians. Take time to swim
and snorkel before the boat trip
back to Cruz Bay.

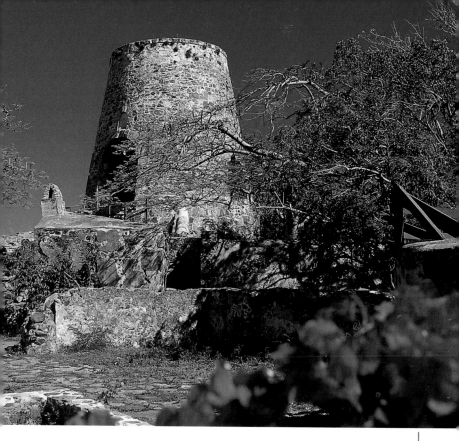

The park's 5,650-acre (2,287-ha) **marine preserve** offers excellent snorkeling in the calm, clear waters off the north coast beaches (see below) and the less accessible south coast around Saltpond and Lemeshur Bays. Parrotfish, angelfish, tangs, grunts, rays, snappers, jacks, and tarpon are frequent visitors to the reef areas and shallow sandy bays. One reason for the wealth of marine life is the mangrove nurseries where fish and marine species breed in the safe, nutrient-rich waters of the coastal swamp. The **Francis Bay Trail,** just around from Maho Bay, has a boardwalk section leading out into the mangroves where herons, Western Indian whistling ducks, pintails, teals, sandpipers, and other waterbirds come to feed. ∎

Constructed on a hilltop to catch the breeze, the conical ruins of the Annaberg Windmill date from around 1810–30.

Beneath the waves

Snorkeling is something of a specialty in St. John, and Trunk Bay even offers a 225-yard (205-m) self-guided trail with underwater signs indicating coral reef features. Snuba is a cross between snorkeling and diving with air pumped from the surface *(Tel 340/693-8063).* Slightly off the beaten track, there is snorkeling at Hawksnest Bay and Watermelon Cay in Leinster Bay. The best diving is farther offshore and in the British Virgin Islands. Contact Coral Divers *(Tel 340/776-6850)* or East End Divers *(Tel 340/779-4994).* ∎

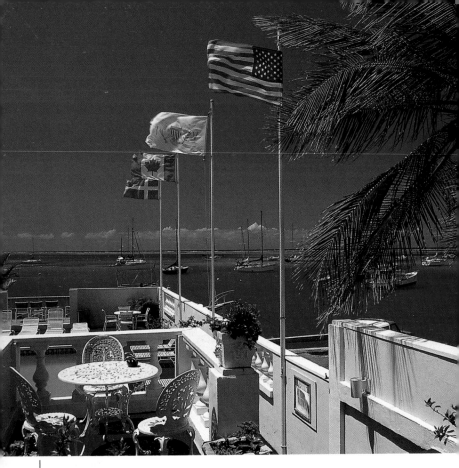

St. Croix

A welcome breeze sets the flags flying above the Christiansted waterfront as waves break against the distant reef.

THE LARGEST OF THE USVI AT 82 SQUARE MILES (212 SQ KM), St. Croix lies 40 miles (64 km) to the south of St. Thomas and the main body of the Virgin Islands. A former sugar island with mountains in the west and flat, fertile agricultural plains in the central district, St. Croix has little agriculture today but is not entirely reliant on tourism either: A huge oil refinery is out near the airport, and locally distilled Cruzan Rum is a popular souvenir item.

St. Croix

🅰 151 E1

Christiansted National Historic Site

✉ Steeple Bldg.

☎ 340/773-1460

🕐 Closed weekends

$ $

Columbus made landfall at Salt River Bay on the north shore in 1493. He beat a hasty retreat on encountering the belligerent Carib but claimed the island for Spain and named it Santa Cruz (Holy Cross). Claimed by France in 1650, the name was translated to St. Croix, and it stuck when the Danes purchased the island in 1733.

The capital of St. Croix is Christiansted (see p. 167), a delightful little Danish-style town with a miniature fortress and shops tucked into a clutch of 18th- and 19th-century arcaded buildings. The island's main sight-seeing attractions lie off Centerline Road, heading west, although there are lovely drives along the North Shore

Road (Rte. 80) and on Mahogany Road (Rte. 76) through the rain forest.

On the west coast, Frederiksted (see p. 169) is where the cruise ships dock. It is another pretty town, splendidly renovated in 1998 to celebrate the 150th anniversary of the abolition of slavery in the Danish colonies. Denmark was the first nation to abolish the slave trade in 1803, although King Frederik VIII made no move toward emancipation until 1848, when he issued an edict stating that all slaves would be freed in 1859. The slaves on St. Croix and St. John rose up in revolt at the news, and the Danish governor, Peter von Scholten, taking the law into his own hands, declared the slaves free on July 3, 1848, at Fort Frederik.

CHRISTIANSTED

St. Croix's pint-size capital was laid out around a calm, reef-sheltered bay in 1733 and named in honor of the king of Denmark, Christian VI. Overlooking the waterfront in the **Christiansted National Historic Site,** spick-and-span **Fort Christiansvaern** looks like a child's toy carved out of yellow marzipan. It was built between 1738 and 1749, and its battlements are still guarded by neatly blacked cannon, which have never fired a shot in anger; there are historical displays on the upper level.

Around the small park in front of the fort are the **Old Danish Customs House** dating from 1751; the 19th-century **Scale House,** where ship's cargoes were inspected and weighed; the 1735 **Steeple Building,** a former Lutheran church housing a small museum; and the original **West Indies & Guinea Company Warehouse,** where slave auctions were once held in the courtyard. One block north on King Street is **Government House,**

Fort Christiansvaern was built on the site of earlier French fortifications guarding the harbor. It has been restored to its appearance circa 1830–40.

Cruzan rum

The Cruzan Rum Distillery is the largest commercial rum-producer in the Virgin Islands and opens its doors for factory tours during working hours.

Visits to the rebuilt factory include a video presentation followed by a guided tour and explanation of the production process, tastings, and a chance to buy the award-winning finished article. (Rte. 64, off Centerline Road, Tel 340/692-2280, weekends and 11:30 a.m.–1 p.m. Mon.–Fri.) ■

Strolling along the harborside boardwalk at Kings Wharf in downtown Christiansted

which occupies two fine 18th-century town houses converted into a residence for Peter von Scholten in the 1830s.

Between King Street and the bay is the **Kings Wharf open-air mall**—a pleasant place to shop or find a café table in the sun before taking a stroll up Strand Street, past boutiques and shops squirreled away beneath picturesque,

creeper-clad arcades. The small but utterly fascinating **St. Croix Aquarium,** located in the Caravelle Arcade, is a big hit with kids and provides divers with a firsthand introduction to local marine life. The aquarium is run by marine biologist Lonnie Kaczmarsky, who collects the exhibits and then releases them back into the sea after a few weeks. ∎

St. Croix Aquarium
- ✉ Caravelle Arcade
- ☎ 340/773-8995
- 🕐 Closed Sun.–Mon.
- 💲 $

Sports & activities

Bicycling: Guided tours and rentals from St. Croix Bike and Tours (Tel 340/772-2343).

Day sails: Bilinda Charters (Tel 340/773-1641); Diva (Tel 340/778-4675).

Diving: Anchor Dive Center, Salt River (Tel 340/778-1522 or 800/532-3483); Cane Bay Dive Shop (Tel 340/773-9913).

Golf: Eighteen holes at the Buccaneer Hotel (Tel 340/773-2100) and the Robert Trent Jones-designed Carambola Golf Club

(Tel 340/778-5638).

Horseback riding: Paul and Jill's Equestrian Stables, Sprat Hall (Tel 340/772-2880).

Sportfishing: Capt. Pete's Sportfishing (Tel 340/773-1123); Lisa Ann Charters (Tel 340/773-3712).

Tours: Christiansted and Frederiksted walks from St. Croix Heritage Tours, for schedules and reservations (Tel 340/778-6997). Minibus tours from St. Croix Safari Tours (Tel 340/773-6700). ∎

Murals like these shopping and domestic scenes are a popular Caribbean art form, brightening up homes and public buildings throughout the region.

Around St. Croix

BUCK ISLAND REEF NATIONAL MONUMENT

Located 5 miles (8 km) off Christiansted (about an hour's sail), uninhabited Buck Island is renowned for its excellent reef snorkeling and diving. Here corals can grow up to 30 feet (9 m) tall and the offshore reefs are home to a rich and varied selection of fish and other marine life. On land there are walking trails, pristine sandy beaches, and picnic facilities.
🅐 167 C2 ☎ 340/773-1460 💲 $$$$$
(includes transportation from Christiansted)

FREDERIKSTED

A 30-minute drive west of Christiansted, this sleepy small town is startled to life when the cruise ships arrive during the winter season. Guarding the harbor, bloodred **Fort Frederik** *(closed weekends)* was founded in 1752 and named for King Frederik V. Governor von Scholten announced the slave emancipation in the courtyard, and several rooms contain island history and cultural displays. The tiny town center is worth exploring for its pretty Victorian gingerbread houses and the trim row of arcaded buildings facing the waterfront. North of town, a sandy beach extends beyond the fort to Sprat Hall, now a guesthouse.
🅐 167 A1

ST. GEORGE VILLAGE BOTANICAL GARDEN

This 17-acre (6.8-ha) spread of lawned gardens and colorful plantings is set amid the ruins of a 19th-century sugar plantation built on the site of a pre-Columbian Amerindian settlement. The marked trail is lined with more than 800 species of tropical plants. The site has a rain forest section and a cactus garden.
🅐 167 B1 ✉ Centerline Rd., Frederiksted
☎ 340/692-2874 🕐 Closed Sun. 💲 $$$

WHIM PLANTATION MUSEUM

St. Croix's Danish colonial past is on display at this restored 18th-century great house. The interior is kept remarkably cool by 3-foot-thick (90-cm) stone walls and an air moat. The rooms are furnished with antique mahogany pieces, including a splendid four-poster bed with typical pineapple carvings, the colonial symbol of hospitality. On the grounds are the remains of the old sugar mill.
🅐 167 B1 ✉ Centerline Rd., Frederiksted
☎ 340/ 772-0598 🕐 Closed Sun. 💲 $$$

British Virgin Islands

KNOWN LOCALLY AS NATURE'S LITTLE SECRETS, THESE RUGGED SMALL islands with amoebic outlines are scalloped into sheltered coves and bays. Once a haven for pirates and smugglers, the British Virgin Islands (BVI) now offer an escapist paradise for yachtsmen and a surprising choice of luxurious resorts for vacationers happy to venture off the beaten track and play at Robinson Crusoe with a gold credit card. Part of the charm of the British Virgin Islands, however, is to savor them as the islanders themselves do—island-hopping by ferry, snorkeling, or having a quiet drink in a harborside bar.

Most of the islands and islets of the BVI group, from the verdant heights of Tortola and Virgin Gorda to the rocky jumble of Fallen Jerusalem, are arranged in two irregular lines flanking the 3-mile-wide (5-km) Sir Francis Drake Channel. Only 15 of the 60 or so volcanic outcrops are inhabited, including Anegada, which is the only coral island in the group.

It took some time for the British to show a proper interest in their Virgin Island colonies and clear them of the piratical likes of Blackbeard, Henry Morgan (1635–1688), and Jost van Dyke (who has an island named after him). In the heyday of the 18th-century plantation era, settlers imported African slaves to plant and tend cotton and sugarcane on the challenging terrain, but their efforts were only

Above: In the wake of Sir Francis Drake, a
modern-day flotilla explores the scattered
islets of the British Virgin Islands.
Right: Tidal pools form around the
huge Jurassic boulders of The Baths,
Virgin Gorda.

moderately successful, and many planters
sailed away, abandoning their slaves before
emancipation in the 1830s. In order to survive, the freed slaves turned to small-scale
farming. The BVI muddled along as part of
the Leeward Islands federation of British
colonies until independence. They toyed with
the idea of political union with the USVI but
opted to become a Crown Colony of Britain.

The BVI remain charmingly sleepy and
rural, and they are noticeably friendlier than
their better developed neighbors. But tourism
is bringing increased prosperity, and a mini-
construction boom is underway. ■

Tortola

TORTOLA WAS NAMED FOR ITS TURTLE DOVES, WHICH still outnumber the 14,000 inhabitants. It is the largest island in the BVI, measuring just 11 miles (18 km) east to west and 3 miles (5 km) north to south. To cross from the capital Road Town on the south coast to the beaches in the north, you have to tackle the central island ridge, where Mount Sage peaks at 1,708 feet (521 m), the highest point in the Virgin Islands archipelago.

Tortola
🅰 151 C4

J.R. O'Neal Botanic Gardens
🅰 173 C2
✉ Botanic Rd.
☎ 284/494-4557
💲 Donation

Most visitors use Tortola as a springboard for yacht charters and visits to the outer islands. However, it is a relaxing place to stay for a few days, soak up the sun, hop aboard a couple of ferries (see box, p. 174), and generally unwind.

A handful of streets running parallel to the reclaimed waterfront, Road Town is the administrative and commercial center of the BVI, but it is somewhat short on charm.

The harbor is usually a lively spot, with ferries coming and going, and yachts checking in and out of the busy marinas. Occasionally a moderate-size cruise ship drops off passengers for an island tour and a bit of shopping.

There is no need to allocate much sight-seeing time to the town itself, although one very pleasant stop is the small **J.R. O'Neal Botanic Gardens.** A short walk

West Indian house on Main Street (*hours vary*). Among the exhibits are Amerindian relics and articles salvaged from the wreck of R.M.S. *Rhone* (see p. 176).

(see p. 176)

AROUND THE ISLAND

Tortola's hotels and best beaches are strung out along the north coast. Starting in the west, secluded **Smuggler's Cove** is recommended for snorkeling and reached by a bumpy unpaved road from Long Bay. **Long Bay** itself is a mile-long (1.5-km) strip of blonde sand backed by palm trees and a hotel. **Apple Bay** is the surfers' favorite and home to Bomba's Surfside Shack, a great beach bar notorious for its full-moon parties. **Carrot Bay** has a couple of bars and a waterfront restaurant. Curving **Cane Garden Bay** is the island's best equipped beach, with windsurfing, waterskiing, and boating opportunities as well as beach restaurants and a few hotels. **Brewers Bay** is a good spot for snorkeling when the sea is quiet; the sandy beaches at **Trunk Bay, Josiah's Bay, Lambert Long Bay,** and **Elizabeth Beach** are good for

The striking golden trumpet flower can be seen all over the island.

from the town center, the lush palm-tree-shaded oasis of indigenous and exotic tropical plants is arranged around a water lily pond, orchid house, and pergola walk.

Another possible detour is the **V.I. Historical Society Folk Museum,** housed in a traditional

Tortola (U.K.)

Rough Point
Shark Bay
Brewers Bay
Mt. Healthy 212m
Trunk Bay
Josiah's Bay
Lambert Long Bay
Lambert
East End
Parham Town
Wesley Hill
Long Swamp
Cane Garden Bay
J.R.O'Neal Botanic Gardens
Leonards
385m Mt. Belle Vue
East End Bay
Hans Creek
Beef Island International Airport
Cane Garden Bay
Road Town
Doty
Road Bay
Kingstown
Hodges Creek
Buck Island
The Bluff
Carrot Bay
Apple Bay
521m
Mount Sage Nat. Park
Hannah
Sea Cow Bay
Brandywine Bay
Long Bay
Smuggler's Cove
West End
Freshwater Pond
Nanny Cay
Hannah Bay
Sir Francis Drake Channel
Soper's Hole
Frenchman's Cay
Little Thatch I.

Guana Island
North Bay
The Hollow
North Bay
Great Camanoe
Cam Bay
White Bay
Lee Bay
Little Camanoe
Marina Cay
Scrub Island
Beef Island
Long Bay
Trellis Bay

0   6 kilometers
0   4 miles

A   B   C   D

Sage Mountain National Park

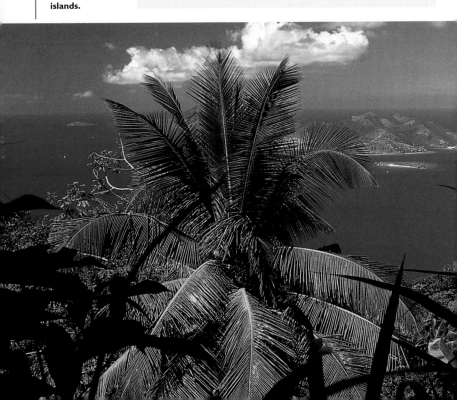

171 B2

Ridge Rd.

284/494-3134

swimming. Attached to Tortola by a causeway is **Beef Island,** with fine beaches at **Trellis Bay** and **Long Bay.**

In the center of Tortola is the 92-acre (37-ha) **Mount Sage National Park,** which was established in 1964 to protect the remnants of the native forest that once covered the whole of Tortola. The park's **Rainforest Trail** features many typical rain forest plants, such as giant elephant ear vines, tree ferns, bromeliads, and philodendrons flourishing beneath an umbrella of 100-foot-high (30-m)

bulletwood trees and buttress-trunked ficus. The **Mahogany Forest Trail** leads off the main path up through white cedar, West Indian, and broadleaf mahogany plantations.

Ferries for Jost van Dyke and the U.S. Virgin Islands depart from **Soper's Hole** harbor on Tortola's West End. Across the bay on Frenchman's Cay is the **Soper's Hole marina,** which packs in the private yachts and charter boats like sardines. On the dock, clapboard buildings house a few shops. ■

The winding route up to Mount Sage National Park is rewarded with fine views across to Tortola's neighboring islands.

Island-hopping by ferry

To see the Sir Francis Drake Channel, take one of the regular inter-island ferries between Tortola and Virgin Gorda. Contact Smiths Ferry Services *(Tel 284/495-4495);* Inter-Island Boat Services *(Tel 284/495-4166).* Ferries make a

number of daily round-trips to Jost van Dyke and St. John (USVI) from Tortola's West End dock; services for St. Thomas (USVI) generally originate in Road Town. Travel between the BVI and USVI requires proof of citizenship. ■

Other British Virgin Islands

ANEGADA

North of Virgin Gorda—and accessible via flights from Tortola—lies Anegada, the second largest of the BVI at 15 square miles (39 sq km). Its name means "the drowned one" in Spanish: The island barely reaches 28 feet (8.5 m) above sea level, and most of the western end is lagoon and marshland.

Anegada's main attraction is its offshore **coral reefs,** which have snared literally hundreds of shipwrecks over the centuries, and the diving is superb. The island has one small hotel with its own dive and sportfishing facilities, a couple of guesthouses, and campgrounds.

COOPER ISLAND

Cooper Island's dinghy dock and bar-restaurant attract yachtsmen sailing the Sir Francis Drake Channel. Those who linger will find a good beach, dive shop, and a few cottages for rent around Manchioneel Bay.
▲ 151 D3

JOST VAN DYKE

A 4-mile (6.5-km) ferry hop across from

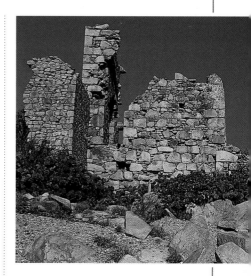

Ghostly relics of the mining industry preside over Copper Mine Point, Virgin Gorda.

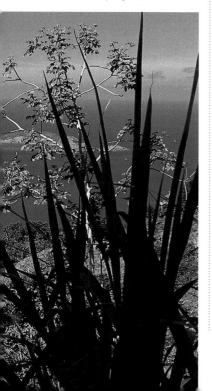

Tortola's West End is the terminally laid-back island of Jost van Dyke, which is a popular day trip for beach lovers. The details are sketchy, but local legend claims van Dyke was a 17th-century Dutch pirate, one of many who rampaged around the islands at the time. A notable historic figure who is definitely connected with the island is William Thornton (1759–1828), a physician and champion of the abolitionist movement, who won the competition to design the Capitol Building in Washington, D.C. He was born here; little appears to have happened since.

Jost van Dyke boasts several magnificent white sand beaches, although few visitors bother to venture beyond **Great Harbour,** where the ferry docks. Here there is a simple inn, a water-sports concession, and a couple of beach bars, which also serve West Indian food and snacks. **Foxy's,** at the east end of the beach, is the epi-center of one of the Caribbean's most excessive New Year's parties. It takes the island 364 days to recover in time for the next one. ▲ 151 C4

NORMAN ISLAND

Uninhabited, save for a handful of goats, Norman Island is reputed to have been the setting for Robert Louis Stevenson's *Treasure Island.* Snorkeling is good around **the Indians** (four jagged pinnacles accessible by yacht), and a floating restaurant is popular with the yachting crowd. ⚔ 151 D3

PETER ISLAND

Just across the Sir Francis Drake Channel from Tortola is Peter Island, occupied by the exclusive and well-equipped **Peter Island Resort.** Even if you are not staying there, you can sample the luxury lifestyle on a day trip from Road Town by ferry. ⚔ 151 D3

SALT ISLAND

Salt Island's three salt ponds once supplied passing ships with their vital salt rations, and in an appropriate variation of the traditional peppercorn (nominal) rent system, the island still pays an annual tax of one bag of salt to the British monarch. While the minuscule local populace (two at a recent count) still harvest salt in the old-fashioned way, the island is chiefly known for the wreck of R.M.S. *Rhone,* one of the most attractive and best preserved wreck diving sites in the Caribbean. The British royal mail ship went down with 300 crew during a hurricane in 1867, and it lies in 30–80 feet (9–24 m) of water on the reefs south of the island. Other notable local dive sites are **Blonde Rock** and **Painted Walls** to the west. ⚔ 151 D3

VIRGIN GORDA

Christopher Columbus is to blame for Virgin Gorda's rather unflattering sobriquet, the "Fat Virgin." From the low and rock-strewn southern end, the island bulges up to a height of 1,359 feet (414 m) at **Virgin Gorda Peak** and

is supposed to resemble a pregnant woman lying on her back. The majority of Virgin Gorda's 2,500 inhabitants live in The Valley (often marked as **Spanish Town** on maps), a meandering collection of old West Indian houses and more modern concrete villas on the southwest coast. Ferry passengers from Tortola disembark here, and there is also a small airstrip.

To the south of town is the island's chief sight-seeing attraction, **The Baths,** a bizarre Jurassic jumble of monumental boulders piled along the shore. From the drop-off point (accessible by shared taxis from the dockside), a path leads 350 yards (320 m) downhill to the beach and the boulders. Turn left here and enter the caves for a ten-minute scramble up and down the giant rocks and across slapping, bubbling tidal pools to secluded **Devil's Beach,** which girdles an idyllic snorkeling spot.

Heading north from The Valley, the landscape becomes greener and more hilly. The road passes twin crescents of powdery white sand beach edging **Savannah Bay** on the west coast, and then it climbs toward Virgin Gorda Peak. (Hiking trails are signed from the roadside; the steep climb takes about 45 minutes round trip.) The views from the mountain road are fantastic, stretching down the Sir Francis Drake Channel to the south; and across the North Sound, a spectacular turquoise bay hemmed in by Mosquito and Prickly Pear Islands, with airline tycoon Richard Branson's private Necker Island in the background. When the road divides, the northern spur leads on to **Leverick Bay;** the other ends at **Gun Creek,** where small motorboats shuttle guests out to the Bitter End and Biras Creek resorts. ⚔ 151 E4 ■

Sports & activities

Day sails: Day trips with lunch and snorkeling from *Patouche II (Tel 284/494-6300);* (half days also available); *Silmaril (Tel 284/495-9225); Tamarin II (Tel 284/495-9837).*

Diving: Baskin in the Sun *(Tortola, Tel 284/494-5854 or 800/233-7938, fax 284/494-5853);* Blue Water Divers *(Tortola, Tel 284/494-2847, fax 284/494-0198);* Dive BVI *(Virgin Gorda, Tel 284/495-5513).*

Sportfishing: Pelican Charters *(Tortola, Tel 284/496-7386).*

Water sports: Windsurfer rentals and tuition, and kayaks from Boardsailing BVI, Tortola *(Tel 284/495-2447, fax 284/495-1626);* kayaks, dinghies, waterskiing, and parasailing from Leverick Bay Watersports *(Virgin Gorda, Tel 284/495-7376).* ■

The Dutch Caribbean islands are divided into two groups: one amid the northerly Leeward Islands; the other, off the coast of Venezuela. From these strategic bases, Dutch merchants once controlled the rich Caribbean trade.

Netherlands Antilles & Aruba

Dutch colonial gable

Netherlands Antilles & Aruba

MORE THAN 500 MILES (800 KM) SEPARATE THE TWO GROUPS OF ISLANDS that make up the Netherlands Antilles (Dutch Caribbean). To the north are the Dutch territories of Sint Maarten, Sint Eustatius, and Saba, and to the south are the islands of Aruba (autonomous since 1986), Bonaire, and Curaçao, (commonly referred to as the ABCs). The northern group is known as the Dutch Windward Islands, which is rather perplexing, as their closest neighbors are the British and former British Leeward Islands.

The confusing terms date from the days of sail, when they described an island's geographical location in relation to its home country's preferred outbound and inbound Caribbean trading routes. The ABCs, lying within plain view (on a clear day) of South America, are the Dutch Leewards. From the early days of European exploration and settlement in the Caribbean, the Dutch were involved as brokers and traders. The extensive fleets of the Dutch West India Company looted the Spanish New World armadas with as much enthusiasm as the next man-of-war, and the emerging French and British colonies depended on Dutch ships for supplies and exports. Although the Dutch are credited with introducing the sugar industry to the region, they didn't choose their possessions with an eye to sugar growing but as trading posts. Hence, they took control of arid, mountainous **Sint Maarten,** two tiny volcanic blips known as **Sint Eustatius** (shortened to Statia in local parlance), **Saba,** and the ABCs, three low, wind-blasted, cactus-strewn islets close to South America and the Dutch colonies in Brazil. Before long the calculated gamble paid off, and the islands of Sint Eustatius and **Curaçao** boasted two of the richest mercantile ports during the 17th and 18th centuries.

Like other Caribbean islands, the Netherlands Antilles changed hands on several occasions. The bulging warehouses of Sint Eustatius were ransacked almost two dozen times. In an unusually pragmatic arrangement the island of Sint Maarten/St.-Martin was divided between Dutch and French colonists in 1648. Despite frequent incursions by both sides and the occasional pesky British intervention, Dutch Sint Maarten and French St.-Martin continue to occupy the 37-square-mile

(96-sq-km) island, the smallest in the world shared by two sovereign states.

The Dutch secured the six Netherlands Antilles islands under the Treaty of Paris in 1816, but by then the sugar boom was over and by the mid-19th century the Caribbean trade had dried up. The discovery of oil in South America brought renewed prosperity to the ABCs in the 1920s, when North American and European oil companies built vast refineries on **Aruba** and Curaçao. The capital of Curaçao, Willemstad, became the administrative capital of the Netherlands Antilles and seat of the Staten (parliament), which was granted autonomy within the Kingdom of the Netherlands in 1954.

The collapse of the local oil industry in the mid-1980s was a time of major upheaval for the ABCs and forced the islands to rely on tourism. Aruba's festering resentment at

Curaçao's domination in the Staten hardened into demands for independence, and the island was granted autonomy in 1986. Although Aruba is no longer one of the Netherlands Antilles, it remains within the Kingdom of the Netherlands.

Aruba is now the tourism leader in the Dutch Leewards. Its hotel-lined shores, casinos, and busy cruise-ship terminal are the envy of the Curaçaoans, whose tourist industry is taking longer to develop. Quiet **Bonaire** has built up a reputation as one of the world's top diving destinations. Meanwhile, 500 miles (800 km) to the north, tourism is also the mainstay of the Dutch Windward Islands. Sint Maarten flourishes as a duty-free enclave in the old Dutch West India Company tradition. Sint Eustatius and Saba maintain a more low-key approach. With few beaches, their rustic charm endears them to visitors in search of peace and quiet. Although Dutch street names abound and the official currency of the Netherlands Antilles is the Netherlands Antilles guilder (Aruba has its own Aruban florin), English is the most widely spoken language in the Dutch Windwards. In the Dutch Leewards you'll hear Papiamento (see p. 201), a linguistic curiosity derived from Dutch, Spanish, French, Portuguese, African, and English tongues in the 17th century. Papiamento is unintelligible to all but the islanders. ∎

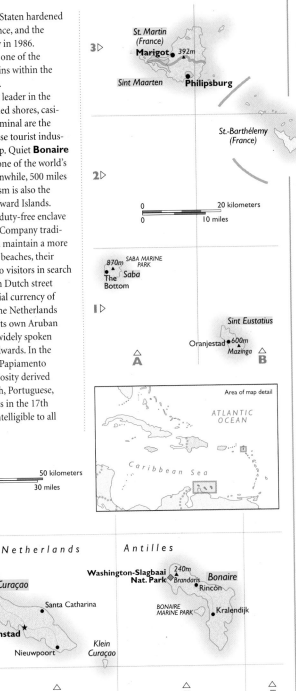

Sint Maarten/St.-Martin

SINT MAARTEN/ST.-MARTIN, ONE OF THE SMALLER ISLANDS in the region at just 37 square miles (96 sq km), celebrated 350 years of dual nationality in 1998. The French occupy the slightly larger northern portion. Although there are no border controls between the two sides of the island, local people are proud of their separate identities. This is particularly noticeable in French St.-Martin, which cultivates a distinctive Gallic air.

Philipsburg

🏛 180 C1

Visitor information

✉ Wathey Sq.

☎ 5995/22337

Sint Maarten Zoological Botanical Garden

🏛 180 C2

✉ Arch Rd., Madame Estate

☎ 5995/32030

💲 $

According to local legend, the division of the island was settled by a Frenchman and a Dutchman who set out to walk around the island in opposite directions, the former armed with a bottle of brandy, the latter with a bottle of gin. The Frenchman, refreshed by brandy, fared better and when the dividing line was drawn up between the point of their departure and the point where they met up, the French had secured a territory of 21 square miles (54 sq km), the Dutch only 16 square miles (41 sq km).

In spite of its diminutive proportions, Sint Maarten/St.-Martin attracts more than a million visitors a year. The Dutch capital of Philipsburg is the major gateway. This top Caribbean cruise-ship destination and duty-free port is well stocked with shopping bargains. The island is also famed for its beautiful beaches, which encircle the steep, scrub-covered hinterland. Most of the development is on the west coast between Philipsburg and the French capital, Marigot (St.-Martin), where hotels and time-share apartments jostle for space around Simson Baai lagoon. You can travel between the two island capitals on minibuses, which depart regularly from early morning until late evening.

PHILIPSBURG

Squeezed onto a narrow sandbar between Grand Bay and the land-locked expanses of Great Salt Pond, Philipsburg unfurls along four long, parallel streets linked by alleys known as *steeges*. The heart of town is **de Ruyterplein,** or Wathey Square, where day-trippers arrive by boat from the cruise ships anchored in the bay. At the top of the square is the restored 19th-century **courthouse,** which has a carved pineapple topknot. To either side of the courthouse, bustling Front Street stretches off in a rich line of duty-free shops, boutiques, and galleries. Follow the narrow steege down the right-hand side of the courthouse to a street market offering bargains on T-shirts, Haitian carvings, and beachwear.

A ten-minute walk east on Front Street will bring you to the **Guavaberry Factory Shop,** housed in a luridly painted ginger-bread cottage on the sidewalk, dating from the 1830s. You can sample locally produced guavaberry liqueur (made from the fruit of *Eugenia floribunda,* not guavas).

A little farther up on the right, on an unnamed steege, is the **Sint Maarten Museum** (*off Front St., Tel 5995/24917, closed Sun.*). Laid out on the second floor above a shop, the tiny museum is a mine of local information. Geological displays include a relief map illustrating how the island was once linked to neighboring St. Barthélémy and Anguilla. Check out the colonial artifacts, old musket balls, and other relics salvaged from the 1801 wreck of the frigate H.M.S. *Proselyte,* as well as a nostalgic collection of antique ice-cream makers, flatirons, and century-old photographs. More recent history is documented in the video of Hurricane Luis, which tore through the island on September 4, 1995.

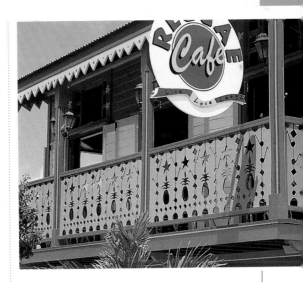

Beyond the museum the steege ends at the sandy bayfront, a short walk from **Bobby's Marina,** with its pair of popular restaurants, daily ferries to Marigot, and boat trips to the islands of St. Barts and Saba. Minibuses depart for the French capital of Marigot from Back Street (one block behind Front Street).

AROUND SINT MAARTEN

The only sight-seeing attraction on the Dutch side is the **Sint Maarten Zoological Botanical Garden,** on the far side of Great Salt Pond. Caribbean birds are displayed in walk-through aviaries, and there's a small but interesting selection of South American reptiles and mammals such as capybaras (the world's largest living rodents), as well as a bat cave that's popular with children.

Beyond Philipsburg, Sint Maarten's chief lure is the beach. On the south side is **Simson Baai Beach,** which has good swimming and windsurfing, although it does lie in the flight path for Princess Juliana Airport. Head northwest along the coast for **Mulletbaai,** a

Modern gingerbread-style decoration featuring pineapple motifs

Rum and spices also flavor the local guavaberry liqueur.

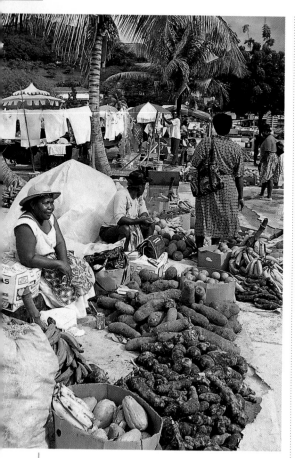

Squashlike christophene, yams, eddoes, and plantains are staples of the Caribbean diet.

market lines the waterfront, and the old warehouses along the boulevard de France have been converted into a string of restaurants and cafés.

The ruins of 18th-century **Fort St. Louis** survey the scene from the heights above the harbor, where the daily ferry service to Anguilla and boat trips to St. Barts depart from the pier (*White Octopus, Tel 5995/24096 or Edge, Tel 5995/542640*).

A grid of shopping streets leads back to rue de Hollande and the minibus pick-up/drop-off points for Philipsburg and Grand Case. To the west are the yacht-filled slips of the marina, edged by a collection of cafés and boutiques selling souvenirs and French fashions.

Beyond the marina is the **Musée de Marigot;** its excellent Amerindian section (in English) provides an informative introduction to pre-Columbian island culture accompanied by tools, religious objects, pottery shards, and shell ornaments.

AROUND ST.-MARTIN

The French side offers a further range of fine beaches (and topless bathing), starting with the alluring mile-long (1.5-km) expanse of **Baie Longue** on the southern tip of the Simson Baai lagoon peninsula. Around the corner is **Baie aux Prunes,** popular with surfers and snorkelers; **Baie Rouge,** where beachgoers can hire sun loungers and umbrellas or swim around the point at the eastern end to a secluded cove; and hotel-lined **Baie Nettlé,** which is good for water sports.

North of Marigot is **Grand Case,** its one pretty, sandy street lined with some of the island's best restaurants. Boats bob at anchor farther east in the well-protected harbor fronting **Anse Marcel,** which has safe swimming for children and

tourist favorite with water sports concessions. For something quieter, try **Cupecoy Beach,** which is backed by low cliffs; nude bathing is permitted at the northern end.

MARIGOT

The appealing and unmistakably French capital of St.-Martin appears to have been plucked straight from the Côte d'Azur and grafted onto a Caribbean island. This is café-and-croissant country, where the sidewalk terraces blossom with bright umbrellas. The town center is laid out between the twin poles of the waterfront and the **Marina Port La Royale.** A craft

Marigot
◪ 180 B2
Visitor information
✉ Marigot Pier
☎ 5908/75721

water sports concessions. Off the east coast are glorious bayside beaches on the **Îlet Pinel,** accessible by ferry from Cul de Sac, and undeveloped **Île Tintamarre.** On the mainland is **Baie Orientale,** nicknamed *Le St.-Tropez des Antilles Françaises* for its sophisticated restaurants and shops.

Continuing south on the main road (Rte. N7) around the base of **Pic du Paradis**—at 1,390 feet (424 m) the island's highest peak—

you'll come to a detour leading to the **Ferme aux Papillons** (Butterfly Farm) at Baie de l'Embouchure. Hundreds of exotic butterflies flutter about the tropical gardens, miniature waterfalls, and koi ponds inside a huge climate-controlled sphere. Exhibits trace the evolutionary cycle from microscopic eggs to caterpillar, chrysalis, and full-fledged insect, and tours provide an entertaining blend of butterfly fact and trivia. ∎

Musée de Marigot
- 180 B2
- Rte. de Sandy Ground
- 590/29 22 84
- Closed Sun.
- $$$

Ferme aux Papillons
- 180 C2
- Rte. du Galion
- 590/87 31 21
- $$$$$

Sports & activities

Bicycling: Mountain bike rentals and guided tours from Tri Sport *(Simson Baai, Sint Maarten, Tel 5995/54384),* and Frog Legs *(Marigot, St. Martin, Tel 590/87 05 11).*

Diving & snorkeling: Dive trips to reef and wreck sites, equipment rental, and instruction are available through Ocean Explorers *(Simson Baai Beach, Sint Maarten, Tel 5995/45252, e-mail: divesm@megatropic.com)* and Scuba-Fun *(Anse Marcel, St.-Martin, Tel 590/87 36 13).*

Golf: The island's only 18-hole golf course is at the Mullet Bay Resort *(Sint Maarten, Tel 5995/52801).*

Horseback riding: Nature trails and beach rides from Caïd & Isa *(Anse Marcel, St.-Martin, Tel 590/87 45 70)* and Bayside Riding Club *(Rte. du Galion, St.-Martin, Tel 590/87 36 64).*

Kayaking: Kayak rental and guided tours from Tri Sport *(Simson Baai, Sint Maarten, Tel 5995/54384).* ∎

Yachts gather in the inner harbor at Anse Marcel.

Sint Eustatius

A SLEEPY CARIBBEAN BACKWATER SOME 35 MILES (56 KM) south of Sint Maarten, Sint Eustatius is the undeveloped Rip van Winkle of the Dutch Windwards, dozing quietly in the lee of its imposing volcanic cone, the Quill. Better known as Statia (pronounced STAY-sha), the island attracts a handful of curious visitors and a motley crew of American and European expatriates who revel in the absence of chic resorts, shopping malls, discos, and other manifestations of mass tourism.

There are no decent beaches on Sint Eustatius, but therein lies the island's quirky charm.

Statia's glittering past looms from the history books out of all proportion to its modest physical dimensions. The island is just 2 miles (3 km) wide and 5 miles (8 km) long from its hilly northern tip through the low central plain to the southern slopes of the Quill. The 1,600 islanders live in the capital, Oranjestad, on the central west coast.

The Dutch West India Company set up shop in Oranjestad in 1636 and developed the port into such a phenomenally successful trading center and slave market that Statia was nicknamed the Golden Rock. Merchant vessels flying every conceivable national flag crowded the harbor, and as business expanded, land was reclaimed to build additional warehouses. On November 16, 1776, the cannon of Fort Oranje fired an 11-gun salute in reply to the merchant ship *Andrew Doria,* an American colonial brig flying the Stars and Stripes, and unwittingly Holland became the first nation to recognize the United States of America. This act earned the tiny island the sobriquet "America's Childhood Friend," although the unfortunate governor at the time was called home in disgrace after the British complained. In 1781, in retaliation, a British naval expedition under

Adm. George Brydges Rodney (1718–1792) descended on Statia, taking possession of all the ships and goods in the port—a prize worth about 8 million dollars.

Statia never recovered, and her beachless shores have hampered the tourist industry. Today, the island is quietly developing a reputation as the new Saba for attracting divers in search of pristine dive sites. With good walks around the Quill and incredibly friendly local people, the island makes an interesting offbeat escape for visitors with a no-frills, no-problem attitude.

ORANJESTAD

A small cliff divides the villagey island capital into two parts. Hurricanes and Admiral Rodney's handiwork have all but destroyed the Lower Town around the harbor, so everybody lives in the **Upper Town,** perched on the clifftop guarded by 17th-century **Fort Oranje.** The **Sint Eustatius Historical Foundation Museum** is housed in a restored 18th-century brick home occupied by Rodney during his stay. Here pre-Columbian artifacts, blue glass trading beads used during the slave era, and porcelain from the Nanking cargo salvaged from the South China Sea, where it foundered in 1752 en route to Statia, can be seen alongside rooms furnished in colonial style.

**Opposite:
Spreading
buttress-type
roots help anchor
giant rain forest
trees such as
the santinay
in thin rocky
mountain soil.**

Unforced smiles express the relaxed Statia way of life.

The town has several historic ruins, including the **Honen Dalim Synagogue,** the second oldest temple in the Western Hemisphere, dating from 1742. It fell into disrepair after Rodney took the Jewish community's money and then deported them.

AROUND THE ISLAND

A trek up the Quill (Mount Mazinga) is a must during any visit to Sint Eustatius. Several routes go right to the lip of the crater; the most direct follows a moderately steep path and takes about 45 minutes. Beneath the high point of **Mount Mazinga** (1,968 feet/600 m), the 550-foot-deep (168-m) crater is carpeted with lush vegetation. On the southwest coast are the ruins of **Fort de Windt,** which afford fine views across to the neighboring island of St. Kitts. Even though fortresses once ringed Statia, the island still changed hands with monotonous regularity.

Statia does have a couple of beaches, but with grayish volcanic sand. Close to the Lower Town is **Oranje Beach,** popular with locals, and **Crooks Castle** is

farther south. Because of dangerous currents, swimming is not safe in the bays on the Atlantic coast. Statia's underwater landscape—even more dramatic than its textbook-perfect volcano—is protected by a new marine park opened in 1998. There are 30-plus official sites ranging from coral reefs and canyons to the **Supermarket** wreck site, where rare flying gurnards occasionally put in an appearance. The site is comprised of two shipwrecks around a section of reef. The easily accessible **City Wall** site, just outside the harbor, was the original sea wall for the old Lower Town warehouse district. Contact local dive operators Dive Statia (*Tel 5993/82435*), Golden Rock Dive Center (*Tel 5993/82964*), or Blue Nature Watersports (*Tel 5993/82725*). ■

Saba

FROM A DISTANCE, TINY SABA (PRONOUNCED Say-ba) RISES out of the sea like a witch's hat from its 5-square-mile (13-sq-km) base. On closer inspection, the dramatic outline of Mount Scenery (2,909 feet/870 m) doesn't stand alone but among a supporting cast of lesser peaks and ridges that make up the dramatically rugged, green interior. The cliffs that edge the island drop away beneath the waves into an underwater world no less fantastically sheer and rated one of the top dive destinations in the Caribbean.

Life on Saba moves at a sedate pace. The 1,100 Sabans live in attractive villages where little white cottages with uniform red roofs perch precariously one above the other on steep hillsides. The capital of the island is The Bottom, but most visitors head up The Road (see p. 188) for the upland village of Windwardside.

Columbus sighted Saba in 1493, but it took a shipwreck to land the first Europeans on the island more than a century later. Dutch colonists from Sint Eustatius founded the first permanent settlement in the 1640s. In 1665 the infamous Welsh pirate Henry Morgan (1635–1688) captured Saba and banished all non-English

Sheer cliffs frame Ladder Bay, where Saba's early settlers landed and carved a stone staircase into the rock face.

Saba

🗺 179 A1

Visitor information

✉ Windwardside

☎ 5994/62231 or
5994/62322,
fax 5994/62350

Saba Museum

✉ Windwardside
🕐 Closed weekends
💲 $

THE ROAD

A minor miracle of engineering and a monument to Sabian stubbornness, The Road traverses Saba from Fort Bay in the southwest to Flat Point in the northeast. When the Sabians first investigated the possibility of a road to augment the old footpaths and donkey tracks in the 1930s, civil engineers from Holland said it couldn't be done. Josephus Hassell's response was to sign up for a correspondence course in civil engineering, and, utilizing his newly acquired knowledge, work began at Fort Bay in 1938. The Road reached The Bottom five years later, crept into Windwardside in 1951, and eventually arrived in Flat Point after carving a 19-mile (31-km) corkscrew passage across the island. ∎

Intricate hand-drawn lacework has been a cottage industry on Saba since the 19th century.

speakers during his short stay. Thereafter the almost impregnable island changed hands by treaty rather than invasion, supported a few small sugar plantations, and lived very quietly.

AROUND THE ISLAND

Saba's capital, The Bottom, lies in a sloping valley and probably takes its name from the Dutch word *botte* (bowl). Among the traditional clapboard homes are several small businesses, shops, and bars and the **Lieutenant-Governor's Residence,** an attractive old Saban house with balconies and gingerbread decoration.

To the south for about a mile (1.5 km), The Road wriggles steeply down to **Fort Bay,** the main port. A leg-trembling flight of 500-plus steps descends to the harbor on **Ladder Bay.** In pre-Road days this was the only route on and off the island, and everything from a box of nails to a tin bathtub had to be carried up on somebody's back.

Tucked into the lee of Mount Scenery, with fantastic views down to the coast, **Windwardside**

clings tenaciously to the slopes, its neat cottages linked by a cat's cradle of narrow alleys. Housed in a 19th-century Dutch sea captain's cottage, the **Saba Museum** serves up a modest history of the island.

Although diving may be Saba's chief draw, hiking Mount Scenery is an excellent land-based diversion. The 1,064-step path to the summit passes through secondary rain forest to a gnarled and stunted world of elfin woodland carpeted with mosses and ferns and is frequently wreathed in mist. The tourist office and **Saba Trail Shop** *(Tel 5994/62630)* in Windwardside have details of other trails and local guide services.

From Windwardside, The Road continues its serpentine way for just under a mile (1.5 km) to the settlement of **Hell's Gate** and on to the airport at Flat Point. ∎

Saba Marine Park

Established in 1987 to protect Saba's pristine marine environment, the park rings the island. Most of the dive sites are marked by permanent buoys off the west coast.

The astonishing diversity of the park's underwater landscapes is matched by vibrant marine life. Excellent visibility ranges upward from 125 feet (38 m) in winter. Varied, challenging diving is ensured by elkhorn forests, giant boulders encrusted with sponges, soft and hard corals, submerged pinnacles that attract big groupers, jacks, and rays, and walls dropping to depths of 1,000 feet (300 m) within half a mile (800 m) of the shore.

The park is partially funded by the small fee paid for each dive. Further information about dives can be obtained from Saba Marine Park *(P.O. Box 18, The Bottom, Tel 5994/63295, fax 5994/ 63435)* or by contacting local dive operators such as Saba Deep Dive *(Tel 5994/63347, e-mail: diving@sabadeep.com, www.sabadeep.com/~diving);* Saba Reef Divers *(Tel 5994/62541, fax 5994/ 62653, e-mail: Sabareef@aol.com, www.sabareef.com);* and Sea Saba *(Tel 5994/62246 or 800/ 838-SABA, fax 5994/62362, e-mail: seasaba@aol.com, www.seasaba.com).* ∎

A tiger grouper and a scuba diver size each other up in the rich coastal waters of Saba.

Curaçao

Curaçao

⚠ 179 D1

Visitor information

✉ Willemstad at Pietermaai 19

☎ 5999/461-6000

CURAÇAO IS THE LARGEST ISLAND OF THE DUTCH Leewards. These lie amid the larger group of Caribbean islands known as the Lesser Antilles, running parallel to the northern coastline of Venezuela. The ethnic mix of the islanders is as beguiling as the grandeur of the scenery on Curaçao. It seems fitting that the island should also be known for its vividly colored liqueurs.

The Koningin Emmabrug pontoon bridge spans the Sint Annabaai channel to the Otrabanda district in Willemstad.

The chief Dutch possession in the Caribbean since the 17th century, Curaçao is the largest of the five Netherlands Antilles islands at 38 miles (61 km) by 9 miles (14.5 km). It lies only 35 miles (56 km) off the coast of Venezuela. Curaçao's rocky shoreline, with its cliffs and coves, is indented with fingernail slivers of white sand beach and lapped by staggeringly blue waters. Inland, giant cactuses straight out of a cowboy movie lord it over the rugged *cunucu*, a scrub-covered landscape that receives less than 23 inches (580 mm) of rain a year.

The Spanish landed on Curaçao in 1499 and dubbed it the Isla de los Gigantes (Island of Giants) for the tall, seafaring Caquetio people they encountered. The native population was soon shipped off to work in the gold mines of Hispaniola, and the ABCs were declared *islas inútiles* (useless islands). In 1634 the Dutch West India Company spotted the potential of Sint Annabaai, Curaçao's huge natural harbor, the largest in the region and seventh largest in the world. The company ejected a handful of Spanish settlers and set about fortifying the harbor entrance and constructing Willemstad within sturdy defensive walls.

Under the Dutch, Curaçao grew wealthy. A notable early governor of the island was Peter Stuyvesant (1592–1672), who lost his leg fighting the Spanish for possession of Sint Maarten in 1644 before sailing off to take up the governorship of Nieuw Amsterdam (New York). Willemstad's duty-free port handled all manner of goods from sugar to gold bullion; it also developed into the Caribbean's busiest slave market. A few plantations were established on the island, but the struggle with the arid climate and infertile soil was a difficult one. Their legacy is a collection of pretty Dutch colonial *landhuizen* (plantation houses) in the rolling hinterland.

The Dutch didn't abolish slavery until 1863, and Curaçao idled along until 1918, when construction of the world's largest oil refinery refueled the island's prosperity. Workers poured in from around the Caribbean, the Americas, and beyond creating a multiracial society. The present-day population of 145,000 is concentrated around Willemstad and the southwestern beaches. The northern part of the island contains Sint Christoffel National Park (see p. 194). This area is very quiet, with just a few small hotels, restaurants, and dive shops on the shore backed by acres of green-gray cunucu backcountry.

WILLEMSTAD

A little pocket of the Caribbean that will be forever Amsterdam, Willemstad's **Handelskade** waterfront is stunning. Dutch gables and terra-cotta roof tiles adorn buildings painted pastel pink and pistachio, with a dash of citrus yellow here and curlicue white stucco plasterwork there. Though modern excrescences now outnumber historic buildings, the effect is still startlingly attractive and a favorite photo opportunity for the scores of visitors who arrive by cruise ship to plunder the capital's duty-free stores and explore its beautifully preserved streets.

Willemstad was recently added to the World Heritage List.

The city is divided by the Sint Annabaai channel, which leads into Schottegat Harbor. On the west side is the

A Curaçaoan celebrates a diverse cultural heritage.

Otrabanda quarter, where the cruise ships dock; to the east Handelskade fronts the central **Punda district,** where the main shops and sights are found. One of the Punda's most popular attractions is the busy daily **Mercado Flotante** (Floating Market). Located around the corner from Handelskade, on the watery cul-de-sac of Waaigat, Venezuelan schooners line the **Sha Caprileskade** waterfront and goods spill out onto colorful market stalls arranged with fresh fruit and vegetables grown on the South American mainland.

A tour of historic Willemstad should begin on the waterfront along Handelskade at **Fort Amsterdam.** Government offices now occupy the former Dutch West India Company headquarters. There's free access to the courtyard and the 1769 fort church, which houses the small **Fortkerk Museum,** with its displays of antique silverware and maps. The church's high ceiling is supported on two pairs of fat white pillars and doubled up as a sail loft. The rainwater cisterns are built of the tiny yellow and red bricks shipped from Holland as ballast and used in many buildings around town.

Several years before Fortkerk was completed, Willemstad's Jewish community had begun to worship in the **Mikvé Israel-Emanuel Synagogue,** the oldest synagogue in continuous use in the Western Hemisphere. Portuguese Jews arrived in Curaçao in the 1650s and founded the first synagogue in 1674; Mikvé Israel was dedicated in 1732. Located in the heart of Punda, the synagogue occupies an attractive courtyard complex alongside a Jewish Museum displaying religious artifacts and memorabilia. The floor of the synagogue is covered with a thick layer of sand said to symbolize both the desert where the Israelites camped and the journey undertaken by persecuted European Jews. Curaçao's Jewish population is largely Sephardic, descendants of those who were expelled from Spain in the 16th century. The old Jewish residential district of **Scharloo,** across Waaigat, is slowly being restored.

Scharlooweg, one block behind the waterfront, is lined with some of Willemstad's best preserved 18th- to 19th-century town houses. Their classical facades are adorned with stucco medallions

Fortkerk Museum
- ✉ Fort Amsterdam, Gouvernementsplein
- ☎ 5999/461-1163
- 🕐 Closed weekends
- 💲 $

Mikvé Israel-Emanuel Synagogue & Jewish Museum
- ✉ Hanchi di Snoa
- ☎ 5999/461-1139
- 🕐 Closed for Jewish holidays
- 💲 $

Curaçao Museum
- ✉ Van Leeuwenhoestraat
- ☎ 5999/462-3873
- 🕐 Closed Sat.
- 💲 $

Sports & activities

Adventure tours: Various sporting options from Adventure Fun & Excitement *(Tel 5999/560-2058)*; also Wild Curaçao *(Tel 5999/561-0027)*.

Cycling: Guided bike tours with Dutch Dream Adventure *(Tel 5999/465-3575)*.

Day sails: Day sails and weekend trips to Bonaire and Venezuela with Insulide *(Tel 5999/560-1340)*; dive,

snorkel, and sunbathing trips aboard *Bounty (Tel 5999/560-1887)*.

Diving & snorkeling: Dive off the leeward coast and visit challenging sites in the Banda Aboa Underwater Park. Princess Divers *(Tel 5999/465-8991)*; Underwater Curaçao *(Tel 5999/461-8131)*.

Hiking & horseback riding: See Christoffel National Park, p. 194. ∎

and reliefs depicting baskets of fruit and flowers, and the front doors stand guard over flights of steps.

The Otrabanda district is reached by the **Koningin Emmabrug** (Queen Emma Bridge) from Handelskade. The impressive swinging pontoon bridge was designed by U.S. consul Leonard B. Smith and installed in 1888. (A free ferry operates when the bridge is opened to allow ships through.) Otrabanda is home to the cruise-ship terminal and the **Riffort,** a 19th-century fort that guards one side of the harbor.

One mile (1.5 km) north of the city center is the **Curaçao Museum,** located in a former seamen's hospital. The museum exhibits monumental colonial furniture, pre-Columbian relics, and works by local artists. ∎

Curaçao cocktails

If the name Curaçao rings a bell but you know nothing about the island of the same name, think of bizarrely tinted cocktail additives. Bottles of vivid blue, red, orange, and green Curaçao liqueurs lurk behind cocktail bars the world over. Visitors to **Landhuis Chobolobo** *(Mercuriusstraat, Salinja, Tel 5999/461-3526, closed Sat.– Sun.)* in the eastern suburbs of Willemstad, can sample the local brew, which is flavored with the sun-dried peel of a small bitter orange. The Curaçaoan soil and climate give the orange its distinctive flavor. ∎

Elaborate stucco decorations on Handelskade are one of the highlights of Willemstad's Dutch colonial architecture.

Around Curaçao

SINT CHRISTOFFEL NATIONAL PARK

The 4,650-acre (1,880-ha) Sint Christoffel National Park, in the north of the island, comprises three former plantations on the slopes of **Mount Sint Christoffel** (1,220 feet/372 m), the highest point in the Dutch Leewards.

The park center, on the grounds of **Landhuis Savonet** plantation, has a small museum describing the island's geology, flora, and fauna, and it is the starting point for a network of trails that strike off into the cunucu or down to the wave-lashed cliffs at **Playa Grandi.** There are fascinating guided walks on Friday mornings, and special evening walks offer a chance to spot the rare Curaçaoan deer, a subspecies of the North American white-tailed deer introduced to the island in pre-Columbian times. Guides can also be arranged for private hikes and bird-watching. Horseback riding and mountain bike rental are available from the concession *(Tel 5999/864-0535).*

◪ 191 B3 ✉ Savonet ☎ 5999/864-0363 💲 $

CURAÇAO SEAQUARIUM

A marine life showcase with more bite than most, the Seaquarium offers outdoor lagoons for sea lions and sharks, tanks housing toothsome eels and tropical fish, and touch tanks to entertain the kids. Two more unusual aspects are an underwater observatory anchored to the shore and the Animal Encounters program *(reservations required).* The encounters take place in a natural reef pool, which is home to stingrays, sea turtles, jacks, tarpons, and sharks. After an introductory dive with a qualified instructor, participants can snorkel and scuba dive among the nondangerous residents on one side of the pool and hand-feed the segregated lemon and nurse sharks through holes in a plexiglass wall.

Adjacent **Seaquarium Beach** is one of the island's best, with access to the 12-mile-

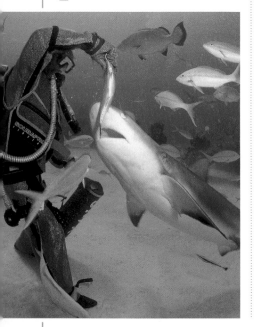

A scuba diver feeds fresh fish to the Caribbean reef sharks at the Curaçao Seaquarium.

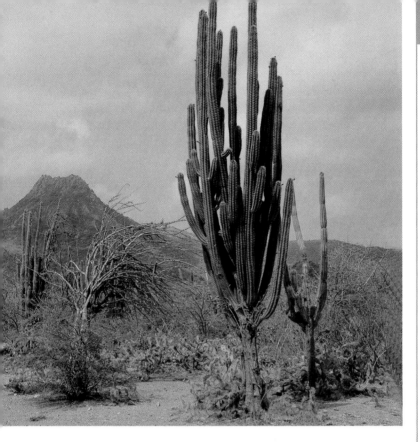

Candle cactuses flourish in the scrublands around Mount Sint Christoffel.

long (19-km) **Curaçao Underwater Park,** and the headquarters of dive operator **Underwater Curaçao** *(Tel 5999/461-8131, fax 465-7826; e-mail: lionsdive@ibm.net).* ⚠ 191 C1 ✉ Bapor Kibra, southeast of Willemstad ☎ 5999/461-6666 💲 $$$$$

LANDHUIS BRIEVENGAT

The most interesting of Curaçao's historic *landhuizen,* Brievengat dates from the 1730s. The interior is furnished in a haphazard fashion with mahogany four-poster beds, armoires, hydra-like hat stands, and rocking chairs known as *ki-mi-ki-hasi* (what can I do about it?) in Papiamento. The pièce de résistance is the red-and-white spotted kitchen, a device to disorient evil spirits and flies. ⚠ 191 C1 ✉ Brievengat (ten-minute drive northeast of Willemstad ☎ 5999/737-8344 🕐 Closed weekends 💲 $ ■

Landhuizen

About 300 country estates had spread across the island's interior by the early 19th century. Most of them had a modest little yellow-and-white Dutch colonial *landhuis* (plantation house) for the owner's family. A handful of these have been restored, notably **Landhuis Brievengat** (see left). You can also visit **Landhuis Jan Kok,** St. Willibrordus. **Landhuis Papaya,** which is painted blood red (the rarer of the two traditional Curaçaoan color schemes), and **Landhuis Daniel,** both on the Westpunt road outside Willemstad, have been transformed into a bar-restaurant and a rather spartan hotel respectively.

For information about all these sites, contact the Curaçao Tourism Development Foundation *(Tel 5999/461-2305).* ■

Bonaire

Bonaire

🗺 179 E1

Visitor information

✉ Kaya Simon Bolivar 12

☎ 5997/78322 or 5997/78649, fax 5997/78408

SHAPED LIKE A DISTORTED BOOMERANG AND LYING 30 miles (48 km) east of Curaçao, Bonaire is a diver's paradise—and that's official, according to the legend adorning local car license plates. Along the sheltered leeward coast of the island and around the offshore islet of Klein (Little) Bonaire, more than 80 dive sites give access to some of the most spectacular and varied marine landscapes in the entire Caribbean.

Bonaire, a derivation of the Arawak word *bojnaj,* meaning "low country," was first noted by Italian explorer Amerigo Vespucci in 1499. When the Dutch wrested control of the island from Spain in 1634, they introduced slaves to harvest the salt pans in the flat southern portion of the island and raised cattle on the scrub-covered *cunucu* backcountry to supply the burgeoning colony of Curaçao.

Activity on the island stuttered to an almost complete halt with the abolition of slavery in 1863, but after a century's break Bonaire's salt industry was revived in the 1960s. The decade also saw the first divers venturing to the out-of-the-way island, and Bonaire's special brand of low-key, dive-oriented tourism was born. Although the news about Bonaire's spectacular underwater world is well and truly out, and hotels are mushrooming, the island atmosphere is still quiet and definitely casual. Nondivers can find fantastic snorkeling from walk-in sites directly off the shore, as well as hiking, mountain biking, horseback riding, and bird-watching.

The modest capital of Bonaire is

The dramatically colored angelfish can be seen in the water around Bonaire.

12 steps to heaven

Bonaire's Guided Snorkeling Program is a great way for nondivers to learn about the reefs and get the best out of the marine park. Offered through dive shops and a dozen resorts, the program features 12 guided snorkel tours at selected sites around the island. Each tour is prefaced with a short slide show. There are snorkeling tips for beginners, safety checks, and a guide to reef etiquette to minimize damage to the delicate environment. Though transportation is included, you'll need to bring your own equipment or rent it. ∎

Sports & activities

Diving & snorkeling: Captain Don's Habitat Dive Center *(Tel 85997/290, fax 5997/8240);* Dive Bonaire *(Tel 5997/8285, fax 5997/8238);* Sand Dollar Dive *(Tel 5997/5252).*

Fishing: Piscatur Fishing Charters *(Tel 5997/8774, fax 5997/4784).*

Horseback riding: Kunuku Warahama Ranch *(Tel 5997/5558).*

Mountain biking: Cycle Bonaire *(Tel 5997/7558).*

Windsurfing & kayaking: Jibe City *(Tel 5997/5233).* ∎

Kralendijk (coral dike), a small town of tidy yellow and gold Dutch Caribbean buildings, restaurants, and hotels facing the rounded outline of Klein Bonaire. From Kralendijk a road circles the southern portion of the island, passing the glittering white salt stacks awaiting shipment from the solar saltworks, which conceal flamingo nesting grounds.

Northwest of Kralendijk is Bonaire's oldest settlement, the sleepy inland village of **Rincon,** on the road to the national park. A short distance away on the Atlantic coast, at Boca Onima, Caquetio Indians left their marks scribbled in red dye on cave walls.

To the north of Rincon, and covering the northwestern portion of the island, is **Washington-Slagbaai National Park.** This 13,500-acre (5,463-ha) tract of land covering one fifth of the island has operated as a wildlife preserve since the 1960s. It is crisscrossed by four-wheel-drive trails and hiking paths, one of which scales the high point of Mount Brandaris (784 feet/240 m). The park is home to most of Bonaire's 190 bird species, including parrots, hummingbirds, and a flamingo colony on the Gotomeer lagoon. Several snorkel and dive sites lie off the leeward coast, such as **Boca Slagbaai** (Slaughter Bay), where the colonial ranchers killed their cattle before shipping the meat to Curaçao.

The island is surrounded by **Bonaire Marine Park.** Designated a marine preserve in 1971, the park rings the entire island and extends from the shore to the 200-foot-deep (60-m) contour through shallow, sloping terraces of fringe reefs to the drop-off. More than 80 species of corals have been identified, including elkhorn, staghorn, leaf, and brain corals, and the reefs are patrolled by a dazzling array of electric blue tangs, angelfish, parrotfish, grunts, and seahorses. All these delights are accessible to snorkelers. Simply locate one of the yellow dive markers and wade out. ■

Palm-thatched slave huts bake on the treeless shore.

Bonaire Marine Park

🗺 179 E1

☎ 5997/8444,
www.bmp.oro

💲 $

Washington-Slagbaai National Park

🗺 179 E1

☎ 5997/8444

💲 $

Aruba

Aruba

178 A2

Visitor information

✉ L.G. Smith Blvd. 172, Eagle Beach

☎ 297/823777

FIFTEEN MILES (24 KM) AS THE PELICAN FLIES FROM THE coast of Venezuela, with a population of 72,000, diminutive Aruba—20-by-6 miles (32-by-10-km)—is the one that got away. The island achieved *Status Aparte,* or independence, from the Netherlands Antilles in 1986 in the wake of the oil boom collapse and then turned wholeheartedly toward tourism. It is now one of the Caribbean's hottest vacation destinations, with a choice of luxurious hotels lining white sand beaches, 24-hour casino action, and duty-free shopping guaranteed to tempt even the most jaded cruise ship visitor.

Dismissed as an *isla inútil* (useless island) by its Spanish discoverers, Aruba was eventually used for ranching and developed something of a reputation for horse breeding. In 1824 gold was discovered, prompting a small-scale gold rush, but the mining became unprofitable and ceased altogether in 1914. Remains of the old mines and smelting works can be seen around Balashi and Bushiribana. Aloe vera plantations sprouted in the early 1900s, but oil refineries built in the mid-1920s made the island's fortunes, caused a population explosion, and gave Aruba one of the highest standards of living in the Caribbean region.

Arubans still live comfortably. They are ruled by a 21-member democratic parliament presided over by the prime minister. The Kingdom of the Netherlands, which handles defense and foreign affairs, is represented by a governor. Aruba has its own legal system, currency, and an excellent education system, which gives foreign languages a high priority. Most people speak English and Spanish as well as Papiamento (see p. 201). The islanders' Amerindian heritage is reflected in their looks, though there are now more than 40 nationalities bubbling in the Aruban melting pot.

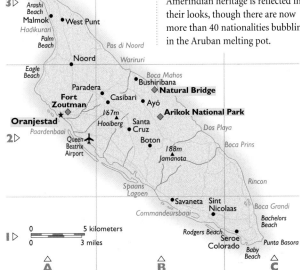

Sun worshippers head for the soft sands of Palm Beach.

Ornate gabled buildings proclaim Aruba's colonial heritage with a flourish in downtown Oranjestad.

Fort Zoutman Historical Museum
- 199 A1
- Off L.G. Smith Blvd.
- 297/826099
- Closed weekends
- $

Numismatic Museum
- Zuidstraat 27
- 297/828831
- Closed weekends

ORANJESTAD

The island capital, Oranjestad was named in honor of the Dutch ruling family, the House of Orange. The town is a mixture of old Dutch Caribbean buildings and modern pastiches that house boutiques and busy shopping malls. The oldest building on the island is **Fort Zoutman,** constructed on the waterfront in 1796. Now a short distance inland due to land reclamation, it still affords a good view over the yacht harbor. The Willem III Tower was added to the fort in 1868, doubling as a lighthouse and the island's first public clock. In its shadow a small **historical museum** exhibits artifacts from the Spanish and Dutch colonial era. Every Tuesday evening year-round, the Bom Bini Festival, an entertaining folkloric show featuring local crafts, food stalls, music, and dancing, takes place in the fort precincts.

Oranjestad has two other small museums. The **Numismatic Museum** boasts a collection of some 30,000 historic coins and banknotes from around the globe. The **Archaeological Museum** displays Amerindian tools, pottery, and 2,000-year-old skeletons unearthed from around the island.

Down on the waterfront **Atlantis Submarines** offers a popular mini-submarine excursion to the Bacadera Reef. There's a motorboat transfer to the dive site before boarding the window-lined sub for a trip 150 feet (46 m) beneath the waves for a fish-eye view of the *Mi Dushi I* shipwreck or the *Sonesta* airplane wreck. The dives are narrated, and identification charts are good guides. ∎

Papiamento

The mother tongue of the Dutch Leewards, Papiamento (from the Spanish *papia* meaning "talk" or "babble") emerged from the pidgin speech of the early colonists and their African slaves. Dutch merchants, Portuguese Jews, Spanish missionaries, South American traders, and local Indians all added to the vocabulary. The language is now spoken throughout the ABCs, with slight island variations (Aruban Papiamento is more Spanish sounding), and taught in schools. Islanders will be hugely entertained if you try a few words.

Welcome	*Bon bini*
Good morning	*Bon dia*
Good afternoon	*Bon tardi*
Good evening	*Bon nochi*
How are you?	*Con ta bai?*
I am fine	*Mi ta bon*
Good-bye	*Aye*
Thank you very much	*Masha danki*
Beautiful	*Bunita*
Very good	*Hopi bon* ∎

**De Olde Molen:
This 19th-century
windmill was
brought to Aruba
as a tourist
attraction
in 1961.**

**Archaeological
Museum**
✉ Irausquinplein 2-A
☎ 297/828979
🕐 Closed weekends

**Atlantis
Submarines**
✉ L.G. Smith Blvd. 82
☎ 297/836090
💲 $$$$$

Natural Bridge is the most famous feature of Aruba's rugged windward coast.

Around Aruba

ARUBA'S BEACHES

Northwest of Oranjestad, Aruba's twin tourist poles are the magnificent sandy sweeps of **Eagle Beach** (the "low-rise strip") and **Palm Beach** (the "high-rise strip"). Both are busy and hotel lined, with water sports concessions.

Two more smaller, less crowded beaches are to the north—**Malmok Beach** (a windsurfers' favorite) and **Arashi Beach.**

Sports & activities

Diving and snorkeling: Aruba Pro Dive *(Tel 297/825520)*; Red Sail Sports *(Tel 297/861603 or 800/255-6425, fax 297/866657, e-mail: infro@redsail.com, www.redsail.com).*

Golf: Aruba's best golfing is the 18-hole Tierra del Sol Golf Course on the northwest coast, designed by Robert Trent Jones *(Tel 297/860978, fax 297/860671).*

Horseback riding: Rancho Del Campo *(Tel 297/820290)*; Rancho El Paso *(Tel 297/873310).*

Touring: The leading island tour operator De Palm Tours *(Tel 297/824400)* offers everything from round-island bus and jeep excursions to sportfishing charters, cruises, and parasailing. ■

AYÓ

Inland, around the village of Ayó, giant boulders litter the dusty cunucu (backcountry), and there are Amerindian rock paintings in the **Arikok National Park** *(see Aruba tourism information p. 199)*. Nestled in among the scrub and tortured divi-divi trees bent into shape by the prevailing trade winds, Aruban farmsteads decorated with talismanic symbols crouch behind cactus fences erected to keep grazing animals out.

THE HOOIBERG

Located right at the center of the island, the Hooiberg (541feet/165 m) is a local landmark. Steps lead all the way up to the top of the hill, which does look a bit like the haystack its Dutch name suggests. The view stretches across the island from coast to coast.

NATURAL BRIDGE

On the north coast near Andicouri is another popular attraction, Natural Bridge, a 100-foot-long (30 m), 23-foot-high (7 m) span of coral rock eroded by wave action.

SINT NICOLAAS

Aruba's largest settlement (population 25,000), located at the eastern end of the island, is undergoing a major facelift. A clutch of good beaches at the very tip of the island include palm-fringed **Rodgers Beach,** the quiet cove of **Baby Beach,** and the breezy strands of **Bachelors Beach** and **Boca Grandi.** ■

B ridging the gap between the Virgin Islands and the Windward Islands, the Leeward Islands of Antigua, Barbuda, and Anguilla are coral islands. St. Kitts, Nevis, and Montserrat are mountainous miniatures of the volcanic Windwards.

Leeward Islands

A Leeward Island student

Leeward Islands

THE SIX ENGLISH-SPEAKING LEEWARD ISLANDS HEAD UP THE CHAIN OF THE Lesser Antilles mingling with the Dutch Windward Islands and the French possessions of St. Martin and St.-Barthélemy (St. Barts). Antigua is the main gateway to this corner of the Caribbean, and it has been since the British established their chief Caribbean naval base here in the 18th century. The British influence lingers on throughout the region in a handful of notable historic sites, the occasional red mailbox, and, of course, the islanders' beloved sport of cricket.

The main European influence on the Leeward Islands might be British, but indigenous Caribbean culture is here, too, in the exuberant local carnivals, reggae, rasta, and the studied art of relaxation. There are beaches galore, water sports, and hiking, plus accommodations ranging from family-friendly resorts to gorgeous plantation hotel retreats.

England's first successful Caribbean colony was **St. Kitts,** settled in 1623. **Nevis** followed in 1628, and a decade later Antigua and Montserrat were added to a growing portfolio of Caribbean possessions. At first, English and French settlers agreed to share St. Kitts, banding

together to rid the island of inhospitable Carib people. Once the Carib were defeated, the good neighbors soon fell out. And so began the battle for control of the eastern Caribbean islands, which would continue into the 19th century and cause the demise of the sugar industry.

While **Antigua** was systematically stripped of its native forest to make way for sugar plantations—and settlers did their best to plant cane wherever the topography allowed on St. Kitts, Nevis, and **Montserrat**—barren, low-lying **Anguilla** became a nest of pirates and smugglers. Slaves brought to the island by prospective planters were soon turned loose to scratch a living from the thin, sandy soil; they developed a local reputation for carpentry and boatbuilding. This early self-reliance fostered the Anguillans' fiercely independent spirit, typified by the bizarre circumstances of the Anguillan "revolution" (actually a reactionary desire to remain British and avoid independence as a satellite of St. Kitts) in the late 1960s.

Slavery was abolished throughout the British Caribbean in 1834, although a term of forced "apprenticeship" legally bound former slaves to their masters for a further period of years. In the end European sugar beets undermined the Caribbean trade to emancipate the slaves for good in the late 1830s. The islands sunk into an impoverished backwater status, administered under the presidency of the Leeward Islands until 1967, when associated statehood brought a degree of autonomy. The twin-island nation of **Antigua** and **Barbuda** achieved independence in 1981, followed by St. Kitts and Nevis in 1983. Anguilla and Montserrat elected to remain British Crown Colonies.

Plantation hotels in beautifully restored colonial houses offer a relaxed and stylish alternative to beachfront accommodations.

Sugar continued to be grown in Antigua until the 1970s and still provides a modest income for St. Kitts, but for more than a century the Leeward Islands' precarious economies had been almost entirely dependent on remissions—money sent by islanders working overseas. In the last 30 years tourism has gradually injected new life into the region, and the top beach islands of Antigua and Anguilla, in particular, have seen considerable hotel development.

Although the Leewards share a common background, each island enjoys its own identity. For the ultimate laid-back Caribbean beach vacation, it would be hard to beat Anguilla, which focuses all the attention on its fabulous white sand strands and super-luxurious resorts. Very quiet and relatively undiscovered Barbuda boasts a selection of delectable and often deserted beaches, where the only crowds are propelled by fins and inhabit magical coral reefs.

Antigua is altogether a more lively choice. In addition to claiming a beach for every day of the year (a wild but forgivable exaggeration), the island's historical sites make for interesting excursions, and friendly pubs provide live reggae and impromptu jump-ups at night. Lush St. Kitts and tiny Nevis combine colonial history with romantic plantation retreats and some fine upland hiking and riding country. Sadly, lovely Montserrat is currently held hostage by its active volcano, which erupted in 1995 and continues to rain ash, rock, and mud over a wide area. The main settlement of Plymouth has been engulfed and the population evacuated to the northern end of the island. ■

Antigua

AT 108 SQUARE MILES (280 SQ KM), ANTIGUA (PRONOUNCED
An-TEE-gah) is the largest of the Leeward Islands. Its irregular coastline, resembling a ragged Rorschach inkblot, incorporates hundreds
of scalloped inlets and bays. The locals boast there are 365 beaches to
choose from, many of them secluded coves backed by sea grape trees
and accessible only by boat.

Antigua
205 D2
Visitor information
Lower St. Mary's St.,
St. John's
268/462-0374

The interior of the island is rolling
and dry. The lush carpet of sugarcane has disappeared and been
replaced by yellow-gray scrubland
dotted with the shells of abandoned
windmills. Small country villages
provide a brief burst of color and
greenery, painted wooden cottages
and modern villas with flower
gardens straggle along the roadside,
and tethered goats and cattle graze
in the dust. Antigua's coastal
heights are generally topped with
the remains of British ramparts; the
most interesting is Shirley Heights
(see p. 212), in Nelson's Dockyard
National Park, overlooking English
Harbour Town.

The first human traces on
Antigua date back to the Stone Age

Ciboney people, who migrated
from South America to settle the
island about 3000 B.C. Peaceable
Arawak arrived on the scene about
A.D. 100, and raiding parties of
Windward Island Carib were mov-
ing up the island chain by the time
Christopher Columbus sighted
the island on his second voyage in
1493. He named it Santa Maria de
la Antigua after a miraculous statue
of the Virgin in Seville Cathedral.
The Spanish and French showed
little interest in the island, discour-
aged by its shortage of fresh water,
but English colonists from St. Kitts
established a base in 1632. Sugar
was introduced in the 1650s, and by
the height of the 18th-century
plantation era, Antigua had more

than 200 cane-crushing windmills, with African slaves forming 93 percent of the population.

Antigua's protected harbors (an important consideration in the Caribbean hurricane belt) and strategic position at the apex of a rough triangle between the major-league sugar colonies of Barbados and Jamaica made the island a natural choice for Britain's chief naval and military base in the Leewards. Fortresses sprang up along the coast, with the main defenses concentrated in the south around English and Falmouth Harbours. The result was so formidable that Britain's enemies gave the whole island a wide berth.

After British emancipation of the slaves in 1834, Antigua's fate mirrored that of other colonial possessions. The dockyard was closed, most of the plantations failed, and the islanders slipped into an unremitting pattern of subsistence agriculture. They were consequently largely ignored by Britain.

Appalling working conditions inspired the first organized labor movement in 1939. It gained strength during World War II, which heralded an influx of U.S. servicemen sent to man military bases on the island. The postwar Labour Party, under the leadership of Vere C. Bird, led Antigua and the neighboring island of Barbuda to self-governing associated statehood in 1967 and full independence in 1981.

Antigua and Barbuda's combined population numbers around 66,000, of which some 85 percent are of African descent. Most Antiguans live in the capital,

Natty paintwork spruces up even the simplest wooden cottage in the countryside outside St. John's.

Sports & activities

Day sails: Sight-seeing and sporty day trips with Kokomo Cat *(Tel 268/462-7245)*; sail to Barbuda with Wadadli Cats *(Tel 268/462-4792)*; or do the traditional booze cruise with Jolly Roger Pirate Cruises *(Tel 268/462-2064)*.

Diving & snorkeling: Antigua's best reef sites are off the south and west coasts. Dive operators include Dive Antigua *(Dickenson Bay, Tel 268/462-3483)*; Dockyard Divers *(Nelson's Dockyard, Tel 268/460-1178)*; and Jolly Dive *(Jolly Harbour, Tel 268/462-0061)*.

Golf: Antigua's two 18-hole golf courses are found at the Cedar Valley Golf Club, near St. John's *(Tel 268/462-0161)*, and at Jolly Harbour *(Tel 268/480-6950)*.

Horseback riding: Spring Hill Riding Club *(Falmouth, Tel 268/463-8041)* and the St. James's Club *(Mamora Bay, Tel 268/460-5000)*.

Sailing: Sailing is concentrated around English Harbour, Falmouth Harbour, and the Jolly Harbour marina complex. Charter companies can supply yachts of all sizes, with or without crew, by the day, week or longer. Contact Nicholson's Yacht Charters *(Tel 268/460-1530, fax 268/460-1531)* or Sun Yacht Charters *(Tel 268/463-2113 or 800/772-3500, fax 268/463-2115)*.

Tours: Off-road four-wheel-drive, hiking, and mountain biking tours from Tropikelly Trails *(Tel 268/461-0383)*. ∎

The sturdy stone windmill tower at Betty's Hope plantation

St. John's, a bustling port city and cruise-ship destination on the west coast, well worth a visit. Antigua has several diversions for the inquisitive traveler who would like to get off the beach and have a look around. Nelson's Dockyard National Park (see p. 210) showcases the finest surviving Georgian naval complex in the world, while the history of the island's sugar industry is explained at the restored Betty's Hope sugar mill (see p. 213) in the center of the island.

A favorite out-of-the-way detour on the southeast coast is a trip to Harmony Hall (see p. 213), a charming old sugar mill complex housing an arts-and-crafts gallery.

Tourists are generally welcomed wherever they go, although some American visitors detect a hint of British reserve when they wander off the well-beaten tourist trail. To capture Antiguans at their most spontaneous, consider a visit during the summer **Carnival** (late July to early August), or join the regattas and riotous partying that accompany the annual **Antigua Race Week** at the end of the December-to-April yachting season. For a more modest hit of the local atmosphere, the Sunday afternoon jump-ups (impromptu dances) at Shirley Heights are entertaining rum-and-reggae-soaked affairs.

ST. JOHN'S & SURROUNDINGS
St. John's is an appealing West Indian town sloping gently back from the downtown waterfront in an orderly pattern of streets and narrow alleys, laid out in 1702. Old wooden buildings with drooping balconies cluster on the hill below the cathedral and its landmark silver cupolas. Charmingly

time-worn, they appear anchored together for support by a web of telephone wires above the road.

The sidewalks of St. John's are always crowded. More often than not during the winter high season, armies of day-tripping cruise passengers pile ashore intent on plundering the duty-free stores in the modern **Heritage Quay** mall at the foot of the pier.

The compact waterfront district remains the focal point of town. Next to Heritage Quay, there's a covered vendors' market full of souvenir stalls, and on its far side is **Redcliffe Quay,** a pretty shopping street lined with restored wood and stone town houses and former warehouses now occupied by boutiques, galleries, and restaurants. The area behind the Quay was once part of a large barracoon, or dockside slave-holding compound, before emancipation.

It's a short walk up Long Street to the **Museum of Antigua and Barbuda,** housed in the neoclassic Old Court House, built in 1750 from stone quarried on Antigua's offshore islets. The fusty, old-fashioned layout conceals a remarkably informative introduction to the islands' history and geology. The archaeological finds are particularly interesting and include Stone Age Ciboney tools, an Arawak ax with a special hole designed to allow tree spirits to escape, and a collection of *zemi,* small stone or carved bone objects believed to attract benevolent powers.

At the top of the hill is the **Cathedral of St. John the Divine,** flanked by its twin towers and presiding over the town center. Constructed on the site of a previous stone church demolished by an earthquake in 1843, the cathedral has a cool, lofty interior clad in

The Cathedral of St. John the Divine looms over the capital's harbor.

Museum of Antigua & Barbuda

✉ Corner of Long & Market Sts., St. John's

☎ 268/462-4930

🕐 Closed Sun.

💲 Donation

pitch pine to protect it against hurricane and earthquake damage. Take a little time to inspect the grand memorial plaques bedecked with coats-of-arms and flowery inscriptions. At the south gate of the tumble-down graveyard (a popular lunchtime picnic spot with local office workers) are the statues of "St. John the Divine" and "St. John

A Rasta musician lets down his dreadlocks and entertains in a local restaurant.

Nelson's Dockyard National Park
🅰 207 B2
☎ 268/460-1379
💲 $$$

the Baptist," said to have been captured from an 18th-century French warship bound for Martinique.

The entrance to St. John's Harbour is overlooked by the ruins of two historic forts with good views. On the north side, reached by Fort Road, is **Fort James,** which was founded in 1706 shortly after the death of King James II. Continuing up the coast, there are a few hotels lining the beach at **Runaway Bay.** Just around a small headland is Antigua's most developed pocket of shoreline— **Dickinson Bay.** This is no Miami Beach high-rise strip but a half-mile (800-m) swath of fine, powdery white sand that turns the water a translucent opal. The beach is backed by just four low-rise hotels set in landscaped gardens. A good spot for active beachgoers, Dickinson Bay has several water sports concessions renting

Windsurfers and Sunfish sailboats.

On the south side of St. John's Harbour is 17th-century **Fort Barrington,** one of Antigua's earliest (and most active) fortresses. The site was already fortified when it was named in honor of Admiral Barrington, who captured St. Lucia from the French in 1665, though most of the present defenses were constructed in 1779. From the fortress ruins there are views across to the neighboring islands of St. Kitts and Nevis on a clear day.

A handful of Antigua's best beaches are tucked into the bays and coves of the southwest coast. Out on the peninsula, near Fort Barrington, are **Deep Bay, Galley Bay,** and the assorted coves and hotel beaches of **Hawksbill Bay,** so named for the hawksbill turtle-shaped rock they overlook. The **Jolly Harbour** complex incorporates a busy marina, shops, and hotels, as well as a beach on Lignumvitae Bay. Farther south, **Dark Wood Bay** lost most of its palm tree fringe in 1995's Hurricane Luis, but it's still a lovely strip of sand with a beach bar, and it is almost deserted on weekdays.

NELSON'S DOCKYARD NATIONAL PARK

The national park covers 12 square miles (31 sq km) on the south coast around Falmouth Harbour, the original capital site of Antigua. A popular yachting center on its own sheltered bay, Falmouth is divided by a narrow isthmus from the virtually landlocked confines of English Harbour. English Harbour served as the British Royal Navy's eastern Caribbean headquarters during the 17th and 18th centuries.

Shirley Heights is the best place to begin a visit to the park. The sprawling 18th-century military complex was named for Gen. Sir Thomas Shirley, governor of the

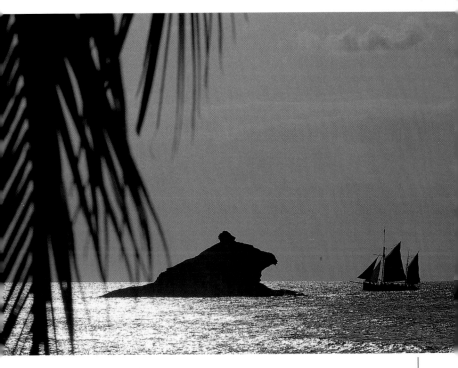

Leeward Islands between 1781 and 1791. It occupies a commanding position on the high ground above the dockyard, which is reached by a well-signed road from English Harbour. Make an initial stop at the **Dow Hill Historical Centre,** where a 15-minute multimedia presentation covers Antiguan history and culture from the Carib to cricket. The road continues to wind uphill, past the elegant stone colonnade of the officers' quarters, now open to the sky and studded with cactuses, until it reaches **Shirley Heights Lookout.** Eagle-eyed sentries could scan the horizon all the way south to the French island of Guadeloupe, giving the British plenty of advance warning in the event of an attack. The French were never foolhardy enough to attempt it.

Hawksbill Rock stands silhouetted against the sunset off Antigua's southwest coast.

Horatio Nelson

England's 18th-century naval hero spent a miserable posting in Antigua between 1784 and 1787. As captain of the 28-gun frigate H.M.S. *Boreas,* Nelson was dispatched to enforce the extremely unpopular Navigation Act, which banned planters and merchants from trading with the newly independent United States of America. At times his mission so incensed the islanders that he was afraid to put into shore and took refuge on Nevis, where he met and married Fanny Nesbit. "Woefully pinched by mosquitoes," Nelson felt so ill when he left for England that he ordered a barrel of rum be taken on board to preserve his body for a home burial if he died during the voyage. ■

Perched high above English Harbor, Fort Shirley's Georgian-era guardhouse dates from 1791.

Down at sea level is **Nelson's Dockyard National Park,** which was considered a hardship posting and "an infernal hole" by its famous namesake, Admiral Lord Nelson (1758–1805). He was plain Captain Nelson in 1784, when he and his shipmates aboard H.M.S. *Boreas* arrived in the Leeward Islands for a three-year tour of duty (see p. 211). The dockyard was decommissioned in 1889 and fell into disrepair until the 1960s, when it was restored, renamed, and opened to the public. It is a delightful place for a stroll, guided by a series of signs that identify the various stores and workshop buildings. You can take a guided tour from the entrance gate. Top sights include the **Admiral's Inn,** housed in a former pitch and tar store, with the coral rock pillars of a sail loft in the gardens. Note the rounded water cisterns flanking the brick walls of the charming **Copper & Lumber Store Hotel,** and visit the **Dockyard Museum,** laid out in the Admiral's House, the last house to be completed in the dockyard, in 1855. There's a short walk out to **Fort Berkeley,** the dockyard's first line of defense, built on a rocky spit of land in 1704. The path starts by the dinghy dock in the marina, and there are grand views back across the harbor basin to **Clarence House.** ∎

Exploring Shirley Heights

The military abandoned Shirley Heights in the 1850s, and since then many of its buildings have simply disappeared behind a screen of scrub. But signposts and footpaths still lead to an assortment of crumbling barracks and batteries, water cisterns, powder magazines, and the Military Cemetery, where the numerous victims of tropical fevers were laid to rest. The signals station at the highest point of the complex (490 feet/149 m) used flags to send messages to Fort George at Monk's Hill, above Falmouth, which were then relayed across a chain of hilltop signals-stations to St. John's. ∎

Around Antigua

BETTY'S HOPE

Antigua's pioneer plantation, Betty's Hope was established in St. Peter's Parish during the 1650s. In 1668 it passed into the hands of the Codrington family of Barbados, who introduced sugar production to the island and remained in control until 1944. For 250 years Betty's Hope was one of the island's most prosperous estates. Its sugar factory didn't close until the 1920s, and sugarcane continued to be grown here until the 1970s. Today, thorny yellow-flowering acacia bushes and wild tamarind trees have swallowed up the former canefields, but one of two windmills has been carefully restored. Refitted with broad wooden sails and cane-crushing machinery, it is the only working sugar mill in the Caribbean.

Inside the small **visitor center** are exhibits explaining sugar processing and the work of the slave gangs. Betty's Hope employed about 310 West African slaves, each responsible for an average 2-acre (0.8-ha) plot of sugarcane. There are also maps and drawings relating to the history of the plantation, as well as a detailed scale model of the now demolished great house, complete with machete-wielding cane cutters, farmyard animals, and smartly dressed Europeans strolling in the great house gardens, shaded from the sun by lacy parasols. In reality, most plantation owners preferred to live in Europe and leave their overseas estates in the hands of managers.

🗺 207 B2   ✉ Southeast of Pares
☎ 268/462-1469   🕐 Closed Sun.–Mon.

FIG TREE DRIVE

A rare pocket of lush natural vegetation in the southwest of the island, Fig Tree Drive runs 5 miles (8 km) from the inland village of **Swetes** down to **Old Road,** on the coast at Carlisle Bay. To the west is **Boggy Peak** (1,319 feet/402 m), Antigua's highest point, rising above the Shekerley Mountains, where escaped slaves once took refuge.

🗺 207 A1   ✉ St. Mary's Parish

FORT GEORGE

An easy hiking expedition for history buffs, Fort George perches on the modest heights of Monk's Hill, behind Falmouth Harbour. To reach the fort, turn off the main road at the village of **Liberta** (one of the first settlements founded by freed slaves) in the direction of Table Hill Gordon. The mile-long (1.5-km) marked track is on the right, navigable by four-wheel-drive vehicles or on foot. The fort, which dates from 1689, was intended as a stronghold for livestock, women, and children if Falmouth was attacked. Sections of the high defensive walls, water cisterns, powder magazines, and cannon emplacements have survived around the 8-acre (3-ha) site.

🗺 207 B1   ✉ Monk's Hill, near Liberta

HARMONY HALL

A delightful spot on the east coast, Harmony Hall is well worth a detour. The former great house on the Brown's Bay Mill sugar estate has been transformed into a gallery of Caribbean arts and crafts and a six-room B&B inn. The old windmill houses a bar overlooking **Nonsuch Bay,** and there is a restaurant serving lunch and afternoon tea. Call ahead, and they will even pack up a picnic and arrange a boat trip to a local beach from the dinghy dock. Visitors can also use the pool. A short drive (3 miles/5 km) southeast of Harmony Hall, beyond Freetown, is the alluring curve of **Half Moon Bay,** which is popular with swimmers, sunbathers, and bodysurfers.

🗺 207 C2   ✉ Brown's Bay (north of Freetown)   ☎ 268/460-4120   🕐 Closed mid-May to mid-Nov.

INDIAN TOWN POINT & DEVILS BRIDGE

Way out at the northeast tip of the island, a side road leads off 1 mile (1.5 km) to Indian Town Point and the site of Devils Bridge. On a blustery day the Atlantic surf crashes against the coastline, where it has hollowed out a natural limestone archway, and blasts through blowholes in the rock, creating fountains of windblown salt spray. Archaeologists have made several excavations in the Indian Town Point area, which was declared a national park in the 1950s. A short drive to the north is sandy **Long Bay.**

🗺 207 C2   ✉ East of Willikies ∎

Magnificent
frigatebirds roost
in the coastal
mangrove
thickets of
Codrington
Lagoon.

Barbuda

A 28-MILE (45-KM) PUDDLE-JUMPER FLIGHT FROM
Antigua, Barbuda bakes quietly in the sun and takes things very, very
easy. The 14-by-8-mile (22.5-by13-km) coral atoll is almost two-
thirds the size of its more developed, upbeat sister, Antigua, but there
are just 1,500 islanders, who live mainly by fishing, farming, and
hunting. Barbuda's top attractions are mind-blowing, pinkish white
sand beaches and superb snorkeling; ornithologists can also enjoy the
frigatebird nesting grounds on Codrington Lagoon.

Magnificent frigatebirds roost in the coastal mangrove thickets of Codrington Lagoon.

BARBUDA ON FOOT

In the northern part
of the island a low
stone passage
plumbs the depths
of **Dark Cave,**
where rare blind
shrimp live in sub-
terranean pools.
Darby Sink Cave,
in The Highlands
region, reaches a
modest 150 feet (45
m) above sea level.
The 70-foot-deep
(21-m) sinkhole
harbors an unex-
pected flourish of
palmetto palms and
other greenery. ■

Any visit to Barbuda comes
with an important caveat:
Accommodations at either of the
island's exclusive resorts are strato-
spherically expensive. If you've mis-
laid the number of your Swiss bank
account, consider a day trip.

Barbuda's only settlement is
Codrington, a handful of streets
leading back from the saltwater
lagoon. Both were named for
Christopher Codrington, a 17th-
century governor-general of the
Leeward Islands who leased the
whole island from the British
crown in 1691. (It remained in the
family's hands until 1872.) Poor soil
and an annual rainfall of only

about 38 inches (965 mm) meant
sugar cultivation was impossible on
Barbuda, but Codrington introduced deer, wild boar, and guinea
fowl for hunting, raised cattle, and
grew provisions to supply his five
Antiguan estates. He also, so it was
reported, used his private island to
encourage slave breeding among his
strongest and healthiest West
African workers.

Barbuda is almost completely
ringed by breathtaking beaches.
One magnificent 14-mile (22.5 km)
stretch starts at the southerly tip of
Cocoa Point and sweeps up the
west coast, past the landmark River
Fort defensive tower to **Palmetto**

Redonda

An uninhabited volcanic rock 30 miles (48 km) southwest of Antigua, Redonda is the third territory of Antigua and Barbuda. It has a rather bizarre recent history. In the mid-19th century, some enterprising souls recognized there was money to be made from Redonda's guano deposits. Thousands of tons of bird droppings were shipped off the island for use as fertilizer. Subsequently, Britain annexed Redonda to its Leeward Island possessions. But an Irishman from Montserrat proclaimed himself king of Redonda, and the title has since passed to a succession of colorful (nonresident) literary types who have generously created Redondan peers out of any famous people who attract their attention, from Welsh writer and poet Dylan Thomas to British film actress Diana Dors. ■

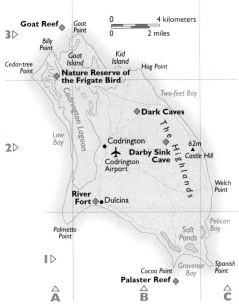

Point, where it takes a sharp turn around the headland and continues on up the outer arm of **Codrington Lagoon.**

In the south, there's excellent snorkeling around **Gravenor Bay** and the 2-mile-long (3-km) **Palaster Reef,** a protected marine reserve off Cocoa Point. Goat Reef, in the north, is renowned for its wreck diving. As yet, Barbuda has no organized dive operation, so divers will need to bring all their equipment. Local fishing boats are available for charter.

Make it a point to take a boat trip out into the mangrove-lined **Nature Reserve of the Frigate Bird** (*Earl's Tours, Tel/fax 268/462-5647. Map 215 A13*) at the north end of Codrington Lagoon. (*You pay the boatmen by the hour. The trip should take 1–2 hours.*) Here is the largest nesting colony of magnificent frigatebirds in the world, with an estimated 2,500 pairs. The glossy black birds have an 8-foot (2.5-m) wingspan and can soar at altitudes of up to 2,000 feet (600 m). During the mating season

(Aug.–Nov.), male birds try to attract a female by puffing out their scarlet neck pouches like a huge balloon, trembling their outstretched wings, and emitting a strange drumming sound. A pair then builds a ragged, twig-lined nest and await the hatching of their ungainly, pure white young (Dec.–Feb.). More than 400 other bird species have been identified in the lagoon area. ■

Barbuda
🗺 205 D3
Visitor information
✉ Thames & Lon Sts., St. John's, Antigua
☎ 268/462-0374

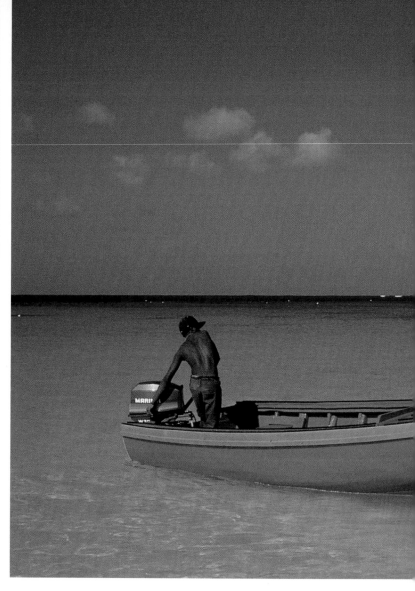

Anguilla

Anguilla

🅜 205 A3

Visitor information

✉ Social Security Bldg.,
The Valley

☎ 264/497-2759 or
800/553-4939, fax
264/497-2710

🕓 Closed weekends

LONG BEFORE A WEALTH OF SUPERLATIVE SANDY BEACHES was considered an attraction, Spanish explorers took one look at the flat, desiccated, and most northerly of the Leeward Islands, christened it Anguilla, meaning "eel," and sailed on in search of richer, greener, and more promising territories. Only 16 miles (25 km) long and 3 miles (5 km) wide at its broadest point, Anguilla has 33 dazzling white beaches with sand so fine and deep that you have to wade rather than walk along them.

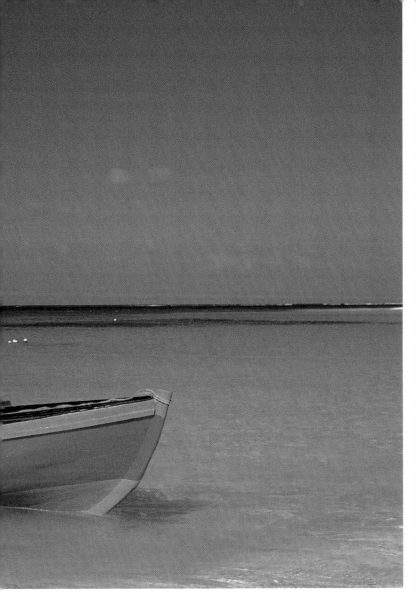

Forget rain forest hikes, historic forts, casinos, and duty-free shopping (although commercialized Sint Maarten/St. Martin is only a 40-minute ferry ride away), and prepare to get horizontal. Anguilla has been neatly summed up in a one-line T-shirt slogan: "Life's a beach, and then you dine." And it is possible to dine very well on Anguilla. The island may be lacking in the general interest and activities department, but it does boast a selection of the Caribbean's most luxurious and architecturally striking hotels, with dining opportunities to match, plus some very good independent restaurants often romantically placed on the shore in earshot of gently lapping waves.

Working up an appetite can be more problematical. Wind-assisted

Many Anguillans build their own sleek, brightly painted fishing boats destined to ply the island's electric blue coastal waters.

St. Gerard's Catholic Church displays a certain individualistic take on island architecture.

swapping one beach for another. In the middle of the island is **The Valley,** Anguilla's capital and administrative center. The settlement has no real focus, but there are some attractive shingled and shuttered traditional houses in jaunty poster-paint colors.

Set back from the main street is the **Anguilla National Museum** *(see Anguilla tourist information, p. 216),* which presents changing exhibitions on local themes, from flora and fauna to history and culture. The museum is also the home of the **Anguilla National Trust,** which can arrange natural history bush walks, bird-watching, visits to Amerindian sites, and tours to see hawksbill turtle nesting grounds in summer.

Near the airport is the 1787 **Wallblake House,** an annex of the museum currently undergoing restoration, together with its old stable block and bakery.

Northeast of The Valley lies **Shoal Bay,** the island's liveliest beach, a broad belt of ankle-deep sand with a handful of beach bars, hotels, and water sports concessions renting out snorkeling gear, Windsurfers, and dinghies.

Five miles (8 km) farther east by road, opposite the fishing village of

water sports are available (Jet skis are banned to protect the reefs), and most of the larger hotels have tennis courts and fitness centers, although golf is not an option as yet. Anguilla has six marine parks, seven wreck dives, and terrific snorkeling.

AROUND THE ISLAND

Exploring Anguilla really only takes a day, but most visitors enjoy a change of scene, even if it's just

"The eel that squealed"

Laid-back Anguilla seems the last place on earth to harbor revolutionary tendencies, but in the late 1960s it became the first British colony to stage a successful revolution against independence. In 1967, faced with the prospect of an unwanted union with St. Kitts and Nevis, the Anguillans rounded up and deported a detachment of Kittitian policemen, rolled an antique cannon onto the beach, and appealed to Britain for continued

colonial status. Embarrassingly out of touch, the British government dispatched armed paratroopers to reestablish order two years later. They were greeted by cheering Anguillans waving Union Jacks and singing "God Save the Queen." The fiasco was dubbed Britain's Bay of Piglets. For an entertaining account of the whole saga, pick up a copy of Donald E. Westlake's *Under an English Heaven,* available on the island. ∎

Island Harbour, is **Gorgeous Scilly Cay,** a tiny offshore islet with a palm-thatched restaurant and good snorkeling. If it's too far to swim, wave for the water taxi.

In the southeast corner of the island, seek out the **Heritage Collection** (*East End at Pond Ground, Tel 264/497-4440*), a fascinating privately owned museum. The bulk of the exhibits are devoted to the revolution (see p. 218), with a detailed account of the proceedings and some entertaining photographs. There are also pieces of Amerindian pottery decorated with pelican heads and antique kitchen implements made out of coral.

You'll find other attractions to the west of The Valley. The island's deepwater port is located on the north coast at **Sandy Ground,** balanced on a curved spit of sand dividing the old salt pans from the ocean. There are a few restaurants, and a ferry dock for a regular boat service to **Sandy Island,** another offshore beach and snorkeling spot with a snack bar.

Continuing west, several hotels and good restaurants are gathered in the **Meade's Bay** and **Barnes Bay** area.

On the south coast, the futuristic apartments of Cove Castles preside over **Lower Shoal Bay;** the Cap Juluca resort fronts **Maunday's Bay;** and Anguilla's longest beach, **Rendezvous Bay,** stretches out in a curving ribbon of dunes facing St.-Martin. ■

Boats or a cliff-hugging trail are the only way to reach secluded Little Bay on the central north coast.

see p. 218

Sports & activities

Diving: Dive Shop Anguilla (*Tel 264/497-2020, fax 264/497-5125*) or Anguilla Divers Ltd. (*Tel 264/497-4750, fax 264/ 497-4632*).

Hiking: Guided hikes with Oliver Hodge (*Tel 264/ 497-3696*).

Horseback riding: El Rancho Del Blues (*Tel 264/497-6164*). ■

St. Kitts

THE TWIN-ISLAND NATION OF ST. KITTS AND NEVIS LIES
near the northern tip of a 500-mile-long (800-km) arc of volcanic
peaks that stretches from Saba to Grenada along a curving submarine
fault between the Atlantic Ocean and the Caribbean Sea. St. Kitts
is the larger of the two islands at 68 square miles (176 sq km), with
three distinct mountain ranges squeezed into its lush, green tadpole-
shaped body. A spine of dry, rugged hills form the tail, which trails
southeast toward Nevis.

The best beaches and a small
collection of hotels are gathered at
the top of the tail section, close to
the bustling island capital of
Basseterre (see p. 222), on the south
coast. To the north, billowing fields
of sugarcane blanket the lower
slopes of the ranges, which peak at
Mount Liamuiga (3,792 feet/1,156
m), and a single perimeter road hugs
the coast, linking quiet rural villages.

The Amerindian name for
St. Kitts was Liamuiga (meaning
fertile land), but when Christopher
Columbus sailed by in 1493, he
named it St. Christopher after
his own patron saint and the
patron saint of travelers. Just over
a century later, British colonists,
led by Sir Thomas Warner
(1575–1649), settled on St. Kitts
and set about cultivating tobacco.
Having defeated the resident Carib
population at Bloody Point in 1626,
they ousted French colonists from
the southern portion of the island,
around Basseterre, and adopted
St. Christopher as a base for colo-
nizing the other Leeward Islands
and Tortola in the Virgin Islands.

The island's Spanish name was Anglicized and shortened, and St. Kitts became known as the Mother Colony of the West Indies.

Naturally the French refused to give up easily. The island and neighboring Nevis were important sugar producers, and St. Kitts, or parts of it, changed hands regularly despite the vast fortress built by the British at Brimstone Hill (see p. 222), grandly but inaccurately touted as the Gibraltar of the West Indies. Britain finally secured sovereignty of the islands under the Treaty of Versailles in 1783. When the sugar bubble burst half a century later, the high-living plantocracy quit the islands in droves, and St. Kitts and Nevis shared the same dismal fate as other Caribbean sugar islands, largely ignored and left to fend for themselves by their uninterested colonial masters.

As Britain prepared to divest itself of its Leeward Island territories in the 1960s, plans were drawn up for a new tri-island state comprising St. Kitts, Nevis, and Anguilla. The Anguillans reacted immediately, staging a mini-revolution to avoid certain domination by larger and more populous St. Kitts. Despite similar reservations, Nevis entered into the state of St. Kitts and Nevis but inserted an escape clause in the constitution that would allow the smaller island to secede should the majority of Nevisians decide they would prefer to go it alone. In recent years the Nevisian economy, boosted by off-shore tax status, has outstripped that of St. Kitts, and traditional inter-island rivalries have been further exacerbated by what the Nevisians feel is undue Kittitian interference in their affairs. At present Nevis is limited to three representatives out of the 11-member Assembly of St. Kitts and Nevis, and the question of secession is being openly discussed. There is a very real prospect that Nevis will go solo in the near future.

While local politicians sharpen their rhetoric in the House of Assembly, island

---

4▷

Dieppe Bay   Dieppe Bay Town
Sandy Bay
St. Paul's   **Rawlins** •Sadlers
Newton   **Plantation**   ◆ **Black Rocks**
Ground•   Tabernacle
Northwest Range   Nicola Town
Belle   1156m   Molineaux•   *Grange Bay*
Tete   Sandy ▲Mt. Liamuiga   •Ottley's
3▷   Point Town *Central Range*   *Hermitage Bay*
Pump Bay **Brimstone Hill**   Cayon•
Half Way Tree **Fort**
        ◆ **St. Thomas'** *Southeast Range*
          Parish Church 900m   *Barkers Point*
Middle Island• **Romney** ▲
        ◆ **Manor**   *St. Kitts*
Old Road Town • **Amerindian**
Old Road Bay **petroglyphs** Robert Llewelyn *Upper Conaree*
        Challengers   Bradshaw Airport✈
      Bloody Point Trinity   *Half Moon Bay*
2▷   Palmetto Point• •Boyd's   *Muddy Point*
          Camp Bay **Basseterre**
                  ★   *North Frigate Bay*
△   △   *North Friar's Bay*
A   **B**   *Frigate Bay* *Turtle Bay*
                    Friar's Bay *Canoe Bay*
                          South Bank Bay
              White House Bay
              Guana Point 319m *Mosquito*
              Ballast Bay *Great Salt* *Bluff*
                     Pond *Scotch*
              Green Point   *Bonnet*
                        Cockleshell
         I▷   *Major's Bay*
                     Bay *The Narrows*
0   10 kilometers   *Nag's Head*
0   6 miles   △   △
              C   **D**

life moseys gently on. Almost two-thirds of St. Kitts' population of 36,000 live in and around Basseterre, with its boisterous street life and markets, restaurants tucked away in pretty stone courtyards, and a brand-new cruise-ship pier. In addition to tourism, St. Kitts' 40-plus working plantations harvest sugarcane for export, and the local brewery has plastered the entire island with its blue-and-yellow logo. Beyond the town and the beach, rain forest hikes are popular. It takes a full day to hike the round-trip up to Mount Liamuiga's crater lip, but local guide companies offer several other less strenuous options, as well as jeep safaris to ruined plantation houses and sugar mills.

BASSETERRE

Originally settled by the French, as its name implies, Basseterre (low ground) skirts a broad bay at the foot of the Southeast Range. The British moved their capital here from Old Road in 1727, but most of the attractive skirt-and-blouse buildings (so-called for their stone ground floors and wooden uppers) postdate the major fire of 1867.

The heart of town is arranged around the twin poles of **The Circus**—where the traffic makes its way around a fancy Victorian clock tower cum public seating area and meeting place—and **Independence Square.** The grassy square has a gaudily painted fountain, a few palms, and a single poinciana, the national tree, which sports brilliant red blooms in summer. On the east side of the square the Catholic church dates from 1670 but has been reconstructed several times. Behind a row of metal railings on the south side of the square stands the handsome Old Georgian House, looking as though it has been transplanted from a centuries-old market town in the English Cotswolds.

The Basseterre waterfront is undergoing a major facelift. An ambitious new marina, shopping area, and commercial development is planned for the 30-acre (12-ha) reclaimed site extending out to the **Port Zante** cruise-ship pier. Follow Bay Road west, past fishing boats and old warehouse buildings, for ferry services for Nevis (*round-trips Mon., Wed., Fri., and Sat.*) depart from behind the bus station. Street sellers lay out small piles of local produce along the roadside on weekdays, but the area really comes alive on Saturdays when small-scale farmers travel into Basseterre from around the island for the main market of the week.

BRIMSTONE HILL FORT & THE NORTH

A circumnavigation of northern St. Kitts makes a good day trip, with several historic sites, excellent scenery, and a choice of plantation

---

Old Georgian House

✉ Independence Sq., Basseterre

☎ 869/465-4049

Local life revolves at a gentle pace around The Circus in downtown Basseterre.

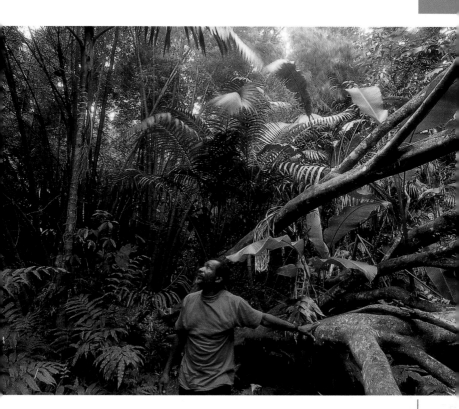

house lunch stops along the way. Take the coast road northwest from Basseterre out into the cane fields above the Caribbean coast.

South (0.25 mile/0.4 km) of the village of Challengers is **Bloody Point,** the scene of the last pitched battle between St. Kitts' European settlers and Carib Indians. At **Old Road Town,** the first permanent British settlement and island capital for a century, there are **Amerindian petroglyphs** carved into a boulder on the side road leading up to **Romney Manor.** Badly damaged by fire, the partially rebuilt 17th-century manor houses the textile workshops of Caribelle Batik.

A local guide shares his knowledge of rain forest plants and wildlife on the slopes of Mount Liamuiga.

Romney Manor
🗺 221 B2
✉ Old Road Town
☎ 869/465-6253
🕐 Closed weekends

Monkey business

The French legacy of St. Kitts extends beyond a couple of place-names, such as Basseterre and the former sugar port of Dieppe Bay Town. The poinciana tree, with its flamboyant red blooms, is named after the first French governor of the island, Philippe de Poincy. The French also introduced green vervet monkeys, which were kept as pets. An estimated 50,000 descendants of the original monkeys are now living in colonies in the mountains. They feed off insects, berries, and fruit, and during summer (when food in the forest is more limited) they make forays to pillage small-scale farms on the edge of villages, where they are considered pests. ■

Close to the site of an old Carib Indian settlement, rock carvings of male and female figures adorn a volcanic stone outcrop.

Brimstone Hill Fort
🅰 221 B2
✉ Brimstone Hill
☎ 869/465-2609
💲 $$$

At Middle Island the tomb of Sir Thomas Warner lies in the overgrown graveyard of **St. Thomas' Parish Church.** Beyond the village the hulking volcanic outcrop of **Brimstone Hill** looms above a sea of sugarcane, with views across to the Dutch Windward Islands of Sint Eustatius and Saba.

The colossal **Brimstone Hill Fort,** founded by the English in 1690, covers a 37-acre (15-ha) site 800 feet (240 m) above the coast. Built from blackened volcanic stone, the Gibraltar of the West Indies was considered impregnable until 8,000 French troops laid siege to it in 1782. It took a month of constant bombardment to destroy every building and breach the 7-foot-thick (2-m) walls, forcing the 1,000-strong garrison of defenders to surrender. The British regained control in 1794 and rebuilt the fortifications, crowned by **Fort George Citadel** (*see St. Kitts visitor information, p. 220*), which is once again bristling with cannon. Inside are Amerindian artifacts and military memorabilia.

Sports & activities

Day sails: Blue Water Safaris (*Tel 869/466-4933*) and Leeward Island Charters (*Tel 869/465-7474*) both offer trips to Nevis with snorkeling and a barbecue lunch.

Diving: Pro Divers, Frigate Bay (*Tel 869/465-3223, fax 869/465-0265*) and Turtle Beach (*Tel 869/465-9086*).

Golf: There are 18 holes of golf at the Royal St. Kitts Golf Club in Frigate Bay (*Tel 869/465-8339*).

Hiking: There are no marked trails on St. Kitts, so it's best to join a guided walk with Greg's Safaris (*Tel 869/465-4121, fax 869/465-0707*); Kriss Tours (*Tel 869/465-4042*); or Addy's Nature Tours (*Tel 869/465-8069*).

Horseback riding: Rain forest trail rides and beach canters from Trinity Stables (*Tel 869/465-3226*). ■

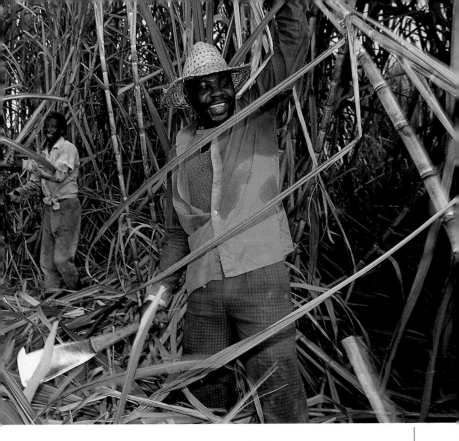

As the main road rounds the north end of the island, it runs through the village of St. Paul's and past a bumpy track leading up to the **Rawlins Plantation.**

Continuing down the east coast, make a stop at **Black Rocks.** These jagged volcanic formations were created by lava from Mount Liamuiga.

FRIGATE BAY & THE SOUTH

Just south of Basseterre lies **Frigate Bay,** St. Kitts' hotel enclave, with an 18-hole golf course and beaches on both sides of the isthmus. The broad, sandy beach on the more sheltered (southern) Caribbean coast is the island's busiest. It has a beach bar and several restaurants. On the Atlantic side of the isthmus the water is rougher, but there's good bodysurfing and the swimming is safe. Swimming isn't recommended at **North Friar's Bay,** however, which has dangerous currents, but its opposite number, South Friar's Bay, is lovely, sandwiched between palm trees and glassy calm water.

A 10-mile (15-km) highway roller coasters down to the southern tip of the island, rounding the old salt ponds where several species of wading birds can be spotted, and egrets balance on the backs of well-fed cattle grazing by the roadside.

Facing Nevis across The Narrows are the small, undeveloped beaches on **Major's Bay, Banana Bay,** and **Cockleshell Bay; Turtle Bay** is served by a lively bar-restaurant. There's a dive operator here, snorkeling off the beach, and wind surfer and ocean kayak rental. ■

Fieldworkers wielding machetes harvest sugarcane in the old-fashioned way.

Nevis

Nevis

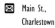 205 B2

Visitor information

✉ Main St., Charlestown

☎ 869/469-1042

DIVIDED FROM ST. KITTS BY A 2-MILE-WIDE (3-KM) channel known as The Narrows, Nevis rears up precipitously to an imposing volcanic cone. Columbus named the island Nuestra Señora de las Nieves (Our Lady of the Snows) in a rather fanciful allusion to the almost permanently cloud-capped heights of Nevis Peak (3,232 feet/985 m); his poetic name was later mangled by British settlers to less romantic but more serviceable Nevis (pronounced NEE-viss).

Colonists established a toehold on the island in 1627, and by the mid-18th century the planters of Nevis were so prosperous and fashionable that the pint-size island was hailed as the Queen of the Caribbees, renowned for its grand plantation houses, fabulous parties, and the spa in Charlestown's Bath Hotel. Nevis was not immune to the French raiding parties that targeted St. Kitts, and suffered several attacks that destroyed buildings and crops. African slaves captured from the famed and highly profitable slave market on Nevis were regarded as an additional prize and were shipped away to work the cane fields of Guadeloupe and Martinique. A century and a half after the abolition of slavery, Nevis accepted independence from Britain as part of the Federation of St. Kitts and Nevis.

A dense mantle
of rain forest
greenery cloaks
Nevis Peak,
which dominates
the interior of
the island.

Charlestown
🅜 227 B2
Visitor information
✉ Main St.
☎ 869/469-1042

Museum of Nevis
✉ Low St., Charlestown
☎ 869/469-5786
🕐 Closed Sun.
💲 $

The smaller (36 square
miles/93 sq km) and quieter part-
ner in the two-island coalition,
Nevis retains vestiges of its rich
colonial past in a clutch of gracious
plantation house hotels and the
sturdy stone buildings of the main
settlement, Charlestown.

The 9,000 Nevisians are among
the most hospitable hosts in the
Caribbean region, and the island's
unhurried pace and gentle charm
are soothing antidotes to world-
weariness. Tourism Nevis-style is
relatively upscale but determinedly
low-key. Nevis has no casinos or
air-conditioned malls, not even a
major historical site, although Lord
Nelson got married on the island,
with a future king of England in
attendance. Instead, guests at
most of the plantation hotels
have to journey to the beaches
on the Caribbean (west) coast,
work up an appetite horseback
riding or hiking in the rain forest,
and make a round-island tour that
takes all of half a day.

CHARLESTOWN

Located two-thirds of the way
down the Caribbean west coast,
Charlestown is the capital of Nevis
and the liveliest spot on the island.
Founded about 1660 and named
in honor of King Charles II in 1671,
the town straggles along the main
round-island road to its hub, a
grassy triangle that doubles as a
meeting place and minibus depot
a short walk from the pier.
Traditional two-story stone and
wood colonial buildings with balconies and gingerbread trim line
the street, and a selection of shops,
cafés, and small businesses has
moved into the alleys leading down
to the rejuvenated waterfront, where
ferries from St. Kitts unload passengers and provisions onto the dock.

At the north end of Main Street
is the **Museum of Nevis,** housed
in Alexander Hamilton House,
birthplace of the American states-
man (1757–1804) whose image
graces the $10 bill (see p. 228).
The one-room museum's modest

Nelson Museum

- ✉ Bath Rd., Charlestown
- ☎ 869/469-0408
- 🕐 Closed Sun.
- 💲 $

Botanical Garden

- ⛰ 227 B1
- ✉ Montpelier Estate, St. John's Parish
- ☎ 869/469-3680
- 💲 $$$

KIDS' STUFF

Family style attractions tend to be something of a rarity in the Caribbean, but Nevis boasts an honorable exception in the **Caribbean Cove Amusement Park** at Stoney Ground, southeast of Charlestown (*Tel 869/469-1286; Closed Mon.–Tues. mid-May–Sept., $$*). Designed with a piratical theme, the park offers bumper boats, miniature golf, a games arcade, dining, a bar, and live evening entertainment. ■

collections cover a broad spectrum of island history and culture, from Amerindian pottery sherds to independence.

An early European visitor to Nevis was Capt. John Smith and a party of 144 Englishmen. They spent six days on Nevis in 1607 en route to found the colony at Jamestown, Virginia. The group were revived by a dip in the hot spring that would later feature as the centerpiece of the **Bath Hotel** at the southern end of town. Today the hotel buildings are sadly dilapidated and partially occupied by the local police, but the steaming waters can still be seen.

Just up from the hotel is the **Nelson Museum,** which examines the life and times of the great English naval hero. Nelson married local girl Fanny Nesbit at the Montpelier Estate in 1787, during an uncomfortable posting to Antigua (see p. 211). Exhibits include a plate from the wedding feast, a portion of the Union Jack

flag under which Nelson stood when he was fatally wounded at the Battle of Trafalgar in 1805, and items from the mountain of Wedgwood, Staffordshire, and other memorabilia commissioned to commemorate his death.

AROUND THE ISLAND

Just north of Charlestown, parallel to the coast road, is **Pinney's Beach,** which unfurls in a 4-mile (6.5 km) reel of golden sand backed by palm trees. Along the way you'll pass **St. Thomas Anglican Church,** sitting on a small rise with views along the coast and across to St. Kitts. Founded in 1643, it is believed to be the oldest congregation on the island.

Farther north is **Oualie Beach,** which has good snorkeling and water sports. Beyond Newcastle Airport is the **Newcastle Pottery,** set in a small roadside workshop, where simple handmade bowls, candleholders, and jugs are fashioned from local red clay.

Alexander Hamilton

Born on Nevis on January 11, 1757, Alexander Hamilton served as aide-de-camp to Gen. George Washington during the American Revolution. He was nicknamed the Little Lion on account of his relatively diminutive stature (5 feet 7 inches/170 cm) and fero-

cious temper, which, it was said, turned his blue eyes to black when he was angry. Hamilton trained as a lawyer, and Washington appointed him the first secretary of the treasury. He died in a duel with Vice President Aaron Burr (1756–1836), his political rival, in 1804. ■

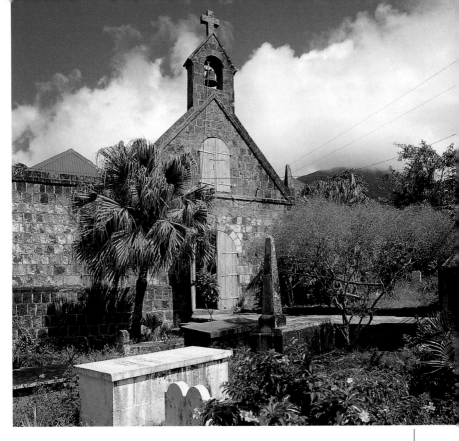

There is more reef snorkeling off the white coral sands of **Nisbet Beach** as the road circles around to the rougher Atlantic coast.

Four of Nevis' five plantation house hotels nestle beneath **Nevis Peak,** overlooking the south coast between Gingerland and Fig Tree Village. A glorious **Botanical Garden** has been established on the grounds of Montpelier Estate. The 8-acre (3-ha) site is still a work in progress, but there's plenty to interest the plant lover, from the fragrant rose and flower garden to a rain forest conservatory and the shady terraces of the orchid and palm garden. Nelson and Fanny Nesbit's marriage at Montpelier Estate is recorded in a copy of the marriage register on display at **St. John's Church** in Fig Tree, on the road back to Charlestown. ■

Sports & activities

Diving: Scuba Safaris *(Oualie Beach, Tel 869/469-9518, fax 869/469-9619).*

Golf: Excellent 18-hole Robert Trent Jones course at the Four Seasons Hotel *(Pinney's Beach, Tel 869/469-1111).*

Hiking: Gentle rambles from Eco-Tours Nevis *(Tel 869/469-2091)* or more challenging excursions, including treks to Nevis Peak, with Top to Bottom *(Tel 869/469-9080).*

Horseback riding: Nevis Equestrian Centre *(Cole Hill, Tel 469-3106);* Hermitage Inn *(St. John's Parish, Tel 869/469-3477).* ■

Visitors can still enter the church where Lord Nelson married Nevis girl Fanny Nisbet.

Montserrat

Montserrat
⚠ 205 C1

**Visitor
information**
✉ Church Rd.
☎ 869/491-2230

THE MOST SOUTHERLY OUTPOST OF THE LEEWARD ISLAND group, Montserrat was long regarded as a haven of peace and tranquility. A real slice of the old Caribbean with a smattering of beaches and hotels, it has a lush, mountainous interior that invites exploration. Today, however, the future of the island is uncertain; the peaceful idyll was shattered by the devastating eruption of the Soufrière Volcano in 1995.

The island was named by Columbus for the famous Montserrate Abbey in the mountains near Barcelona, Spain, and settled in the 17th century by Irish Catholics seeking refuge from Protestant persecution on St. Kitts. The Irish connection earned Montserrat its nickname, the Emerald Isle, and the Montserratians celebrate St. Patrick's Day as well as the Queen's birthday (the island is a British Crown Colony). Additional outbreaks of Irishness include the Irish harp design on postage stamps, and the barest trace of an Irish brogue in local speech.

Life was a gentle round of fishing, farming, and a little low-key tourism until Montserrat's quiet repose was destroyed by ominous grumblings from the Soufrière Volcano in the summer of 1995. In August a major ashfall rained down on the capital, **Plymouth;** a few days later the southern portion of the island was evacuated. By October a glowing lava dome protruded from the crater, and further evacuations saw Plymouth abandoned and a safe zone established in the northern third of the island. Although some Montserratians relocated to Britain and neighboring Antigua, most preferred to stay and brave the increased volcanic activity. **Olveston** has been named the temporary capital. Ash eruptions have been thrown 30,000 feet (9,000 m) in the air and lethal pyroclastic flows of superheated rock, mud, and gasses stream down the mountainsides. In June 1997 the dome collapsed, causing a pyroclastic flow that destroyed eight villages and killed 20 people tending their fields on the flanks of the volcano outside the safe zone.

At present, volcanologists are unable to predict an end to Montserrat's volcanic activity, and the southern portion of the island remains uninhabitable. There are few tourist facilities, and the only access is by ferry or helicopter from Antigua. ■

Volcanic origins

Geologically, Montserrat is part of the volcanic Windward Island chain poised on the brink of the Atlantic and Caribbean tectonic plates. As these grind slowly against each other, molten magma escapes from the Earth's core. These volcanic eruptions have created a chain of massive peaks. All the major Windward Islands have an active volcano, called a soufrière from the French word for sulfur. In the Grenadines a new subterranean sea mount known as Kick 'em Jenny is gradually taking shape and promises to be the youngest Caribbean island when it eventually breaks the surface. ■

The French Caribbean islands of Guadeloupe and Martinique sashay to a vibrant Creole beat, while sybaritic St.-Barthélemy lends an unmistakable aura of European chic to the laid-back tropics.

French Antilles

Traditional Creole headdress

French Antilles

TWO OF THE LARGEST ISLANDS IN THE LESSER ANTILLES (AFTER TRINIDAD), Guadeloupe and Martinique flank Dominica midway down the chain of eastern Caribbean islands. These islands are the heart of the French Caribbean, exuding a zesty Creole atmosphere that permeates every aspect of daily life from the insistent rhythms of zouk music and the rapid-fire Creole language to local cuisine and the colorful checked madras cotton tucked into complicated women's headdresses. Some 150 miles (240 km) away among the Dutch islands and former British colonies of the Leewards, the smaller French territories of St.-Barthélemy (St. Barts) and St.-Martin (half an island shared with the Netherlands, see p. 180) stick to a more traditional French lifestyle modeled on that of the *métropole,* as mainland France is known.

The islets of Les Saintes are a popular destination for day trippers

The first French colony in the Caribbean was founded on St. Kitts in 1624, the year after an English settlement was established on the island. A decade later, ambitious French colonists expanded their horizons and bravely tackled the Cannibal Isles, gaining a foothold on both **Guadeloupe** and **Martinique** between 1635 and 1636. The introduction of sugar cultivation in the latter part of the 17th century heralded *l'age d'or blanc* (the age of the white gold) and the expansion of French influence down the eastern Caribbean chain and north to St. Domingue (present-day Haiti). As slave ships unloaded their human cargo to work the vast tracts of sugarcane, sizable fortunes flowed into the planters' coffers, and the town of St. Pierre on Martinique developed into one of the most prosperous and fashionable cities in the West Indies.

Things did not always run smoothly, of course. Britain challenged France's authority at every turn and by a combination of treaties and brute force occupied virtually every French Caribbean territory during the 18th century. France did her best to return the compliment.

Ironically the supporters of the ancien régime of Martinique actually called the enemy in to assist when the French Revolution decreed the abolition of slavery. The British ruled the island for 20 years without liberating the slaves. Napoleon (whose wife came from a family of Martiniquan planters) reintroduced slavery in 1802, causing widespread chaos and slave rebellions in Haiti and Guadeloupe. The law was not repealed until 1848, when the plantations turned to East Indian indentured laborers to replace the freed slaves.

Unlike the British islands, which were gently but firmly urged down the road to independence in the 20th century, France has bound her Caribbean territories more closely. Guadeloupe and Martinique have been integrated into the republic's political mainstream as semiautonomous overseas *régions*. The islanders have the same rights as their mainland counterparts and elect representatives to the Assemblée Nationale in Paris, vote in French elections, and enjoy the benefits of substantial government subsidies that have elevated local standards of living way above average for the region.

Dramatic volcanic eruptions raised Guadeloupe and Martinique from the seabed, and both islands boast beautiful mountain ranges choked with rain forest greenery and encircled by cane fields and banana plantations. There are well-developed resorts on sandy beaches and upcountry hideaways, frenetic port cities and picturesque fishing harbors, where the catch of the day is flipped straight off the dock

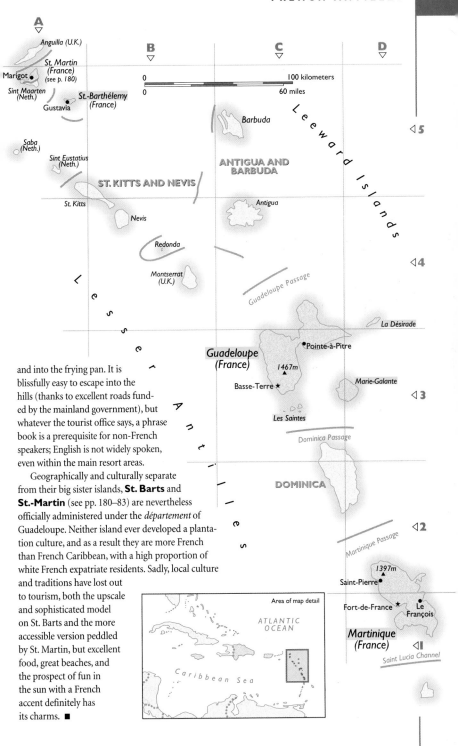

A
▽

Anguilla (U.K.)

St. Martin
(France)
(see p.180)

Marigot ●

Sint Maarten
(Neth.)

St.-Barthélemy
(France)

Gustavia ●

Saba
(Neth.)

Sint Eustatius
(Neth.)

B
▽

0 _____ 100 kilometers

0 _____ 60 miles

C
▽

Barbuda

ANTIGUA AND
BARBUDA

D
▽

Leeward Islands

◁5

ST. KITTS AND NEVIS

St. Kitts

Nevis

Antigua

Redonda

Montserrat
(U.K.)

Guadeloupe Passage

La Désirade

◁4

Guadeloupe
(France)

1467m ▲

Basse-Terre ★

Les Saintes

●Pointe-à-Pitre

Marie-Galante

◁3

Dominica Passage

and into the frying pan. It is
blissfully easy to escape into the
hills (thanks to excellent roads funded by the mainland government), but
whatever the tourist office says, a phrase
book is a prerequisite for non-French
speakers; English is not widely spoken,
even within the main resort areas.

Geographically and culturally separate
from their big sister islands, **St. Barts** and
St.-Martin (see pp. 180–83) are nevertheless
officially administered under the *département* of
Guadeloupe. Neither island ever developed a plantation culture, and as a result they are more French
than French Caribbean, with a high proportion of
white French expatriate residents. Sadly, local culture
and traditions have lost out
to tourism, both the upscale
and sophisticated model
on St. Barts and the more
accessible version peddled
by St. Martin, but excellent
food, great beaches, and
the prospect of fun in
the sun with a French
accent definitely has
its charms. ■

DOMINICA

Lesser Antilles

Martinique Passage

◁2

1397m ▲

Saint-Pierre ●

Fort-de-France ★

Le
François

Martinique
(France)

Saint Lucia Channel

◁1

Area of map detail

ATLANTIC
OCEAN

Caribbean Sea

Guadeloupe

SHAPED LIKE A GIANT BUTTERFLY WITH MISMATCHED wings, Guadeloupe is in fact two separate islands crowded together by seismic upheavals and linked by a bridge over the Rivière Salée (Salt River). The western wing is Basse-Terre, its verdant and volcanic peaks marching south to the crater rim of smoldering Soufrière (4,815 feet/1,467 m). By contrast, the eastern wing of Grande-Terre is a rolling, dry limestone plateau fringed by beaches and coral reefs. Making up the Guadeloupean archipelago offshore are the islands of La Désirade, Marie-Galante, and the eight tiny islets of Les Saintes. Guadeloupe is an inviting mixture of urban buzz and unspoiled scenery, suffused with an unmistakable Creole flavor.

Guadeloupe

🗺 233 C3

Visitor information

✉ Place de la Victoire, Pointe-à-Pitre

☎ 590/82 09 30, fax 590/83 89 22

Perhaps inspired by the dozens of streams and waterfalls that tumble down Basse-Terre's rain-forested flanks, the Carib people called the island Karukera (Island of Beautiful Waters). Christopher Columbus sailed past in 1493 and rechristened it Santa Maria de Guadalupe de Extremadura in honor of a famous Spanish monastery. A century and a half later the French colonized Guadeloupe with indentured settlers who worked for three years to pay off their sea passage. Unaccustomed to tropical conditions, they farmed with limited

success until a four-year British occupation (1759–1763) turned the plantations around. The slow start meant Guadeloupe was administered from more successful Martinique and was forced to trade through the commercial port of St. Pierre on Martinique, whose merchants paid artificially low prices for Guadeloupean sugar. As news of the French Revolution traveled across the Atlantic in 1789, it found the unhappy Guadeloupeans ripe for change.

Guadeloupe's settlers embraced the revolutionary regime with enthusiasm. Bands of armed *patri-otes* (supporters of the revolution) overthrew the planters and installed a revolutionary government led by Victor Hugues (1770–1826). They erected the mandatory guillotine in Pointe-à-Pitre, where more than 300 enemies of the revolution lost their heads, and the slaves were freed in 1794. But their freedom was short-lived. The old regime regained control, and slavery was bloodily reestablished; many former slaves preferred death to submission. The British came and went a couple more times before France secured the colony for good in 1815. The Guadeloupeans' independent cast of mind remains a force to be reckoned with today. There are occasional calls for inde-pendence from *la métropole*, but French cash is a powerful incentive to remain under the old colonial umbrella, particularly in view of the massive grants made available to help the island rebuild in the wake of Hurricane Hugo in 1989.

Guadeloupe encompasses 530 square miles (1,372 sq km) and has a population of about 408,000. The contrasting island wings possess two equally diverse main cities. On the southwest coast of Basse-Terre is Basse-Terre town (see p. 242), the modest administrative capital tucked in the lee of La Soufrière. A circlet of small towns and villages, linked by a round-island road, ring the coast of Guadeloupe's west wing. Only one route, La Traversée, scales the central mountain range, clambering up into the Parc National de la Guadeloupe (see p. 243), a magnificent natural preserve with some of the best—and most challenging—hiking in the Caribbean.

In the southwest corner of Grande-Terre is Guadeloupe's biggest and busiest city—the sprawling commercial center and cruise ship port of Pointe-à-Pitre (see below). No great beauty, it has a frenetic pace at odds with the usual leisurely Caribbean tempo, but it's fun to explore the local markets, and ferries for the offshore islands leave from the waterfront. Dotted east along the coast from Pointe-à-Pitre are the seaside resort towns of **Gosier, Ste.-Anne,** and **St. -François.** Gosier is the most developed, with a wall of large, modern hotels fronting the shore and packed beaches. Ste.-Anne and St.-François have retained more of their local character. Here it is sometimes possible to catch a game of *boules* in progress on one of the dusty, tree-shaded squares before dining out stylishly *à la française* at an excellent (although not inexpensive) fish restaurant along the promenade.

Pointe-à-Pitre
235 B2

POINTE-À-PITRE

A teeming metropolis of 80,000 souls, Pointe-à-Pitre lies on a sheltered bay at the southern end of the Rivière Salée. Although the city dates from the 17th century, hurricanes, earthquakes, and fires have taken their toll, and modern concrete structures outnumber the few remaining colonial buildings.

With the sunlight blotted out by tall, thin buildings, downtown Pointe-à-Pitre is a maelstrom of traffic and pedestrians fighting for space on the narrow streets. At times it appears that there are more cars on the sidewalk than pedestrians, and jaywalking is obligatory. (Avoid driving in the downtown area at all costs.)

The focus of the old town in **La Darse** is the bustling waterfront area, with its ferry dock and jumble of street vendors' stalls selling anything from T-shirts and wood carvings to fresh produce and piping hot *accras* (see p. 238). Behind the dockside hubbub is **Place de la Victoire,** with its fringe of old colonial houses, their balconies full of flowers. A handful of sidewalk cafés provides a restful view of the city's green heart, planted with palm, mango, and African tulip trees.

Plunge into the grid of busy side streets west of the gardens to the **Cathédrale St.-Pierre et St.-Paul** (place Gourbeyre). Nicknamed *la cathédrale de fer* ("iron cathedral") for its elaborate

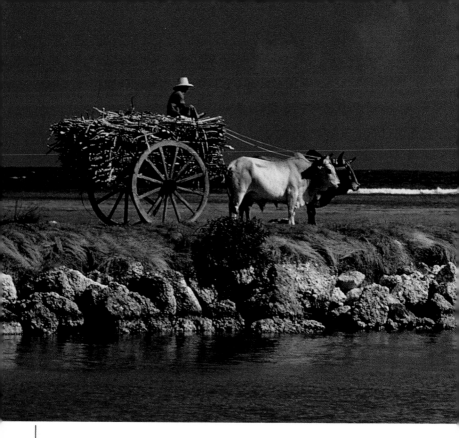

On rural Grande-Terre, a local farmer and his oxen pause to contemplate the antics of water-sport enthusiasts.

Creole cuisine & dining out

The Creole cuisine of Guadeloupe and Martinique is an inspired fusion of French culinary *élan*, traditional African cooking, and local Caribbean ingredients. Seafood is a mainstay of Creole menus and comes in a wide variety of guises, from simple *accras* (shredded salt-cod fritters) to *blaff* (a fish or shellfish stew cooked in a wine and herb court bouillon). Other specialties include *cirique* or *étrille* (little sea crabs), *chatrou* (octopus), *lambi* (conch tenderized with lime for salads), *langouste* (lobster), *ouassous* (crayfish), and *soudrons* (clams). *Crabes farcis* are stuffed land crabs, more meaty than sea crabs, and the locals are known to feed them with dried coconut and hot peppers to improve their flavor. Try *colombo*, a curried stew of chicken or goat *(cabri)* flavored with coriander, cumin, mustard, ginger, and pepper. Other accompaniments are *fruit à pain*, the rather tasteless fruit of the breadfruit tree, and *christophene*, a tropical squash served cooked or grated raw in salads.

Dining out can be expensive, but Creole food is generally cheaper than French. Limited-choice menus, at a fixed price *(menu touristique),* are usually good value, and service is included *(compris)*. It is de rigueur to round off a meal with a *digestif* from among the dozens of locally produced aged or fruit-flavored rums. ■

ironwork, the building was constructed in the early 19th century and has some fine stained glass.

Rue Frébault, the city's main shopping street, is lined with boutiques and stores full of French fashions and European imports. On the corner of Frébault and rue Peynier is the **Marché Couvert** (Covered Market), providing a boisterous slice of island life. Its maze of stalls is piled high with fruits and vegetables, bags of ground spices, and bunches of vanilla pods presided over by garrulous female vendors who giggle and haggle in a machine-gun patter of incomprehensible Creole.

West along rue Peynier is the **Musée Schoelcher,** devoted to the life and times of 19th-century abolitionist Victor Schoelcher (1804–1893), a leading light in the French antislavery movement. When emancipation finally reached the French Caribbean in 1848, Schoelcher was elected a deputy of Guadeloupe. The museum occupies a pretty pink town house with wrought iron decorations and a double staircase leading up to the entrance. Exhibits range from plantation-era artifacts and Schoelcher's campaigning pamphlets to African carved ivories, model ships, and other curios. The statue in front of the building depicts the revolutionary leader Victor Hugues.

AROUND GRANDE-TERRE
Though Grande-Terre's southern beaches act as a magnet for tourists, most of the island is undeveloped, a rural backwater where rolling limestone hills, known as Les Grands Fonds, shelter a smattering of small

Shoppers haggle and adopt a distinctly hands-on approach when selecting fresh local produce at street markets.

Musée Schoelcher
✉ 24 rue Peynier
☎ 590/82 08 04
🕐 Closed Sun.
💲 $

Aquarium de la Guadeloupe
- 235 B2
- Place Créole-Marina
- 590/90 92 38
- $$$

Fort Fleur d'Epée
- 235 B2
- 590/90 94 61

Gosier
- 235 C2
Visitor information
- 5 Square de la Banque, Pointe-à-Pitre
- 590/82-09-30

Distillerie Bellevue
- 235 C2
- D101 (On the road from Moule to Les Abymes)
- 590/23 47 10

farming hamlets, and the sugarcane harvest is still transported to the mill by ox-drawn carts.

Between Pointe-à-Pitre and Gosier is **Bas-du-Fort's** busy marina, which is a good place to stop off and sample the nautical atmosphere from a sunny café or to dine out in restaurants. Next to the marina is the **Aquarium de la Guadeloupe,** the biggest in the Caribbean. A showcase for tropical fish, it also has a mangrove section and a huge shark tank with a walk-through plexiglass tunnel.

On a headland above Bas-du-Fort are the 18th-century coral rock ruins of **Fort Fleur d'Epée,** laid out on a hilltop site shaded by red-flowering flamboyant trees.

Across Grande Baie is the seaside town of **Gosier,** Guadeloupe's chief resort, taking its name from the brown pelican, a familiar sight throughout the Caribbean. The old town has been swamped by an avalanche of hotels, restaurants, cafés, and discos spilling downhill to the shore and stretching for several miles along the narrow sandy beaches. Hotels and concessions are well equipped for water sports, and small boats make the short voyage

out to the tiny offshore pimple of **Îlet du Gosier,** where there's a lighthouse and another public beach (clothing optional).

Midway along the coast is **Ste.-Anne,** where long, sandy Caravelle beach offers water-sport activities and a Club Med resort to the west of town. Nearby is **Ste.-Anne Plage,** a lovely strip of fine white sand on a turquoise bay. It can get crowded, but plus points for families include shady trees, a row of café-restaurants across the street, and carts selling hot, sweet crêpes, and ice cream.

St.-François has a salty tang, with fishermen constructing traditional hexagonal fish traps from wooden battens and chicken wire on the waterfront. The closest beach is **Plage des Raisins Clair,** but to the east of town is the 7-mile (11-km) road out to Pointe des Châteaux, lined with beaches along the southern shore. **Plage Tarare,** on the north side, is a nudist haunt. At the tip of the headland is **Pointe des Châteaux,** with its own small beach cove where surfers ride the powerful Atlantic waves that have hollowed caves from the soft limestone. A rocky path scales the cliffs

Sports & activities

Bicycling (cyclisme): Cycling is a hugely popular weekend sport when Guadeloupeans take to Basse-Terre's mountainous hinterland in a blur of Lycra. Grande-Terre offers gentler cycling. Rentals from Easy Location (Tel 590/24 21 54).

Diving & snorkeling (plongée sous-marine & plongée avec tuba): Best off Basse-Terre's west coast; also around Îlet du Gosier. Contact Les Heures Saines (plage de Malendure, Tel 590/98 86 63, fax 590/98 77 76);

Aquafari (Gosier, Tel 590/84 51 57).

Golf: Golf de St. François (Tel 590/88 41 87), Guadeloupe's only 18-hole course, designed by Robert Trent Jones.

Hiking (randonnée): See p. 243.

Horseback riding (équitation): Le Martingale (Grande-Terre, Tel 590/26 28 39); La Manade, St. Claude (Basse-Terre, Tel 590/81 13 85). ∎

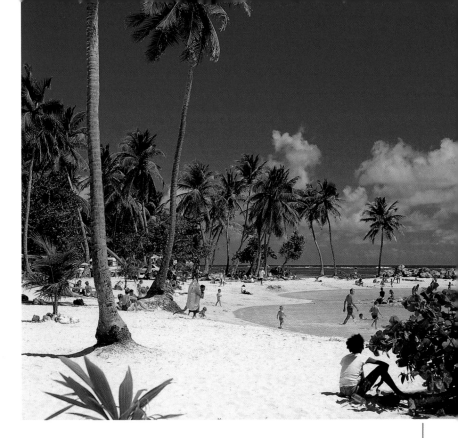

to an orientation table with blustery views to the out islands and peaks of Basse-Terre.

From St. François, Rte. N5 runs north to **Moule,** once the capital of Guadeloupe. On a back road west of town is the **Distillerie Bellevue** (open for visits), the only rum distillery on Grande-Terre.

A country road continues up to the northern tip of the island, past a viewpoint at **Porte d'Enfer** (Gate of Hell), before reaching **Pointe de la Grande Vigie** (Grand Lookout), where French sentries once scanned the horizon for signs of British activity on Antigua.

Beach stops on the west coast include **Anse Laborde** (just north of Anse-Bertrand) and **Anse du Souffleur** (at Port-Louis). In the center of the island is **Morne-à-l'Eau,** famous for its classic French Caribbean cemetery. ■

Families flock to the shallow sheltered bay fronting Ste.-Anne.

Nature preserved

On the west coast of Grande-Terre is the **Réserve Naturelle du Grand Cul de Sac Marin,** an annex of the Guadeloupe national park. Its 9,000-acre (3,600 ha) territory encompasses mangrove swamps, coastal forest, and an adjacent marine preserve. The foreshore is a prime feeding ground for waterfowl and wading birds, and the Aquarium de la Guadeloupe offers glass-bottomed boat trips to the marine preserve *(Tel 590/90 77 17).* ■

Around southern Basse-Terre

Basse-Terre
🅰 235 B1
Visitor Information
✉ Maison du Port,
off blvd. du Général
de Gaulle
☎ 590/81 24 83

Rhumerie Longueteau
🅰 235 B2
☎ 590/86 46 39
🕐 Closed Sun.

Plantation Grand Café
🅰 235 B2
☎ 590/86 33 06
🕐 Closed Sun. year-round & Sat. May–Oct.
💲 $$$

VIEWED FROM THE SUNNY BEACHES OF GRANDE-TERRE, the towering, luxuriantly green bulk of neighboring Basse-Terre appears to brood like some giant leviathan beneath a blanket of clouds. About two-thirds of the island is the unspoiled Parc National de la Guadeloupe with *traces* (walking trails) ranging from short, muddy scrabbles to waterfall beauty spots to serious long-distance hikes across the ridgeline or up to the Soufrière volcano. A fast modern road (Rte. N1) whisks you down the east coast from Pointe-à-Pitre to the capital of Basse-Terre in less than an hour, although there are several minor detours en route.

Just south of **Ste.-Marie,** a small coastal town where Christopher Columbus is thought to have come ashore and encountered his first Carib in 1493, there are signs off the main road to the **Rhumerie Longueteau** distillery and **Plantation Grand Café,** a banana plantation. Cane fields march right up to the palm-shaded lawn of the modern Longueteau estate house and its tiny, old-fashioned steam mill, which lurks in a corrugated iron shelter full of heat and noise and the rich, sticky scent of molasses. Informal tours operate year-round, but the mill is only working (and interesting) during the January-to-July harvest season. After the visit, you can sample straight rums and potent homemade rums spiked with guava, pineapple, carambola, or banana flavorings.

Just up the road is the Plantation Grand Café, which celebrates the not-so-humble banana. A banana garden displays different varieties from around the world—little plump pink velutinas from India, crocodile's fingers from Indonesia. The 30-minute tours rattle around the plantation in open-sided trucks.

On the southern edge of the town of Capesterre-Belle-Eau a side road leads up to the trailhead for the third and least spectacular of the **Chutes du Carbet,** a series of three waterfalls in the national park (see p. 243) fed by the Rivière Grand Carbe, which originates on La Soufrière. The third fall is a mere 65 feet (20 m) high, but it's a peaceful 45-minute trek into the rain forest beneath giant mahogany, gommier, and bois rouge trees. Although the path continues on to the two upper falls, the most popular access point is another side road about a mile (1.5 km) farther along Rte. N1, which takes a scenic route up to a parking area and collection of roadside barbecue stalls. It's a 20-minute uphill hike to the popular 360-foot-high (110-m) second fall. It takes two hours to reach the 410-foot-high (125-m) top fall and three hours to get up to **Soufrière.**

At the southern tip of the island is **Basse-Terre** town, which offers little to detain the dedicated sight-seer, although it has a bustling provincial charm. Across the street from its French-style, palm-lined seafront esplanade, stalls are weighed down by succulent mangoes and pineapples, and teetering pyramids of fresh vegetables tumble out of the covered market. A tight grid of shopping streets squeezes in

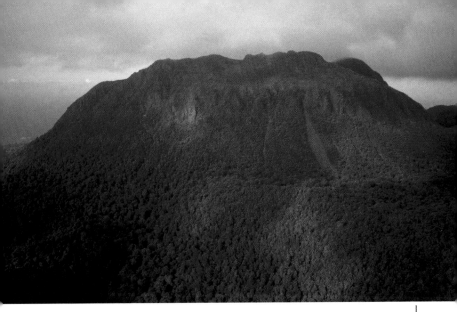

between the Hôtel de Ville and the gray stone Catholic cathedral. To the south, **Fort Delgrès** stands guard over the harbor and houses a small history museum. Behind the city center are residential suburbs spreading up the hillsides to St.-Claude, where a few old Creole houses cling doggedly to slopes hedged in by exuberant gardens.

Above St.-Claude, Rte. D11 strikes on up through the encroaching rain forest to the **Maison du Volcan,** a small museum that charts the origins of volcanoes and the history of Soufrière. The narrow road grinds on up to **Savane à Mulets,** 1,000 feet (305 m) below the volcano's summit. From here the round-trip hike to the summit takes around two and a half hours along a well-marked trail past lava flows, boulders, and sludge deposited as recently as 1976, when Soufrière last erupted. The climb is generally accompanied by a steady drizzle and cool winds, so bring appropriate clothing. At the summit, not one crater but a chain of reeking, sulfur-spewing pits are staggered along the fault line, and heat radiates from the ground.

To complete a tour of southern Basse-Terre, the slow west coast road (Rte. N2) parallels the shore to **Mahaut,** where the Route de la Traversée (see p. 244) crosses back to the east coast for Pointe-à-Pitre. If you're in a hurry, however, it's quicker to return along the east coast. ■

Soufrière volcano dominates the southern half of Basse-Terre.

Fort Delgrès
235 B1
590/81 24 83

Maison du Volcan
235 B2

Parc National de la Guadeloupe

For additional information about the national park in Guadeloupe, contact the park headquarters at Habitation Beausoleil *(Montéran, 97120 St.-Claude, Tel 590/80 24 25, fax 590/80 05 46).* The main access points to the park's trail network in Basse-Terre are along the Route de la Traversée (see p. 244) and around Soufrière. Guided hikes (some in English) can be arranged through the Bureau des Guides de Moyenne Montagne *(Tel 590/81 24 83)* and Les Amis du Parc National *(Tel 590/81 45 53).* ■

A drive around northern Basse-Terre

This clockwise circuit of northern Basse-Terre begins with a spectacular rain forest drive along the Route de la Traversée before looping around the top half of the island. You can experience a variety of suggested diversions along the way, from a glass-bottomed boat trip to museums of cocoa and rum.

From **Pointe-à-Pitre** ❶ (see p. 236) follow signs for Basse-Terre west across the Rivière Salée, and south on the fast Rte. N1 to the exit for La Traversée (Rte. D23). The cross-island road skims west through the cane fields before ascending into the rain forest, where it enters the Parc National de la Guadeloupe (see p. 243).

Just inside the park boundaries is the pretty **Cascade aux Écrevisses** (Crayfish Falls) ❷, a popular picnic spot at the foot of a pretty waterfall edged by dripping mosses and creepers. Beneath the forest canopy it's hard to resist scrambling around on the boulders that litter the stream like giant stepping-stones.

Just over a mile (1.5 km) on is the **Maison de la Forêt,** which provides an excellent introduction to the 74,000-acre (29,950-ha) park with exhibits covering geology, flora, and fauna (unfortunately only in French). Hiking maps are available giving details of the well-maintained, 190-mile (306-km) trail network within the park, and there are several round-trip walks from the maison.

One of the park's more challenging hikes is the **Trace des Crêtes,** which follows the mountain ridge above the west coast and crosses La Traversée at the **Col des Mamelles** ❸ (1,922 feet/586 m), a mountain pass between twin volcanic peaks. This is the highest point on the road, with fantastic views of the park on a clear day, although the vista is frequently obscured by cloud and rain (the annual rainfall here is about 250 inches/6,350 mm).

After the hairpin descent to the coast at **Mahaut,** there's an optional short (3 miles/5 km) detour south to **Plage de Malendure** ❹, where glass-bottomed boat trips depart for the marine preserve surrounding the tiny Îlet de Pigeon. The **Reserve du Commandant Cousteau** honors one of its

early champions, oceanographer Jacques Cousteau (1910–1997), who helped introduce a fishing ban and named Pigeon Island one of the world's top ten dive sites (some considerable time ago). The coral reef site is rather crowded with divers and pleasure boats these days, but the excellent visibility (averaging 100 feet/30 m) ensures there's always something interesting to see.

1.5 miles (2.5 km) north of Mahaut on

Ginger plant

Rain forest waterfall

Rte. N2 is **Maison du Cacao** *(Tel 590/98 25 23)*, which delves into the history, cultivation, and manufacture of cocoa, introduced to Guadeloupe by Arawak Indians. The French went mad about the stuff in the 18th century, and drinking hot chocolate became a national obsession. Blocks of 100 percent natural cocoa are on sale.

It's worth stopping at **Maison du Bois** *(Tel 590/82 09 30)*, a few minutes' drive up the coast. The House of Wood has built up an impressive collection of antique wooden tools and utensils. Among the coffee grinders, cassava root crushers, wicker lobster pots, and hand whisks is a crafty machine for deseeding cotton flowers, as well as displays depicting boatbuilding and furniture-making.

The drive continues past the attractive fishing village of **Deshaies** and the broad bay at **Grande Anse,** graced by one of Guadeloupe's finest beaches. The 2-mile-long (3-km) sweep of rosy gold sand is backed by palm trees, and

there's a choice of snack bars or a Creole restaurant, Le Karacoli (see p. 377), which makes an inviting lunch break.

The road (Rte. N2) rounds the tip of the island and continues on to **Ste.-Rose;** follow signs for the **Musée du Rhum** *(Tel 590/28 70 04, closed Sun.)* at nearby Bellevue. Exhaustive signboards and displays examine every last detail of three centuries of rum-making in the Caribbean along with such antique artifacts as an enormous cane juice vat hewn out of a single tree trunk. The interesting insect gallery displays some 5,000 butterflies, beetles, and bugs from around the world. After watching a short film (some showings in English), take a tour of the **Distillerie Reimonenq** *(Tel 590/82 09 30)*.

Back on the main road (Rte. N2), it's a swift run back to Pointe-à-Pitre. ■

- See area map page 235
- Pointe-à-Pitre
- 58 miles/88 km
- A full day with stops
- Pointe-à-Pitre

NOT TO BE MISSED
- Col des Mamelles
- Maison du Cacao
- Musée du Rhum

Place de la Victoire, Pointe-à-Pitre

Terre-de-Haut (foreground) and the neighboring islands of Les Saintes group

The Guadeloupean Archipelago

LA DÉSIRADE

An arid, flat-topped table mountain 6 miles (10 km) off Pointe des Châteaux (the eastern tip of Guadeloupe), La Désirade was the first landfall sighted by Christopher Columbus on his second voyage to the New World in 1493. Only 8 miles (13 km) long and one mile (1.5 km) wide, the island has a population of 1,600 mainly white inhabitants, several hundred sheep, and thousands of iguanas. The islanders lead a simple life farming or fishing.

The main settlement is **Grande-Anse** (*Visitor information, Ave. de L'Europe 97118, St.-François, Tel 590/88 48 74)* on the sheltered southern shore; farther up the coast, past the golden sands of Grande-Anse and **Le Souffleur,** you can see the ruins of an old leper colony at **Baie-Mahault.**

Daily ferry services (*Tel 590/88 48 63)* depart from St.-François in Guadeloupe (one hour); you can also take scheduled flights (15 minutes). Bicycle rentals and island tours are available through Location 2000 (*Tel 590/20 03 74)*. There are a few basic lodgings on the island, and locals offer B&Bs.

🅰 235 D1

MARIE-GALANTE

Twenty miles (32 km) south of Grande-Terre is the flat limestone island of Marie-Galante, which was named for Columbus's flagship the *Santa Maria de Galante.* Shaped like a beech leaf, Marie-Galante was settled in 1648 and once carpeted with sugarcane. Dozens of old windmills dot the remaining cane fields that are still harvested to produce the island's famous rums.

Grand-Bourg (*Visitor information, Grand Bourg, Tel 590/97 56 51)* is Marie-Galante's main settlement. South of town is the 18th-century **Château Murat** (*see Grand-Bourg visitor information)* plantation house, which has a windmill and a museum illustrating local customs. Along the bottom of the island awaits good swimming at **Petite Anse,** and plantation island with a couple of good beaches, one hotel, and rooms to rent. **Terre-de-Haut,** on the other hand, greets the daily invasion of day-trippers with equanimity and helps lighten their wallets in the welcoming restaurants and boutiques of **Le Bourg.** A fishing port, Le Bourg is set on a magnificent bay sheltered by the **Îlet à Cabrit** (Goat Island). Nowhere on the island is more than a 30-minute walk from Le Bourg, although it's a stiff uphill climb to **Fort Napoléon** *(Tel 590/97 56 51, closed p.m.).* The fortress houses a museum of local history, with a section devoted to the Battle of the Saints (see below).

Terre-de-Haut's best beach is the **Plage Pont Pierre,** in the east. Two quieter beaches are **Petite Anse Pain de Sucre,** west of Le Bourg, and **Anse du Figuier,** on the south coast (clothing optional).

Daily ferry services *(Tel 590/83 12 45 or 590/90 04 48)* run to Terre-de-Haut and Terre-de-Bas from Pointe-à-Pitre (one hour) and Trois-Rivières (30 minutes). There are also daily sailings between Le Bourg and Terre-de-Bas, and flights from Guadeloupe. Scooters and bicycles can be rented in Le Bourg. ■

▲ 235 B1

water sports at **Pointe de la Feuillère,** near Capesterre. Inland, a maze of country lanes burrows through tunnels of sugarcane; several rum distilleries offer tours and tastings. Another tourist stop is the **Trou à Diable** (Devil's Hole), an underground cavern that requires a flashlight and sturdy footwear to explore.

Fine beaches run the length of the northwest coast between **Vieux Fort** and the fishing village of **St.-Louis.** Daily ferry services *(Tel 590/83 12 45 or 590/90 04 48)* to Grand-Bourg and St.-Louis leave from Pointe-à-Pitre (one hour); scheduled flights are available (15 minutes). Cars and scooters are rented from Magauto *(Grand-Bourg, Tel 590/97 34 49).* For hotel information contact the tourist office *(Tel 590/97 77 48).*

▲ 235 C1

LES SAINTES

A cluster of tiny islands 7 miles (11 km) south of Basse-Terre, Les Saintes were supposedly named for All Saints' Day (November 1) by Columbus. Only two of the jagged volcanic islets are inhabited. The quieter and less visited is **Terre-de-Bas,** a sleepy former

The Battle of the Saints

One of the most famous naval battles of the 18th century, the Battle of the Saints was the decisive factor in determining British supremacy in the Caribbean. In the spring of 1782, the French fleet was in Martinique, readying itself for an invasion of Jamaica calculated to destroy British credibility in the region. The preparations were being monitored by Adm. George Rodney (1718–1792) of the Royal Navy from his base on Pigeon Island, St. Lucia. On April 7, under Admiral de Grasse, 33 French ships of the line set sail; Rodney gave chase, meeting the French off Les Saintes on the morning of April 12. In a surprise maneuver, which owed more to the weather conditions than design, Rodney broke the French line in not one but three places and carried the day. The tactic was later used by Admiral Nelson at the Battle of Trafalgar. ■

Slavery

Sugar and slavery, the twin bastions of the West Indian colonial era, arrived in the New World with Columbus. Spanish conquistadores created the first Caribbean slaves when they put the native Amerindians to work on the plantations of Hispaniola (in the present-day Dominican Republic) and gold mines of South America. It took less than 20 years to decimate the indigenous population through disease and ill-treatment, prompting the Spanish to import African slaves to Hispaniola as early as 1511. (See pp. 308–309.)

The triangular trade

Portuguese merchants introduced the first African slaves to Europe in the 1450s, as exotic ornaments for the court. Domestic slavery of captured enemies was accepted practice among the tribes of the West African coast, and local traders were keen to exchange slaves for European manufactured goods such as textiles, glass, and weapons. The colonization of South America added a new dimension to this modest two-way traffic, bringing a steady trickle of African slaves across the Atlantic during the 16th century.

At first the British and French West Indian colonies relied on European laborers, but a combination of unaccustomed heat and tropical diseases killed as many as three out of four white settlers within two years of their arrival. When the sugar boom in the mid-1700s unleashed an urgent requirement for plentiful, cheap labor better prepared for the climate and backbreaking plantation work, the "triangular trade" was born. Ships from Europe headed to Africa where manufactured goods paid for African slaves. The slaves then embarked on the infamous Middle Passage to the New World, where the living cargo was exchanged for raw materials such as sugar, tobacco, cotton, and rum bound for Europe.

The Middle Passage

For the terrified slaves destined for the New World, their ordeal often began months ahead of transportation. Slavers selected their cargo from the vast barracoons (slave forts) that dotted the West African coast from Cape Verde to the Bight of Biafra, journeying from port to port until their vessels were filled to capacity. In preparation for the five- to eight-week voyage, food and water were taken on board and the cargo holds were subdivided into "slave decks," wooden shelves often no more than 2.5 feet (0.75 m) apart, where the slaves were packed in lying flat, the males shackled together left leg to right leg and wrist to wrist. Sickness, disease, and despair were rampant on the slave ships: One in eight slaves died on the Middle Passage. The survivors were oiled up to make them look healthier and auctioned off to the highest bidder in the slave markets of Curaçao, Martinique, Nevis, and Sint Eustatius, or on the wharf where the ship came into land.

It has been estimated that more than four million African slaves survived the journey to the West Indian colonies. British slave traders

Working patterns

West Indian planters devised two basic work regimes, the harshest of which was the "gang system" preferred on sugar estates. Slaves were divided into groups according to their strength, with the strongest first gang allocated the hardest manual tasks. Youths and old people in the second gang undertook lighter work, and the children in the third gang weeded and tidied. The gangs worked 10–12 hours a day, six days a week, and up to 18 hours during the harvest. The more liberal "task system" adopted on smaller farms and by slaves working as skilled craftsmen involved specific tasks that had to be completed in a given time. Slaves were then free to work their vegetable plots or undertake other jobs. ∎

alone imported 2.5 million live slaves between 1690–1807, and the French added at least another million. By the 1750s, black slaves already represented 90 percent of the population on sugar-growing islands, though the proportion was much lower in the Bahamas, Cayman Islands, and Netherlands Antilles where plantations were impractical. The dramatic imbalance between black and white meant the planters lived in constant fear of slave rebellions and ruled their private fiefdoms with a rod of iron. Ferocious slave drivers, armed with whips, disciplined the slave gangs in the fields and savage penalties were meted out for acts of disobedience or theft.

Opposite: A slave auction, from The Negro's Complaint **(1826) by A. Opie**
Top: The crossing, c. 1840
Above: A sugar estate in Antigua, as depicted in 1823 by William Clark

Rebellion & emancipation

Despite the planters' best efforts to suppress their workforce, there were slave rebellions throughout the colonies in the 18th century. Most lasted no more than a couple of weeks or months before being ruthlessly crushed, though a successful revolt in the French colony of St. Domingue led to the creation of the black Republic of Haiti in 1804. In the 1780s, European intellectuals who long opposed slavery on moral grounds were joined by churchmen and the combined pressure of forceful pamphleteering campaigns and sermons caused widespread antislavery sentiment. The British outlawed the slave trade to their colonies in 1808, and decreed the abolition of slavery in 1834. Sweden (1846), France and Denmark (1848), and Holland (1863) followed suit, while the Spanish held out until 1873 in Puerto Rico. ■

During the winter season, Gustavia harbor showcases the dizzy heights of luxurious yachting.

St.-Barthélemy

KNOWN AS MANHATTAN-SUR-MER TO THE COGNOSCENTI, St.-Barthélemy is the epitome of French Caribbean chic and arguably the most exclusive and expensive speck of volcanic rock in the region, give or take a private island or two. This is the winter playground of the super-rich and super-casual, where the shops overflow with Chanel and champagne, but dressing for dinner is frowned upon.

St.-Barthélemy

233 A5

Visitor information

Quai du Général de Gaulle, Gustavia

590/27 87 27, fax 590/27 74 47, www.st-barths.com

One of the first things to strike visitors to St. Barts (or Saint-Barth in French) is the paucity of black faces; almost all 6,000 permanent inhabitants are white, affluent, and of French descent. French culture defines every detail, from the humble baguette to the rarefied heights of gourmet cuisine, from designer labels to traditional *calèche* bonnets, the old-fashioned women's sun hats (now rarely seen except on high days and holidays) that recall St. Barts' pioneering colonists from Normandy and Brittany.

St. Barts was not born with a silver spoon in its mouth. The 8-square-mile (21-sq-km) island was named San Bartolomé for Columbus's brother and colonized by 60 French settlers from St. Kitts in 1648. The first colony was wiped out by a Carib raiding party, but the strategic position of St. Barts amid the English Leeward Island colonies prompted a second attempt by Protestant Huguenots in 1674. While other islands planted cotton and cane, St. Barts' stock in trade was piracy. Buccaneers frequently took refuge in its convenient coves. In 1784 French King Louis XVI exchanged St. Barts for trading rights in the Baltic, and the island became Swedish for a century. The Swedes declared their sole Caribbean possession a free port, and for a while it profited handsomely, trading with the newly independent United States. When business tailed off, the island was sold back to France in 1878, and subsided into obscurity until quietly emerging as a stylish jet-set hideaway in the 1980s.

pointy-roofed **Swedish belfry** is a local landmark. On the western side of the harbor is the **Musée de Saint-Barth,** which provides a quick roundup of local history and customs. Its collections include Amerindian votive objects, colonial documents, fish traps, straw hats woven out of latanier palm fronds, and stiff-sided calèche bonnets, also known as *quichenottes* (or kiss-me-not) and once regarded as the best defense against amorous Englishmen and Swedes. The closest beach is **Shell Beach,** a ten-minute walk south of town at **Anse de Grand Galet.**

St. Barts peaks at less than 1,000 feet (300 m), but its tightly packed folds of perpendicular green hills make it seem much taller, while lovingly cultivated gardens create an impression of tropical lushness. The 18 small villages dotted about the island are linked by narrow roads that crawl doggedly up into the hills and then plummet back to the coast. At the bottom of a particularly vertiginous descent north of Gustavia is the charming fishing village of **Corossol.** Turn left at the waterfront for the **Inter-Oceans Museum,** an intriguing

GUSTAVIA

Postcard-pretty Gustavia was named in honor of the Swedish king Gustav III and hems in three sides of its sheltered harbor, guarded by four hilltop forts. During the height of the winter season, splendiferous gin palaces line the docks, berthed sleek cheek-by-elegant jowl, and the boutiques, jewelers, and terrace cafés of the tiny town center are packed with serious shoppers and gawking day-trippers from Sint Maarten. The

Gustavia

◪ 251 A2

Musée de Saint-Barth

✉ rue Alvar

☎ 590/27 89 07

🕐 Closed Sun.

💲 $

Inter-Oceans Museum

✉ Corossol

☎ 590/27 62 97

🕐 Closed Mon.

💲 $

French designer labels elevate duty-free shopping to an art form in the island capital.

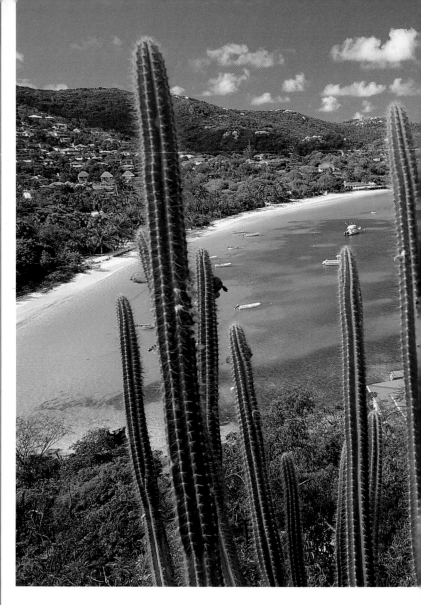

seashell collection said to be the second largest in the world, with several world-record-size exhibits. Basket-weaving is another specialty.

On the north coast is St. Barts' chief tourist hub, **St.-Jean** (*Visitor information, Gustavia Pier, Tel 590/27 87 27*), where a small group of hotels, restaurants, and shops have sprung up along the roadside. A road circles the east end of the island, past the beach at Anse du Grand Cul-de-Sac and around **Morne du Vitet** (938 feet/281 m).

The two best beaches are on the south coast: **Anse de Grande Saline,** reached via St.-Jean, and **Anse du Gouverneur,** south of Lurin. Both are undeveloped, with deep white sand and terrific views of Saba, Sint Eustatius, and St. Kitts in the distance. ■

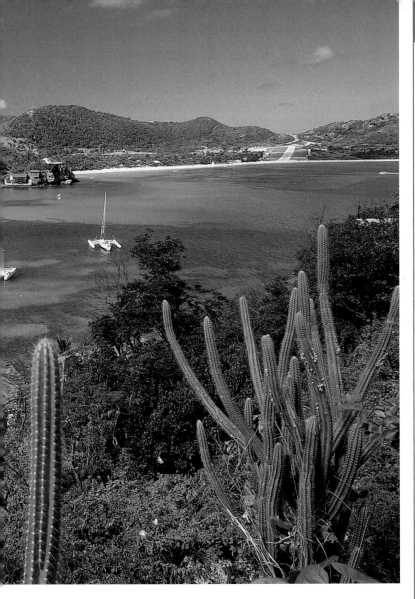

Sports & activities

**Day sails & water sports
(voile & activités nautique):**
Marine Service (Tel 590/27 70 34, fax
590/27 70 36) or Océan Must (Tel
590/27 62 25, fax 590/27 95 17).

**Horseback riding
(équitation):** Ranch des

Flamands (Tel 590/27 80 72).

Mountain biking (VTT):
Rentals from Rent-Some-Fun
(Gustavia, Tel 590/27 70 59).

Tours: Contact Gustavia Office
du Tourisme (Tel 590/27 87 27). ■

Tall branches of
torch cactus rise
above the hardy
scrub on the
sunbaked hills
surrounding
Baie-de-St.-Jean.

Mont Pelée looms
above the ruined
city of St.-Pierre,
destroyed in the
eruption of 1902.

Martinique

MARTINIQUE IS ONE OF THE MOST BEAUTIFUL OF ALL THE
Caribbean islands. The Amerindians called it Madinina, the Island
of Flowers, and Martinique is still celebrated for its glorious gardens
and rampant rain forest, as well as its lovely women, fine beaches, and
distinctive Creole culture. Measuring 50 miles (80 km) long and 22
miles (35.5 km) wide, it is flanked by the Windward Islands of
Dominica to the north and St. Lucia to the south.

Martinique

🅰 233 D1

Visitor information

✉ 2 rue Ernest
Deproge

☎ 596/63 79 60,
fax 596/73 66 93,
e-mail: martinique
@nyo.com,
www.martinique.org

Northern Martinique is tall and
explosively green, swathed in dense
rain forest that swoops down from
the heights of Mont Pelée, the
island's only active volcano,
through the lesser but still impressive peaks of the Pitons du Carbet
(see p. 260) to a fringe of banana
plantations clinging to the lower
slopes. The central plain, stretching
east from Fort-de-France (see p.
256), the island's capital on the west
coast, is Martinique's sugarcane
belt. The south of the island is characterized by the dry, hilly folds of
the *mornes,* which back a scattered
collection of beaches and small
coastal resorts.

Columbus may have spotted
Martinica, as he called it, on his
second voyage, but he definitely
stopped off here on his fourth
expedition in 1502. He waxed lyri-
cal about the beauty of the island
and the Carib women who greeted
his arrival with cries of "Madinina."
It is uncertain whether Martinica is
a corruption of Madinina or maybe
a homage to St. Martin. The Carib
were still in possession of the island
when French settlers first came
ashore near Le Carbet on the west
coast in 1635. After a quarter of a
century of violent skirmishes, a
treaty ceded the Atlantic-facing east
coast to the Carib, but before long
the French had the whole island to
themselves and proceeded to carpet
it with sugarcane.

Martinique's administrative
capital was established at Fort Royal
(present-day Fort-de-France) in

Grand' Rivière
Macouba
Cap St-Martin
Basse-Pointe
Plantation Leyritz-
Musée de Figurines Végétales
Anse Céron
Les
Ombrages
Ajoupa-
Le Lorrain
Marigot
1397m
Bouillon
N1
Le Précheur
Mont
Pelée
Gorges de
la Falaise
Anse Charpentier
Le Morne
Rouge
Musée de
la Banane
Musée du Rhum
Ste.-Marie
Pointe du Diable
Château Dubuc
884m
Bézaudin
Tartane
Presqu'île de
la Caravelle
St.-Pierre
Morne Jacob
Fond-
St.-Denis
Morne des
Esses
La Trinité
D2
Rade de St-Pierre
694m
Le Carbet
Morne
Bellevue
D2
Baie du Galion
Le Morne-Vert
1196m
Galion
Gros-Morne
Îlet Ramville
Bellefontaine
Pitons
du Carbet
Jardin de
Balata
Le Robert
Havre du Robert
St.-Joseph
N1
Pointe Larose
Case-Pilote
Balata-Tourlet
Cul-de-Sac des Roseaux
Anse Coilat
Schœlcher
N1
Le Lamentin
Baie du François
Le François
Fort-de-France
Fort
St.-Louis
Aéroport-de-Fort-de-
France-le Lamentin
N6
Baie du Simon
Habitation
Clément
Baie des Flamands
Baie de Fort-de-France
Pointe du
Bout
Ducos
Le St.-Esprit
Pointe du
Vauclin
Anse Mitan
Baie de
Genipa
Salée
504m
Baie du Vauclin
Anse à l'Ane
D7
Montagne
du Vauclin
Le Vauclin
Musée de la Pagerie
Les Trois-Îlets
Maison
de la Canne
Rivière-Salée
Cul-de-Sac
de Paquemar
Grande Anse d'Arlet
La Mauny
N6
Grande Anse
Macabou
Les Anses-d'Arlets
D7
Le Diamant
Trois
Rivières
Rivière-Pilote
Petite Anse du Diamant
Grande Anse
du Diamant
Ste.-Luce
Le Marin
Cap Ferré
Pointe du Diamant
Ecomusée de
Martinique
Cul-de-Sac
du Marin
Rocher
du Diamant
Pte.
du Marin
Ste.-Anne
Passe des Fours
Grande Anse
des Salines
Anse Trabaud
Pointe des Salines

0   10 kilometers
0   6 miles

A   B   C   D

1681, but the real focus of the island was St.-Pierre, a gracious harbor city at the foot of Mont Pelée, which became the hub of French trade and culture in the region. The British captured the island in 1762 but returned it a year later (along with Guadeloupe) in exchange for Dominica, Grenada, St. Vincent, and Tobago, plus French territories in Senegal and North America. The extent of the French concessions reflected the importance they attached to their Caribbean possessions. In 1793 the French Revolution arrived in Martinique, and initially the republicans carried the day. But within a year the planters had restored the old regime, with the help of the British. Although relatively stable,

Martinique witnessed several slave uprisings before the abolition of slavery in 1848 and the subsequent decline in wealth and importance of the sugar economy. Yet the most devastating day in the island's history occurred 54 years later, on May 8, 1902, when Mont Pelée erupted, destroying the city of St.-Pierre and killing all but one of its 30,000 inhabitants.

While life has returned to St.-Pierre in a small way, it remains quite literally a shadow of its former self. In contrast, Fort-de-France has boomed. A big and bustling port city with more than 100,000 inhabitants, the capital is gobbling up the wooded hillsides behind the Baie des Flamands and spreading eastward to the industrial quarter of Le

The colorful bracts of the lobster claw are a familiar rain forest sight.

HARBOR FERRIES (VEDETTES)

Ferries make a neat way to pop into Fort-de-France from the beach resorts across the bay (or vice versa). There are frequent and inexpensive ferry services from the downtown waterfront near Fort St.-Louis to Plage du Bout, Anse Mitan, and Anse à l'Ane. Ferries operate from 6 a.m. until about midnight to the main resort of Pointe du Bout; the crossing takes 20 minutes. There are also services to Ste.-Anne on the far south of the island (*La Vedette runs from the waterfront downtown, La Savane*). ■

Fort-de-France
🅰 255 B2

Fort St.-Louis
✉ blvd. Chevalier Ste. Marthe
☎ 596/60 54 59
🕐 Call for openings
💲 $$$$$

Lamentin and the airport. Facing the city from across the broad mouth of the Baie de Fort-de-France are the well-developed hotel strip of Pointe du Bout and quieter Anse à l'Ane. The island's other two leading resort areas are the yachting center of Le Marin and Ste.-Anne, found down on the southeast peninsula close to Grande Anse des Salines, Martinique's best beach.

The Atlantic shore is rough and rocky, with another peninsula, the Presqu' ile la Caravelle, about halfway up the coast, home to a few small hotels, sugar mill ruins, and a nature reserve.

The rain forest luxuriance of the north is dominated by the cloud-capped bulk of simmering Mont Pelée. It's not a particularly interesting volcano to climb, but there are several pretty walks out of the village

of Ajoupa-Bouillon and a memorable drive north through the Pitons du Carbet from Fort-de-France (see pp. 260–61). Although distances are modest and the roads good, leave plenty of time to explore, and allow at least three or four days for a really good look around.

FORT-DE-FRANCE

A vibrant and attractive city, Fort-de-France enjoys a splendid position on the Caribbean coast, set against a backdrop of dark green hills. Its compact heart is inviting and easy to explore on foot, with a busy shopping district and narrow streets of flat-fronted buildings adorned with elaborate ironwork balconies.

The original settlement grew up around **Fort St.-Louis,** founded by the French in 1639. The sturdy fortress has been considerably extended and sits on a headland

---

Sports & activities

Mountain biking (VTT):
Rentals from VT Tilt (*Les Trois-Îlets, Tel 596/68 16 75. Also see Tours, below*).

Diving & snorkeling (plongée sous-marine & plongée avec tuba):
Martinique's best coral reef sites are off the south coast, and there's good snorkeling at Les Anses d'Arlets. St.-Pierre's harbor offers wreck sites dating from the 1902 eruption of Mont Pelée. L'Ile Bleue (*Marina Pointe du Bout, Tel 596/66 06 90*); Sub Diamond Rock (*Le Diamant, Tel 596/76 25 80*); Histoire d'Eau (*Ste.-Anne, Tel 596/76 92 98*); Tropicasub (*St. Pierre, Tel 596/78 38 03*).

Golf:
The Martinique Golf & Country Club (*Les Trois-Îlets, Tel 596/68 32 81, fax 596/68 38 97*)

has an 18-hole course designed by Robert Trent Jones.

Horseback riding (equitation):
Black Horse (*Les Trois-Îlets, Tel 596/68 37 80*); Ranch Jack (*Les Anses d'Arlet, Tel 596/68 37 69*).

Tours:
Guided walking, kayaking, mountain biking, and 4x4 safaris from Aventures Tropicales (*Fort-de-France, Tel 596/64 58 49*); shopping and historical tours of Fort-de-France from Azimut (*Tel 596/60 16 59*).

Water sports (activités nautiques):
Hotels and concessions offer water sports in main tourist areas. Experienced windsurfers will find more challenging conditions on the Atlantic side at Le Vauclin; contact Club Nautique de Vauclin (*Tel 596/74 50 83*). ■

jutting out into the water, where it guards the **Baie des Flamands** waterfront to the west and the yacht harbor to the east. It is still occupied by the military but open for tours, which scout around the dungeons and the battlements while guides recall episodes from the fort's history. There is always plenty of activity down on the wharf, where cruise-ship passengers arrive, ferries depart for the beaches across the **Baie de Fort-de-France** (see p. 256), and kids dive off the piers just for fun.

Across the street from the wharf is a colorful craft and souvenir market, which lays out its wares on the edge of **La Savane**. These 12-acre (4.5-ha) gardens are shaded by magnificent royal palms, and it's a pleasant place to take a stroll and admire the flowers or sit on a park bench and watch the world go by. Overlooking the gardens from rue de la Liberté is the **Musée Départemental d'Archéologie Précolumbienne et de Préhistoire de la Martinique,** where you can find displays of pottery and other Amerindian artifacts, as well as exhibits on slavery and colonial life illustrated with the help of period furnishings, crafts, clothing, and documents.

Continue along the west side of the gardens to the fabulously eccentric **Bibliothèque Schoelcher,** a library named in honor of the great French abolitionist Victor Schoelcher and housed in an exotic Byzantine-Romanesque-art nouveau structure designed for the 1889 Paris Exhibition. When the show was over, the building was taken to pieces, shipped to Martinique, and reconstructed. Opposite the library is a headless statue of the Empress Joséphine (1763–1814). Once the pride of her Martiniquais

compatriots, the empress was removed from her position at the center of La Savane, and beheaded in 1991, after a guidebook revealed her role in encouraging Napoleon to reintroduce slavery in 1802.

Across the street from the library is rue Victor Sévère, which marks the top end of the main shopping district, bounded by rue de la Liberté, rue Victor Hugo, and rue de la République. The **Préfecture** is the first of several imposing colonial government buildings along this handsome street. Among the fashionable boutiques, patisseries, and stores chock-full of French luxury goods at the heart of the grid is the **Cathédrale de St.-Louis,** which stands on rue Victor Schoelcher. The brown-and-cream painted building, with its clock tower, steeple, and fancy ironwork, was erected on the foundations of six former churches in 1878.

AROUND SOUTHERN MARTINIQUE

Visible across the bay from Fort-de-France, Martinique's most

The interior of the Cathédrale de St.-Louis is illuminated by fine stained-glass windows.

Musée Départemental
✉ 9 rue de la Liberté
☎ 596/71 57 05
🕑 Closed weekends
💲 $

Bibliothèque Schoelcher
✉ Corner of rue de la Liberté & rue Perrinon
☎ 596/70 26 679

The stone cottage housing the Musée de la Pagerie was once a separate kitchen for the estate great house.

Les Trois-Îlets
ⓜ 255 B2
Visitor information
✉ Place Gabriel Hayot
☎ 596/68 47 63

Musée de la Pagerie
ⓜ 255 B2
✉ Les Trois-Îlets
☎ 596/68 34 55
$ $

Maison de la Canne
ⓜ 255 B2
✉ Les Trois-Îlets
☎ 596/68 32 04
⊕ Closed Mon.
$ $

developed tourist enclave is the promontory of Pointe du Bout and the adjacent beach at Anse Mitan. This vacation center has a lively concentration of hotels, restaurants, beaches and water sports concessions frequented by day-tripping cruise passengers who hop across from the city by ferry (see p. 256).

Neighboring **Les Trois-Îlets** is an attractive little seaside village. A Saturday market is held on the square in front of the church where Napoleon's future empress was christened Marie-Rose Joséphine Tascher de la Pagerie in the summer of 1763. Just outside the village is the former family estate, now the home of the **Musée de la Pagerie,** which is laid out in a simple stone cottage among the ruins of the sugar mill. It houses collections of domestic utensils, period prints, and a few personal possessions of the empress, including letters from the emperor. On the main road (Rte. D7) east of the village is the informative **Maison de la Canne,** occupying another restored old sugar mill. Exhibits cover the history of the early plantations and the slave trade amid a

welter of antique paraphernalia, models, and bilingual signboards.

Heading counterclockwise around the coast from Trois-Îlets, you reach the narrow sandy beach at **Anse à l'Ane** and its popular beach bars. The lovely village of **Les Anses-d'Arlets** has several dark sand beaches nearby, including the tiny black sand strip of Petit Anse du Diamant, where dozens of traditional fishing boats painted orange, turquoise, and green ride the gentle swell in the bay. Around the headland there's a fine view of the **Rocher du Diamant,** an offshore islet shaped like a giant brioche with a slice carved out of it. In 1804 British troops from St. Lucia captured the rock to harass French shipping. It was "commissioned" into the British Navy, armed with cannon and nicknamed H.M.S. *Diamond Rock.* The British garrison held out for 18 months, hoisting provisions ashore from visiting ships until a concerted French bombardment forced the occupiers to withdraw.

East of Ste.-Luce, across the Rivière-Pilote, is the **Ecomusée de Martinique,** providing a detailed and fascinating account of island history. Note, however, that the signs are all in French (although there's talk of providing English subtitles in the future). The excellent sections on Amerindian society and culture are accompanied by artifacts, models, and a list of common words derived from Amerindian languages, such as alligator, barbecue, and tobacco.

Continuing eastward, visit the yachting center of **Le Marin** at the foot of a deep, sheltered bay behind its packed marina. On the waterfront you can choose from a clutch of seafood restaurants serving up the catch of the day, accompanied by the creak of rigging in the breeze. Around the bay is the **Pointe du Marin** headland, with its crescent of sandy beach fringed by palms; a zigzagging hillside Calvary dominates the approach to the pretty resort town of **Ste.-Anne.** South of Ste.-Anne, the road passes the dry, sunbaked peninsula and salt ponds to **Grande Anse des Salines,** a refreshingly undeveloped curve of blonde sand. Palms, sea grape trees, and Australian pines provide a shady retreat, and there are snack wagons, vendors selling fresh pineapple, and a restaurant.

From Le Marin, Rte. N6 cuts across to the east coast town of **Le François.** In the rolling countryside just south of town is the old **Habitation Clément** sugar estate, which opens its doors to the public. Rum hasn't been distilled here since 1988, but the fully equipped distillery is on display, as are the *chais* (storehouses) where up to 1,400 barrels of Rhum Clément mature in oak imported from France. The highlight of the visit is the lovely 19th-century **plantation house.** In the dining room, carved colonial furniture is highlighted by oil lamps and antique silver. Go upstairs to see the embroidered coverlets on the four-poster beds. ■

Ecomusée de Martinique
- 🅰 255 C1
- ✉ Anse Figuier
- ☎ 596/62 79 14
- 🕐 Closed Mon.
- 💲 $

Habitation Clément
- 🅰 255 C2
- ✉ Le François
  (2 miles/3 km
  from St-François
  on Rte. D18)
- ☎ 596/54 62 07
- 💲 $$$

Seine fishermen check their nets on the beach at Bellefontaine. The nets are suspended vertically from floats and weighted.

A drive through the Pitons du Carbet to St.-Pierre

The first leg of this tour follows the historic inland trail to St.-Pierre, La Route de la Trace, carved through the highlands back in the 17th century. Martinique's tropical profusion is on display in the Jardin de Balata and in the untamed rain forest, while the grim but compelling story of St.-Pierre unfurls among century-old ruins.

From **Fort-de-France's** ❶ (see p. 256) inner city ring road, boulevard du Général de Gaulle, Rte. N3 follows the Rivière Madame north (toward Morne-Rouge) and then climbs into the hillside suburbs. Stop off at the church of **Sacré Coeur** ❷ for a tremendous view over the capital. The domed *Montmartre Martiniquais* was inspired by its famous Parisian namesake and erected in 1923 as a memorial to the dead of World War I.

The air is noticeably cooler as the road winds on up to the **Jardin de Balata** ❸ (*Rte. de Balata, Tel 596/64 48 73*), a gorgeous tropical garden laid out around a Creole home some 1,475 feet (450 m) above the coast. Meandering paths trail through flaming red-and-pink torch ginger, orchids, fruit trees, spice bushes, and swaths of leafy anthuriums gathered in the shade cast by palms, immortelles, and flamboyant trees.

The road begins to twist and turn in earnest as it passes through the Pitons (peaks) flanked by soft banks of ferns, 100-foot-high (30-m) stands of bamboo, and huge rain forest trees dangling ropes of liana and festooned with bromeliads.

At the town of **Deux Choux** take Rte. D1 8 miles (13 km) west to **St.-Pierre** ❹ and the Caribbean coast, passing through the banana plantations. (See panel for a possible detour.) Overlooking a handsome bay in the shadow of Mont Pelée, St.-Pierre was once the gracious Paris of the Antilles, a thriving colonial city renowned for the wealth of its merchants and the elegance of its buildings and inhabitants. Old photographs show the port filled with clipper ships waiting to load sugar and rum from the docks, and some private homes even boasted electricity in 1902. In the spring of that year, after centuries of inactivity, Mont Pelée rumbled. On May 5 the crater split, releasing a torrent of lava and mud, but local government officials in the crucial stages

of an election campaign decided against evacuating the city. A warning was given on May 7, but only a thousand Pierrotins packed their bags and headed for Fort-de-France. A little before 8 a.m. on May 8, Mont Pelée erupted, sending a giant cloud of burning ash and poisonous gases into the sky. The pyroclastic flow, reaching temperatures of over 3700°F (2040°C), swept down over the town and caused the sea to boil.

St.-Pierre's present-day population of 6,000 lives among the gaunt ruins of the cataclysmic eruption. The **Cyparis Express** (*place des Ruines du Figuier, Tel 596/55 50 92*) tourist train, named for the only survivor, makes a narrated (in French) circuit, or visitors can roam freely around the shell of the old theater, inspect Cyparis's cell, and visit the cathedral rebuilt behind its surviving facade. The **Musée Vulcanologique** (*rue Victor Hugo, Tel 596/78 15 16*), founded by U.S. volcanologist Franck Perret in 1932, displays photographs of the old city, melted glass bottles, fused nails, and other curios salvaged from the wreckage.

Take the Rte. N2 coast road a couple of miles (3 km) south of St.-Pierre to **Anse Turin** ❺, which once played host to Paul Gauguin (1848–1903). The celebrated French painter spent five months living by the beach in 1887 as he searched for a tropical isle where he could live like a "noble savage." Martinique was not a success, judging from letters home full of complaints and self-pity, and he wound up in Tahiti. Several of the letters and reproductions of his paintings are housed in the **Musée Gauguin** (*Anse Turin, Tel 596/78 22 660*), which also exhibits local artwork.

Rte. N2 hugs the coast back to Fort-de-France, passing the village of **Le Carbet** ❻, where the founder of St.-Pierre, Pierre Belain d'Esnambuc, landed with a hundred Norman colonists to claim Martinique for France in 1635. ■

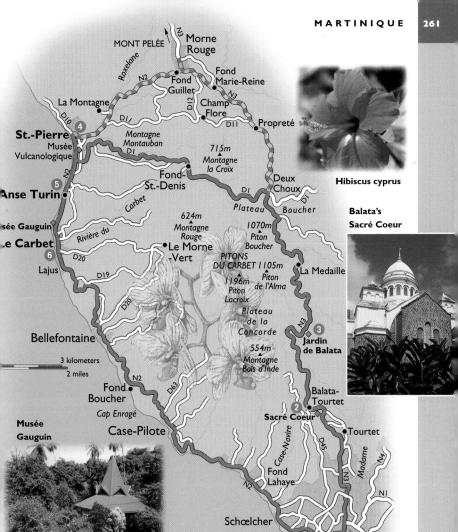

MONT PELÉE

Morne Rouge

N3

Roxelane

N2

La Montagne

Fond Guillet

Fond Marie-Reine

Champ Flore

N3

Propreté

D12

D12

D1

D10

St.-Pierre

Musée Vulcanologique

Montagne Montauban

D1

715m Montagne la Croix

Fond-St.-Denis

Deux Choux

Plateau Boucher

D1

sée Gauguin

Anse Turin

N2

Carbet

624m Montagne Rouge

Le Morne -Vert

1070m Piton Boucher

.e Carbet

Rivière du

D20

Lajus

D19

D20

PITONS DU CARBET 1105m

1196m Piton Lacroix

Piton de l'Alma

La Medaille

Plateau de la Concorde

N3

Jardin de Balata

Bellefontaine

3 kilometers

2 miles

554m Montagne Bois d'Inde

Musée Gauguin

Fond Boucher

Cap Enragé

Case-Pilote

N2

D63

Balata-Tourtet

Sacré Coeur

Tourtet

Case-Navire

D45

Madame

N4

N3

Fond Lahaye

N1

Schœlcher

N2

Pointe des Nègres

START

Fort-de-France

Hibiscus cyprus

Balata's Sacré Coeur

St.-Pierre on film

An interesting detour is a visit to the **Maison des Volcans** (Tel 596/52 45 45, Fri. and Sun. 2–4:30 p.m. only) in Morne Rouge. As well as information on volcanism, this small museum on the main street provides a 45-minute video compiled from film footage of St.-Pierre before and after the 1902 eruption (English version on request). ■

See map page 255

► Fort-de-France

↔ 40 miles/65km

🕐 An easy day trip with stops

► Fort-de-France

NOT TO BE MISSED

- Jardin de Balata
- St.-Pierre
- Musée Gauguin

The heavy purple-red flower of the banana plant hangs beneath a bunch of ripening fruit.

The North & Northeast

AJOUPA-BOUILLON

This self-proclaimed "ville florale" displays its roadside banks of wild begonias, massed crotons, and shrimp plants with pride. Ajoupa is also home to **Les Ombrages** *(Tel 596/53 31 90)*, a lush botanical garden clambering up a rain forest ravine, and the starting point for walks to the **Gorges de la Falaise** *(Tel 596/53 37 56)*. The 30-minute trail starts just west of town and leads through the rain forest to a swimming hole fed by a waterfall.
255 B4 ✉ Immeuble Boulon, Quartier Racine ☎ 596/53 32 87

CARAVELLE PENINSULA

From the main road follow signs for **Tartane** (Rte. D2), a small resort on the north coast of this wooded peninsula. At the end of the road a section of rough track leads to the ruins of 17th-century **Château Dubuc** *(Tel 596/73 19 30)*, which crown a rise overlooking a protected bay and the foundations of an old sugar mill. A quirky little museum houses old belt buckles, broken bottles, and clay pipe stems unearthed around the estate. From the parking lot, footpaths strike off into a natural reserve and to the cliffs and coves lining the shore.
255 C3

PLANTATION LEYRITZ-MUSÉE DE FIGURINES VÉGÉTALES

An attractive hotel-restaurant converted from an old sugar estate, this popular lunch stop is on the tour bus trail. It has a small museum of figurines in historical costume fashioned out of leaves, seeds, grasses, and other plant matter.
255 B4 ✉ Rte. D21 from Basse-Pointe
☎ 596/78 53 92 💲 $

STE.-MARIE

Two of Martinique's most conspicuous products are showcased in museums just west and north of the town: rum and bananas. The **Musée de la Banane** *(Rte. de Bézaudin, Tel 596/69 45 52)* sits at the heart of a working banana plantation. Check out the history of the banana and amazing banana trivia (Germans devour more than 33 pounds/15 kg of bananas per person per year). Stroll along the banana walk and visit the packing houses on weekdays.

The **Musée du Rhum** *(Tel 596/69 30 02)* also believes in transporting visitors to the business end of its operations with guided tours of the Distillerie Saint-James. The actual museum is an old plantation house with collections of antique tools and memorabilia.
255 C3 ■

Tethered in a row like giant green men-o'-war, the Windward Islands of Dominica, St. Lucia, St. Vincent, and Grenada lie broadside to the rain-bearing Atlantic winds that feed their towering, forested peaks.

Windward Islands

Dressed for Carnival

Windward Islands

THE MAJESTIC QUARTET OF WINDWARD ISLANDS TAPERS OFF TOWARD THE tail end of the Lesser Antilles, rising sheer from the Atlantic surf on one side and the gentle wavelets of the Caribbean Sea on the other. The islands are the mere tips of a volcanic mountain range that has sprouted along a rift in the earth's crust where the Atlantic and Caribbean tectonic plates collide. Three of the four main Windward Islands have an active *soufrière*, a sulfurous volcanic vent liable to erupt every hundred years or so (Grenada, the exception, has bubbling hot springs). Tall enough to create their own microclimates by trapping the winds off the Atlantic and converting them to rain clouds, the Windwards are fantastically fertile. Islanders grow bananas, coconuts, and spices for export, and farmers have their work cut out for them trying to keep the encroaching sea of green at bay. In the high country, rare parrots add a flash of brilliant color to the dense rain forest canopy towering above a steaming jungle of ferns, creepers, and twisted tree roots.

Today **Dominica, St. Lucia, St. Vincent** (with its chain of islands known as **the Grenadines), and Grenada** are independent nations, but their long association dates back to the days of sail when they fell to the windward side of the English colonial trading routes between Europe and the Caribbean. Later the term was adopted by 19th-century British administrators who governed the Windward Islands as a group distinct from British colonies in the Leeward Islands.

The earliest inhabitants of the Windward Islands were Arawak Indians, farmers and fishermen whose peaceful reign ended abruptly with the arrival of warlike Carib people about A.D. 1000. Spanish explorers gave the "Cannibal Isles" a wide berth, and they became the focus of Carib resistance in the region until the mid-17th century, when the sugar trade spurred French and English colonists into action. Initially the two most topographically challenging islands, Dominica and St. Vincent, were left to the Carib, who were joined by escaped African slaves. But a century later, white settlers had forced Dominica's few remaining Carib into exile on the Atlantic coast; on St. Vincent mixed-race black Carib took refuge in the hills and continued a dogged resistance until the early 19th century.

Throughout the plantation era Europe's conflicts were mirrored in the Caribbean arena, where Britain and France squabbled over the Windwards incessantly and won, lost, and regained territories with bewildering frequency. The islands inherited a confused legacy of French and English place-names, as well as the French-influenced Creole patois that is still widely spoken in Dominica and St. Lucia, although the islands have been officially English speaking for 200 years. When slavery was abolished in 1834, former slaves turned to the land and carved small-scale farms out of the rich soil. The islands slid into an agricultural backwater administered by a British governor based in Grenada. Several attempts to federate the British Caribbean territories came to nothing, and eventually the individual Windward Islands were granted self-government in the 1960s and full independence in the late 1970s. They are now members of the British Commonwealth.

Part of the Windward Islands' appeal is the coexistence of tourism and traditional island life. This is particularly true on Dominica, where vast tracts of primal rain forest and uplands remain in pristine condition, and fishing and farming still underpin the local economy. Also unspoiled and under-appreciated, St. Vincent is another rain forest wilderness and tropical market garden but generally consigned to the role of stepping-stone for yachtsmen heading for the Grenadines. The Grenadines are a yachting paradise, an alluring chain of minuscule islands with great beaches, some uninhabited, some harboring exclusive resorts. Others, such as pretty Bequai, fall somewhere between the two. To the south is charming Grenada. Easygoing and friendly, the Spice Island is

Spectacular waterfalls plummet hundreds of feet through a Dominican rain forest.

Area of map detail

ATLANTIC
OCEAN

Caribbean Sea

overloaded with natural beauties and ringed by sandy beaches, spice plantations, and pretty villages. St. Lucia is the most developed of the Windwards, but even here it's easy to escape the resort beaches of the northwest and take a trip to the mountains, where villages nestle amid fabulous tropical flowers and vegetable plots on the edge of the forest. ■

0   60 kilometers

0   40 miles

7 ▷

Dominica Passage

Portsmouth ●   ● Marigot

1447m ▲   **DOMINICA**

Roseau ✪

6 ▷

Martinique Passage

Fort-de-France ★

Martinique
(France)

5 ▷

St. Lucia Channel

Castries ✪

950m ▲

Soufrière ●   **ST. LUCIA**

4 ▷

Vieux Fort ●

St. Vincent Passage

1074m ▲   ● Georgetown

St. Vincent

Kingstown ✪

3 ▷

ST. VINCENT   *Bequia*
AND THE
GRENADINES

♪ *Mustique*

Canouan I.

Mayreau I.   Tobago Cays

Union ◦ Palm I. (Prune I.)
Petit St. Vincent

Carriacou   Petit Martinique

2 ▷   ● Saline I.

Frigate I.

● Ronde

Victoria ● 840m ▲

GRENADA

✪ **St. George's**

I ▷

△   △   △
A   **B**   **C**

L e s s e r   A n t i l l e s

W i n d w a r d   I s l a n d s

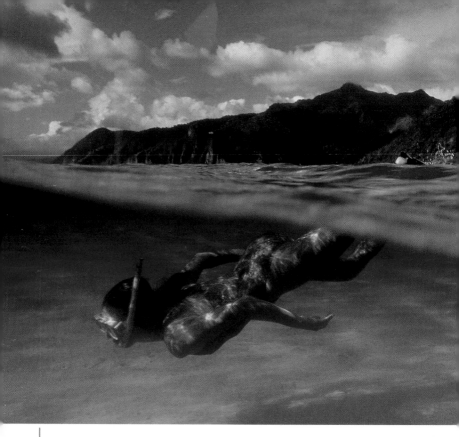

Dominica

DOMINICA (PRONOUNCED DO-MIN-EE-KA) WAS KNOWN TO the Carib as Wai'tukubuli ("tall is her body"). From a 29-by-16-mile (47-by-26-km) base, the soaring interior peaks at Morne Diablotin (4,747 feet/1,447 m) within five miles (8 km) of the coast, and the jagged mountains of the central north-south spine average more than 3,000 feet (900 m). Dominica is generously endowed with natural wonders. The island is home to one of the world's last untouched rain forests, more than a thousand species of flowering plants, a boiling lake, 300-plus rivers, and almost as many waterfalls coursing down the mountainsides in a flash of shimmering silver and spray. Off the coast the underwater landscape is similarly breathtaking and fast gaining a reputation as an exciting dive destination.

The population of about 75,000 is 98 percent black, mainly Catholic, and most people still struggle to make a living from the land. Despite its undoubted beauty, Dominica is one of the Caribbean's poorest islands. Small-scale farming and fishing, augmented by traditional crafts, are the economic mainstays of one of the world's last surviving Carib communities, living on the Carib Territory in the northeast. With few beaches (and those that exist tend toward narrow strips of gray volcanic sand), tourism is still in its infancy here. Dominica has only 700 or so hotel rooms, and facilities are mostly modest and unsophisticated. On the plus side, Dominica is a rare Caribbean haven for adventurous travelers keen to hike, dive, and explore without the usual tourist distractions.

Dominica lies between the French islands of Guadeloupe and Martinique. (It is not to be confused with the Dominican Republic in the Greater Antilles, see pp. 95–124.) Christopher Columbus sailed around Wai'tukubuli's northern tip on his second voyage to the New World in November 1493. It was a Sunday, so he christened his find Dominica and noted in his logbook that the island was "remarkable for the beauty of its mountains…and must be seen to be believed." They say he would have little difficulty recognizing it today. French colonists laid claim to Dominica in the 1750s but ceded it to Britain under the Treaty of Paris in 1763. Despite a century of French raids, slave rebellions, and isolated attacks by bands of marauding Maroons (escaped slaves who hid in the near-impenetrable mountains), the British remained more or less in control. From the mid-18th century Dominica was administered with the Leeward Islands until 1939, when it was transferred to the Windward Islands. Independence arrived in 1978, and two years later the Dominicans elected the Caribbean's first woman prime

minister, Dame Eugenia Charles, who retired at the age of 76 in 1995.

The capital of the island, Roseau (see p. 268), is a small weather-beaten town and cruise-ship stopover with around 20,000 inhabitants. It lies at the mouth of the Roseau River on the southwest coast. Inland along the river lies the Trafalgar Falls (see p. 269), one of Dominica's most popular tourist attractions. The nearby village of Laudat is the main drop-off point for hikes in the Morne Trois Pitons National Park (see p. 270). South of Roseau there are several hotels and dive outfits on the water at Castle Comfort, and a narrow road hugs the shore to the southern tip of the

Dominica

🅰 265 B6

Visitor information

✉ National Development Corporation, Dominica

☎ 767/448-2045, fax 767/448-5840

Dominica Museum
✉ Bay St., Roseau
🕐 Closed Sun.
💲 $

island. Here divers and snorkelers can explore the spectacular Scotts Head/Soufrière Marine Park (see p. 273).

Dominica's second largest settlement is Portsmouth, in the northwest, which also has a cruise-ship facility in nearby Cabrits National Park (see p. 272). Above the coast, endangered sisserou and jaco parrots are protected in the Northern Forest Reserve on the slopes of Morne Diablotin, and a road crosses over to the Atlantic coast, running through the coconut plantations to Melville Hall Airport. South of Melville Hall the Transinsular Road carves a splendid route to Roseau through the Central Forest Reserve and the pretty mountain village of Bells. The drive takes 90 minutes and affords grand views of cloudy peaks and the rain forest. Remaining on the windward side, the coastal road runs through Carib Territory, passing roadside stalls selling traditional basketwork, to Castle Bruce and an alternative route back to the capital via the waterfall at Emerald Pool (see p. 271).

ROSEAU & THE ROSEAU VALLEY

Dominica's capital, which moved to Roseau (pronounced Row-so) from Portsmouth in the late 18th century, is laid out in a neat grid between the banks of the Roseau River and Fort Young. Roseau has a certain dilapidated charm, with a motley collection of sturdy stone colonial buildings and a handful of modern concrete structures built since Hurricane David smashed through the island in 1979. It's easy to explore on foot, and there are several small galleries, cafés, and craft shops around Cork Street.

Roseau's most animated corner is the local **produce market,** which spills out from the shade of its tin roof and onto the sidewalk at the river end of the waterfront.

The hub of colonial Roseau was the Old Market Place on **Dawbiney Square,** off King George V Street. Slave auctions were once held in the small cobbled, tree-shaded plaza, now annexed by a café and souvenir stalls squeezed in around a curious cast-iron centerpiece decorated with a regal crown. On one side of the square, facing the waterfront and downtown cruise-ship berth, is the **Dominica Museum,** which provides an interesting overview of island history and culture. Among the exhibits are Carib tools and a thatched *carbet* (hut), a section on Dominican writers, including Jean Rhys, and a series of fascinating 18th-century prints by Agostino

Jean Rhys

Writer Jean Rhys was born in Roseau in 1894; her mother's family were white Creole planters. Rhys traveled to Europe at age 16 and drew on her own experiences as a chorus girl, artist's model, and poet's wife for her first collection of short stories, *The Left Bank* (1927), which explores the role of women on the edge of bohemian society. After a checkered literary career, she returned to her Caribbean roots for *Wide Sargasso Sea* (1966). It recounts the imagined history of the first Mrs. Rochester, a white Creole heiress who became the mad wife of Charlotte Brontë's novel *Jane Eyre.* Set in Jamaica and Dominica in the early 1800s, it describes the decadence of a Caribbean lifestyle on the verge of extinction. ■

Brunias, an Italian-born artist employed by Dominica's first British governor, Sir William Young, to record scenes of island life.

Sir William's name lives on at **Fort Young,** a short walk away along the seafront. Now a hotel (see p. 378), the fort was constructed of blackened volcanic stone in 1775. It retains few reminders of its military heyday, except for a couple of fancy brass cannon and workmanlike snipers' embrasures in the walls of the dining room.

Opposite the fort is the **Anglican Church,** which contains memorial tablets eulogizing 19th-century British colonial officials, and stained-glass windows behind the altar. The **Roman Catholic Cathedral,** on Turkey Lane, is in rather better shape, built of dark river rocks between 1800 and 1916. To the east are the **Botanical Gardens** *(off King George V St., Tel 767/448 2401. Map 267 B2),* stretching over a 40-acre (16-ha) former cane field on the lower slopes of Morne Bruce. Teams play cricket in the large grassy park, and an aviary houses indigenous sisserou and jaco parrots. Among the botanical exhibits are flowering cannonball trees with their strange waxy blooms, teaks, flamboyants, cassia trees, and a monstrous African baobab tree blown onto an empty bus during Hurricane David and now sprouting a trio of secondary trunks.

The **Trafalgar Falls** lie about 5 miles (8 km) east of town at the head of the Roseau Valley. *(Take King George V St. out of central Roseau, cross the Roseau River in the direction of Laudat, and follow signs. Map 267 B2)* Carving an imposing cleft deep into the green buttress of the Morne Trois Pitons highlands, the valley walls swoosh up to either side of the road, carpeted in a tangled mass of rain forest jungle and terraced vegetable plots grafted onto almost perpendicular slopes. The bumpy track runs out near the **Papillote Wilderness Retreat** *(Tel 809/683-2501. Map 267 B2),* a delightful small hotel and restaurant set in pretty gardens, where guides offer their services. From here it's a steep 10- to 15-minute hike to the twin waterfalls, known as "mother" and "father." The father fall on the left is warm, while the

Tropical downpours are a frequent occurrence, but it is business as usual for the traders and shoppers in Roseau's waterfront market.

mother is cold, and they plummet down the 200-foot (60-m) cliff face in a roar of tumbling water and spray to a pool below, bouncing off giant boulders streaked orange with mineral deposits. Below the viewing platform are paths leading around to swimming areas. There's good native bird spotting in the gardens, where semidomesticated jungle fowl and imported peacocks roam and occasionally shatter the peace with raucous cries.

Morne Trois Pitons National Park

🅰 267 B2

✉ Roseau

☎ 767/448-2733

💲 $$$

Syndicate Estate

🅰 267 B3

✉ Division of Tourism, Valley Rd., Roseau

☎ 767/448-2045

MORNE TROIS PITONS NATIONAL PARK

Most of Dominica's best known natural attractions are found in the 17,000-acre (6,880-ha) national park stretching south of Morne Trois Pitons (4,550 feet/1,387 m), the second highest peak on the island. Sprinkled with mountain lakes, hissing volcanic fumeroles, sulfur springs, and an annual rainfall of almost 300 inches (7,600 mm), this is superb (if rather damp) upland hiking country. Together with the Northern Forest Reserve (see p. 271), the national park showcases the many different faces of the rain forest, from the grandeur of 100-foot-tall (30 m) secondary forest to stunted, high-

altitude elfin woodlands, and a treasury of island plant life that numbers some 74 species of orchids and 22 types of fern.

Dominican wildlife is fairly difficult to spot, but there are occasional sightings of opossums, agoutis, iguanas, and five non-venomous snakes, including elusive boa constrictors. More than 170 bird species have been identified. Locals catch freshwater shrimp, fish, crabs, and frogs for food. (Frog's legs are served up under the pseudonym "mountain chicken" in local restaurants.)

The easiest starting point for explorations in the park is the village of **Laudat,** east of Roseau. **Freshwater Lake,** 2,500 feet (760 m) above sea level, is accessible by car, and **Boeri Lake** is an attractive 40-minute walk farther on over two steep ridges cupped in a volcanic crater.

The park's most challenging and celebrated hike is the trail to **Boiling Lake,** a 200-foot-wide (60-m) flooded volcanic fumerole that bubbles and steams at 180° to 200°F (82–93°C). It's best to engage a guide before undertaking the strenuous seven- to eight-hour round-trip trek. Local guides wait

---

Sports & activities

Diving: In the south of the island contact Anchorage Hotel and Dive Center (Tel 767/448-2638, fax 767/448-5680); Dive Dominica (Tel 767/448-2188 or 800/544-7631, fax 767/448-6088, e-mail: dive@tod.dm, www. divedominica.com); or Nature Island Dive (Tel 767/449-8181, fax 767/ 449-8182, www.natureislanddive.dm). In the north, Cabrits Dive Centre, (Portsmouth, Tel 767/445-3010, fax 767/445-3001).

Hiking & tours: Boiling Lake

and Morne Diablotin hikes, and botany and bird-watching tours from Ken's Hinterland Adventure Tours (Tel 767/448-4850, e-mail: khatts@tod.dm, www.delphis.dm/ khatts.htm); Indian River and hiking tours from Cobra Tours (Tel 767/445-4668, fax 767/445-4453); and Dominica Tours (Tel 767/448-2638, fax 767/448-5680). Mountain bike and kayak rentals and tours from Nature Island Dive (Tel 767/449-8181, fax 767/ 449-8182, www.natureislanddive.dm). ∎

at the trailhead, or you can hook up with a reputable guide company (see p. 270). En route to Boiling Lake, the trail crosses the **Valley of Desolation,** a suitably hellish, barren landscape cluttered with huge boulders, where the fumes from noxious sulfur springs and sinister pools of bubbling gray mud have killed off all but the hardiest sprigs of vegetation.

At the western edge of the park are the **Middleham Trails** (3 hours round-trip), which strike out from Cochrane or Laudat for the dramatic 500-foot-high (150-m) **Middleham Falls** via the **Stinking Hole bat caves.**

A challenging 4- to 5-hour round-trip trail from Pont Cassé tackles **Morne Trois Pitons** itself, climbing into the eerily quiet world of elfin forest frosted with lichens and wrapped in mosses and mist.

A few miles farther east, outside the park and just off the Castle Bruce road, is **Emerald Pool.** The small green-blue swimming hole is fed by a waterfall and set in a fern-flanked rain forest grotto beneath lianas and elephant ears.

NORTHERN FOREST RESERVE

Larger than the national park, the 22,000-acre (8,900-ha) Northern Forest Reserve (*Tel 767/448 2733. Map 267 B3*) on the slopes of Morne Diablotin is a refuge for Dominica's two endemic parrot species: sisserou and jaco. The green-and-brown sisserou is the national bird and the rarer of the two. Captive breeding programs have helped swell numbers in the wild to approximately 300. There are about a thousand of the more colorful jaco, or red-necked parrots.

A road from Dublanc, on the west coast south of Portsmouth, clambers up to the **Syndicate Estate.** At this former citrus and banana plantation 1,800 feet (550 m) above sea level, a short trail provides good bird-watching opportunities. The best way to see the birds is on a tour (see p. 270).

A guide is also recommended for a strenuous 6- to 7-hour round-trip ascent of **Morne Diablotin.** The mountain was named for the black-capped petrel that inhabited the forest before being hunted to extinction. ∎

Hikers trek around the steaming cauldron of Boiling Lake high in Dominica's desolate central highlands.

Syndicate Estate

🅰 267 B3

✉ Division of Tourism, Valley Rd., Roseau

☎ 767/448-2045

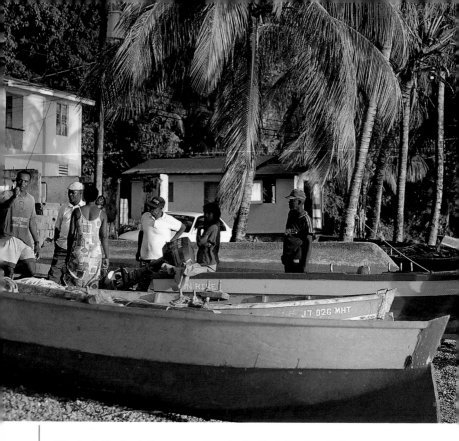

Wooden fishing boats drawn up on the volcanic shingle beach at Soufrière

Around Dominica

CARIB TERRITORY

Established in 1903, the 3,700-acre (1,500-ha) Carib Territory *(Map 267 C3)* encompasses eight small villages strung along the Atlantic coast between Atkinson and Castle Bruce. Some 3,000 Carib people live in the territory, descendants of Amerindian migrants who paddled their dugout canoes from the Amazon Basin to occupy the Caribbean islands in A.D. 1200–1300. Although most are now of mixed race, the Dominican Carib display their South American heritage in their facial features, bronze skin, and straight black hair.

Modern Carib have abandoned traditional thatched huts in favor of more comfortable wooden Creole homes balanced on stilts overlooking the sea. A few ancient ceremonies and traditions such as boatbuilding survive, and

there's a program under way to preserve the rarely spoken Carib language. Basket-weaving is a local specialty on display at roadside stalls alongside model boats and other wood carvings. The Carib Territory's one other sight is the **St. Marie of the Caribs Catholic Church** at Salybia, which has an altar carved in the shape of a dugout canoe.

PORTSMOUTH & CABRITS NATIONAL PARK

Portsmouth, once the island capital until malarial mosquitoes in the nearby swamps sent the British scurrying down to Roseau, is a scruffy little town of 5,000 souls set on Prince Rupert Bay. There's little reason to linger here.

On the southern edge of town take a boat trip on the **Indian River** (see p. 270). You can paddle upstream through a leafy green

A Rasta oarsman paddles visitors up the Indian River near Portsmouth.

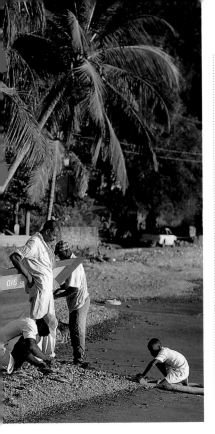

tunnel of swamp ferns, bwa mang trees, wild hibiscus, and anthuriums. Herons and egrets stalk the shallows, and turquoise king-fishers flit past.

Just over a mile (1.5 km) north is **Cabrits National Park** (*Map 267 A4, Portsmouth, Tel 767/444-2401*), occupying the forested peninsula at the top of the bay. It's said that this sheltered anchorage attracted 16th-century explorers Sir Francis Drake (1540–1596) and Sir John Hawkins (1532–1595). They would stop off to resupply their ships, trading with the Carib and hunting goats (*cabrits*) left by previous expeditions for fresh meat. In 1765 the British founded **Fort Shirley** to defend the harbor. Its scattered remains, linked by footpaths, litter the hillside. Some of the old volcanic stone and redbrick buildings have been overtaken by jungle, but several others have been partially restored, and the former **Powder Magazine** houses a small museum.

Black sand beaches fringe Prince Rupert Bay, with several hotels and a dive shop at

Picard Beach. The best snorkeling and coral reef and wall diving sites are located in **Douglas Bay,** north of Cabrits Peninsula.

SCOTTS HEAD & THE SOUTH
A half-hour drive from Roseau around the curve of Soufrière Bay, the narrow finger of Scotts Head Peninsula juts out from the Caribbean coast at the southern tip of the island. From the ruins of **Fort Cashacrou,** the view stretches off to the French island of Martinique 20 miles (32 km) to the south and back up the Dominican coast to the mountains.

Beneath the waters of the bay is a sub-merged volcanic caldera a mile (1.5 km) across and almost 1,000 feet (300 m) deep, forming the centerpiece of the **Scotts Head/Soufrière Bay Marine Park** (*Map 267 B1*), Dominica's top dive site. Around the crater rim lava pinnacles and reef sites are fre-quented by a kaleidoscope of marine species. Hard and soft corals and forests of sponges stud the walls of dramatic dropoffs. One site with particular appeal for snorkelers is **Champagne,** which lives up to its name in a cloud of tiny bubbles released from a volcanic vent in the seabed.

The fishing village of **Soufrière** takes its name from the hot sulfur springs reached by a winding road up into the hills. You can also reach the springs from the Tête Morne road above Berekua, on the shore at Grand Bay, near the Geneva Estate once owned by the family of writer Jean Rhys (see p. 268). ∎

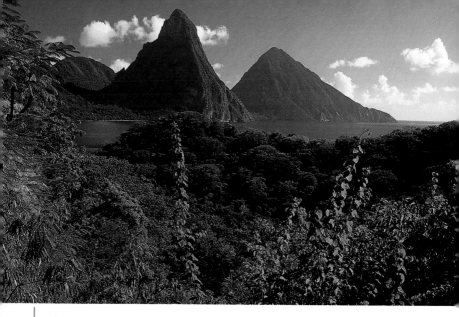

St. Lucia

LAVISHLY BESTOWED WITH DENSE GREEN RAIN FOREST, landmark peaks rising sheer from the sea, golden beaches, rare parrots, and a profusion of vivid tropical flowers, St. Lucia is a first-rank Caribbean beauty. The 27-by-14-mile (43-by-23-km) island is shaped like a pear and lies between Martinique to the north and St. Vincent in the south.

The twin volcanic peaks of the Pitons on the southwest coast are St. Lucia's most famous landmarks.

St. Lucia

🅼 265 B4

Visitor information

✉ Point Seraphine Cruise Ship Complex

☎ 758/452-4094, fax 758/453-1121, e-mail: slutour@ candw.lc, www.st-lucia.com.lc

St. Lucia (pronounced LOO-sha) is the most developed and populous of the Windward Islands. Nevertheless, the entire central portion of the island is mountainous forest ringed by rolling acres of banana plantations, sugarcane, and coconut groves. Small fishing villages dot the coast, mountain hamlets cling perilously to absurdly verdant valleys, and most telltale signs of tourist development have been tucked neatly into the northwestern corner of the island above the capital, Castries (see p. 276), home to more than a third of St. Lucia's 150,000 inhabitants.

Christopher Columbus may have set foot on St. Lucia on his fourth voyage to the New World in 1502, but the island's earliest recorded European resident was one François Le Clerc, a 16th-century French pirate who established a base on Pigeon Island and attacked passing Spanish galleons. Also known as Jambe de Bois for his wooden leg, Le Clerc appears to have survived the attentions of the island's resident Carib people, who had already dispatched two attempted British settlements before the French finally established a colonial toehold in 1651. St. Lucia was one of the most hotly contested plantation islands in the eastern Caribbean, nicknamed the Fair Helen of the West Indies for all the ships launched in the battle for her favors. Strategically placed next to the flourishing French sugar colony of Martinique and just as cultivable, the colony represented a considerable prize and changed hands

14 times, shuttling between her French founders and British usurpers. The British finally gained the upper hand after a fierce battle culminating on the slopes of Morne Fortune (see p. 277) above Castries in 1796, although French revolutionaries continued a guerrilla war from hideouts in the mountains for some time afterward. St. Lucia was secured by Britain under the Treaty of Paris in 1814. The island, which became independent in 1979, remains a member of the British Commonwealth.

Despite a century and a half of British occupation, St. Lucia displays her Gallic heritage at every turn. French place-names are more common than English, and the local patois is based on Creole. Creole cooking, Creole architecture with its fancy gingerbread trimmings, and a lingering fondness for the checkered madras fabrics, more usually seen on the French islands, conspire to make St. Lucia stand out from her Windward Island neighbors. St. Lucians are spontaneous and party loving. The island's pre-Lenten Carnival is a riot of costumes, music, and food, and the Friday night jump-up street party at Gros Islet (see p. 278) is an island institution where locals and visitors alike hook up to dance the night away. Musical events are scheduled throughout the year, including a world-class summer Jazz Festival, and any number of fêtes, sailing regattas, and impromptu jump-ups will add a memorable note to an island vacation.

African traditions also maintain a hold on the local imagination. Although the majority of the population is Catholic (another French legacy), St. Lucia has a rich folkloric culture. Evil spirits are banished by the beating of drums, and houses are made safe by magical wreaths of thorny acacia and special herbs.

VIEWS OF THE PITONS

Drivers have their work cut out on the stretch of serpentine road that drops briefly to sea level at Canaries, a small fishing community, before carving a path up through the rain forest and emerging above Soufrière. This is one of the best views of the Pitons, with the Petit Piton (2,461 feet/743 m) in the foreground and the Gros Piton (2,619 feet/798 m) 1.5 miles (2.5 km) behind. ■

Cloven-hoofed *diablesses* are reputed to shrink from the sign of the cross, and an *obeahman* (black magic practitioner) is consulted in times of trouble.

Although St. Lucia's tourist heartland is the northwest, most of the island's attractions are found south of Castries along the Caribbean coast and in the rain forest highlands.

Near the town of Soufrière are the Pitons ("peaks"), St. Lucia's most famous landmarks, which are depicted on the national flag. A brace of lofty volcanic plugs, they soar dramatically from the shore, easily upstaging the island's tallest peak, Mount Gimie (3,118 feet/ 950 m) a few miles inland. Close by are a marine park, a "drive-in" volcano, the gardens at Diamond, a working cocoa plantation, and the rain forest reserve at Morne Fond St. Jacques. Soufrière itself has several hotels and makes a good base for visitors interested in exploring the rain forest, diving, or enjoying the low-key atmosphere.

Castries

🏛 275 B4

✉ St. Lucia visitor information, p. 274

CASTRIES

St. Lucia's unremarkable capital lies at the foot of a sheltered inlet encircled by steep, forested hills. Castries was founded in the 1760s and named for the French Minister of the Marine, the Maréchal de Castries, who would have appreciated the well-protected natural harbor. But the city has a bad habit of burning down, and most of its uninspiring concrete architecture dates from the last conflagration, in 1948. St. Lucia is a regular feature on cruise-ship itineraries, and as the

Rain forest birds

A bananaquit perches by a cluster of berries.

Of the 43 or so bird species that inhabit the St. Lucian rain forest, 33 are endemic, such as the rare white-breasted thrasher, St. Lucia oriole, St. Lucia wren, and the endangered St. Lucian parrot. Conservation measures established in the 1970s brought this last species back from the edge of extinction. Known as the *jacquot* locally, the 16- to 18-inch-tall (40- to 45-cm) parrot is one of the most colorful inhabitants of the rain forest. It has a green back, blue head, red throat patch, and flashes of yellow and red under its wings.

A good way to find the parrots is to look for a stand of towering santinay trees, where they like to nest and feed on the small pink fruits. Their raucous screech is another telltale sign. ■

giant liners enter the harbor, they pass the old French battery at Vigie (Lookout) Point before berthing at the modern Pointe Seraphine cruise complex or right up against the downtown waterfront.

Set back from the waterfront is **Jeremie Street,** a terrific bustle of market stalls, traffic, and pedestrians. T-shirt sellers and souvenir stalls perch on the dockside. Across the street the old covered market building has been hijacked by vendors of carvings, basketware, and beach bags, while the produce market has been relegated to a concrete monstrosity with orange pyramid-shaped roofs. This is still the place to find a healthy dash of local color among the piles of citrus fruits and bananas, squashlike *christophené,* yams, ginger roots, and hot peppers.

A couple of blocks inland, past the Parliament and Court House on Laborie Street, lies the 19th-century **Cathedral of the Immaculate Conception.** The interior is painted from floor to ceiling with murals depicting biblical figures, African clerics, and pineapple motifs (the traditional Caribbean symbol for hospitality). Next to the cathedral is **Derek Walcott Square,** which honors the St. Lucian poet and playwright who won the Nobel Prize for Literature in 1992. There's a massive samaan tree on the square and a few old-style West Indian buildings around the edge.

Running south from the city center, Government House Road labors up Morne Fortune (pronounced For-TU-nay), past the Governor General's residence, and on to the **Morne Fortune Historic Area** (*Tel 758/452-4094*).

The brig *Unicorn* makes regular excursions along the west coast from Castries to Soufrière.

In 1796 British soldiers of the
27th Inniskilling Regiment spent
two days fighting their way to
the summit of the morne, forcing
the French to surrender. Their
bravery is commemorated by
the Inniskilling Memorial in the
grounds of **Fort Charlotte** (*Tel
758/452 4094*), where old military
buildings have been transformed
into a college.

RODNEY BAY & THE NORTH

From Castries the main road
north swings alongside the local
airport, which is edged by 2-mile-
long (3 km) **Vigie Beach,** and on
past the Gable Woods Mall and
Choc Bay hotel enclave to Rodney
Bay, St. Lucia's busiest resort area.
On the southern side of the bay,
hotels line the soft white sands
of Reduit Beach. At the head of
the beach a narrow channel gives
access to the yacht harbor and
Rodney Bay Marina. This bustling
Caribbean sailing center is
bordered to the north by the
waterfront village of **Gros Islet,**
home to the famous Friday night
jump-up.

The north shore of Rodney Bay
curves around to **Pigeon Island,**
the *gros islet* (big island) that gave
the neighboring village its name.
The former pirate lair of notorious
Capitaine Jambe de Bois is now the
**Pigeon Island National
Historic Park,** linked to the
mainland by a sandy causeway. In
1778 Adm. George Rodney of the
British Royal Navy set up a naval
base in Gros Islet Bay (later
renamed in his honor) and established a lookout post on the island.
According to one story, the sentries
on hilltop Fort Rodney used carrier
pigeons to report sightings of passing vessels and developments on the
French island of Martinique, clearly
visible 20 miles (32 km) to the
north. (A more prosaic explanation
attributes the name to the quantities
of red-necked pigeons that congre-
gated here before the native forest
was stripped away.) The ruins of
Fort Rodney still afford spectacular
views north to Martinique, and
south down the serried peaks of St.
Lucia's mountainous interior to the
Pitons. A botanical trail meanders
around the 40-acre (16 ha) island,
and there are several old military

ruins, such as barracks buildings, powder magazines, and a sunken musket redoubt, to explore.

The restored 1824 Officers' Quarters contain an interpretation center with exhibits tracing Adm. Rodney's famous victory at the Battle of the Saints in 1782. Look for the tavern under the arches of the cellars and bring beach towels for a swim.

To the east of Rodney Bay, the exclusive **Cap Estate** residential quarter occupies the hilly northern tip of the island. There are several stunning private houses, a golf course (see p. 280), and a lovely

restaurant in the estate's original 250-year-old great house.

SOUTH TO SOUFRIÈRE

There are two ways to explore the sights of southern St. Lucia, and visitors staying in the north of the island should reckon on a full-day to visit the Soufrière area (a two-hour drive from Castries). A hassle-free option is to take a day sail from Castries or Rodney Bay, which includes a land tour of the attractions around Soufrière. On the other hand, you can rent a car and tackle the beautiful switchback road down the Caribbean coast, with the

A guided walk tour picks up a trail into the St. Lucian rain forest.

Rain forest hikes & nature reserves

The trails in St. Lucia's 19,000-acre (7,700-ha) **National Rainforest** are maintained by the Forestry Department (see p. 280), which supplies good guides. Above Soufrière, several hikes depart from the trailhead near **Morne Fond St. Jacques.** Farther north is the **Barre de l'Isle Rainforest Trail,** which scales **Morne La Combe** (1,446 feet/441 m).

Bird-watching blinds have been set up in the **Mankote Mangrove** area near Vieux Fort, maintained by the **St. Lucia National Trust** (Tel 758/452-5005). The Trust also controls access to the **Maria Islands Nature Reserve,** with several unusual species of lizards and snakes; and the **Fregate Island Nature Reserve,** a frigatebird nesting ground. ■

option of continuing right around the island on a tour from the capital.

The road south to Soufrière starts from Morne Fortune, south of Castries, and swoops downhill into the banana plantations and cane fields of the Cul de Sac Valley. Across the ridge at the end of the valley, there is a turn on the right to **Marigot Bay,** an idyllic little hurricane hole surrounded by steep wooded hills where Rex Harrison talked to the animals during the filming of *Doctor Dolittle* in 1967.

The bay is a popular sailing center, with a marina and small hotel complex. The free *Gingerbread Express* ferry runs a regular two-minute service across the harbor mouth to a beach with a bar-restaurant.

A short run farther south is **Anse la Raye** (Skate Bay, named after the fish once caught here), a picturesque West Indian fishing village. Its narrow streets are lined with sun-bleached wooden cottages, and down on the waterfront you'll see a few fishing boats hollowed out of gommier trees.

Set in attractive gardens in the river valley behind the village is **La Sikwe Sugar Mill.** The old mill buildings contain antique plantation artifacts and a restored 40-foot (12-m) waterwheel. ■

Sports & activities

Day sails: Companies that offer sight-seeing tours to Soufrière and the Pitons from Castries or Pigeon Island include Brig Unicorn *(Tel 758/452-6811)*; Endless Summer *(Tel 758/450-8651)*; M/Y Vigie *(Tel 758/452-3762)*; and Surf Queen *(Tel 758/452-8351)*.

Diving & snorkeling: St. Lucia's underwater scenery is every bit as impressive as its terrestrial landscape, promising excellent visibility, a diverse collection of corals and marine life in top condition, and wreck dive opportunities. For example, Soufrière Marine Park offers reef dives straight off the beach. The island's largest operators are Scuba St. Lucia *(Anse Chastanet, Tel 758/459-7755)*; Dolphin Divers *(Rodney Bay Marina, Tel 758/452-9485)*; Rosemond's Trench Divers *(Marigot Bay, Tel 758/451-4761)*.

Golf: Attractive nine-hole course at the St. Lucia Golf & Country Club, Cap Estate *(Tel 758/450-8523, fax 758/450-0674)*.

Hiking: Guides are mandatory for hikes in the National Rain Forest; contact the Forestry Department in advance *(Tel 758/450-2231 or 758/450-2086)*.

Horseback riding: Estate and rain forest trails for a couple of hours or a week are available from Trekkers *(Morne Coubaril Estate, Soufrière, Tel 758/459-7340, fax 758/459-5759, e-mail: coubaril@ candw.lc)*. Plantation trails and beach picnics from Country Saddles *(Tel 758/450-1231) and* Trim's Riding Stables *(Tel 758/450-8273)*.

Sportfishing: Annie Baby *(Rodney Bay Marina, Tel 758/452-0412)*; Captain Mike's Watersports *(Vigie Marina, Tel 758/452-7044)*.

Water sports: Reduit Beach, in Rodney Bay, is well supplied with hotel water-sports concessions. The best windsurfing is off the southern tip of the island; Island Windsurfing *(Vieux Fort, Tel/fax 758/454-7400)*. ■

A solitary bell-ringer summons churchgoers in Vieux Fort.

Around Soufrière

DIAMOND BOTANICAL GARDENS, WATERFALL & MINERAL BATHS

Set in the hills above Soufrière, these lovely botanical gardens harbor a glorious profusion of tropical plants and trees crowding narrow pathways; a waterfall that tumbles down from La Soufrière.

🅰 275 A2 ✉ East of Soufrière 💲 $

LA SOUFRIÈRE SULPHUR SPRINGS

Because you can drive to within a few yards of La Soufrière's sinister and smelly volcanic vent, this attraction has been billed as "the world's only drive-in volcano." At the heart of the 7-acre (3-ha) crater, pools of boiling mud belch in the chalky moonscape.

🅰 275 A2 ✉ Southeast of Soufrière

MORNE COUBARIL ESTATE

The Morne Coubaril Estate, established in 1713, is still a working plantation producing cocoa and coconuts. During an hour-long tour, visitors learn how copra, coconuts, sugarcane, cocoa, and cassava were processed over a century ago and visit a reconstructed slave settlement.

🅰 275 A3 ✉ East of Soufrière ☎ 758/459-7340 💲 $$$

AROUND TO THE ATLANTIC COAST

Not far beyond Soufrière, the round-island route exchanges its border of lush green forest for open countryside. The roadside **Livity Art Studio**, located in the village of Victoria, is worth a stop for souvenir hunting, as is the **Arts and Crafts Development Centre** in Choiseul.

Down on **Choiseul Bay** the village lines a half-moon crescent of sand where brightly painted fishing boats unload their catch at the waterfront market.

The town of **Vieux Fort** crouches at the neck of the Moule à Chique, St. Lucia's most southerly point, facing St. Vincent in the distance. It is the site of Hewanorra International Airport. Off the east coast is the **Maria Islands Nature Reserve** (see p. 279), with its range of seabirds and several endemic wildlife species.

The relatively swift return route to Castries passes the hamlet of Micoud and an observation point overlooking the **Fregate Island Nature Reserve** (see p. 279). At the banana town of Dennery, the road heads inland, crossing the Barre de l'Isle Ridge on its journey back to the island capital. ∎

St. Vincent & the Grenadines

St. Vincent

▲ 265 B3

Visitor information

✉ Bay St., Kingstown

☎ 784/457-1502,
fax 784/456-2610,
e-mail: tourism @
caribsurf.com,
www.stvincentand
grenadines.com

**Famous for
its diving, the
uninhabited
Grenadine island
of Tobago Cays
can only be
reached by boat.**

ST. VINCENT HEADS THE CHAIN OF THE GRENADINE Islands like an emerald green kite with a 75-mile-long (120-km) tail trailing down toward Grenada. At 18 by 11 miles (29 by 18 km), it's the smallest and probably the least discovered of the Windward Islands, with a nearly impenetrable jungle heart where generations of Carib once hid out and kept the Europeans at bay for over two centuries.

ST. VINCENT

St. Vincent is still relatively over-looked today, outshone by the golden beaches and yachting havens of the Grenadines (see pp. 288–91) and the more widely publicized attractions of St. Lucia and Barbados. But while St. Vincent is no classic Caribbean idyll, all palm-fringed sands and rum punches (although the latter can be found), it does offer a quiet backwater charm, a miraculously undeveloped hinterland, and several hotels with discreet appeal for less hide-bound travelers.

Successive waves of Ciboney, Arawak, and Carib settlers paddled their way from South America to Hairoun, as they called St. Vincent before Europeans added it to the New World map. But the island's rugged terrain and the prospect of ending up at the sharp end of a Carib barbecue curtailed further investigation, and St. Vincent became a refuge for Carib people forced from other islands. They were joined by escaped African slaves, some the survivors of shipwrecks off the coast, while others set sail on rafts from Barbados and were

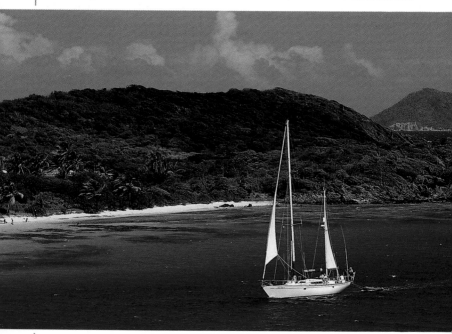

blown to St. Vincent by the westerly trade winds. Mixed Afro-Carib Black Carib soon outnumbered the original Yellow Carib, and started to take their lands. In retaliation the Yellow Carib allowed the French to establish a small colony in 1719. The Black Carib took to the hills to continue their resistance, surviving the First Carib War, initiated by a British invasion in 1763—a Caribbean extension of Britain's and France's long-running conflicts.

The French snatched the island back with embarrassing ease in 1779. When the challengers sailed in for the attack, the entire British garrison was away working the governor's plantation in the north of the island, and no one could locate the key to the gun battery. With the British reinstated by the Treaty of Versailles in 1783, the French switched allegiance to the Black Carib and backed the uprising that became known as the Second Carib War, or Brigands' War, lasting from 1795 to 1797. British plantations and settlements were torched and planters fed through the cane-crushing gear of their own sugar mills until the army regained control. The surviving 5,000 Black Carib were deported to British Honduras (present-day Belize). The last Yellow Carib retreated to the far north of St. Vincent, where their descendants still live today. The wars over, St. Vincent settled down to a quiet agrarian existence, growing a little sugar, Sea Island cotton, and arrowroot. It was granted independence from Britain in 1979, and it remains a member of the British Commonwealth.

Agriculture is still a mainstay of St. Vincent's economy, and the island is rampantly fertile. There's no escaping the evidence, from the stranglehold of its creeper-clad rain forest peaks to the vegetable plots

and tropical fruit orchards clinging to steep-sided valleys. Jagged mountains rip the underbellies of lowering gray rain clouds, so it always appears to be raining somewhere on the island. Regular dustings of volcanic fertilizer from Soufrière, one of the Caribbean's most active volcanoes, further enrich the crumbling red earth. They say you could plant a pencil here, and it would take root.

The capital of St. Vincent and the Grenadines is Kingstown on the south coast of St. Vincent, a 20-minute drive from the main tourist enclave at Villa. A busy working port, Kingstown is a transportation hub for the Grenadines and is served by regular ferries and small island-hopper aircraft.

Fresh produce spread on a Kingstown sidewalk

Fresh and canned goods are loaded onto the inter-island ferry at Kingstown for transport down the Grenadines.

Kingstown
🅜 283 B1

Fort Charlotte
✉ 10 minutes' drive W of Kingstown
☎ 784/456-1830

Botanical Gardens & National Museum
🅜 283 B1
✉ Off Leeward Hwy.
☎ 784/457-1003
🕐 Museum closed Sun.
💲 Museum $

It's also a good place to begin any exploration of the island. Look to the west coast for quiet volcanic sand beaches and secluded coves only accessible by boat. Yachting is a major attraction, and day sails can be combined with diving and snorkeling. Hikers can plan some great days out around La Soufrière and the Buccament River Valley, where the beautiful, rare St. Vincent parrot makes its home.

Kingstown
Hemmed in by a crown of steep, wooded ridges, the capital of St. Vincent and the Grenadines hugs the mile-long (1.5-km) curve of Kingstown Bay and pushes back up the hillside. Down on the waterfront there's a lively bustle of cargo ships, ferries, and fishing boats, and a brand-new cruise-ship berth is taking shape at the eastern end of the harbor. Behind the docks is Kingstown's pocket-size downtown district, which still has a few bumpy, old-fashioned cobbled streets and rows of arcaded shops sheltering the sidewalk from the sun and occasional cloudbursts.

Heading west on Halifax Street, take a detour down Hillsboro Street (by the Cenotaph) to investigate the **produce market.** The busiest days are Friday and Saturday, when farmers venture into town from all around the island. On the opposite side of Halifax Street, iron railings fence in the imposing gray stone **Law Courts,** where the St. Vincent Parliament meets. Pastel-painted **St. George's Anglican Cathedral,** founded in 1820, is just a little farther on. The interior of the church has an unusual stained-glass window depicting a red-robed angel. Supposedly commissioned by Queen Victoria to celebrate the birth of her first grandson, it was destined for St. Paul's Cathedral in London. But the monarch preferred her angels white, so the homeless window was presented to St. George's by the dean of St. Paul's. Among the many memorial plaques set in the walls of the cathedral, one commemorates Maj. Alexander Leith, a British war hero, who killed the Carib leader Chatoyer in a fencing duel on Dorsetshire Hill in 1795.

Across the way from the cathedral is Kingstown's most bizarre architectural monument, the 19th-century **St. Mary's Roman Catholic Church.** A riot of conflicting styles with a playful assortment of turrets, towers, pinnacles, and twisted barley-sugar columns, it was designed by a Belgian priest who drew his inspiration from pictures of famous European cathedrals.

On top of Berkshire Hill, at the western end of town, stands **Fort Charlotte,** which affords magnificent views down the Grenadines from its eyrie 600 feet (180 m) above the bay. Named for George III's queen, the sprawling fortress was constructed in 1806 but never fired a shot in anger. A pictorial history of "St. Vincent and the Carib Wars" by William Linzee Prescott adorns the former cells.

Kingstown's pride and joy are the **Botanical Gardens,** set in the hills above the town center. The gardens are the oldest of their kind in the Western Hemisphere, founded in 1763. They were intended as a research and breeding station for useful tropical plants run as a distant adjunct of Kew Gardens in London. Their most famous success story concerns the breadfruit tree, introduced from the South Pacific to provide cheap, nutritious food for slaves working on the Caribbean plantations. Capt. William Bligh (1754–1817) set sail with the first consignment of saplings from Tahiti aboard H.M.S. *Bounty* in

1787, but the small matter of a mutiny delayed his arrival until 1793. At first the slaves refused to touch the bland, alien fruit, but now the breadfruit's starchy flesh is a staple vegetable dish.

The gardens are free, but guides loiter near the entrance, and their services certainly liven up a visit. They know all the good stories, such as how the traveler's palm tree automatically aligns itself east-west and contains a reservoir of water for the lost and thirsty adventurer.

Within the 20-acre (8-ha) grounds is the rarely open but fascinating **National Museum,** which contains dozens of Amerindian artifacts, including a Carib skull with a classic flattened forehead achieved by binding a baby's head with wooden battens. There's no need to search for the aviary; the piercing screech of the St. Vincent parrot is guide enough. Predominantly yellow-gold with a glorious lilac head, these parrots are part of a captive breeding program.

Founded in 1823 and remodeled by Don Charles Verbeke in the 1930s and '40s, St. Mary's Roman Catholic Church combines Romanesque and Moorish elements.

Sports & activities

Day sails: For sight-seeing and snorkeling trips on St. Vincent, contact Baleine Tours *(Tel 784/457-4089)*; Fantasea Tours *(Tel 784/457-4477)*; Sea Breeze Nature Tours *(Tel 784/458-4969)*. On Bequia, contact Passion *(Tel 784/458-3884)*.

Diving: Dive St. Vincent *(Tel 784/457-4928, fax 784/457-4948, e-mail: bill2s@caribsurf.com, www. divestvincent.com)*; Dive Bequia *(Tel 784/458-3504, fax 784/458-3886)*; Dive Canouan *(Tel 784/458-8044,*

fax 784/458-8851); Grenadines Dive, Union Island *(Tel 784/458-8138, fax 784/458-8122)*.

Hiking & island tours: See p. 286.

Sailing charters: Barefoot Yacht Charters *(Tel 784/456-9526, fax 784/456-9328, e-mail: barebum@caribsurf.com)*; Nicholson Yacht Charters (U.S.) *(Tel/fax 617/661-0554 or 800/662-6006, e-mail: nicyacht@tiac.net)*. ∎

A short boat ride from Villa, Young Island was one of the region's first private island resorts.

Villa & Young Island resort
 283 B1
Visitor information
✉ Bay St., Kingstown
☎ 784/457-1502, fax 784/456-2610, e-mail: tourism@caribsurf.com, www.stvincentand grenadines.com

Montreal Estate Gardens
 283 B2
✉ N of Mesopotamia
🕐 Closed Sept.–Nov.
💲 $$$

Villa & the east coast

Most visitors will embark on their explorations from hotels in the small town of **Villa,** southeast along the coast from Kingstown. It makes an ideal starting point for touring the east coast of St. Vincent, along with its adjacent—and highly productive—agricultural hinterland.

Facing Villa's narrow sand beaches is the **Young Island resort,** which you can reach by water taxi from the waterfront. According to legend, the island was a gift from a Carib chief to Sir William Young, a British governor of St. Vincent who had presented the local leader with a horse. Behind Young Island are the ruins of **Fort Duvernette,** hugging another rocky islet. A staircase carved into the cliff leads to the 200-foot (60-m) summit, from which there are fine views.

North of Villa via the Vigie Highway, a panoramic vista extends over Kingstown to the Grenadines and inland to the misty mountains from a lookout point on the knife-edge ridge of **Ayri Hill.** The road continues to the fertile Marriaqua (or Mesopotamia) Valley, where much of the island's fresh produce is grown. A side road leads up to the gorgeous **Montreal Estate Gardens,** set in a circlet of cloudy peaks scoured by waterfalls. Giant orchids and tulip trees shade

Hiking & island tours

You can undertake short walks such as the Vermont Nature Trails easily without a guide, but local knowledge adds greatly to the rain forest experience. Guides are recommended for volcano hikes. The Forestry Department *(Tel 784/457-8594)* can assist, or contact Clint and Millie Hazell of HazeECO Tours for excursions to Trinity Falls, Soufrière, and other hikes, island tours, and boat trips *(Tel 784/457-8634, fax 784/457-8105, e-mail: hazeco@caribsurf.com);* SVG Tours *(Tel 784/458-4534, fax 784/458-4534);* Petit Byahaut nature resort *(Tel/fax 784/457-7008, www.outahere.com/petitbyahaut).* ■

tropical flowers on terraces built of river rocks.

The Yambou River flows down from the village of Mesopotamia, past rocks carved with Arawak petroglyphs, and through the Yambou Gorge toward the Atlantic coast. Here the Windward Highway wriggles along the shore to Georgetown, through banana and coconut plantations, and continues around to the north of the island, dominated by the impressive bulk of Soufrière volcano (4,048 feet/1,234 m). At **Rabacca Dry River,** just north of Georgetown, a four-wheel-drive track strikes up the trailhead for the 3.5-mile (5.5-km) hike up the east side of Soufrière. It's a rewarding walk to the mile-wide (1.5-km) crater rim and back. A more challenging route sets out from Chateaubelair on the Caribbean side, and the two can be combined for a really strenuous expedition (see p. 286).

The west coast & Falls of Baleine

The Leeward Highway clambers north out of Kingstown and begins a roller-coaster journey past a series of small fishing villages to the beaches around Barrouallie and Richmond. Beyond these coastal attractions are a series of diverting stops, ranging from archaeological artifacts to exotic wildlife and scenery on a grand scale.

About 5 miles (8 km) from Kingstown, as the highway runs through the Buccament River Valley, a side road leads to the **Vermont Nature Trails.** The connecting trails are well marked and easy to follow, making a 2-mile (3-km) rain forest loop between the 1,000- to 2,000-foot (300- to 600-m) levels of Grand Bonum Mountain in the 10,870-acre (4,440-ha) **St. Vincent Parrot Reserve** (*Tel 784/457 1502. Map 283 B2*). One path follows the Dalaway River, which supplies 45 percent of St. Vincent's drinking water, and heads on through an area of Caribbean pine trees dripping with epiphytes. It continues into the rain forest proper, where giant buttressed santinay trees are a favorite parrot habitat. Between 500 and 700 parrots live in colonies spread about the preserve. It's usually easiest to spot them in the late afternoon at the **Parrot Lookout,** perched on the edge of a deep green wooded valley. Also keep an eye out for brilliantly colored hooded tanagers found only on St. Vincent and Grenada, several species of hummingbirds, and broad-winged and black hawks.

Back on the highway, at **Layou,** 1,300-year-old Arawak petroglyphs adorn a 20-foot (6-m) rock. *(The site is on private land, so call the Kingstown Tourist Office, Tel 784/457-1502, in advance, or ask for permission to visit the site.)* **Peter's Hope Bay** and **Keartons Beach,** lying on either side of the fishing village of Barrouallie, are good spots for a dip in the Caribbean Sea, and there's another beach near **Richmond** at the end of the highway.

A popular excursion from here is the 45-minute hike to **Trinity Falls** *(Map 283 B3),* which you can reach from a trail several miles north of town. The lovely rain forest walk emerges at a swimming hole fed by the waterfall.

In the north end of the island, accessible only by boat (*Baleine Tours, Tel 809/457 4089, or Fantasea Tours, Tel 809/457 4477*), are the **Falls of Baleine,** tumbling down from Soufrière in a 60-foot (18-m) cascade to a rock pool. Several vessels combine a visit to the falls with snorkeling (see p. 285). ■

Captain Bligh's bounty: Huge glossy-leaved breadfruit trees and their edible fruits are a familiar feature of many backyards.

St. Vincent

4▷

Young
Island

Bequia   Old-Hegg
                Turtle Sanctuary
Port Elizabeth   ◇ Industry Bay
Admiralty Bay ✈ ▲ Mt. Pleasant

3▷ West Cay   Derrick   Petit Nevis   Battowia

                         Isle a
                         Quatre   Baliceaux I.
         Pigeon
         Island
                                      The Pillories
                    Endeavour Bay   Mustique

                    Britannia   Macaroni Bay
                    Bay   ○ Rabbit Island

                              Petit
                              Mustique I.
            Petit Canouan   Savan Islands

2▷

         Pt. Jupiter   Pt. Moody
      Canouan I.   ▲ 267m
         Grand Bay   Mt. Royal

      Glossy Bay   ✈ Charlestown
                    Friendship
                    Bay

      Mayreau I.
      Station Hill ▲   ◇ Horseshoe Reef
1▷ Bloody Bay
Chatham Bay ✈ Clifton   Tobago Cays   Sail Rock
     305m ▲
Mt. Parnassus Ashton   Palm Island (Prune I.)
Union
Island   Petit St. Vincent

   △   △   △
   A   B   C

0   20 kilometers
0   10 miles

**Stunning a fish
with rum**

📍 265 B2

Visitor information

✉ Bay St., Kingstown,
   St. Vincent

☎ 784/457-1502,
   fax 784/456-2610,
   e-mail: tourism@
   caribsurf.com,
   www.stvincentand
   grenadines.com.

THE GRENADINES

An irregular chain of 30-plus tiny islands and cays interspersed with a host of lesser sandbars and reefs, the Grenadines trail off from St. Vincent for about 35 miles (56 km) toward Grenada and the Grenadian Grenadine islands of Carriacou and Petit Martinique (see p. 300).

Fewer than a quarter of the islands are inhabited (part of their charm for yachtsmen), while some welcome no-frills sailors and divers, and others have been transformed into tiny oases of barefoot luxury.

Although it may be quicker to get around by island-hopper plane, the real way to see the Grenadines is by boat.

The M/V *Barracuda* mail boat sails from St. Vincent to Bequia and Canouan, Mayreau, and Union Islands on Mondays and Thursdays, making the return trip on Tuesdays and Fridays, and a round-trip minus Bequia on Saturdays.

Further information about excursions and day sails is available from the Kingstown tourist office (*Tel 784/457-1502*).

Bequia

An hour's ferry ride from St. Vincent is Bequia (BECK-way; *Map 288 C3),* the largest of the St. Vincent Grenadines at 6 square miles (15 sq km) and an utterly beguiling tourist retreat. The quaint main settlement of Port Elizabeth fringes Admiralty Bay, where the ferry docks within a stone's throw of shops and waterfront restaurants overlooked by the 18th-century Hamilton Battery. Water taxis shuttle around the bay to the palm-backed sands of Princess Margaret Beach and Lower Bay.

You can tour the island on foot or by taxi, or rent a scooter for a trip up to **Mount Pleasant,** with its view south to the tip of Grenada on a clear day. Down on the wind-ward side there's safe swimming and snorkeling at **Industry Bay,**

and it's worth visiting the **Old-Hegg Turtle Sanctuary** *(Park Beach, Tel 473/458-3245)* at the end of the track to Park Beach.

Canouan Island

Midway down the Grenadines, dry and hilly Canouan Island (pronounced CAN-oo-ahn; *Map 288 B2)* has beautiful sandy beaches around the port settlement of **Charlestown** in the curve of Grand Bay. A quiet spot with fewer than 800 inhabitants, the island is being slowly developed.

Mayreau Island & Tobago Cays

Two fabulous beaches flank the 1.5-square-mile (4-sq-km) scrubby island of **Mayreau** (pronounced MY-row; *Map 288 B1).* It's a steep climb from the makeshift dock to the village on **Station Hill** (population

Heading for a day on the beach away from it all in the Grenadines

Above: Carved wooden gingerbread decorations adorn porches and gables in Mustique. Opposite: Yachtsmen play castaway for the day on Sandy Island at the tail end of the Grenadine chain.

money-is-no-object accommodations in 70 or so private villas, a 20-room hotel, and a distinctly upscale B&B.

Yachts gather in **Britannia Bay,** and day-trippers are permitted ashore (no ferry service) to sample the gleaming white sands of **Macaroni Bay** or enjoy a drink at Basil's Bar. There are good walks around the 1,350-acre (546-ha) island and more swimming and snorkeling at secluded **Gallicaux Bay** and the hotel beach at **Endeavour Bay.**

Union Island

While not the most alluring Grenadine, **Union** (Map 288 A1) is certainly the most visually arresting, with a range of peaks culminating in Mount Parnassus (999 feet/305 m), the island chain's highest point. It's a busy transportation hub, with a lively yacht harbor and a couple of hotels at **Clifton,** the main town (visitor information, Tel 473/458-8350).

The best beaches are Chatham Bay on the west coast and **Bloody Bay** to the north, both only accessible on foot or by boat. ∎

fewer than 200). A couple of bar-restaurants cater to yachtsmen, and there are rooms to rent and a low-key resort on **Salt Whistle Bay.**

The four deserted **Tobago Cays** (Map 288 B1) lie east of Mayreau, surrounding **Horseshoe Reef,** a wildlife reserve and fabulous snorkeling spot accessible by day sails.

Mustique
The ultra-chic Caribbean hideaway of **Mustique** (Map 288 C2) offers

Palm Island & Petit St. Vincent

The Grenadine Islands make idyllic miniature resorts. Young Island, off the south coast of St. Vincent, is a prime example, and there are two more pint-size beach hideaways in the southern Grenadines. A mile off Union Island is Palm Island, which had to change its name from Prune Island after owners John and Mary Caldwell planted hundreds of coconut palms in their laid-back resort. Three miles farther south is Petit St. Vincent (better known as PSV; Map 288 B1), another barefoot paradise to welcome yachtsmen. ∎

Room service local style on Petit St. Vincent

Grenada

A picturesque huddle of West Indian houses is sandwiched between St. George's Anglican Church and the Carenage waterfront.

TYPICALLY GREEN AND MOUNTAINOUS, GRENADA IS THE southernmost Windward Island, only 100 miles (150 km) or so from the coast of South America. Its smaller sister islands, Carriacou and Petit Martinique, are part of the Grenadines chain, which stretches north to St. Vincent. Grenada is wrapped in rain forest and sprinkled with sandy beaches. It's the Spice Island of the Caribbean, one of the world's top nutmeg producers (even the national flag incorporates a nutmeg). Visitors can hike and dive, bathe in rain orest waterfalls, stock up on spices from stalls run by pipe-chewing old biddies, and generally kick back and relax on one of the friendliest small islands (21 by 12 miles/34 by 19 km) in the region.

Grenada

🅜 265 A2

Visitor information

✉ S side of The Carenage, St. George

☎ 473/440-2001 or 473/440-2279

Christened Concepción by Columbus in 1498, Grenada (pronounced Gren-AY-dah) was renamed by Spanish sailors homesick for the hills of southern Spain. French settlers from Martinique purchased the island from indigenous Carib for a handful of beads and tools in 1650, but the peace was short lived and the French soon routed the opposition. The last Carib are said to have jumped to their deaths from the cliffs at La Morne de Sauteurs (Caribs' Leap) in 1651 (see p. 298). The French and English fought for control of

the plantation island until it was ceded to Britain in 1783. During the French Revolution, Grenada was the scene of a bloody slave revolt led by Julien Fédon, a French planter, from his isolated coffee and cocoa estate at Belividere. Arms were smuggled in from Guadeloupe, and the rebels overran most of the island, slaughtering British settlers, including the governor, during the 15-month insurrection. When the British finally regained control in June 1796, Fédon disappeared and the plantations were in ruins.

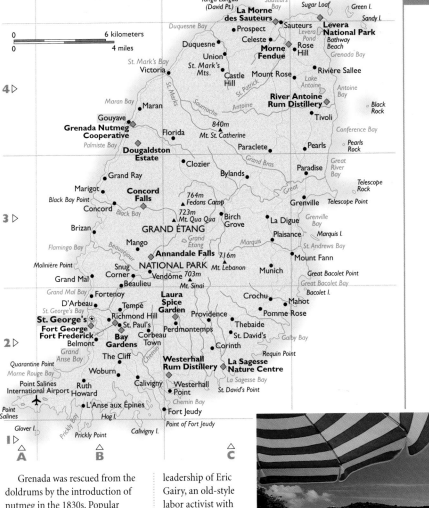

Yachts lie at anchor in Mount Hartman Bay on Grenada's south coast.

Grenada was rescued from the doldrums by the introduction of nutmeg in the 1830s. Popular legend has it that a doctor from the East Indies arrived with a couple of nutmeg trees in his baggage and jazzed up the local rum punch with a dusting of grated nutmeg. Grenada's nutmeg industry took off in the 1850s, when East Indian plantations were stricken with a fatal disease, and other spices were introduced. Thus the West Indies finally achieved a spice island by default, 400 years after Columbus set out to find one.

Grenada took full independence from Britain in 1974, under the leadership of Eric Gairy, an old-style labor activist with considerable local support. Freed from colonial restraints, Gairy's regime became increasingly despotic. In March 1979 the opposition New Jewel Movement staged a bloodless coup led by Maurice Bishop, who initiated a program of socialist reforms that revitalized the economy, but soon he began to look equally repressive. Democratic elections were not called, the opposition was gagged,

Above: Costumed carnival-goers wait to take their place in the main parade through St. George's.

Opposite: Two spices in one: Freshly opened nutmeg fruit show how strings of red mace enclose the nutmeg shell.

ties with Cuba and the Eastern Bloc caused uneasiness abroad, and in October 1983 Bishop was ousted by a hard-line Marxist-Leninist faction of his own party and placed under house arrest. As demonstrators rallied in support of Bishop, troops opened fire, killing more than 50 people. Bishop was executed in Fort George alongside five of his closest supporters. Four days later, on October 25, a joint U.S.-eastern Caribbean "friendly invasion" of Grenada restored order.

Most Grenadians supported the "intervention," as it is referred to locally, and U.S. visitors are very welcome. The upheavals of the 1980s, which kept tourists away, have been overcome, and the island has benefited from its enforced isolation. There's a heartening awareness of environmental issues, and tourism has been allowed to develop at a gentle pace. But development is heating up, and the advice is to get here soon, before it gets too touristy to see Grenada at its best.

ST. GEORGE'S

There's no better introduction to Grenada than sailing into St. George's Harbour. It is one of the most picturesque ports in the Caribbean, nestled within the steep-sided walls of an extinct volcanic crater and guarded by a battery of old fortresses. St. George's was founded by the French but renamed in honor of England's King George III, and there are numerous examples of Georgian colonial architecture among the church steeples and neat rows of red-roofed homes that cling to the precipitous hillsides like contour lines.

A sharp ridge divides St. George's into two parts linked by a Victorian tunnel bored through the rock in 1895. On the harbor side is the horseshoe-shaped **Carenage** (harbor), which hugs the waterfront, edged by shops and restaurants. The wharves where ships were once careened (tipped on their sides to have their hulls cleaned) are now a bustle of cargo boats and ferries, fishing sloops from nearby Carriacou, and tenders delivering cruise-ship passengers into the hands of predatory spice ladies selling their wares.

In the shadow of the ridge is the **Grenada National Museum,** housed in former French barracks dating from 1704. Island history and culture are explored in an assortment of Amerindian finds, colonial knickknacks, and a

Grenadian spices

Grenada is an olfactory banquet of spices redolent with the pungent tang of nutmeg, cloves, and sweet woody cinnamon. Nutmeg is the island's most important spice and easy to find by the roadside and in the hills. The nutmeg tree (*Myristica fragrans*) produces an apricot-like yellow fruit that splits when ripe to reveal a brown shell covered with a waxy red web of mace. The fruit is used to make preserves, the mace is processed as a separate spice, the inedible shell is recycled as a path-building material, and the inner kernel is the spice used in cooking and pharmaceuticals.

Like the nutmeg tree, cinnamon trees were imported from the East Indies. The bark is used as a food flavoring. Allspice (*Pimenta officinale*) originated in Jamaica. As its name implies, it tastes like nutmeg, cinnamon, and cloves all rolled into the one tiny unripe fruit. ∎

Grenada National Museum

✉ Monckton St. (off Long St.)

☎ 473/440-3725

🕐 Closed Sun.

💲 $

Fort George

✉ Church St.

detailed, well-balanced account of the 1983 intervention.

Close to the museum is the 350-foot-long (107-m) **Sendall Tunnel,** which burrows beneath the ridge to the seafront **Esplanade** on the bay side of St. George's. Protecting the town from the headland at the harbor mouth is **Fort George,** which now serves as a police station. It is open to the public, and there are great views over town from the 18th-century battlements. A block back from the minibus depot on the bayfront is the **market square,** a hive of activity best visited on a Saturday morning. Women in headscarves and bright cotton dresses preside over an edible carpet of fresh fruit, vegetables, and spices spread out on the sidewalk as they banter with customers from the shady recesses of large, striped umbrellas. A strenuous climb up Market Hill leads to **Church Street,** where several of St. George's finest Georgian buildings perch on the

hillside. Eighteenth-century **York House** is where the Grenadian Parliament sits and the Supreme Court presides. **St. George's Anglican Church,** constructed in 1825, contains memorial plaques commemorating the British planters and governor, Sir Ninian Home, killed during Fédon's Rebellion (see p. 292). Market Hill continues up to a busy junction orchestrated by a white-gloved traffic officer. Lucas Street heads past **Government House,** the governor-general's official residence guarded by pith-helmeted sentries, to tumble-down **Fort Matthew** and the rather better-preserved remains of **Fort Frederick** (*Tel 473/440 2001*).

GRAND ANSE & THE SOUTH COAST

Lying just over 2 miles (3 km) south of St. George's is Grand Anse, Grenada's main tourist enclave. A clutch of low-rise hotels lines the two-mile (3-km) stretch of white sand beach facing the Caribbean

Sports & activities

Bicycling: Ride Grenada (Grand Anse, Tel 473/444-1157).

Day sails: The Moorings (Tel 473/444-4439 or 800/437-7880, e-mail: yacht@moorings.com, www.travelgrenada.com/secret.htm); Starwind Enterprises (Tel 473/440-3678).

Diving & snorkeling: Dive Grenada (Tel 473/444-1092, fax 473/440-6699, e-mail: dive'da@caribsurf.com, www.divegrenada.com); Grand Anse Aquatics (Tel 473/444-1046, fax 473/444-4808); Scuba Express (Tel 473/444-2133; fax 473/444-0156, e-mail: trueblue@cpsnet.com).

Hiking: Expeditions from Henry's Safari Tours (Tel 473/444-5313, fax 473/444-4460, e-mail: safari@caribsurf.com, www.travelgrenada.com/safari.htm); Telfor Hiking Tours (Tel 473/442-6200).

Tours: Minibus tours and boat trips from Henry's Safari Tours (see above); Eco-Tours (Tel 473/444-9367, fax 473/444-8104, e-mail: victoria@travelgrenada.com, www.travelgrenada.com/victoria.htm).

Sportfishing: Bezo Charters (Tel 473/443-5021); Evans Chartering Services (Tel 473/444-4422). ■

Sea. The swimming is safe, and water-sports concessions rent Windsurfers, dinghies, and kayaks. Waterskiing and parasailing are also available, and dive operators arrange trips to the reef sites off Molinière Point just north of St. George's, the Kick 'em Jenny submarine volcano, and the scuttled wreck of the *Bianca C*, a cruise ship that caught fire in St. George's Harbour in 1961.

West of Grand Anse, en route to the very tip of the island at Point Salines, is **Morne Rouge Beach,** set in a quiet cove. There are sandy crescents at **Dr. Grooms Beach, Magazine Beach,** and the deliciously named **Pink Gin Beach,** which nestles beneath a fashionable spa hotel. Tucked into the rocks at the end of **Tamarind Beach** is a great bar-restaurant with kayak rentals and snorkeling. On the southern shore of the peninsula is another handful of hotels, apartments, and private homes inhabiting the secluded coves of **Prickly Bay** and the narrow strip of sand beach at **L'Anse aux Épines.**

As the main road heads east from St. George's and the beaches, it swiftly runs into the countryside and cane fields growing at the foot of steep, forested hills. **Bay Gardens,** set in the hills, make an interesting detour. More than 5,000 species of tropical plants display their finery along nutmeg shell paths winding around the site of an old sugar mill. You could also drop in at the **Laura Spice Garden,** on the road to Windsor Castle, where top-quality herbs and spices are grown and packaged for export. At **Westerhall Rum Distillery,** they will probably provide an impromptu factory tour on weekdays. A few pieces of antique distilling equipment can still be seen.

Midway along the south coast, look for signs to **La Sagesse**

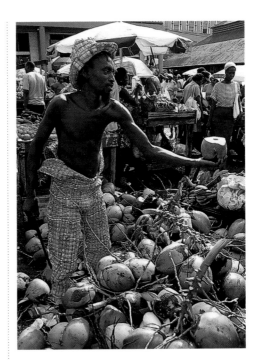

A coconut seller offers fresh coconut milk straight from the shell in St. George's market.

Nature Centre. Follow the bumpy track to the beach, past a carefully tended checkerboard of vegetable gardens edged by banana plants and huge mango and soursop trees. The nature center is rather less official than it sounds. In reality it is a charming guesthouse and alfresco restaurant arranged around a little pink plantation house on a lovely beach.

AROUND NORTHERN & CENTRAL GRENADA

A clockwise circuit of northern Grenada, returning to St. George's via the central highlands, reveals a landscape of rich diversity from sea-level mangrove swamps to rain forest mountains, and scenes from island life in spice plantations, a nutmeg factory, and charming Creole villages.

Heading north of St. George's, the main road hugs the twisting coastline, edged by cliffs and the

Bay Gardens
- 293 B2
- St. Paul's
- 473/440-5338
- Closed Sun.
- $

Laura Spice Garden
- 293 C2
- Perdmontemps, St. David's
- 473/440-3458
- Closed weekends
- $

Caribbean Sea. At Concord, follow signs for **Concord Falls** inland up into the hills through spice plantations and cocoa walks (cocoa tree groves) to the lowest of the three falls. It's an energetic 30-minute climb to the second fall and one and a half hours to the upper fall; both have swimming holes. The trail (4.5 hours) continues all the way to **Grand Étang** (see p. 299).

Back on the main road just south of the fishing village of Gouyave, look for the **Dougaldston Estate** on the right. In a sweet-smelling clapboard barn learn how nutmeg, mace, cloves, allspice, cinnamon, and cocoa are still harvested and processed in the old-fashioned (technology-free) way. In Gouyave (French for "guava"), you'll find the **Grenada Nutmeg Cooperative,** which welcomes visitors interested in sniffing around its processing plant, stuffed full with sacks of nutmeg kernels ready for market. On the beach behind the main street, brightly painted fishing boats are drawn up on the sand.

Beyond Gouyave the round-island road circles the St. Mark's Mountains and **Mount St. Catherine** (2,757 feet/840 m), Grenada's highest peak. The clifftop known as **La Morne des Sauteurs** (Leapers' Hill) on the north coast, is where, in 1651, the island's last Carib threw themselves to their deaths (see p. 292).

South of Sauteurs is the **Morne Fendue plantation house** (*Tel 473/440 2001*), which makes a great lunch stop.

In the northeast is **Levera National Park** (*Map 293 D5; Tel 473/440 2001*), with its mangrove swamp and fine stretch of golden sand where leatherback turtles come ashore to lay their eggs in summer (April–June). The swimming is safer, however, at nearby **Bathway Beach.** Bird-watching is good around **Levera Pond,** a wild-fowl breeding and feeding ground where scarlet ibis are occasionally spotted. Nearby is the Rivière Sallee Boiling Spring, which provides Grenada's token volcanic activity.

The main road runs inland above the Atlantic coast, through the pretty villages of Mt. Rose, Tivoli (see p. 299), and Paradise, past Creole cottages and colorful gardens, giant mango trees, wandering goats, and posses of giggling schoolchildren wearing neat uniforms. From **Grenville,** Grenada's second-largest town, the cross-island road climbs into the rain forest and **Grand Étang** (Big Pond) **National Park.** Natural history displays at the park center detail local geology, flora, and fauna, and

Barn doors flung open to catch the breeze, workers sort and prepare spices by hand.

RIVER ANTOINE

On the coast road east of Tivoli, the River Antoine Rum Distillery is worth a detour on weekdays. One of the oldest working distilleries in the Caribbean, it uses antique cane-crushing equipment still powered by a water mill fed by Lake Antoine, a mile (1.5 km) away. The brave can sample the local brew. The 18-acre (72-ha) crater lake is another notable birding spot visited by snail kites, limpkins, and whistling ducks, among others. ∎

a 15-minute nature trail offers sweeping views off to the coast and a chance of spotting Mona monkeys, introduced to Grenada from Africa more than 300 years ago. Across the road a path leads to the **Grand Étang crater lake,** circled by a 90-minute shoreline trail. The trailhead for longer hikes to Mount Qua Qua and Concord Falls is a short distance west of the park center.

On the road back to St. George's, **Annadale Falls** is a popular beauty spot with a swimming hole fed by the 30-foot (9-m) cascade. ∎

Hiking in Grand Étang National Park

Grenada's best hiking opportunities lie within this national park in the central highlands. The **Mount Qua Qua Trail** is a moderately energetic, three-hour round-trip from the park center through elfin woodlands to the rocky summit of Mount Qua Qua. For a more challenging hike, take the Concord Trail, which continues from Mount Qua Qua for a further three hours to the Concord Falls.

Other popular hiking destinations include the **Honeymoon Falls** and the **Seven Sisters waterfalls,** both of which are best tackled with a guide (see page 296). Birds of the rain forest include tanagers, doves, thrushes, and broad-winged hawks, while armadillos *(tatoo)* and opossums *(manicou)* live at ground level. ∎

Grenada Nutmeg Cooperative
- 293 B4
- Gouyave
- Closed Sun.
- $

Grand Étang National Park & center
- 293 C3
- S of Gouyave
- 473/442-7425
- Closed Sun.
- $

Carriacou

Carriacou
📍 265 B2
Visitor information
✉ Main St.,
   Hillsborough
☎ 473/443-7948

Some 23 miles (37 km) north of Grenada (a three-hour ferry ride), Carriacou (pronounced CARRI-ah-cou) is the largest of the Grenadines (8 by 5 miles/13 by 8 km), with a population of about 6,000.

The island is hilly and dry, largely undeveloped, and fringed by white sand strands. It takes its name from the Carib word for "land of reefs," and there's good snorkeling and diving offshore (see below). Carriacou was once planted with cotton and sugar, but when the plantations died out in the 19th century, the islanders turned to fishing, boatbuilding, and smuggling. **Hillsborough,** the tiny capital, is built on a curving bay. Close by are several waterfront restaurants and the small **Carriacou Museum** (*Paterson St., closed Sun.*).

Its collections of Amerindian and colonial relics are laid out in a former cotton ginnery.

Just north of town, the village of **Windward** is a good place to watch the local boatbuilders in action, working the white cedar wood grown on the island. Farther up the coast, Anse la Roche has a pretty and secluded beach.

South of Hillsborough, **Paradise Beach** boasts a lovely sweep of white sand with a beach bar facing a palm-shaded island.

The village of **L'Esterre** is home to Carriacou's living legend, naïve artist Canute Calliste, who welcomes visitors to his tiny studio. Farther afield on the southwest shore is Tyrrel Bay, a yacht anchorage with a modest "restaurant row." ∎

Sports & activities

Diving & snorkeling

Carriacou's best dive and snorkel sites are found around the offshore islets in Hillsborough Bay and uninhabited Saline and Frigate Islands to the south. Water taxis will ferry passengers out to Sandy Island from the Hillsborough waterfront. Sharks, rays, and eels are among the marine inhabitants of the Mabouya Island dive sites. Contact local operators Carriacou Silver Diving *(Tel/fax 473/443-7882);* or Tanki's Watersport Paradise *(Tel 473/443-8406, fax 473/443-8391).* ∎

Petit Martinique

Petit Martinique
📍 265 B2

The diminutive island of Petit Martinique is a volcanic cone lying 2.5 miles (4 km) off the northeast coast of Carriacou.

Served by ferries from Hillsborough, Petit (pronounced PETT-y) Martinique is pretty much a closed community of 900 or so islanders said to have one of the highest per capita incomes in the eastern Caribbean. As fishing and boat-building could hardly account for this, smuggling would appear to be the key, and the Petit Martinicans are currently very unamused by the joint U.S.-Grenadian coastguard base that has been set up on the island supposedly to combat drug trafficking throughout the region. Tourist facilities are limited to one small guesthouse. ∎

Once known as the Gateway to the West Indies, Barbados has welcomed travelers for centuries. The island's exquisite beaches, sophisticated lodgings, and a wealth of things to see and do add greatly to its present-day allure.

Barbados

Celebrating the Crop Over festival

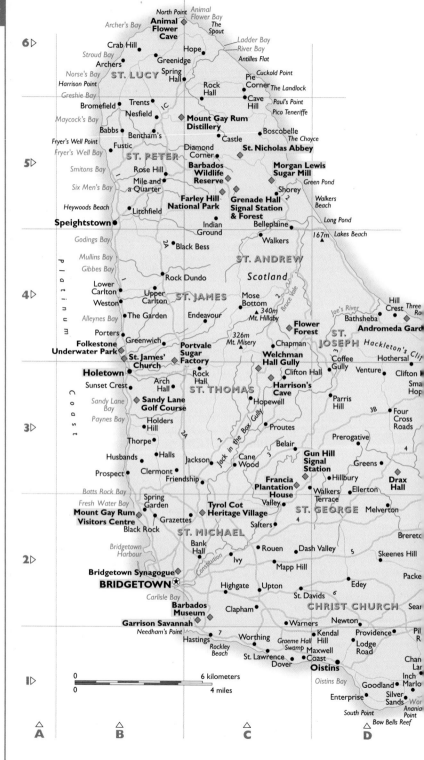

North Point
Animal Flower Bay
Animal Flower Cave
The Spout
Archer's Bay
6▷
Crab Hill
Hope
Stroud Bay
Greenidge
Archers
Ladder Bay
River Bay
Antilles Flat
Norse's Bay
Spring Hall
ST. LUCY
Cuckold Point
Harrison Point
Rock Hall
Pie Corner
Greshie Bay
Cave Hill
The Landlock
Bromefield
Trents
Paul's Point
Nesfield
Pico Teneriffe
Maycock's Bay
Mount Gay Rum Distillery
Babbs
Boscobelle
Bentham's
Castle
The Choyce
Fryer's Well Point
Fustic
Diamond Corner
St. Nicholas Abbey
Fryer's Well Bay
ST. PETER
5▷
Smitons Bay
Rose Hill
Barbados Wildlife Reserve
Morgan Lewis Sugar Mill
Mile and a Quarter
Shorey
Green Pond
Six Men's Bay
Walkers Beach
Farley Hill National Park
Grenade Hall Signal Station & Forest
Heywoods Beach
Litchfield
Belleplaine
Long Pond
Speightstown
Indian Ground
Walkers
167m
Lakes Beach
Godings Bay
Black Bess
ST. ANDREW
Mullins Bay
Scotland
Gibbes Bay
Rock Dundo
4▷
Lower Carlton
Upper Carlton
ST. JAMES
Mose Bottom
Hill Crest
Three Ro
Weston
340m
Mt. Hillaby
Joe's River
Bathsheba
Alleynes Bay
The Garden
Endeavour
326m
Flower Forest
Andromeda Gard
Porters
Mt. Misery
Chapman
ST. JOSEPH
Hackleton's
Greenwich
Welchman Hall Gully
Coffee Gully
Hothersal
Clif
Folkestone Underwater Park
Portvale Sugar Factory
Venture
Clifton
St. James' Church
Rock Hall
Clifton Hall
Sma Hop
Holetown
Arch Hall
Harrison's Cave
Sunset Crest
ST. THOMAS
Parris Hill
3B
Four Cross Roads
Sandy Lane Bay
Sandy Lane Golf Course
Hopewell
Holders Hill
Proutes
4
Paynes Bay
3▷
Thorpe
Belair
Prerogative
Husbands
Halls
Gun Hill Signal Station
Greens
Prospect
Clermont
Jackson
Cane Wood
Hillbury
Drax Hall
Friendship
Francia Plantation House
Walkers Terrace
Ellerton
Batts Rock Bay
Valley
Fresh Water Bay
Spring Garden
Tyrol Cot Heritage Village
ST. GEORGE
Melverton
Mount Gay Rum Visitors Centre
Grazettes
Salters
4
Breretc
Black Rock
ST. MICHAEL
Bridgetown Harbour
Bank Hall
Rouen
Dash Valley
Skeenes Hill
2▷
Ivy
Mapp Hill
Packe
Constitution
Upton
Edey
Bridgetown Synagogue
Highgate
St. Davids
BRIDGETOWN ✪
Carlisle Bay
Clapham
CHRIST CHURCH
Sear
Barbados Museum
Warners
Newton
Garrison Savannah
Needham's Point
Providence
Pil R
Hastings
Worthing
Kendal Hill
Lodge Road
1▷
Rockley Beach
Graeme Hall Swamp
Maxwell
Chan Lar
St. Lawrence
Dover
Coast
Inch
Oistins
Marlo
0   6 kilometers
Goodland
Silver Sands
Wor
0   4 miles
Oistins Bay
Enterprise
Ananía Point
South Point
Bow Bells Reef

△   △   △   △
A   **B**   **C**   **D**

Barbados

BARBADOS LIES 100 MILES (150 KM) EAST OF THE WINDWARD ISLANDS, surrounded by the Atlantic Ocean. Unlike its volcanic neighbors, the island is an undulating limestone massif. Its coral rock underpinnings are responsible for the famous Platinum Coast beaches, the island's upscale tourist heartland. The more informal (and affordable) side of Barbados is the south coast resort area, with a string of equally appealing beaches by day, some of the best dining on the island, and a lively nightlife after dark.

The British ruled Barbados for 340 uninterrupted years before independence and left an indelible, slightly formal imprint on this former sugar colony. There's considerable pride in the Barbados Parliament and more than a touch of Little England in the local passion for cricket, the ritual of afternoon tea, and dressing for dinner in some quarters.

Barbados takes its name from the huge, native bearded fig tree, also known as a banyan, which drops a curtain of aerial roots to the ground. Portuguese explorers called them *los barbados* (bearded ones). Although Amerindian settlers discovered the island almost 4,000 years ago, it was uninhabited when British colonists landed near the site of Holetown on the west coast in 1627. Dutch settlers played a significant part in developing the early plantations, and they introduced sugarcane from Brazil in 1637. As the colony prospered, indentured laborers were shipped out from Britain, and soon African slaves were brought in to swell the plantation workforce.

With the abolition of slavery in 1834, the sugar industry lurched from virtual failure to moderate success in the early 20th century, but another downswing in the economy in 1937 led to rioting and the establishment of a strong labor union movement, which worked toward independence from Britain in 1966.

Beyond the sprawling capital city of Bridgetown, and the resort areas to either side, the landscape is remarkably rural. Cane fields and pockets of woodland roll back from the leeward coast, while Mount Hillaby (1,089 feet/340 m), and the 1,000-foot (300-m) crest of Hackleton's Cliff are poised dramatically above the Atlantic on the windward coast. The island is divided into eleven parishes (Christ Church and ten named after saints), which are frequently given as an address rather than the name of a village. ∎

Congor Rocks
Castle Congor Bay
Conset Bay
Coach Hill Conset Point
Codrington College
Palmers Bell Point
JOHN Bayfield Ragged Point
Massiah Street Deebles Point
Thicket Marley Vale The Chair
Kitridge Bay
Kitridge Point
ottage le Merricks
Church Palmetto Bay
ST. PHILIP Bottom Bay
Robinsons Cave Bay
ezer Sunbury Plantation House Sam Lord's Castle Long Bay
Six Cross Roads Shark's Hole
n Factory & eritage Park Blades The Crane
dbourne Crane Bay
atricks Mangrove Cobbler's Rock
Foul Bay
Walronds St. Martins
Cobbler's Reef
Salt Cave Point
rantley Adams nternational irport
arlowe Point

E F

Area of map detail
ATLANTIC OCEAN
Caribbean Sea

Bridgetown

BRIDGETOWN, THE ISLAND'S ENERGETIC CAPITAL CITY, IS an important Caribbean business center and home to about 100,000 residents. The heart of the city lies on The Careenage, a narrow inner harbor at the mouth of the Constitution River, where an English expedition discovered an Amerindian bridge in 1625. A few fishing boats and pleasure craft now tie up to the wharves, where ships were once tipped onto their sides to have their hulls cleaned and repaired (careened). A handful of waterfront cafés makes The Careenage a pleasant place to take a break and watch the world go by.

Bridgetown's tribute to Admiral Lord Nelson predates Nelson's Column in London by more than half a century.

On the north bank of the inlet is **National Heroes Square,** known until recently as Trafalgar Square. Here the mellow complex of coral rock public buildings contains the House of Assembly, the seat of the Barbados Parliament where the island's legislators meet. Although the buildings only date from the 19th century, the historic assembly was first established in 1639.

A statue of Lord Nelson has stood on the square since 1813, when it was erected by British settlers to commemorate Nelson's victory and death at the Battle of Trafalgar. However, the good admiral may soon be on the move to a new location and his place taken by a Barbadian figure.

A short walk east on St. Michael's Row leads you to **St. Michael's Cathedral,** which has been rebuilt several times (most recently in 1831) on the site of the original church, founded in 1625. George Washington (1732–1799) is said to have worshiped in one of its former incarnations in 1751, during his only trip outside what is now the United States.

West of Trafalgar Square is **Broad Street,** the city's main shopping and business district. Among modern offices and department stores are a number of fine old colonial buildings dressed up with fancy ironwork balconies.

A few blocks away, off Magazine Lane, is the ice-cream pink-and-white **Bridgetown Synagogue,** built in the 19th century and now

Bridgetown
- ⬛ 302 B2
- **Visitor information**
- ✉ Harbour St.
- ☎ 246/427-2623
- 🕐 Closed weekends

Bridgetown Synagogue
- ✉ Magazine Lane
- 🕐 Closed Sun.
- 💲 $ (or Heritage Passport)

restored. The first synagogue on the island (the second in the Americas, after Curaçao) was established by Jewish migrants from Brazil in 1651. Bridgetown's prosperous Jewish community acted as financial agents and export brokers for the fledgling colony, and it grew considerably in the mid-17th century, when the British islands offered freedom of religious practices under the direction of Oliver Cromwell (1599–1658). The present synagogue was built in 1833, but many tombs in the cemetery date back much further.

From the city center the Princess Alice Highway heads west to **Bridgetown Harbour** and the cruise-ship complex.

To the south, across The Careenage on the Chamberlain Bridge, Bay Street follows the curve of Carlisle Bay into the **Bayville** district, where a few pretty 19th-century town houses with gingerbread trimmings have survived on quiet back streets shaded by palm and mango trees.

A mile (1.5 km) south of Bridgetown is **Garrison Savannah**, once a British parade ground. The enclosure now doubles as a jogging track and a small racecourse where the Barbados Turf Club hosts weekend race meetings

Drinking in the view of downtown Bridgetown from a waterfront café on The Careenage

Barbados Museum

✉ St. Ann's Garrison,
St. Michael

☎ 246/427-0201

💲 $$$ (or Heritage Passport)

The national flag flies over Bridgetown's Victorian coral rock parliament buildings.

Sports & activities

Day sails: Day sails or sunset cruises from Limbo Lady (*Tel 246/420-5418*); Secret Love (*Tel 246/437-7490*); Tiami Catamaran Cruises (*Tel 246/425-5800*).

Diving & snorkeling: Reef diving and wrecks on the west coast, with good snorkeling at Paynes Bay and Folkstone. Contact Coral Isle Divers (*Tel 246/434-8377, fax 246/431-9068, e-mail: coralis@caribnet.net*); Hightide Watersports (*Tel 246/432-1311 or 800/513-5763, e-mail: hightide@sunbeach.net, www.gti.net/hightide*); West Side Scuba Centre (*Tel/fax 246/432-2558, e-mail: chriscj@gocarib.com*).

Golf: Eighteen championship holes at Sandy Lane Golf Club, Holetown (*Tel 246/432-1145*); also at the Royal Westmoreland (*Tel 246/422-4653; access is restricted*).

Hiking: Barbados National Trust Sunday hikes (*Tel 246/426-2421*).

Horseback riding: Caribbean International Riding Centre, St. Andrew (*Tel 246/422-7433*).

Sportfishing: Billfisher II (*Tel 246/431-0741*); Blue Marlin Charters (*Tel 246/422-2098, fax 246/435-6655, e-mail: bluemrln@caribsurf.com, www.world-traveler.com/barbados/bluemarl.html*).

Surfing: Dangerous swimming but excellent surfing on the east coast around Bathsheba. ∎

(*alternate Saturdays Jan.–March and May–Oct.*). Around the track are several imposing 19th-century buildings, including the distinctive red **Main Guard** (also known as the Savannah Club), the former barracks and crumbling ramparts of 17th-century **Fort Charles,** and **St. Anne's Fort,** founded in 1704 but never completed.

The old military prison houses the excellent **Barbados Museum.** A circuit of the exhibits begins with an overview of the island's natural history and early Amerindian inhabitants accompanied by copious background notes.

In the plantation-era section, the Aall Gallery displays rare antique maps, including a second edition of Richard Ligon's original map of Barbados, published in 1657. It shows the island still partially covered in native forest, with plantations blocked neatly along the leeward coast and wild boars rampaging about the interior. Prisoners once broke stones in the museum's lower courtyard and lived in cells around the leafy upper courtyard, now occupied by a series of rooms furnished in 19th-century style.

The Chancellor Gallery has a small selection of military memorabilia, and a fascinating collection of 17th- and 18th-century engravings is a highlight in the Cunard Gallery. Island views and studies of plantation great houses compete for attention with portraits of fashionable planters, dandies, dancers, and Rachel Pringle, Barbados's most famous 18th-century madame. ∎

Bridge Gate spans the route south from The Careenage to Garrison Savannah.

1627 and all that…

The exuberant "1627 and all that…" is a folkloric show that takes place on Thursday and Sunday evenings in the historic **Barbados Museum.** Singers and dancers trace island history and the fusion of African and British cultures accompanied by the music of traditional drums and a steel band. For information and reservations, call 246/428-1627. For a more homogeneous Caribbean experience (calypso, cabaret, limbo, steel-band music), try the Tropical Spectacular dinner show, hosted Wednesday and Friday evenings at The Plantation Restaurant, St. Lawrence (Tel 246/428-5048). ∎

Sugar

At the height of the 17th- to 18th-century sugar era, Barbados was one of the most powerful islands in the Caribbean. For two centuries sugar was the backbone of the West Indies, the "white gold" that lined the planters' coffers, shaped the foreign policy of distant European countries, and instigated the largest forced transportation of human beings in history (see pp. 248–49).

Sugar arrives in the New World

The Spanish conquest of the New World in the 16th century was fueled by South American gold and precious gems. Lacking the mineral wealth of the mainland, the success of the West Indian colonies founded in the early 17th century depended on finding a profitable crop that could not be grown in Europe yet one that would survive the vagaries of transatlantic transportation. Cotton, indigo, and coffee were early contenders, but tobacco proved the most profitable option until new plantations in Virginia flooded the market with better quality tobacco, leaving the Caribbean settlers searching for an alternative.

Sugarcane was among a selection of experimental crops brought to the Spanish colony of Hispaniola by Christopher Columbus in 1493. Although the cane flourished, it was more than a century before Dutch planters from Brazil introduced sugarcane and their vital expertise to Barbados in the 1630s. By this time the new fashion for coffee and chocolate drinking in Europe provided a burgeoning home market, and the success of the first sugar crops ignited a planting frenzy that carpeted Barbados with cane by the 1650s and spread rapidly throughout the region.

Cultivation & processing

Compared with tobacco, which could be grown profitably on small holdings, sugar required larger plantations and extensive capital outlay for buildings and processing equipment. The labor force on the islands was also insufficient, so slaves were imported from West Africa to work the cane fields.

To prepare the land for sugar cultivation, the planter's first task was to clear native vegetation and divide his estate into large fields arranged around the central mill and processing facility. A crop grown from cane tops planted in well-prepared earth could be harvested after 18 months; but the Dutch introduced *ratooning*, a less expensive and faster method of propagation using shoots grown on cane roots left in the ground after the previous harvest and ripe for harvesting within a year.

The crop was cut by hand during the dry season (Jan.–May) and carried to the mill, which could be powered by wind, water, animal, or slave labor. Here the cane was crushed by rollers, the *bagasse* (cane trash) removed for fuel, and the cane juice diverted into a series of copper boiling pans. Lime water was added to assist clarification, and as the boiling syrup progressed through pans of ever decreasing size and increased temperature, it was skimmed to remove impurities. From the final pan, liquid sugar was poured into wooden cooling troughs where it separated into *muscovado* sugar crystals and molasses. The molasses was then drained off and distilled to make rum, and the semirefined sugar was packed into hogsheads to await shipment overseas.

The origins of sugar

The recorded history of sugar begins in India, though how sugarcane reached the subcontinent from its probable origins in Polynesia is unknown. Discovered by Persian invaders circa 510 B.C., sugarcane and the secret of "honey without bees" traveled to the Middle East. A few centuries later, the ancient Greeks and Romans prized it as a luxury and a medicine, and during the Middle Ages small quantities of sugarcane were cultivated around the Mediterranean region. It was still regarded as a rare and expensive alternative to honey when crusaders returning from Syria introduced the "new spice" to Britain in 1099. ■

Boom & bust

At the beginning of the 18th century, the lucrative spoils of the booming Caribbean sugar trade were shared equally between Britain and France, and trade was at the core of a century of bitter rivalry between the two countries. European wars were an excuse to impose sanctions and mount invasion expeditions; peace treaties inevitably involved the transfer of colonial powers to the victors.

Peace with France in 1814 brought Britain a handful of former French West Indian colonies and a glut of sugar accompanied by a dramatic reduction in profits.

Across the Channel, the French turned to sugar beets, grown in Europe as a vegetable since Roman time, and a far cheaper and easier way of producing sugar since the discovery of a viable method of sugar extraction in 1812. The widespread cultivation of sugar

Top: Farmers burn stubble on a Guadeloupe cane field. Above: Early 19th-century views of an Antiguan boiling house

beets in Europe, coupled with the emancipation of the slave workforce spelled the end of the sugar industry in the smaller West Indian colonies in the 1840s. Only the big producers such as Barbados, Jamaica, and Trinidad survived by importing indentured labor from overseas. ■

Sunbury
Plantation House
recalls the elegant
lifestyle enjoyed
by plantation
owners during the
sugar boom.

Plantation houses & gardens

THE COLONIAL HERITAGE OF BARBADOS COMES ALIVE IN
its wonderful plantation houses and lush tropical gardens. Plantation
owners built gracious residences to reflect their exalted social standing. In doing so, they achieved a refinement that matches that of the
sugar that underpinned their wealth. Lush gardens reinforce the
notion of living in an island paradise.

**Francia Plantation
House**

- 🅰 302 C3
- ✉ St. George
- ☎ 246/429-0474
- 🕐 Closed weekends
- 💲 $ (or Heritage
  Passport)

THE SOUTHERN HEARTLAND

The rolling countryside of southern
Barbados cuts a swath eastward
from Bridgetown and north of
Grantley Adams Airport. The
atmosphere here is redolent of
two Barbadian mainstays: sugar-
processing and rum. Two lovely residences here evoke the feel of three
centuries' worth of plantation life.

One of the last plantation houses
to be built on the island, in the
early part of the 20th century, is
the **Francia Plantation House.**
This charming blend of European
and Caribbean architectural styles,
located just 4 miles (6 km) northeast of Bridgetown, is still inhabited
by descendants of its original
French owner. The ground floor is
open to the public and furnished in

elegant 19th-century fashion with a magnificent mahogany dining table and Venetian crystal chandeliers in the dining room, and some pretty 18th-century pieces in the drawing room, while antique maps adorn the walls. Take a stroll around the terraced gardens to glimpse the **Gun Hill Signal Station** (see p. 315) poking up above the trees.

About 6 miles (10 km) east of Francia is **Sunbury Plantation House.** A 300-year-old great house, Sunbury was a private home until the 1980s, and it still retains charmingly homey touches such as fresh-cut flowers and potted plants dotted among the traditional Barbadian mahogany furniture and collections of antique china, glass, and silver. The bedrooms upstairs are open for inspection, with Victorian clothes laid out on capacious four-poster beds. The old yam cellar has been turned into a carriage museum and repository of old-fashioned agricultural and domestic implements. The Courtyard Restaurant in the garden serves lunch and afternoon tea. If the idea of a hurricane-lamp-lit dinner in the main house appeals, call and make a reservation for the five-course Plantation Dinner.

HIGHLAND SITES
The central highlands of Barbados lie just to the east of the Platinum Coast. The terrain here was too hilly for large-scale plantations, so the landscape feels more unspoiled.

The first garden you come to is **Welchman Hall Gully,** located about 5 miles (8 km) due east from Holetown along the west coast. Originally laid out as a botanical walk in the 1860s, this fabulously lush mile-long (1.5-km) wooded gorge was created by the collapse of a limestone chamber in part of the Harrison's Cave underground cavern network (see p. 315). Around the fantastical pinnacles and limestone rock formations, more than 200 species of exotic plants and flowers flourish in the cool shade of giant forest trees and towering stands of bamboo. A carpet of ferns and trailing lianas add to the jungle-like atmosphere, and you might hear vervet monkeys crashing about in the treetops in the early morning or late afternoon.

Another haven of exuberant tropical plant life, the 50-acre (20-ha) **Flower Forest** lies just 2 miles (3 km) northeast of Welchman Hall Gully. Flower Forest occupies a commanding position in the Scotland district with views across a ruffle of hills to the wide blue Atlantic. In the woodlands steep paths zigzag down through a forest of gingers, lobster claw heliconias, Chinese hat plants, and red hot cattails to a grassy

An elegant hat stand flanks a staircase at Sunbury Plantation House.

Sunbury Plantation House
🅰 303 D2
✉ St. Philip
☎ 246/423-6270
💲 $ (or Heritage Passport)

Welchman Hall Gully
🅰 302 C3
✉ Welchman Hall, St. Thomas
☎ 246/438-6671
💲 $$ (or Heritage Passport)

Flower Forest
🅰 302 C4
✉ St. Joseph
☎ 246/433-8152
💲 $$

Barbados National Trust Heritage Passports

The Barbados Museum and Bridgetown Synagogue are 2 of 15 historic sites managed by the Barbados National Trust and covered by the money-saving Barbados Heritage Passport scheme. The passports are on sale at many hotels, the Cave Shepherd department store in Bridgetown, and all the sights themselves. A Full Passport ($35) offers a saving of 50 percent on admission to all 15 attractions, including plantation houses, Harrison's Cave, and the Mount Gay Rum Visitors Centre. Three Mini Passports ($18) valid for a selection of five named sites are also available. ∎

Above: Tropical palms add an unusual backdrop to the Jacobean-era St. Nicholas Abbey.
Right: The aptly named Chinese hat plant

Andromeda Botanic Gardens

🏛 302 D4

✉ Bathsheba, St. Joseph

☎ 246/433-9261

💲 $$ (or Heritage Passport)

St. Nicholas Abbey

🏛 302 C5

✉ Cherry Tree Hill, St. Peter

☎ 246/422-8725

🕐 Closed weekends

💲 $ (or Heritage Passport)

lookout. A leisurely inspection of the orchid collection provides a welcome break on the trek back.

THE NORTHEAST COAST

The rolling uplands of the interior end abruptly in a series of dramatic coastal cliffs in the east. Although relatively unpopulated, the northeast coast of Barbados has a pair of memorable sights to visit.

The first is **Andromeda Gardens,** lying only 4 miles (6.5 km) east of Flower Forest. World-renowned for a fabulous collection of indigenous and exotic tropical flowers, these lovely gardens cling to the cliffs above the Atlantic coast like their namesake heroine in

Greek mythology, who was chained to the rocks. The 6-acre (2.5-ha) gardens were established privately by Mrs. Iris Bannochie in 1954 and arranged in outdoor "rooms," where orchids, heliconias, hibiscus, and clouds of bougainvillea abound alongside fragrant bowers, water-lily ponds, and shady corners planted with ferns and striking ornamental foliage.

A shore road runs northward along the rocky eastern coast of Barbados, where there are few settlements but extensive beaches.

Some 9 miles (14.5 km) north from Andromeda Botanic Gardens is **St. Nicholas Abbey.** A rare example of Jacobean architecture in the Caribbean, the "abbey" rejoices in a splendid gabled facade dating from around 1650-1660, but the building never had any religious connections. Tours with a local guide explore a handful of dark wood-paneled rooms containing colonial antiques.

For an entertaining 20th-century perspective, try to catch a showing of an old home movie depicting Bridgetown and plantation life in the 1930s. ■

The south coast

AROUND THE SOUTHWEST TIP OF BARBADOS AT GARRISON
Savannah (see p. 305), the coastal highway runs into the Christ
Church district and a string of beachfront villages.

**Rum Factory &
Heritage Park**
🗺 303 E2
✉ Foursquare
 Plantation, St. Philip
☎ 246/420-1977

Sam Lord's
castle, built by
one of Barbados's
more colorful
characters

Hastings, Worthing, and **Dover**
back the best of the lovely south
coast beaches, while St. Lawrence,
midway between Worthing and
Dover, is a veritable restaurant row
with the best nightlife on the island.

Beyond **Oistins,** a fishing center
and Barbados's third largest town, is
lively **Silver Sands Beach,** a
favorite with windsurfers. East of
Grantley Adams Airport, you'll find
secluded beach coves at Long Bay,
Foul Bay, and Crane Bay.

The interior of the south coast
also has its share of attractions and
activities. Far and away the most
popular is the unashamedly
touristy **Rum Factory and**

Heritage Park at Six Cross
Roads, a mile (1.5 km) south of the
Sunbury Plantation
House (see p. 311).
The south coast
runs out at Ragged
Point, where
the rocks
beneath the
East Point
Lighthouse
are lashed by
the Atlantic,
and views
stretch north
up the east
coast to Pico
Tenerife. ■

Rum punch

Rum is bottled as either clear
white rum, or the slightly
mellower gold rums colored with
caramel and aged in wooden barrels.
On the French islands the blending
and aging of rums is a serious business, and the top producers even
date their top of the range products
to create vintages like wines. Rum
punch was the planters' favorite tip-
ple and a good way of
transforming some of the
rougher local brews into a
palatable drink. The traditional
recipe for rum punch calls
for one measure of sour
(lemon or lime), two of sweet
(cane juice), three of strong
(rum), and four of
weak (water). ■

Rum punch
can deliver a
deceptive
blow to the
unwary.

More places to visit around Barbados

ANIMAL FLOWER CAVE

At the northern tip of the island, dozens of multicolored sea anemones flower in the rock pools of this subterranean cave hollowed out of the cliffs by wave action. Visitors can swim around with a guide, watch the "animal flowers" waving their tiny tentacles, and take a dip in one of the larger pools.

◭ 302 B6 ✉ St. Lucy ☎ 246/439-8797 ⑤ $

BARBADOS WILDLIFE RESERVE & GRENADE HALL SIGNAL STATION & FOREST

The first of three attractions conveniently grouped in the same location, the Barbados Wildlife Reserve is a miniature animal kingdom set in a 4-acre (1.5-ha) pocket of mahogany forest. Vervet monkeys, shy Brocket deer, porcupines, and agoutis (tropical rodent) wander at will in the woodlands and provide real wildlife spotting opportunities that delight children. The reserve has an iguana sanctuary decorated with orchids, a walk-through aviary, and a secure caiman pool, as well as a caged python.

Across the parking lot is the Grenade Hall Signal Station, one of half a dozen lookout towers constructed in the early 1800s to keep a watch on slaves working on the plantations. Sentries used semaphore to relay news of disturbances or approaching ships at sea.

Nature trails in the adjacent Grenade Hall

Above left: This enlarged and creatively decorated chattel house has an air of permanence.

Above: A boatyard near Speightstown

Forest offer a glimpse of how Barbados would have appeared to the first settlers. Native trees such as the whitewood, poison tree, and silk cotton tree are marked along the route.

Nearby, Farley Hill Park is a favorite picnic spot on the grounds of a ruined plantation house with an arboretum.

◭ 302 C5 ✉ Farley Hill, St. Peter ☎ 246/422-8826 ⑤ $$$

CODRINGTON COLLEGE

A magnificent avenue of slender cabbage palms flanks the driveway leading to the imposing facade of this Anglican theological college. The college was founded in 1743 and financed by a bequest from Christopher Codrington (1668–1710), a one-time governor general of the Leeward Islands whose family was among the earliest settlers on Barbados. Access to the college buildings is limited, but visitors can view the outside of the Principal's

Lodge (the original 17th-century estate house where Codrington was brought up), stroll around the gardens that lead down to Consett Bay, and take a turn around the pretty water-lily pond and along a short nature trail through woodland.

🅰 303 E3 ✉ St. John ☎ 246/433-1274
💲 $ (or Heritage Passport)

GUN HILL SIGNAL STATION

A strategic position 700 feet (213 m) above sea level gives this 1818 signal station unparalleled views across the island and off to the Atlantic. The site was first used as a lookout in 1697 and later became a convalescent station on account of the comfortably cool breezes. At the foot of the hill is the whitewashed Military Lion, carved from a single piece of rock by a convalescent British officer.

🅰 302 C3 ✉ Gun Hill, St. George
☎ 246/429-1358 🕐 Closed Sun. 💲 $ (or Heritage Passport)

HARRISON'S CAVE

The island's top sight-seeing attraction is a miniature trolley ride around a subterranean cave carved out of the coral limestone by underground rivers. Passengers don hard hats and set off on a nearly mile-long (1.5-km) ride through a series of spooky, theatrically lit caverns festooned with dripping stalactites, rimstones, flowstones, and a spiky forest of stalagmites. The speleotherms (cave formations) take approximately a hundred years to grow a single cubic inch of solid calcite, but eventually the stalactites and stalagmites can join up to create impressive pillars. There is an

Reef & wreck tours

Scuba diving is one way of seeing local marine life up close (see p. 306), or sign up for a guided snorkeling tour with Atlantis Adventures. For spectacular underwater views without getting wet, take the *Atlantis* minisub to reef and wreck sites at depths of 150 feet (46 m). Or stick to a surface view from the *Atlantis Seatrec*, a reef observation craft with a see-through hull. *(Information and reservations Tel 246/436-8929.)* ■

underground lake fed by a 40-foot (12-m) cascade. The cave lies at one end of the Welchman Hall Gully botanic walk (see p. 311).

🅜 302 C3   ✉ Welchman Hall, St. Thomas ☎ 246/438-6640   💲 $$$

MORGAN LEWIS SUGAR MILL

Hundreds of sugar-grinding mills once dotted the Barbadian landscape, and their crumbling ruins are a common sight along the tiny roads of the sugarcane belt today.

The 250-year-old Morgan Lewis mill was the last old-style mill to close when it ceased operations in 1944. Recently placed on the List of 100 Most Endangered Sites in the World by the World Monuments Fund, its weathered stone cone is the largest surviving windmill in the Caribbean. All its working parts are intact, and the old sails and wooden parts have been repaired with South American hardwoods. Climb up to the sail compartment for panoramic views of the surrounding Scotland district.

🅜 302 C5   ✉ St. Andrew   ☎ 246/426-2421 💲 $ (or Heritage Passport)

MOUNT GAY RUM VISITORS CENTRE

Rum has been produced in Barbados since the 1640s. The Mount Gay distillery is in the north of the island at St. Lucy, but here at the visitor center near Bridgetown Harbour (*Brandons, St. Michael*) the aging, blending, and bottling processes are on display, followed by tastings at the end of the tour.

🅜 302 B2   ✉ Spring Garden Hwy., Bridgetown ☎ 246/425-9066   🕑 Closed weekends (tours every 30 minutes)   💲 $$ (or Heritage Passport)

PLATINUM COAST

The focus of the famed Platinum Coast is **Holetown** *(7 miles, 11 km N of Bridgetown on Rte. 1. Map 302 B3),* where English settlers first disembarked in 1627 and established a small village they called Jamestown after King James I. The original name (it was changed to Holetown after a tidal hole close to the beach) is still preserved in the little coral rock church of St. James, founded in 1629 and originally built of wood, and in the surrounding district known as the Parish of St. James. Many of the

island's most elegant hotels and private houses are located here. **Paynes Bay** is a particularly lively section of the beach, with beach bars and water-sports concessions.

Just north of Holetown there's snorkeling in the **Folkestone Underwater Park.**

Farther north along the coast is another busy beach strip at Heyward's Bay, north of Speightstown.

PORTVALE SUGAR FACTORY

The sugar factory produces about 14,500 tons of sugar a year. The spring harvest season (Feb. to May) is the best time to visit, when tours plunge into the ear-shattering, sweet and steamy atmosphere of the factory floor among the cane cutters, crushers, and boilers.

The informative museum traces the history of the sugar industry.

🅜 302 B4   ✉ St. James   ☎ 246/432-0100 🕑 Closed Sun.   💲 Museum $ (or Heritage Passport), including factory tour $$

TYROL COT HERITAGE VILLAGE

A single-story stone house painted a jaunty white and orange with green louvered jalousies (shutters), Tyrol Cot was built by leading Barbadian architect William Farnum, in 1854. The home of former prime minister Sir Grantley Adams (1898–1971) and his wife from 1929 until her death in 1990, it is furnished with many family pieces.

In the gardens the Heritage Village illustrates how the local architectural style developed from a basic slave hut thatched with cane trash to the first simple post-slavery wooden chattel house and its more elaborate gingerbread-trimmed descendants. After emancipation, workers were permitted to own houses but not land, so the original chattel house (from "goods and chattels") was a single unit easily dismantled and moved if the owner was evicted from a plantation site. As the homeowner prospered or the family grew, further units could be added, along with such refinements as jalousies and glass windows.

Craft work is on sale, and a restaurant is on site.

🅜 302 C2   ✉ Codrington Hill, St. Michael ☎ 246/424-2074   🕑 Closed weekends 💲 $ (or Heritage Passport) ■

Though Trinidad and Tobago share a rich tapestry of natural delights, Trinidad's pulse races to the rhythms of steel pan and calypso and the razzle-dazzle of Carnival, while life on Tobago beats to a more relaxed tempo.

Trinidad & Tobago

Topflight cricket

Trinidad

A TWIN-ISLAND NATION AT THE SOUTHERN EXTENT OF THE LESSER Antilles, Trinidad and Tobago make an odd couple. Boisterous, multicultural Trinidad is the larger of the two and home to the capital, Port of Spain. At 50-by-38 miles (80-by-61-km) it's also the largest of the eastern Caribbean islands. Trinidad is a chunk of South America severed from the Venezuelan coast just 7 miles (11 km) away as recently as 10,000 years ago. Trinidad breaks the traditional Caribbean mold with an industrialized, oil-based economy that has shunned tourism until recently. But for a lesson in how to develop, the Trinidadians need look no further than Tobago, a more typical West Indian escapist haven offering one of the warmest welcomes in the region (see p. 330).

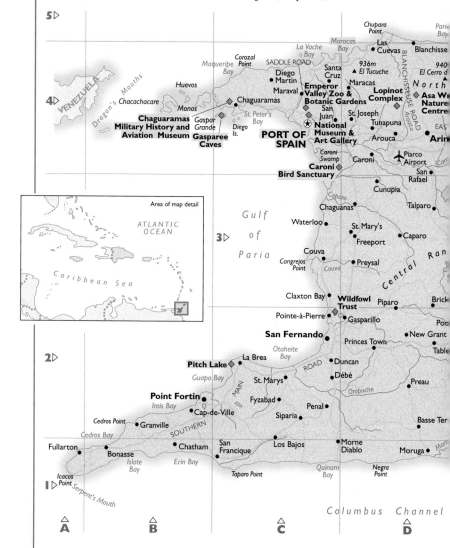

The Iere (Land of Hummingbirds) of the Arawak was rechristened Trinidad (Trinity) by Christopher Columbus, who sighted three peaks in the southeast of the island on his third voyage to the New World in 1498. Although the island was claimed for Spain, its Amerindian inhabitants kept settlers at bay until 1592, when the Spanish established a toehold, grew a little tobacco, and kept watch over their treasure fleets sailing home to Europe from South America. Trinidad was still a backwater by the late 18th century, when the Spanish king offered land grants to Catholic settlers. An influx of French planters keen to escape the revolutionary guillotine on their own islands introduced sugar and cocoa plantations. But Spain never reaped the rewards as Britain snatched the island in 1797, later taking possession of neighboring Tobago in 1814.

Trinidad's plantations foundered after emancipation in 1838, but once again the island found the solution by encouraging migration from abroad. This time the call was answered by East Indian indentured laborers, who were shipped to the Caribbean, worked a five-year term in the cane fields, and then chose between a return passage and a 5-acre (2-ha) plot of land. Many stayed, and their descendants now number 40 percent of the island's unusually diverse population of about 1.25 million. Another 40 percent of Trinidadians can trace their roots back to Africa, while the remaining 20 percent are of European, Chinese, Middle Eastern, and South American extraction.

World War II brought Americans to Trinidad in force. About 80,000 U.S. military personnel were stationed at 225 bases around the island. At about this time the first stirrings of steel-pan music were heard in the "panyards" of Port of Spain as musical Trinidadians recycled old oil drums by beating out the steel surfaces until they could play a range of notes. The versatility of the steel drums (known as pans) added an extra dimension and sophistication to the traditional percussion bands, and the rippling rhythms of steel pan are the heartbeat of Trinidad's famous Carnival, alongside the raucous lyrics of calypso, soca (a fusion of soul music and calypso), and chutney (a fusion of calypso and traditional Indian music).

Trinidad and Tobago gained independence from Britain in 1962 and became a republic within the Commonwealth in 1976. Trinidad's oil wealth insulated the island from the tourism development that swept through other Caribbean islands in the 1960s and '70s, but the 1980s oil slump changed attitudes. Trinidad's tourist industry is still in its infancy (beach hotels are a novelty), but ecotourism is the island's trump card. ∎

Port of Spain

TRINIDAD'S FRENETIC CAPITAL CITY, PORT OF SPAIN, reflects the island's multicultural heritage. Its teeming streets overflow with shoppers and market stalls, while pompous British colonial architecture rubs shoulders with Muslim mosques, West Indian gingerbread houses, and modern concrete office buildings. The heart of the city was laid out after a major fire in 1808, but Port of Spain now stretches for miles along the Gulf of Paria and back into the hills to sought-after residential suburbs such as Maraval.

Port of Spain
🗺 319 C4

National Museum & Art Gallery
✉ 117 Frederick St.
☎ 868/623-5941
🕐 Closed Sun.–Mon.

Port of Spain's main downtown thoroughfare is **Frederick Street,** which links Brian Lara Promenade (named for a famous Trinidadian cricket player) with the grassy expanse of **Queens Park Savannah.** The southern end of Frederick Street resembles an Eastern bazaar, with its Indian fabric shops and boutiques spilling out onto the sidewalk.

Midway up the street is **Woodford Square,** a small park bisected by paths where locals meet to "lime" (hang out and chat) on benches under the trees. The entire west side is flanked by the imposing bulk of the **Red House,** seat of the Trinidad and Tobago

Parliament. On the south side is the mellow, stone **Trinity Cathedral,** dating from the early 19th century. It's worth a visit for its soaring wooden ceiling and patchwork of stained glass (entrance on Queen Street).

A 15-minute walk north on Frederick Street takes you to the **National Museum and Art Gallery.** There's an interesting section on the famous Carnival, complete with sequined-and-plumed costumes, elaborate masks, and a photo montage of Carnival kings and queens dating back to the 1960s. Among the Trinidadian art on display, look for works by Michel Jean Cazabon, as well as

Jackie Hinkson's colorful depictions of Port of Spain in the 1940s.

Frederick Street ends at Queen's Park Savannah, a large open space with a circumference of 2.5 miles (4 km) proudly hailed by Trinidadians as the "largest traffic circle in the world." The Savannah plays a central role in the Carnival festivities and doubles as a sports field during the rest of the year. At one time Trinidad's premier race-course was located in the park.

On the northwest side are seven grand old colonial mansions, which have been nicknamed the **Magnificent Seven** (after the film of the same name), although several are now looking a little tired.

To the north is **Emperor Valley Zoo,** which showcases various South American mammals from capybaras and tapirs to the giant Brazilian otter. Here you can find deer, agouti, and tree porcupines from Trinidad's forests, and aviaries for wetland birds *(Queen's Park Savannah, Tel 868/622-3530).*

Next door to the zoo are the **Botanic Gardens** *(Queen's Park Savannah),* laid out in the 1820s by Sir Ralph Woodford. Although many of the magnificent tropical trees are carefully numbered, there are no names. At the far side of the gardens stands the President's House, a sturdy, L-shaped British colonial affair.

Southwest of the Savannah is the **Woodbrook district,** noted for its attractive gingerbread homes; there are also several good restaurants in the area.

Farther west is the **Western Main Road** in the St. James district. It's known as the "city that never sleeps," thanks to its lively nightlife, bars, ice-cream parlors, and street vendors selling rotis (Indian-style bread pockets stuffed with chicken, meat, or vegetables). ∎

Carnival

Trinidad's famous Carnival originated in the late 18th century with French Catholic settlers, who marked the approach of Lent with a series of elaborate feasts and parties or masquerades (which, shortened to "mas," is the traditional Trinidadian word for Carnival). The buildup to Carnival begins in the New Year with calypso and panorama (steel band) competitions around the island. The main event kicks off in Port of Spain the Friday before Lent and culminates on Shrove Tuesday as the Parade of Bands gathers on Queen's Park Savannah. Anyone can join in Carnival (or "play mas"), whether it's just dancing on the street or signing up with a mas camp and renting a fabulous carnival costume. Check with the tourist office; you can even cruise the mas camps on the Internet *(www.visittnt.com).* ∎

Above: Carnival costumes are often works of art and can take months to design and execute.

Cricket in the Caribbean

Cricket occupies a unique position in the Caribbean region. In many countries, particularly former British colonies such as Jamaica, Barbados, Antigua, and Trinidad, the sport is followed with a passion that verges on the religious. But, more importantly, it is one of the very few successful cooperative endeavors in a region where most other attempts at integration have failed. National rivalries are forgotten and the West Indies team presents a cohesive face as the ambassadors of the Caribbean on overseas tours.

One of contemporary cricket's greats, Trinidadian Brian Lara captains the West Indies team.

reputation for stylish and exuberant playing, bringing a freeflowing athleticism and sense of humor to the game and earning them the nickname of the "calypso cricketers."

During the 1930s West Indian cricket was dominated by the presence of George Headley, judged to be the greatest West Indian batsman ever and globally among the six best of all time. He has a unique place in Caribbean history in that he personified black excellence in a whitedominated sport, a symbol of self-worth for the adoring crowds. During the postwar years the game was dominated by three Barbados players—

The story of the development of West Indian cricket is a fascinating one, and it says much about the importance of the sport in the region that one of the best accounts of its development, *A History of West Indian Cricket* (Andre Deutsch, 1988) should have been written by no less a person than Michael Manley, former prime minister of Jamaica.

When cricket was introduced by the British, it was mostly played by army officers and plantation owners, but in the sweltering heat they preferred to bat rather than bowl (pitch), and it was the slaves and sons of slaves who were drafted in to bowl for them. After emancipation a network of cricket clubs sprang up, and it soon became clear that the descendants of the former slaves were incredibly good at cricket.

The first English team toured the West Indies in 1895, and in 1897 the first All-West-Indies team was picked to play against another visiting English team. The first tour of England by a West Indies team took place in 1900, but the great turning point came in the 1920s, when the West Indies were granted Test status—that is, the right to compete on the international cricket circuit.

The West Indian team soon gained a

Frank Worrell, Everton Weekes, and Clive Walcott. They were followed by one of the great West Indian stars of all time, the legendary Garfield (Gary) Sobers. The Sobers era, from 1960 to 1974, witnessed the highest level attained by the West Indies up to that date, during which they played 67 tests, of which they won 21, lost 16, drew 29, and tied one.

The golden age of West Indies cricket, however, was yet to come. This was the decade, from 1976 to 1986, when they dominated the world of cricket. Out of 17 test matches they won 15, drew one, and lost one—a remarkable record of victories in any sport. They achieved a level of preeminence that was so great that opposing sides were almost beaten before the game began, so formidable was their reputation.

Since then the West Indies team has found itself in a period that many see as a cyclical decline, culminating in a humiliating defeat by the Australians in 1999, when the team scored the lowest total of runs in its 72-year history.

Commentators believe that this malaise will pass, and that the region will continue to produce great cricketers such as Vivian Richards (from Antigua), Clive Lloyd (Guyana), and Brian Lara, the current superstar, who comes from Trinidad. But others

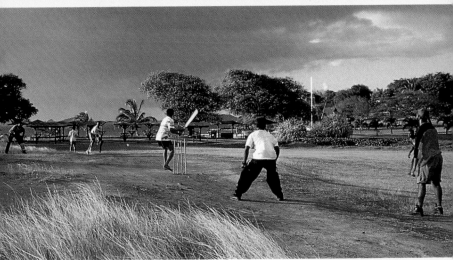

Top: The West Indies take on England in Barbados. Above: Any open space serves as a practice pitch for youngsters to hone their skills.

worry that the ascent of alternative sports will eclipse Caribbean cricket. Soccer, basketball, and track and field are becoming increasingly popular among the younger generations. Baseball has long been the national sport of Cuba, the Dominican Republic, and Puerto Rico, with many Dominicans and Puerto Ricans playing major league baseball—and earning big money—in the United States.

Nonetheless, on many Caribbean islands an impromptu game of cricket will spring up anywhere that the youngsters can find a few sticks to act as stumps and a tennis ball to practice with, be it on the beach or the back streets. The aspirations and hopes of generations have become embedded in a game that symbolizes a rare sense of unity among Caribbean peoples. ■

Sports & activities

Ecotours: Explore the rain forest with Wildways, Port of Spain *(Tel/fax 868/623-7332, e-mail: wildways@trinidad.net)*. For trips in the Caroni Bird Sanctuary, Northern Range, and Nariva Swamp, contact Winston Nanan *(Tel/fax 868/645-1305)* at Caroni.

Golf: St. Andrew's Golf Club, Maraval *(Tel 868/629-2314)*.

Water sports: Windsurfer and kayak rentals at Chagville Beach, Chaguaramas Peninsula. ∎

Around the north

The mountains of the Northern Range stretch right across the north of Trinidad, dividing the coast from the central plain. This is where you'll find the island's two highest peaks, **El Cerro del Aripo** (3,083 feet/940 m) and **El Tucuche** (3,075 feet/936 m). The range is cloaked in a lush tangle of rain forest that is home to many of Trinidad's 430 bird species, 630 types of butterflies, and 2,300 varieties of flowering plants. Only two roads cross the central mountains: the **Saddle Road,** which links Port of Spain and the popular beach at Maracas Bay; and the **Blanchisseuse Road** from Arima, which can also be accessed from

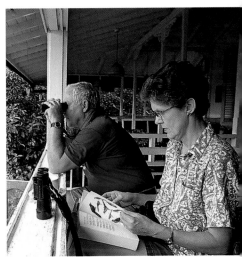

Above: With eyes trained on the bird-feeding stations, guests identify winged visitors to Asa Wright.
Left: Rain forest retreat—relaxing on the veranda at the Asa Wright Nature Centre.

ASA WRIGHT NATURE CENTRE

A visit here provides an unmissable opportunity to sample Trinidad's myriad birdlife and plant life; more than 170 species of birds have been recorded in the Arima Valley, where the nature center sits at a comfortable 1,200 feet (365 m) above sea level, hemmed in by the rain forest.

A series of trails explores the 200-acre (80-ha) estate, and short guided walks provide a window on the rain forest world, where leaf cutter ants share the paths and blue morpho butterflies flutter past like elegant turquoise magic carpets.

There's a ringside seat for the mating dance of the white-bearded manakin, accompanied by what sounds like a salvo of Chinese firecrackers as the male birds snap their wings with a loud popping noise.

Settle down on the veranda at the lodge to watch hummingbirds, honeycreepers, tanagers, and trogons drop in to snack on sugar water or fresh fruits. Guests staying a minimum of three nights at the center qualify for a visit to the world's most accessible colony of oilbirds. Known as guacharos ("one who wails" in

Lopinot. They form the basis of a good circular day tour out of Port of Spain, heading counterclockwise to Arima, then up to the Asa Wright Nature Centre, north to Blanchisseuse, and along the coast to Maracas before the return route over the Saddle Road.

West from Port of Spain is the **Chaguaramas Peninsula** (*Visitor information, 10–14 Phillips St., Port of Spain, Tel 868/623-1932. Map 318 C3*), which has a military history museum (see p. 328), marinas, and boat trips to a clutch of offshore islands, a man-made beach at Chagville, and Macqueripe Beach on the north coast. **Caroni Swamp,** which is only a short drive to the south of the city, also runs naturalist tours.

Above: The cooling swimming hole at Asa Wright. Above right: Scarlet ibis roosting in mangroves at Caroni Bird Sanctuary

Amerindian), these cave-dwelling birds feed their young on oily fruits such as palm, camphor, and laurels. Guacharos were highly prized for their fat, which was used for cooking and fueling oil lamps. They are now a protected species.

Bring sensible footwear as the trails can be very muddy and slippery, as well as a bathing suit for a dip in the swimming hole, and mosquito repellent.

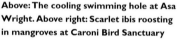 318 D4 ✉ Arima Valley ☎ 868/667-4655
 $$$

CARONI BIRD SANCTUARY

This 40-acre (16-ha) wetlands preserve in the Caroni Swamp is renowned for the evening flight of the scarlet ibis returning to mangrove roosts just before sunset. Flat-bottomed boat tours leave from the dock (follow the signs from the highway) at about 4:30 p.m., puttering through tree-lined waterways to the heart of the swamp. Along the way you can spot caimans, four-eyed fish, mangrove roots festooned with oysters, maybe even a silky anteater, and 186 species of birds from the not-so-common common potoo, a nocturnal bird that is devilishly difficult to spot, to the egrets, herons, and scampering willets feeding on the mudbanks among a lunatic orchestra of fiddler crabs sawing away with their outsize pincers.

About 10,000 scarlet ibis inhabit the sanctuary, nesting between March and September. Ibis chicks are black but develop a dark, silvery color at six to twelve months. The young birds don't achieve their brilliant red-orange adult plumage for another couple of years. Scarlet ibis are now protected from hunters, who once prized the feathers for carnival costumes. About half an hour before sunset the ibis begin to knife through the sky, iridescent red darts congregating in the dark mangrove greenery until it blazes like a Christmas tree caught in the last rays of the sun.

🔺 318 C4   ✉ Uriah Butler Hwy.   💲 $$$

Gasparee Caves

A group of five shore islands lie off the tip of the Chaguaramas Peninsula, colonized by holiday homes and visited by yachtsmen. A 15-minute boat ride from the mainland, Gasparee Island is renowned for its caves. It's also a popular picnic spot, and you can ramble around the old military fortifications.

Inexpensive water taxis depart from the Island Boat Owners marina *(Tel 868/634-4331)*, almost the last boatyard along Western Main Road (20 minutes from Port of Spain). ∎

Sports-mad Trinidadians play soccer on the beach at Maracas Bay.

CHAGUARAMAS MILITARY HISTORY & AVIATION MUSEUM

A 20-minute drive west of Port of Spain, this rambling museum will appeal to military history buffs, especially Americans who served here in World War II. Much of the military hardware and memorabilia relate to the 1940s, but displays trace conflicts dating back to the native Amerindians and Spanish conquistadores, and up to Trinidad's short-lived coup by Muslim extremists in 1990.

318 C4 ☒ Chaguaramas ☎ 868/634-4391 🅂 $

LOPINOT COMPLEX

A twisting scenic route leads up into the Northern Range, passing through small villages with burgeoning gardens and flapping Hindu prayer flags, to the settlement of Lopinot, founded by French cocoa planter Charles Joseph, comte de Lopinot in 1806. The count's simple wooden estate house contains a one-room museum surrounded by magnificent saaman trees, and there's a cocoa barn and old slave quarters.

Lopinot is one of the main centers of *parang*, the Spanish-based traditional music of Christmas in Trinidad. Introduced from Venezuela, parang is played on tiny, four-stringed cuatro guitars.

318 D4 ☒ Lopinot Valley

MARACAS BAY & THE NORTH COAST

Protected by steep wooded headlands and a stately border of palm trees, Maracas Bay is Trinidad's most popular beach and attracts the crowds on weekends. This is the place to sample shark and bake, a seasoned fish sandwich served with hot pepper-and-tamarind sauce. This typically cheap and filling local culinary institution is served up from palm-thatched vendors' stalls.

Five miles (8 km) east of Maracas there's another curve of fine white sand at Las Cuevas, which takes its name from the caves (*cuevas* in Spanish) along the shore. Vacation homes dot the coast road to the fishing village of Blanchisseuse. Neighboring **Damier Beach** is a favorite with windsurfers. ∎

Around the south

The Eastern Main Road from the town of Arima cuts across to Trinidad's Atlantic coast and a long palm-fringed sandy shore stretching down to the southeast tip of the island at Galeota Point. There are good beaches at **Manzanilla Bay** (named for the green, poisonous machineel trees behind the beach), **Cocos Bay,** and **Mayaro Bay.**

Inland is the 3,840-acre (1,554-ha) **Nariva Swamp,** home to a fantastic variety of wildlife. To visit the Nariva's **Bush Bush Wildlife Sanctuary,** get a permit from the Wildlife Division of the Forestry Department (*Tel 868/622-5114*) or approach an accredited tour operator (see p. 324).

On the west coast, just north of Trinidad's second largest city and oil center San Fernando, is the Pointe-à-Pierre **Wildfowl Trust** (*Map 318 C2, Tel 868/662-4040*), where wetlands and forest trails provide splendid bird-watching opportunities (*call ahead for guided walks*).

PITCH LAKE
Around Otaheite Bay from San Fernando is the Pitch Lake at La Brea (*Map 318 C2*), one of Trinidad's most famous (but least exciting) sights. Probably the world's largest natural

A hole in the Pitch Lake's soft, gray crust reveals the liquid bitumen beneath.

bitumen reservoir, the 100-acre (40-ha) "lake" looks like a massive parking lot, although predatory guides aim to liven up a visit with a fund of anecdotes (fix a fee in advance). The endless supply of gloopy black tar was used to caulk the hulls of conquistadores' galleons and to pave the streets of Paris and London, as well as Port of Spain, where it was also employed as fuel for 19th-century street lamps until residents complained about the appalling fumes. A small museum (*Tel 868/648-7697*) outlines the history of the lake. ■

Turtle watch
Endangered leatherback turtles lay their eggs on the beaches of northern and eastern Trinidad during the March-to-August breeding season. Beyond Arima and Valencia is the Toco Main Road, which heads out to the turtle beaches at Matura Bay and then rounds the tip of the island to the beautiful, undeveloped north coast beaches at Grande Rivière and Matelot. The Forestry Department can advise on the best beaches for turtle-watching (*Tel 868/622-3217*), and guided expeditions can be arranged through Nature Seekers (*Tel 868/667-9075*) and G.R.E.A.T. (*Tel 868/670-8274*). ■

Tobago

TRINIDAD'S LITTLE SISTER ISLAND, TOBAGO, ALSO BROKE AWAY FROM SOUTH America several million years ago, but in look and feel it's more similar to the Windward Islands in the north. Just over 20 miles (32 km) from the hustle and bustle of Trinidad, Tobago is a mountainous green oasis of charm and calm, where the Trinidadians come to relax and the Tobagonians take pride in their easygoing hospitality and unspoiled natural surroundings.

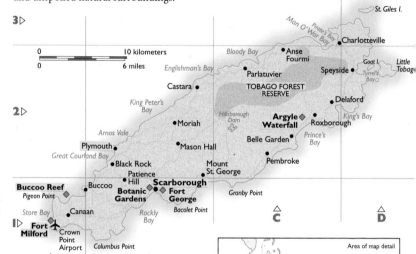

It's probable that Christopher Columbus sighted Tobago when he discovered Trinidad in 1498. He called it Bellaforma (Beautiful Form), although the original Amerindian name (derived from the word for "tobacco") has stuck. The Dutch, English, and French all laid claim to the island, which changed hands more than 20 times and developed into one of the richest sugar islands in the region. Secured by the British in 1814 and administered with the Windward Island group, Tobago found that its fortunes waned after emancipation in the 1830s. It was declared bankrupt in 1888 and appended to neighboring Trinidad. After a century as a poor rural backwater, Tobago now has a small but flourishing tourist industry, concentrated on the northwest coast between Crown Point Airport and Plymouth.

For a mere strip of an island at 20 by 5.5 miles (32 by 9 km), Tobago packs a lot. A central spine of mountains rises in the east and falls sharply through the rain forest to the broad bays of the southern windward coast and sheltered north shore. Here at the eastern end of the island, wooden pirogues from the villages of Speyside and Charlotteville ferry scuba enthusiasts out to Tobago's famous coral reefs. Enriched by nutrients swept along on the Guyana Current from Venezuela's Orinoco River, the reef sites contain 44 species of coral, including the world's biggest brain coral (12 feet by 16 feet/3.5 m by 5 m), a colony of giant manta rays, and occasional visitations by black-tipped, hammerhead, or huge plankton-eating whale sharks. The western end of the island is flat and covered in coconut palms, with stunning white sand beaches created by offshore reefs.

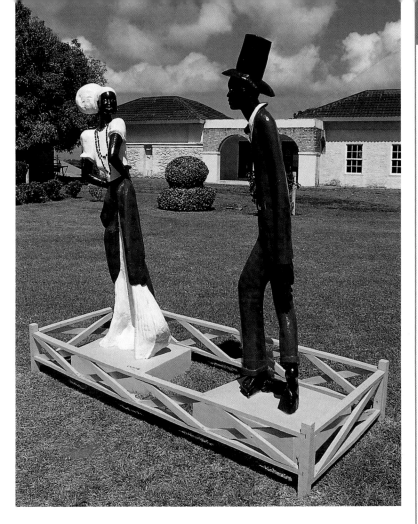

A pair of sculptured figures depicted in 19th-century costume dance the Tobago jig at Fort King George.

SCARBOROUGH

The majority of the 50,000 Tobagonians (almost all of African descent) live in the island's west end and in the pint-size capital of **Scarborough** (*Map 330 B1. Visitor information, N.I.B. Mall, level 3, Tel 868/639-2125*) on the south coast.

This unpretentious town climbs steeply from Rocky Bay into a circlet of hills overlooked by **Fort George.** The Lower Town is a melee of fish sellers and noisy market stalls. Take a break in the charming **Botanic Gardens** (*Greenside St.*), where the grassy slopes are planted with poinciana and poui trees, spreading Indian almonds, a mango grove, and a huge silk cotton tree near the gazebo. ·

Scarborough's few remaining colonial buildings are found in the Upper Town. On the way up to Fort George, look for **Gun Bridge,** with its black metal railings made out of old rifle barrels. The fort dates from the 1780s and affords a commanding view along the coast.

The **Tobago Museum** (*84 Fort St., Tel 868/639 3970, closed weekends*) is next door. It has a collection of Amerindian finds and a military history section. ∎

Around the island

Tobago
Visitor information
✉ N.I.B. Mall, Level 3,
   Scarborough
☎ 868/639-2125

TOBAGO IS AN IDEAL ISLAND TO EXPLORE IF YOU DON'T want to feel pressured to pack too much into a single excursion. The island's compact size ensures that no single trip is too long, and the laid-back atmosphere encourages you to linger along the way, pausing to admire the view, stop for a swim, or chat with local fishermen mending their nets on the shore.

The **Crown Point settlement** occupies the western tip of Tobago, with the airport and a handful of hotels and guesthouses set on Store Bay. Behind the scrap of beach, where fishing boats are drawn up on the sand, is a clutch of stands selling crafts and souvenirs. There are bars

The drive through the hills behind the coast to **Parlatuvier** is charming, and you'll find fine secluded beaches down dirt tracks at King Peter's Bay, Englishman's Bay, and Bloody Bay before the road cuts up into the rain forest (see opposite) and down to the Atlantic coast at

The sun sinks in the west behind the boat pier at Pigeon Point beach.

and snack shops. On Sandy Point you will find the low coral rock battlements of 18th-century **Fort Milford,** which now contain a small garden facing Pigeon Point, a classic Caribbean beach bordered by leaning palms. Offshore is **Buccoo Reef,** Tobago's most visited underwater attraction, although it has suffered somewhat from the glass-bottomed boat crowds.

Beach hotels are scattered along the road to **Plymouth** (Map 330 B2), where the ruins of Fort James are still guarded by antique cannon.

Roxborough. Just short of Roxborough, a side road leads to **Argyle Waterfall** (*Map 330 C2*). From the parking area in an old cocoa plantation, it's a shady 15-minute walk upriver to the falls, which bounce down a series of ledges on the cliff face to a swimming hole.

Speyside and Charlotteville flank the northeastern end of Tobago. Speyside borders Tyrrel's Bay along the Atlantic coast, overlooking **Little Tobago** (*Map 330 D2*) and Goat Island. Little Tobago is a seabird sanctuary and breeding ground for frigate-

Tobago Forest Reserve

The forest reserve was established back in 1764, making it the world's oldest legally protected forest. The dense rain forest heights of the Main Ridge remain almost untouched. The best way to visit the reserve without a guide is to take the **Gilpin Trace** marked off the Parlatuvier-Roxborough Road. It's a 2-mile (3-km) hike from the head of the trail down to The Hut. ■

A glass-bottomed boat hovers above touristy Buccoo Reef, but Tobago's best underwater scenery is in the north.

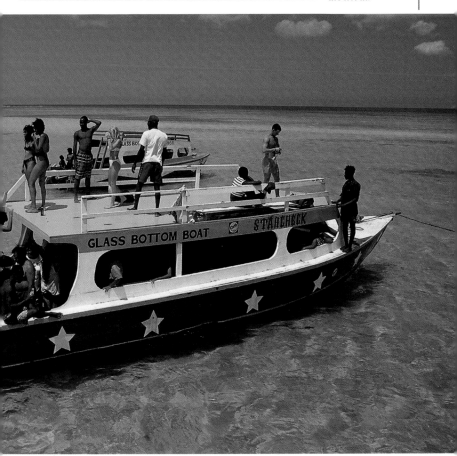

birds, boobies, and tropic birds. Boat trips run from the jetty, where dive operators and glass-bottomed boats depart for the offshore reefs.

Charlotteville, on the Caribbean side, is a sleepy little fishing village and dive center (see below) on the broad expanse of **Man O'War Bay.** Old wooden houses nestle beneath giant breadfruit trees, and the stone seawall is shaded by sea grape trees.

A 15-minute walk to the east of the village takes you to **Pirate's Bay,** a good beach. ∎

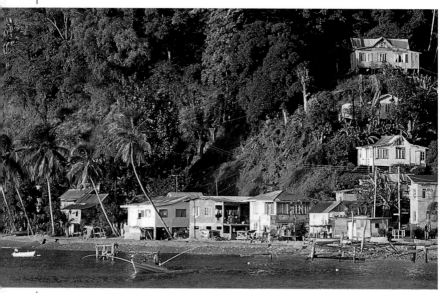

Houses grafted onto the forested hillside behind the fishing village of Charlotteville

Sports & activities

Day sails: Catamaran cruises with snorkeling are available from Kalina Kats *(Tel 868/639-6306)* and Mount Irvine Watersports *(Tel 868/639-9379).*

Diving & snorkeling: Tobago is encircled by excellent dive sites, from Buccoo Reef to the gorgeous Japanese Gardens and challenging Flying Manta. Local dive operators include Aqua Marine Dive *(Tel/fax 868/639-4416, e-mail: amdtobago@trinidad.net);* Black Rock Dive Centre *(Tel 868/639-0191, fax 868/639-9292,e-mail: grafton@trinidad.net);* Man Friday Diving *(Tel/fax 868/660-4676).*

Ecotours: Tobago's eastern highlands are cloaked in fabulously unspoiled rain forest, but unfortunately there are very few established trails that can be followed without a guide.

The Gilpin Trace loops off the Roxborough-Parlatuvier road (see p. 333). Otherwise you can hike with an experienced naturalist and arrange bird-watching trips to Little Tobago through David Rooks Nature Tours *(Tel/fax 868/639-4276, e-mail: rookstobago@trinidad.net).*

Golf: The Mount Irvine Hotel *(Tel 868/639-8871)* has a lovely 18-hole course. ∎

Travelwise

(Information in this section is
arranged by island or island
group.)

Green sea turtle

TRAVELWISE INFORMATION

GENERAL INFORMATION

Airlines

Although price is a factor in your choice of airline, check also on the safety record and frequency of flights. No-frills airlines usually have a limited number of flights per day, but often require no advance reservations. **Major airlines:** Delta Air LInes, Tel 800/241-4141; Northwest Airlines, Tel 800/447-4747; TWA, Tel 800/892-4141; United Airlines, Tel 800/538-2929; US Airways, Tel 800/842-5374. **Smaller airlines:** American Eagle, Tel 800/433-7300; Carnival Air Lines, Tel 800/824-7386; LIAT, Tel 800/468-0482.

Climate

Temperatures average 77°–86°F (25°–30°C) year-round. Northeasterly trade winds are fairly constant and provide respite from the heat and humidity. The higher the latitude, the cooler the temperature, especially from November to January. May to October is the wettest period, and the hurricane season is July to October. The Weather Channel Connection gives up-to-date forecasts (Tel 900/932-8437).

Driving

Driving regulations vary, so consult the Getting Around section for each island. Current and former British dependencies drive on the left-hand side; French and Dutch on the right. Some islands require you to have a temporary visitor license (or local license). Ask where to obtain one when you rent a car or by going to the local police station or tourist board office. The state of main roads is good, although local roads can be poor. Take a road map with you.

Electricity

On most islands 110 and 120 volts AC supply is used, and outlets are identical to those in the United States. On the French and Dutch islands, and those with a British background, you'll need an adapter for U.S. appliances. When making a reservation, ask your hotel which voltage is used. Most hotels have a supply of adapters.

Festivals & events

These are listed by island in this section. Contact local tourist offices for festival information.

Insurance

A comprehensive travel insurance policy is a useful precaution and will include cancellation, interruption, default, trip delay, and full medical coverage.

Time zones

Most islands are on Atlantic Standard Time (AST), which is Eastern Standard Time (EST) plus one hour (GMT -4). AST is not affected by daylight saving time (DST). Jamaica and the Cayman Islands are on EST with no daylight saving, and the Turks and Caicos Islands are on EST with daylight saving.

Tipping

Rules for tipping vary, so check your bill for a service charge. If no service charge is included in the bill, leave a tip of 10 to 15 percent, depending on service. Tipping can be an important source of income.

Travelers with disabilities

The Caribbean travel industry is now more aware of the needs of travelers with disabilities; many new developments reflect this sensitivity to mobility requirements. However, few attractions are equipped for wheelchair access. When making a reservation, ask specific questions concerning your needs. Some local tourist boards supply lists of hotels with wheelchair access, and they may be able to find particular information for you. **Sprout,** 893 Amsterdam Ave., New York, NY 10025, Tel 212/222-9575 or 888/222-9575, fax 212/222-9768; **Disabled People Organisation of the Caribbean,** Tel 876/967-9439.

Exchange rate August 1999			
Country	Currency	Abbreviation	Value/US$1
Jamaica	Jamaican dollar	J$	J$39
Cayman Islands	Cayman Island dollar	CI$	CI$0.81
Turks and Caicos	US dollar	US$	
Dominican Republic	Dominican peso	RD$	RD$15.85
Puerto Rico	US dollar	US$	
Virgin Islands	US dollar	US$	
Netherland Antilles			
(inc. Sint Maarten)	Netherland Antilles florin or guilder	NAf	NAf1.77
Aruba	Aruban florin	Afl	Afl1.77
Leeward Islands	East Caribbean dollar	EC$	EC$2.70
French Antilles			
(inc. St.-Martin)	French franc	F	F6.07
Windward Islands	East Caribbean dollar	EC$	EC$2.70
Barbados	Barbados dollar	BD$	BD$1.98
Trinidad and Tobago	Trinidad and Tobago dollar	TT$	TT$6.15

JAMAICA

PLANNING YOUR TRIP
Arrival/departure
Most tourists heading for the resorts on the north coast arrive at the Donald Sangster International Airport, 2 miles (3 km) east of Montego Bay. However, those going south or east might do better to land at the Norman Manley International Airport, 13 miles (21 km) from Kingston.

Air Jamaica, Tel 876/935-5141, provides an excellent service from gateways such as New York, Los Angeles, Chicago, Miami, Atlanta, Baltimore, and Toronto. Most major airlines serve both airports. Numerous charter airlines also fly from the United States and Canada. Regional services are provided by Cayman Airways, British West Indian Airways (BWIA), and Antilles Luchtvaarkt Maatschappy (ALM). There are also small airstrips in Negril, Ocho Rios, Port Antonio, and Tinson Pen (near the center of Kingston). They are served by Air Jamaica Express, Tel 876/922-466 or 876/952-5401, with several flights each day between these points and the international airports. Many visitors find these short hops a convenient means of cutting down on transfer times to their hotels.
Departure tax is: US$20 (J$750).

Entry requirements
A valid passport, birth certificate, or photo ID is required, along with onward or return ticket.

Festivals & events
January Accompong Maroon festival; Annual National Exhibition of new and emerging artists (Kingston)
February Bob Marley's Birthday Bash (Kingston); Reggae Sunsplash (Ocho Rios)
March Blue Marlin Spring Tournament (Port Antonio); Negril Music Festival; Kite Festival (Ocho Rios)
April Carnival (Kingston to Ocho Rios and Montego Bay)
May Reggae Superjam Vintage Classics (Kingston)
June Ocho Rios Jazz Festival
July Carnival (Negril); Season of Dance (National Dance Theatre in Kingston)
August Jamaica Independence Day Parade (Kingston); Miss Jamaica World Beauty Pageant (Kingston)
September Blue Marlin Tournament (Montego Bay)
October Caribbean Heritage Festival (Kingston); Octoberfest (Kingston)
November International Karting Meet
December Christmas Craft Fair (Devon House, Kingston); National Pantomine (Ward Theater, Kingston); Yacht Race (Montego Bay)

National holidays include New Year's Day (Jan. 1), Ash Wednesday, Good Friday, Easter Monday, Labor Day (4th Mon. in May), Emancipation Day (Aug. 1), Independence Day (Aug. 6), National Heroes Day (3rd Mon. in Oct.), Christmas Day, and Boxing Day (Dec. 26).

GETTING AROUND
Car rental
Major companies include Avis, Tel 876/926-1560; Budget, Tel 876/928-1115; Island Car Rentals, Tel 876/926-8861; and Beaumont Car Rental, Tel 876/926-8021. To rent a car you must be 25 years old with a valid driver's license and major credit card. Driving is on the left.

Although major roads are generally in good condition, you may encounter stray goats, dogs, and chickens, erratic cyclists, pedestrians—and potholes. At intersections, traffic coming from the right has priority, but don't rely on this. Always use your horn when passing, in case the driver in front suddenly swerves to avoid a pothole. There are few good signs, and you can only rely on major towns and resorts being shown. Road markings at junctions are almost nonexistent, except on new roads. In towns, watch out for "No Entry" signs, which are often below hood level where you can't see them.

Public transportation
Local bus timetables are erratic, and the buses are overcrowded. Minibuses travel on many of the same routes and may be slightly quicker, but equally overcrowded. Fares are inexpensive. Buses or minibuses can be flagged down anywhere along the roadside.

Taxis are widely available and most are unmetered: Agree on a fare before setting off (ask at your hotel for advice). Licensed taxis display red PPV (Public Passenger Vehicle) plates; avoid unlicensed cabs. Shared taxis (or route taxis) ply set routes around large towns or between towns and can be flagged down in the same way as buses or minibuses. The Jamaican Union of Travellers Association (JUTA) operates a fleet of tourist buses and taxis, and are often contracted for ground transfers.

PRACTICAL ADVICE
Emergencies
Ambulance or fire: Tel 110.
Police: Tel 119.

Telephones
The area code is 876.

Tourist information
Kingston: 2 St. Lucia Ave., Tel 876/929-9200 or 800/233-4582 (U.S.), fax 876/929-9375, e-mail: jamaicatrv@aol.com, www.jamaicatravel.com.

U.S. & Canada offices
Chicago: 500 N. Michigan Ave., Suite 1030, IL 60611,, Tel 312/527-1296, fax 312/527-1472.
Los Angeles: 3440 Wilshire Blvd., Suite 805, CA 90010, Tel 213/384-1123, fax 213/384-1780.
New York: 801 Second Ave., 20th floor, NY 10017,, Tel 212/856-9727, fax 212/856-9730.
Toronto: 1 Eglinton Ave. East, Suite 616, Ontario M4P 3A1, Tel 416/482-7850, fax 416/482-1730.

CAYMAN ISLANDS

PLANNING YOUR TRIP
Arrival/departure

The Owen Roberts International Airport on Grand Cayman is the main point of entry, with direct flights every week from Miami. The national flag carrier is Cayman Airways, which has direct flights from Miami, Tampa, Orlando, Houston, and Kingston (Jamaica). Other carriers from Miami include United Airlines, Northwest Airlines, and American Airlines. There are also direct flights from Tampa, Washington, Baltimore, Boston, Cleveland, New York, Charlotte,, Philadelphia, Chicago, Montego Bay (Jamaica), Cancun (Mexico),, and Belize City (Belize). Departure tax is US$12.50 (CI$10).

Little Cayman is a 45-minute flight from Grand Cayman, with flights three times daily operated by Island Air, Tel 345/949-0241.

Cayman Brac is 50 minutes from Grand Cayman on direct flights with Island Air (four times daily); Cayman Airways, Tel 345/949-2811, has one flight daily (except Mon. & Tues.) plus direct flights to Miami (1 hour 40 minutes).

Entry requirements

U.S., Canadian, and British citizens require a passport or proof of identity (such as birth certificate, voter registration card, or alien registration card) and onward or return ticket.

Festivals & events

January Wind-surfing regatta
April Batabano Carnival
June Million Dollar Month Fishing Tournament; International Aviation Week; The Taste of Cayman Summer Bash Weekend
October Pirate's Week
National holidays include New Year's Day (Jan. 1), Ash Wednesday (Feb. or March), Good Friday, Easter Monday (March or April), Discovery Day (mid-May), the Queen's Birthday (mid-June); Constitution Day (1st Mon. in July); Remembrance Day (2nd Mon. in Nov.); Christmas Day, and Boxing Day (Dec. 26).

GETTING AROUND
Car rental

Rental companies (or the police station) will issue a temporary driving permit (US$6.50) on production of a valid driver's license. Reputable companies include Andy's Rent-a-Car, Tel 345/949-8111; Budget, Tel 345/949-5605; Cayman Auto Rentals, Tel 345/949-6408; Cico Avis, Tel 345/949-2468; Coconut Car Rentals, Tel 345/949-4037; Economy, Tel 345/949-9550; Just Jeep, Tel 345/949-7263; Marshall's, Tel 345/949-7281; and Thrifty, Tel 345/949-6640.

Driving is on the left. Speed limits of between 20 and 50 mph (30 and 80 kph) are strictly enforced. Seat belts are obligatory. Avoid driving into Georgetown during rush hours.

On Little Cayman, hotels provide free bicycles for guests, and this is just about all you need to explore the western end of the island. Rental cars are available from McLaughlin Enterprises, Tel 345/948-1000, in Blossom Village if you want to reach the more remote beaches and snorkeling areas on the eastern end of the island, such as Point of Sands. Hotels also offer a drop-off/pickup service to Point of Sands for US$15.

On Cayman Brac, Hertz Brac Rent-a-Car, Tel 345/948-1515, has cars and jeeps; B & S Motor Ventures, Tel 345/948-1546, supplies cars, jeeps, scooters, and bicycles.

Public transportation

Grand Cayman: Minibuses run along the length of Seven Mile Beach with a flat fare of CI$1.50. There are no bus services elsewhere on the islands. Taxis can be found outside the major hotels, near the post office in Georgetown, or called from your hotel reception.

Little Cayman and Cayman Brac have no bus services, but taxis are available for transfers or sight-seeing tours.

PRACTICAL ADVICE
Emergencies
Grand Cayman
Police, fire, ambulance: Tel 911. Royal Cayman Islands Police: Tel 345/949-4222. Georgetown Hospital: Tel 345/949-8600.
Little Cayman
Police: Tel 911. Clinic: Tel 345/948-1051.
Cayman Brac
Emergency: Tel 911. Hospital: Tel 345/948-2243.

Media

The *Daily Caymanian Compass* (circulation 25,000) appears on weekdays. The complimentary monthly magazine *What's Hot* has good features on local life.

Telephones

The area code is 345.

Tourist information
Georgetown The Pavilion, Cricket Sq., Grand Cayman, Tel 345/949-0623, fax 345/949-405, e-mail: cscayman@canw.ky, www.caymanislands.ky.

U.S. & Canada offices
Chicago: 9525 W. Bryn Mawr, Suite 160, Rosemont, IL 60018, Tel 847/678-6446, fax 847/678-6675.
Houston: Two Memorial City Plaza, 820 Gessner, Suite 170, TX 77024, Tel 713/461-1317, fax 713/461-7409.
Los Angeles: 3440 Wilshire Blvd., Suite 1202, CA 90010, Tel 213/738-1968, fax 213/738-1829.
Miami: 6100 Blue Lagoon Dr., Suite 150, FL 33126-2085, Tel 305/266-2300, fax 305/267-2932
New York: 420 Lexington Ave., Suite 2733, NY 10170,, Tel 212/ 682-5582, fax 212/986-5123.
Toronto: Toronto Marketing Consultants, 234 Eglinton Ave. East, Suite 306, Ontario M4P 1K5, Tel 416/485-1550, fax 416/485-7578.

TURKS & CAICOS

PLANNING YOUR TRIP
Arrival/departure
There are international airports on Providenciales, Grand Turk, and South Caicos. Providenciales is the main international gateway, with a twice-daily service from Miami with American Airlines. There are also weekly charter flights from Boston, Detroit, New York, Montreal, and Toronto, and scheduled services to Jamaica, Cuba, Haiti, the Dominican Republic, and the Bahamas. Inter-island services are provided by Sky King Airways, Tel 649/941-5170, and Turks and Caicos Airways, Tel 649/946-4255. Departure tax is US$15.

Entry requirements
Visitors from the U.S. and Canada require a valid passport or a birth certificate and photo identification. A valid onward or return ticket is also required.

Festivals & events
April Spring Garden Festival (Grand Turk)
May Regatta Festival (South Caicos)
June Fun in the Sun Festival (Salt Cay); International Billfish Tournament (Providenciales)
July Summer Festival (Providenciales); Game Fishing Tournament (Grand Turk)
   National holidays include New Year's Day (Jan. 1), Good Friday, Easter Monday, Commonwealth Day (last Mon. in May), National Heroes Day (end May), Queen Elizabeth's birthday (mid-June), Emancipation Day (1st Mon. in Aug.), Columbus Day (Oct. 11), International Human Rights Day (Oct. 25), Christmas Day, and Boxing Day (Dec. 26).

GETTING AROUND
Car rental
Rental agencies on Providenciales include Provo Rent A Car, Tel 649/946-4404; Budget, Tel 649/946-4993; and Tropical Auto Rental, Tel,

649/946-5300. Foreign driver's licenses are valid; driving is on the left-hand side of the road.

Public transportation
There are no buses on the islands. Taxis are widely available and cost around US$2 per mile; they can also be hired for island tours (always agree on the price beforehand).

PRACTICAL ADVICE
Emergencies
Call either 999 or 911.

Telephones
The area code is 649.

Tourist information
Grand Turk: Turks and Caicos Islands Tourist Board, Pond St., Grand Turk, Tel 649/946-2321, fax 649/946-2733, e-mail: tci.tourism@ caribsurf.com.
Providenciales: Turtle Cove Landing, Tel 649/946-4970, fax 649/941-5494.

U.S. office
New York: Trombone Associates Inc., 420 Madison Ave., NY 10017., Tel 212/223-323, fax 212/223-0260, www.turksandcaicostourism.com

DOMINICAN REPUBLIC

PLANNING YOUR TRIP
Arrival/departure
The main international gateway is Las Americas International Airport, Tel 809/549-0450, 18 miles (29 km) to the east of Santo Domingo. Several U.S. airlines (American, TWA, and Apa International) have direct flights from Miami, New York, and Boston; from other U.S. cities, connections are in either Miami or San Juan (Puerto Rico).
   Most of the charter airlines use either Puerto Plata, Tel 809/586-0219, or Punta Cana,, Tel 809/686-8790, international airports. There are also international airports at La Romana, Tel 809/556-5565, Santiago, Tel 809/582-4894,

and Barahona, Tel 809/524-7010. Santo Domingo has a small domestic airport, Herrera, Tel 809/567-3900, with daily scheduled services to all the airports within the country on Air Santo Domingo, Tel 809/683-8020.
Departure tax is US$10.

Entry requirements
U.S. citizens must have a valid passport or birth certificate and photo ID. A tourist card (US$10) must be bought on entry.

Festivals & events
January The festival of the patron saint of the Dominican people, Our Lady of Altagracia, is celebrated with all-night vigils, family visits, and singing, and dancing.
July Merengue festival (Santo Domingo)
September Merengue festival (Sousa)
October Merengue festival (Puerto Plata)
   National holidays include New Year's Day, the birthday of Juan P. Duarte (Jan. 26), Independence Day (Feb. 27), Good Friday, Easter Monday, Labor Day (May 1), Restoration Day (Aug. 16), Columbus Day (Oct. 12), and Christmas Day.
   Each town also celebrates its own saint's day with a *fiesta patronal*, which starts with a Mass and then continues with races, sports, street games, and dancing.

GETTING AROUND
Car rental
Santo Domingo offices: Avis, Tel 809/ 535-7191; Dollar, Tel 809/541-6801; Budget, Tel 809/567-0175; Hertz, Tel 809/221-5333. Valid driver's license or international driver's license required, as well as a credit card. Driving is on the right; speed limits are 80 kph on highways, 40 kph in cities, unless otherwise indicated.

Public transportation
Taxis are available in all tourist areas and at the airports, but

they are comparatively expensive; since they are unmetered, always agree on a price before setting off.

The country has a widespread network of public buses, with the better ones featuring air-conditioning and on-board snacks and videos on long-distance routes; it is advisable to reserve seats in advance. On lesser routes, privately operated minibuses known as *guaguas* operate between towns and villages, stopping to pick up or drop off passengers frequently.

Motorbike taxis (*motoconchos*) also operate between many villages and towns.

PRACTICAL ADVICE
Emergencies
Police, fire, ambulance: Tel 711.

Telephones
The area code is 809.

Tourist information
Santo Domingo: Ministry of Tourism, Ave. Mexico corner, 30 de Marzo, Tel 809/221-4660, fax 809/682-3806, e-mail: sectur@codetel.net.do, www.codetel.net.do.
National Hotel and Restaurant Association, www.domrep-hotels.com.do.

U.S. & Canada offices
Chicago: 561 W. Diversey Pkwy., Suite 214, IL 60614-1643, Tel 773/529-1336 or 888-303-1336, fax 773/529-1338.
Miami: 2355 Salzedo St., Suite 307, Coral Gables, FL 33134, Tel 305/444-4592 or 888-358-9594, fax 305/444-4845.
New York: 1501 Broadway, Suite 410, NY 10036,, Tel 212/575-4966 or 888-374-6361, fax 212/575-5448.
Montreal: 2980 Rue Crescent, Quebec, H3G 2B8, Tel 514/499-1918 or 800-563-1611, fax 514/499-1393.
Toronto: 35 Church St., Unit 50 Market Square, Ontario M5E 1T3, Tel 416/361-2126 or 888-494-5050, fax 416/361-2130.

PUERTO RICO

PLANNING YOUR TRIP
Arrival/departure
The main gateway is San Juan's Luis Munoz Marin International Airport, Tel 787/462-3147. There are also small airports at Aguadilla, Mayaguez, and Ponce. American Airlines is the dominant carrier, with daily nonstop flights from Miami, Fort Lauderdale, Chicago, Dallas, New York, and Boston. Other regular scheduled services include Continental from New Jersey, Northwest-KLM from Detroit and Memphis, United from Chicago and New York, TWA from New York, U.S. Airways from Charlotte, Pittsburgh, and Philadelphia, and Delta from Atlanta. There are frequent services to nearby destinations such as the Virgin Islands and the Dominican Republic. American Eagle, LIAT,, and BWIA all offer regional services. Many shorter flights leave from San Juan's Isla Grande airport, which is more centrally located than the international airport. Charter and helicopter operators include MN Aviation, Tel 787/722-5980; Icarus Caribbean Corp, Tel 787/729-0000; and Caribbean Helicorp, Inc., Tel 787/722-1984. Departure tax: None.

Entry requirements
All non-U.S. residents need a U.S. visa, or U.S. visa waiver form for participating countries.

Festivals & events
March/April Carnival (Easter)
April/May Caribbean and Latin American Graphics, usually held in late spring (biennial)
May Heineken Jazz festival
June Celebrations of St. John the Baptist (June 23)
Casals Festival (music festival founded by famed cellist Pablo Casals)
December The Bacardi rum plant is host to the largest gathering of artisans and craftworkers on the island. The Christmas season starts

early in Dec. and lasts through Three King's Day (Jan. 6).

All U.S. **national holidays** are observed in Puerto Rico, and there are also nine local holidays honoring local leaders or events in the island's history.

GETTING AROUND
Car rental
Avis, Tel 787/721-4499; Budget, Tel 787/791-3685; Dollar, Tel 787/791-5500; and National, Tel 787/791-1805. Local rental companies are usually better value; try Charlie's Rental, Tel 787/728-2418; Vias, Tel 787/796-6404; or L & M Rental, Tel 787/725-8416.

Five tourist routes are marked with good signs across the island; each route is identified with symbols connected to the national heritage.

Public transportation
All taxis are metered, except when they are chartered for long-distance rides. A new system of tourist taxis has been introduced, with fixed rates between the airport, ports, and tourist areas (such as Condado or Old San Juan). City buses are a good way to get around in San Juan.

There are no scheduled bus services between cities, although you can catch shared taxis (known as *publicos,* they have yellow number plates with the letters P or PD at the end) that run to most parts of the island.

PRACTICAL ADVICE
Emergencies
Police, fire, and ambulance: Tel 911.
Tourist Zone Police (Condado): Tel 787/722-0738.

Telephones
The area code is 787.

Tourist information
San Juan: La Princesa Building, Old San Juan, Tel 787/721-2400, fax 787/722-5208;
Luis Munoz Marin Airport, Tel 787/791-1014; in Condado,

Tel 787/723-1709, in Old San
Juan, Tel 787/722-1709.

U.S. & Canada offices
New York: 575 5th Ave., 23rd
floor, NY 10017, Tel 212/599-
6262, fax 212/818-1866.
Florida: 901 Ponce de Leon
Blvd., Suite 604,, Coral Gables,
33134, Tel 305/445-9112,
fax 305/445-9450.
Los Angeles: 3575
W. Cahuenga Blvd., Suite 560,
CA 90068, Tel 213/874-5991,
fax 213/874-7257.
Toronto: 43 Colbourne St.,
Suite 310, Ontario M5E 1E3, Tel
416/368-2680, fax 416/368-5350,
www.discoverpuertorico.com,
www.welcome.topuertorico.org.

VIRGIN ISLANDS

U.S. VIRGIN ISLANDS

Entry requirements
U.S. citizens do not require a
passport for the USVI, but need
proof of identity to fly home.

Telephone
The area code is 340.

National holidays
These include New Year's Day
(Jan. 1), Martin Luther King Jr.
Day (3rd Mon. in Jan.),
President's Day (3rd Mon. in
Feb.), Transfer Day (March 31),
Holy Thursday (Thurs. before
Easter), Good Friday, Easter
Monday, USVI Emancipation Day
(July 3), Independence Day (July
4), Labor Day (1st Mon. in Sept.),
Columbus Day (2nd Mon. in
Oct.), Thanksgiving Day (4th
Thurs. in Nov.), Christmas Day,
and Boxing Day (Dec. 26).

ST. CROIX

PLANNING YOUR TRIP
Arrival/departure
Several airlines fly daily to St.
Croix from the U.S., including
American Airlines (from Miami),
Delta (from Atlanta), and US
Airways (from Philadelphia), and
there are numerous connections
via Puerto Rico (see p. 340), and

St. Thomas (see below) with
American Eagle. A twice-daily
hydrofoil service operates
between St. Croix and St.
Thomas (1 hour 15 minutes);
information Tel 340/776-7417.

Festivals & events
December–January The
Crucian Christmas Festival is St.
Croix's version of Carnival,
lasting for a month over
Christmas and the New Year
culminating in the Three Kings
Day parade (Jan. 6).
March LPGA Tournament at
the Carambola golf course
May St. Croix Annual
International Triathlon
November Mumm's Cup
Regatta
For a glimpse of the island's
heritage catch a performance by
Crucian quadrille dancers.

GETTING AROUND
Car rental
Avis, Tel 340/778-9355; Budget
Rent a Car, Tel 340/778-9636;
Olympic Ace, Tel 340/773-8000;
and Thrifty Car Rental, Tel
340/773-7200, can all arrange
airport and hotel pickups and
delivery. U.S. driver's licenses are
valid on the island; driving is on
the left in St. Croix.

Public transportation
It costs just a dollar to take the
bus from Christiansted to
Frederiksted; service every 40
minutes from 5:30 a.m.–9:30
p.m. daily. Taxis are readily available from the airport and hotels
or from taxi stands on King
Street and at Market Square
in Christiansted, or by Fort
Frederik in Frederiksted. Taxis
are not metered, but regulated
by an official tariff carried by
drivers. Check the fare in
advance. Taxi vans offer cut-price
transfers from the airport to
hotels around the island.

PRACTICAL ADVICE
Emergencies
Police, fire, and ambulance:
Tel 911.
St. Croix Hospital, Tel 340/778-
6311, has a 24-hour emergency

room. Hotels have access to a
24-hour duty doctor.

Tourist information
St. Christiansted: Queen
Cross St., Tel 340/773-0495 or
800/372-USVI, fax 340/773-5074,
www.st-croix.com,
www.usvi.net.

U.S. offices
New York: 1270 Ave. of the
Americas, Suite 2108, NY 10020,
Tel 212/332-2222, fax 212/332-
2223.
Coral Gables: 2655 LeJeune
Rd., Suite 907, FL 33134, Tel
305/442-7200, fax 305/445-9044.

ST. THOMAS & ST. JOHN

PLANNING YOUR TRIP
Arrival/departure
The major U.S. airlines provide
daily direct flights to St. Thomas,
and there are connections from
numerous major U.S. cities via
Puerto Rico (see p. 340) with
American Eagle. St. John does
not have an airport, but it is a
short ferry ride from St.
Thomas. Regular service departs
from St. Thomas, either to
Charlotte Amalie (45 minutes)
or Red Hook (20 minutes),
throughout the day. The Westin
and Caneel Bay hotels provide
private boat service for guests.

Festivals & events
March–April International
Rolex Cup Regatta (Easter
weekend, St. Thomas)
April Virgin Islands Carnival
(St. Thomas)
June–July St. John celebrates
Carnival during the run-up to a
big Independence Day party.
July Pillsbury Sound Race
August St. Thomas Open at
Mahogany Run; Atlantic Open
Blue Marlin Tournament

GETTING AROUND
Car rental
Avis, Tel 340/331-1084 and
Budget, Tel 340/626-4516. Local
operators, including Dependable,
Tel 340/522-3076, on St. Thomas,
and Conrad Sutton, Tel 340/776-
6479, on St. John, can offer more

competitive rates. U.S. driver's licenses are valid on the islands, but unlike the U.S. mainland driving is on the left in the USVI.

Public transportation

There is a local bus service on St. Thomas. On St. John, a regular bus shuttles between the ferry dock at Cruz Bay and Coral Bay on the east coast throughout the day. Taxis are readily available from St. Thomas Airport and St. John's Cruz Bay ferry dock, as well as from hotels and taxi stands in tourist areas. They are not metered, but regulated by an official tariff carried by drivers. Check the fare in advance. Taxi vans offer cut-price transfers from the St. Thomas Airport to hotels around the island.

PRACTICAL ADVICE
Emergencies

Police, fire, and ambulance: Tel 911. St. Thomas Hospital, Tel 340/776-8311, has a 24-hour emergency room. There is a clinic in St. John, but medical emergencies will be transferred to St. Thomas. Hotels have access to a 24-hour duty doctor.

Tourist information

Charlotte Amalie: U.S. Virgin Island Department of Tourism, P.O. Box 640, St. Thomas, USVI 00804, Tel 340/774-8784, fax 340/774-4390, e-mail: info@usvi.net, www.usvi.net.

There are also offices at Emancipation Park (downtown Charlotte Amalie), Havensight Mall in St. Thomas, and around the corner from the ferry dock in Cruz Bay, St. John..

U.S. offices:
See St. Croix, p. 341.

BRITISH VIRGIN ISLANDS

PLANNING YOUR TRIP
Arrival/departure

There are no direct flights to the British Virgin Islands from North America, but American Eagle and

several local airline companies offer frequent short-hop services to Tortola from Puerto Rico (see p. 340), and from St. Thomas, USVI (see p. 341). Air St. Thomas flies to Virgin Gorda from Puerto Rico and St. Thomas. The Gorda Aero Service flies to Anegada from Tortola and St. Thomas. With the exception of Anegada, the main BVIs are linked to each other, and St. Thomas and St. John in the USVI, by regular, inexpensive ferry services (see p. 158 and p. 174). Departure tax is US$10 for air travelers, or US$5 for those leaving by sea.

Entry requirements

U.S. citizens are required to produce a valid passport or proof of citizenship (a birth certificate or voter's registration), accompanied by photo ID such as a driver's license, together with a return or on-going ticket

Festivals & events

June–July HIHO windsurfing championships and regatta, conveniently timed to coincide with the Fourth of July
August BVI Festival (Tortola, 1st Mon., Tues., and Wed.)
December Foxy's famous New Year's Party (Jost van Dyke's Great Harbour, Dec. 31)
National holidays include New Year's Day, Commonwealth Day (2nd Mon. in March), Good Friday, Easter Monday, Whit Monday (May), Queen's Birthday (2nd Mon. in June), Territory Day (July 1), St. Ursula's Day (Oct. 21), Prince Charles's Birthday (Nov. 14), Christmas Day, Boxing Day (Dec. 26).

GETTING AROUND
Car Rental

On Tortola, Budget, Tel 284/494-2639, Dollar, Tel 284/494-6093, and Hertz Tel 284/495-4405, offer rental cars and 4WD vehicles.

On Virgin Gorda, contact L & S Jeep Rental, Tel 284/495-5297, or Mahogany, Tel 284/495-5469.

On Anegada, try ABC Car Rentals, Tel 284/495-9466, or DW Jeep Rentals, Tel 284/495-8018. Visitors are required to purchase a temporary license (US$10) in addition to a valid foreign driver's permit. Roads can be rough, and 4WD vehicles are good for negotiating bumpy tracks to the beach. Driving is on the left.

Public transportation

On Tortola, an irregular bus service operates out of Road Town to destinations along the south coast, but most visitors find taxis are more reliable alter-natives.

On Virgin Gorda, day trippers can take an island tour aboard an open truck with seats and an awning or hire a taxi.

There are frequent ferry services daily from Tortola to Virgin Gorda, Jost van Dyke, and the U.S. Virgin Islands of St. John and St. Thomas. Ferries also link Virgin Gorda with St. Thomas several times a week.

PRACTICAL ADVICE
Emergencies

Police, fire, and ambulance: Tel 999. Peebles Hospital: Road Town, Tortola, Tel 284/494-3497. Hotels can assist with locating a duty doctor. Serious medical emergencies are airlifted to St. Thomas, USVI, or San Juan, Puerto Rico.

Telephones

The area code is 284.

Tourist information
Tortola:
BVI Tourist Board, Ferry Terminal, Road Town, Tel 284/494-3134, fax 284/494-3866, e-mail: bvitourb@caribsurf.com. There is also a bureau in the Virgin Gorda Yacht Harbour, Tel 284/495-5181.

U.S. office:
New York: BVI Tourist Board, 370 Lexington Ave., Suite 1605, NY 10017, Tel 212/696-0400 or 800/835-8530, e-mail: bvitouristboard@worldnet.att.net.

NETHERLANDS ANTILLES & ARUBA

Entry requirements
For all islands in the group, U.S. citizens are required to produce a valid passport or proof of citizenship (birth certificate or voter's registration), accompanied by photo ID such as a driver's license, together with a return or on-going ticket. On St.-Martin, stays of three weeks require a full passport. There are no passport controls between the two halves of the island.

National holidays
These include New Year's Day, Good Friday, Easter Monday, Queen's Birthday (April 30), Labor Day (May 1), Ascension Day (May), Christmas Day, and Boxing Day (Dec. 26).
St.-Martin only: Whit Monday and All Saints Day (Nov. 1).

ARUBA

PLANNING YOUR TRIP
Arrival/departure
American Airlines flies direct to Aruba's Queen Beatrix International Airport, Tel 297/848000, from Miami and New York, and also make connections to other cities from Puerto Rico. Air Aruba flies out of Miami, Tampa, Baltimore, and Newark; ALM flies from Atlanta; and there are charter flights from many other U.S. cities. Departure tax is US$10.

Festivals & events
January New Year celebrations
February–March Carnival Monday (beginning Feb.) marks the start of the month-long run-up to Carnival; National Anthem and Flag Day (March 18)
June Windsurfing Festival
October Deep-Sea Fishing Tournament
December Sint Nicolaas's (Santa Claus) Birthday (Dec. 5)

GETTING AROUND
Car rental
Avis, Tel 297/828787; Budget, Tel 297/828600; Optima Rent-A-Car, Tel 297/838874; and TRAC Rent-a-Car, Tel 297/834902, have offices at the airport and other useful tourist locations. Foreign driver's licenses held for a minimum of two years are valid on Aruba; driving is on the right.

Public transportation
Aruba has an inexpensive and reliable bus service that links the hotel areas with Oranjestad, the airport, and San Nicolas; private minibus services offer greater flexibility. Taxis are easy to find at the airport or hotel, or call the Oranjestad depot, Tel 297/822116.

PRACTICAL ADVICE
Emergencies
All Emergencies: Tel 115, Police: Tel 100, Hospital: Tel 297/874300. All hotels have a doctor on call 24 hours.

Telephones
The country code is 297.

Tourist information
For tourist information on the island, contact the Aruba Tourism Authority, L.G. Smith Blvd. 172, Oranjestad, Tel 297/823777, fax 297/834702.

U.S. offices
Weehawken: Aruba Tourism Authority-North America, 1000 Harbor Blvd. (ground floor), NJ 07087, Tel 201/330-0800 or 800-TOARUBA, fax 201/330-8757, e-mail: ata.newjersey@toaruba.com.

BONAIRE

PLANNING YOUR TRIP
Arrival/departure
ALM Antillean Airlines offers direct services to Bonaire's Flamingo International Airport from Miami and Atlanta; Air Aruba flies direct from Newark. American Airlines flies from Miami to Curaçao and New York to Aruba for connections to Bonaire; United Airlines flies from Miami to Aruba; and some charter companies also fly to Aruba from several U.S. cities.

Departure tax is US$10 for international flights, or US$5.75 for trips within the Netherlands Antilles.

Festival & events
February–March Carnival
April Rincon Day
September Bonaire Day (Sept. 6)
October Annual Sailing Regatta

GETTING AROUND
Car rental
Avis, Tel 5997/5182; Budget, Tel 5997/8315; and Hertz, Tel 5997/7221, all have offices at the airport. Local operators include AB Car Rental, Tel 5997/8980, and Sunray Car Rental, Tel 5997/5230. Foreign driver's licenses are valid. Driving is on the right.

Public transportation
A few minibuses shuttle between Kralendijk and Rincon, and taxis are available at the airport and can be booked through hotels.

PRACTICAL ADVICE
Emergencies
Police: Tel 113 or 8000.
St. Francis Hospital in Kralendijk, Tel 5997/8900, has a decompression chamber.

Telephones
The country code is 5997.

Tourist information
Bonaire: Kaya Libertador, Simon Bolivar 12, Kralendijk, Tel 5997/8322, fax 5997/8408.

U.S. office
New York: 10 Rockefeller Plaza, Suite 900, NY 10020, Tel 212/956-5900 or 800/956-5913, e-mail: 102372.3337@compuserve.com, www.interknowledge.com.

CURAÇAO

PLANNING YOUR TRIP
Arrival/departure
Hato International Airport is well served by direct flights from

TRAVELWISE INFORMATION

Miami with American Airlines and the national carrier ALM. ALM also flies out of Atlanta and Fort Lauderdale. Flights to neighboring Aruba offer an alternative route with easy connections for the short hop to Curaçao.

Departure tax is U.S.$12.50 for international flights, or U.S.$6 for trips within the Netherlands Antilles.

Festivals & events
February/March Carnival starts with Carnival Monday.
March Springtime fishing tournaments
April Celebration of the Queen's Birthday (April 30); Sailing Regatta
July Flag Day (July 2)
August Salsa Festival
October Jazz Festival

GETTING AROUND
Car rental
Avis, Tel 5999/868-1163; Budget, Tel 5999/868-3466; National, Tel 5999/869-4433; and Caribe Rentals, Tel 5999/461-3089. Foreign driver's licenses are valid and driving is on the right.

Public transportation
Inexpensive public buses cover main routes around the island from Willemstad. Private minibuses offer a more flexible alternative. Taxis are unmetered.

PRACTICAL ADVICE
Emergencies
Police: Tel 114. Ambulance: Tel 112. Hospital: Tel 110. Help Line Assistance: Tel 5999/461-7991.

Telephones
The country code is 5999.

Tourist information
Willemstad: Curaçao Tourism Development Bureau, Pietermaai 19, Tel 5999/461-6000, e-mail: ctdbcur@ibm.net.

U.S. office
New York 475 Park Ave. S., Suite 2000, NY 10016,, Tel 212/683-7660 or 800/332-8266, fax 212/683-9337, www.curacao-tourism.com.

SABA

PLANNING YOUR TRIP
Arrival/departure
No direct flights from the U.S., but Winair makes the 15-minute hop from Sint Maarten to J.E. Yrausquin Airport several times a day. High-speed ferries from Sint Maarten run twice a week.

Departure tax is US$10 for flights connecting with a same-day international service; or US$2 for flights with a stopover in the Netherlands Antilles.

Festivals & events
April Celebration of the Queen's Birthday (April 30)
July–August Carnival
December Saba Day Festivities

GETTING AROUND
Car rental
Scout's Place, Windwardside, Tel 5994/62205, can arrange car and jeep rental; also Johnson's Car Rental, Tel 5994/62469.

Public transportation
Taxis are available at the airport or can be booked through hotels.

PRACTICAL ADVICE
Emergencies
Police: Tel 5994/62221. Medical Centre, The Bottom: Tel 5994/63288. Medical emergencies are generally flown to Sint Maarten.

Telephones
The country code is 5994. From Sint Maarten and Sint Eustatius, dial 04 and the number.

Tourist information
Windwardside: Saba Tourist Bureau, Tel 5994/62231, fax 5994/62350.

U.S. office
Boca Raton: Saba and Sint Eustatius Tourist Office, P.O. Box 6322, FL 33427, Tel 561/394-8580 or 800/722-2394, fax 561/394-4595, e-mail: sabatourism@juno.com, www.turq.com/saba.

SINT EUSTATIUS

PLANNING YOUR TRIP
Arrival/departure
There are no direct flights from the United States, but Winair operates several daily island-hopper services into F. D. Roosevelt Airport, Tel 5993/82620, from Sint Maarten (see p. 345); the flight takes 20 minutes. There are also connections to St. Kitts.

Departure tax is US$10 for flights connecting with a same-day international service; or US$5 for journeys including a stopover in the Netherlands Antilles.

Festivals & events
April Celebration of the Queen's Birthday (April 30)
July Carnival
November Statia/America Day (Nov. 16)
December Kingdom Day (Dec. 15)

GETTING AROUND
Car rental
Avis, Tel 5993/82421, has an office at the airport, and there are a couple of local rental operators in Oranjestad. Foreign licenses are valid in Statia; driving is on the right.

Public transportation
With no buses on Statia, most visitors tend to walk or cycle. Taxis are available at the airport and can be ordered at hotels.

PRACTICAL ADVICE
Emergencies
Police: Tel 5993/82333. Hospital: Tel 5993/82211. Medical emergencies are generally flown to Sint Maarten.

Telephones
The area code is 5993. From Sint Maarten and Saba, dial 03 and the number.

Tourist information
Oranjestad: Sint Eustatius Tourism Development Foundation, Fort Oranje, Tel 5993/82433.

U.S. office
See tourist information for Saba.

SINT MAARTEN/
ST.-MARTIN

PLANNING YOUR TRIP
Arrival/departure
Princess Juliana Airport, Tel 5995/54211, in Sint Maarten is the main island gateway. American Airlines flies direct from New York and Miami daily and provides connections from other North American cities via Puerto Rico. Continental, US Airways, and Northwest offer services originating in the United States.

The island is a transportation hub for regional carriers LIAT and Winair; ALM Antillean flies to the Dutch Leewards; Air St. Barts, Air Guadeloupe, and Air Martinique serve the French Antilles with some smaller planes departing from St.-Martin's L'Esperance-Grand-Case regional airport, Tel 590/875303.

Departure tax is US$20 for international flights or US$10 for trips within the Netherlands Antilles.

Festivals & events
January Epiphany (Jan. 6, St. Martin)
February/March Carnival (St.-Martin)
March Heineken Regatta
March/April Carnival (Sint Maarten)
April Queen's Birthday celebrations (Sint Maarten, April 30)
June June Fest cultural events
July Bastille Day (St.-Martin, July 14); Schoelcher Day, marked with boat races in Grand Case (St.-Martin, July 21)
November Concordia Day (Nov. 11) unites the islanders to celebrate their dual heritage.

GETTING AROUND
Car rental
Avis, Tel 5995/52316, Budget, Tel 5995/54030, and Hertz,, Tel 5995/54541, operate out of Princess Juliana Airport with local offices in St.-Martin.

Foreign driver's licenses are valid on the island, and driving is on the right.

Public transportation
Frequent and inexpensive (US$1–2) minibus services shuttle between Philipsburg and Marigot with connections to Grand Case. Taxis are quite expensive (rates are fixed in US$).

PRACTICAL ADVICE
Emergencies
Sint Maarten Police: Tel 5995/22222. Ambulance: Tel 5995/22111.
St.-Martin Police: Tel 590/875010. Ambulance: Tel 590/878625.

Telephones
The country code for Sint Maarten is 5995, and 590 for St.-Martin. To call the French side from the Dutch side, dial 00 590 and the local number; to call the Dutch side from the French side, dial 19 5995 and the local number.

Tourist information
Sint Maarten
Philipsburg: W. Nisbeth Rd. 23, Tel 5995/22337, www.st-maarten.com.
There is a tourist information kiosk by the pier on Philipsburg's Wathey Square.

U.S. office
New York: 675 3rd Ave., NY 10017, Tel 212/953-2084 or 800/786-2278, fax 212/953-2145.

St.-Martin
Marigot: Office du Tourisme de St.-Martin, Blvd. de France (waterfront), Tel 590/875721, fax 590/875643, e-mail: stmartin@ megatropic.com www.interknowledge.com/ st-martin.

U.S. office
New York: St.-Martin Tourist Information Office, 10 E. 21st St., Suite 600, NY 10010, Tel 212/529-8484, fax 212/460-8287.

Entry requirements
For all islands in the group, U.S. citizens are required to produce a valid passport or proof of citizenship, such as a birth certificate or voter's registration, accompanied by a photo ID, such as a driver's license, together with a return or ongoing ticket.

National holidays
Holidays common to all islands include New Year's Day (Jan. 1), Good Friday, Easter Monday, Labour Day (1st Mon. in May), Christmas Day, and Boxing Day (Dec. 26).

ANGUILLA

PLANNING YOUR TRIP
Arrival/departure
There are no direct flights from the United States to Anguilla's Wallblake Airport, Tel 264/497-2514. American Eagle operates daily services from Puerto Rico (see p. 340), and there are frequent connections with various airlines from neighboring Sint Maarten/St.-Martin and Antigua.

A frequent (every 30 minutes from 7:30 a.m. to 6:15 p.m.) and inexpensive 15-minute ferry service operates between Blowing Point, Anguilla, and Marigot, the capital of French St.-Martin, Tel 264/497-6665.

Departure tax is US$10, or US$2 for the ferry crossing to St.-Martin.

Festivals & events
May Anguilla Day
June Celebration of the Queen's Birthday
August Carnival
Anguillans are legendary boat-builders and like to celebrate every major event in the calendar with a regatta.

Other national holidays include Whit Monday, Constitution Day (Aug. 6), and Separation Day (Dec. 17).

GETTING AROUND
Car rental
Island Car Rentals, Tel 264/497-2723; Malliouhana Travel & Tours, Tel 264/497-2431; and Hertz-affiliated Triple K, Tel 264/497-2934 or U.S. 800/654-3131. Visitors must purchase a temporary license (US$6) in addition to presenting a valid overseas driving permit. Driving is on the left.

Public transportation
There is no local bus service on Anguilla. Taxis are available at the airport, Tel 264/497-5054, and ferry dock, Tel 264/497-6089, or arranged through the hotel.

PRACTICAL ADVICE
Emergencies
All emergencies: Tel 911. Police: Tel 264/497-2333. Princess Alexandra Hospital, Stoney Ground: Tel 264/497-2551. Serious medical cases are airlifted to Puerto Rico.

Telephones
The area code is 264.

Tourist information
The Valley: Tel 264/497-2759, fax 264/497-2710, e-mail: abtour@anguillanet.com, www.candw.com.ai/~atbtour.

U.S. offices
Centerport: Medhurst and Associates, Inc., 1208 Washington Dr., NY 11721, Tel 516/425-0900, fax 516/425-0903, e-mail: medhurst@ix.netcom.com
San Francisco: Anguilla Tourist Board, World Trade Center, Suite 250, CA 94111, Tel 415/398-3231, fax 415/398-3669, e-mail: soleil@sonic.net.

ANTIGUA & BARBUDA

PLANNING YOUR TRIP
Arrival/departure
Several carriers serve Antigua's V. C. Bird International Airport direct from the United States, including American Airlines out of New York (also via Puerto Rico), Continental (from Newark), and BWIA (from Miami). Antigua is also the hub for the local airline LIAT, offering frequent connections to islands throughout the region.

Barbuda is served by daily LIAT, Tel 268/462-3147, flights from Antigua. Both the K Club and Coco Point hotels have private planes for clients.

Departure tax from Antigua is US$12; there is no tax payable for trips between Antigua and Barbuda.

Festivals & events
April Antigua Sailing Week attracts a world-class field for five major races, as well as a host of smaller events and wild partying (for information contact ASW, St. John's, Tel 268/462-8872).
July Carnival
National holidays include May Bank Holiday (last Mon. in May), public holidays (1st Mon. & Tues. in Aug), and Independence Day (Nov. 1).

GETTING AROUND
Car rental
Avis, Tel 268/462-2840; Dollar Rent-A-Car, Tel 2684/462-0362; and Hertz, Tel 268/462-6450 are found at Antigua's airport and other locations around the island. Visitors have to purchase a temporary driver's permit (US$20) in addition to presenting a valid overseas license.

On Barbuda, Burton Car Rental, Tel 268/460-0078, has a few jalopies for rental. Caribrep, Tel 268/462-0818, can arrange island tours.

Public transportation
Antigua has an irregular daytime bus service geared to commuters heading into St. John's from around the island. Buses only leave when they are full; fares are inexpensive.

Taxis, bookable from the hotel, are not metered, but government fixed rates apply. Agree on the fee in advance. There is no public transportation on Barbuda.

PRACTICAL ADVICE
Emergencies
Police Headquarters in St. John's: Tel 268/462-0125-8. Holberton Hospital: Queen Elizabeth Highway, St. John's, Tel 268/462-0251. Serious cases are airlifted to Puerto Rico or Miami. Most hotels are served by a 24-hour duty doctor.

Telephones
The area code for Antigua and Barbuda is 268.

Tourist information
St. John's: Antigua & Barbuda Department of Tourism, Nevis St. & Friendly Alley, Tel 268/462-0480, fax 268/462-2483, www.interknowledge.com/antigua-barbuda.

U.S. offices
New York: 610 Fifth Ave., Suite 311, NY 10020,, Tel 212/541-4117, fax 212/757-1607.
Miami: 25 S.E. 2nd Ave., Suite 300, FL 33131, Tel 305/381-6762, fax 305/381-7908.

ST. KITTS & NEVIS

PLANNING YOUR TRIP
Arrival/departure
There are no direct scheduled flights from North America to St. Kitts and Nevis, though rare charter flights to St. Kitts' Robert L. Bradshaw International Airport, Tel 869/465-8472, operate during the winter high season. However, there is easy access via Puerto Rico (see p. 340) with American Eagle to St. Kitts, and LIAT to St. Kitts or Nevis' Newcastle Airport, Tel 869/469-9343. LIAT and Nevis Express also fly to both islands from Antigua and Sint Maarten, and provide regular service between St. Kitts and Nevis. Departure tax is US$10.

Festivals & events
June St. Kitts Music Festival
August Culturama, around Emancipation Day (1st Mon. in Aug. Nevis)
September Heritage Festival on Independence Day (St. Kitts

and Nevis, Sept. 19)
December–January National
Carnival kicks off on Dec. 26 and
lasts into the New Year (St. Kitts).
Other **national holidays** include
Whit Monday, Queen's Birthday
(2nd Sat. in June), and National
Heroes Day (Sept. 16).

GETTING AROUND
Car rental
Car and jeep rentals are
available through Avis: St. Kitts,
Tel 869/465-6507; Nevis, Tel
869/469-1240; and local
operator TDC Rentals: St. Kitts,
Tel 869/465-2991; Nevis, Tel
869/469-5690. TDC also offers
an exchange rental arrangement
between St. Kitts and Nevis
(minimum three days). Visitors
must obtain a temporary driver's
permit (US$18.50) in addition to
presenting a valid foreign license.
Driving is on the left.

Public transportation
Inexpensive minibus services
leave the ferry dock in
Basseterre, and from Main Street
Charlestown when they are full
or the driver is ready. Taxis are
readily available and fares are
fixed by the government.

PRACTICAL ADVICE
Emergencies
In St. Kitts contact the police at
Tel 869/469-2241. On Nevis, Tel
869/469-5391. For medical
problems, hotels can call for a
doctor. The Joseph N. France
Hospital in Basseterre, and
Alexandra Hospital in Nevis
treat minor casualties. Serious
medical emergencies are
transferred to Puerto Rico.

Telephones
The area code is 869.

Tourist information
St. Kitts: St. Kitts and Nevis
Department of Tourism, Pelican
Mall, Bay Rd., Basseterre, Tel
869/465-4040, fax 869/465-8794,
www.interknowledge.
com/stkitts-nevis.
Nevis: Independence Square,
Main St., Charlestown, Tel
869/469-1042, fax 869/469-1066.

U.S. office
New York: 414 E. 75th St., NY
10021, Tel 212/535-1234 or
800/582-6208, fax 212/734-6511.

FRENCH ANTILLES

National holidays
Holidays common to all islands
include New Year's Day (Jan. 1),
Shrove Tuesday, Ash Wednesday,
Good Friday, Easter Monday,
Labor Day (May 1), Victory Day
1945 (May 8), Ascension Day
(May), Abolition of Slavery Day
(May 22), Whit Monday, Bastille
Day (July 14), Feast of the
Assumption (Aug. 15), All Saints
Day (Nov. 1), All Souls Day
(Nov. 2), and Christmas Day.

GUADELOUPE

PLANNING
YOUR TRIP
Arrival/departure
Air France operates three direct
services a week between Miami
and Guadeloupe; American
Airlines flies twice daily from
Puerto Rico (see p. 340). Pôle
Caraïbes Airport, Tel
590/21 14 00, lies just east of
Pointe-à-Pitre, convenient for
Gosier and other Grande-Terre
coastal resorts. There are also
daily services from regional
transportation hubs such as
Antigua (see p. 346) and Sint
Maarten/St.-Martin (see p. 345).
Inexpensive daily ferry services
link Guadeloupe with
Martinique (3 hours 45
minutes), and the islands of the
Guadeloupean archipelago (see
pp. 82–83). Ferries to Dominica
(1 hour 45 minutes) operate five
times a week. For schedule
information, contact L'Express
des Îles, Tel 590/83 12 45.
Crossings can be rough, so
travelers might prefer a short
plane ride.

Entry requirements
For stays up to 21 days, U.S.
visitors only need produce a
current or expired passport,
or proof of citizenship plus
government-issued photo ID,

and a return or on-going ticket.
Longer stays require a valid
passport. Airport security tax
on departure of US$20.

Festivals & events
January Carnival preparations
begin early in the New Year and
culminate in a giant three-day
event running up to Ash
Wednesday.
July Creole arts festival
(Ste.-Anne)
August The annual Fête des
Cuisinières is a gastronomic
showcase for female chefs.

GETTING AROUND
Car rental
Avis, Tel 590/21 13 54; Budget,
Tel 590/82 95 58; Euro Rent,
Tel 590/21 13 44; and Hertz,
Tel 590/84 57 94 are among the
rental agencies at the airport
and main tourist areas. Scooter
rentals are also widely available.
Overseas driver's licenses are
valid for 20 days in Guadeloupe;
driving is on the right.

Public transportation
Public buses serve most
destinations around the island
and operate from early morning
until around 6–7 p.m. There is a
useful service along the south
coast of Grande-Terre to
Pointe-à-Pitre with drop-off and
pick-up points near the ferry
terminal on La Darse. Carry
small change in francs for the
fare. To stop the bus, shout
"arrêt" or press a buzzer.
Taxi rates are fixed; agree the
price in advance.

PRACTICAL ADVICE
Emergencies
Police: Tel 17. Medical
emergencies: Tel 590/91 39 39
or Tel 590/89 11 00. There are
hospitals in all major towns, and
duty doctors can be summoned
by hotels.

Telephones
The country code is 590.

Tourist information
Pointe-à-Pitre: Office
Départemental du Tourisme de

la Guadeloupe, place de la Victoire, 97110, Tel 590/82 09 30, fax 590/83 89 22.

U.S. office
New York: Maison de la France, 444 Madison Ave., 16th floor, NY 10022, Tel 212/838-7800, fax 212/838-7855. www.francetourism.com.

ST.-BARTHÉLEMY

PLANNING YOUR TRIP
Arrival/departure
St. Jean Airport, Tel 590/27 65 41, can only take small STOL (Short Take-Off and Landing) aircraft, so the easiest access to St. Barts is from Sint Maarten (see p. 345), which is well served by direct flights from North America, and only a 10-minute hop away. Air St. Barth and Winair offer up to 10 flights a day from Sint Maarten, and there are Winair connections to many other destinations in the Eastern Caribbean (often via Sint Maarten). Air St. Barth also operates services to Guadeloupe, as does Air Guadeloupe. There are flights from St. Thomas and Puerto Rico with Air St. Thomas, Air Guadeloupe, and Virgin Air.
Express ferries make the sea crossing daily from Sint Maarten/St.-Martin. The one-hour trip can be quite rough, however fine the weather.

Entry requirements
For stays up to 21 days U.S. visitors only need produce a current or expired passport, or proof of citizenship plus government-issued photo ID, and a return or ongoing ticket. Longer stays require a valid passport. Airport departure tax is approximately US$6.

Festivals & events
January–February/March Festival de Musique
April–May Sailing regatta season
April Festival de la Gastronomie; Festival du Cinéma Caraobe

November Swedish Marathon
December New Year's Eve Regatta

GETTING AROUND
Car rental
Avis, Tel 590/27 71 52; Budget, Tel 590/27 66 30; and Hertz, Tel 590/27 71 14. Open-top jeeps are popular. Motorbikes and scooters can be rented through Chez Bérenger, Tel 590/27 89 00, and Saint-Barth Motobique, Tel 590/27 67 89, among others. Foreign driver's licenses are valid; driving is on the right. The gas station at St. Jean is closed Sun.; the only other gas station is at Lorient and closes Thurs., Sat. p.m., and all day Sun.

Public transportation
There is no public bus service on the island. Taxis are available from the airport, and the taxi stand on Quai du Général de Gaulle in Gustavia, Tel 590/27 66 31. There is a flat rate for rides up to five minutes, and it goes up every three minutes thereafter.

PRACTICAL ADVICE
Emergencies
Police: Tel 17. Ambulance and fire: Tel 18. The Hôpital de Bruyn in Gustavia, Tel 590/27 60 35, can handle most casualities and hotels can help locate the duty doctor. Serious medical emergencies are taken to Sint Maarten or Puerto Rico.

Telephones
The area code is 590.

Tourist information
Gustavia: Office du Tourisme, Quai du Général de Gaulle, 97133, Tel 590/27 87 27, fax 590/27 74 47, www.st-barths.com.

U.S. office
See Guadeloupe, p. 347.

MARTINIQUE

PLANNING YOUR TRIP
Arrival/departure
The only direct flights to Martinique from the United States are Air France's three weekly flights from Miami to Lamentin Airport (Tel 596/42 16 00), outside Fort-de-France. American Eagle flies twice-daily from Puerto Rico (see p. 340); and there are regular flights from other regional transportation hubs such as Antigua (see p. 346) and Sint Maarten (see p. 345).
Inexpensive ferry services link Martinique to Guadeloupe (3 hours 45 minutes) daily; to Dominica (1 hour 45 minutes) six times a week; and St. Lucia (1 hour 20 minutes) four times a week. For schedule information, contact L'Express des Îles at Tel 596/63 12 11. Crossings can be rough, so travelers might prefer a short-hop plane ride.

Entry requirements
For stays up to 21 days U.S. visitors only need produce a current or expired passport, or proof of citizenship plus government-issued photo ID, and a return or ongoing ticket. Longer stays require a valid passport. No departure tax.

Festivals & events
January Pre-Carnival activities kick off in January and climax on Ash Wednesday.
April Martinique Food Show
July Fort-de-France Cultural Festival
August Round-island yawl (boat) race
December Winter music festival featuring jazz or guitar in alternate years

GETTING AROUND
Car rental
Avis, Tel 596/51 17 70; Budget, Tel 596/63 69 00; Europcar, Tel 596/73 33 13; and Thrifty agents Jumbo Car, Tel 596/42 22 22. Overseas driver's licenses are valid for 20 days and driving is on the right.

Public transportation
Public buses from Fort-de-France operate from early morning until around 7 p.m. They stop at designated bus stops; to get off shout "arrêt."

Ferries from Fort-de-France serve local beaches and Ste. Anne. Taxi rates are fixed; agree on the price in advance.

PRACTICAL ADVICE
Emergencies
Police: Tel 17. Fire: Tel 18. Medical emergencies and ambulance: Tel 596/75 15 15. There are well-equipped hospitals and local clinics. Hotels or the tourist office can assist with locating an English-speaking doctor.

Telephones
The country code is 596.

Tourist information
Fort-de-France: Office Départemental du Tourisme de la Martinique, 2 rue Ernest Deproge, BP 520, 97206, Tel 596/63 79 60, fax 596/73 66 93, e-mail: martinique@nyo.com, www.martinique.org.

U.S. offices
See Guadeloupe, p. 347.

WINDWARD ISLANDS

National holidays
Holidays for the group include New Year's Day, Good Friday, Easter Monday, Whit Monday, Labour Day (1st Mon. in May)/May Day, Dominica (May 1), Christmas Day, and Boxing Day (Dec. 26).

DOMINICA

PLANNING YOUR TRIP
Arrival/departure
There are no direct flights to Dominica from the U.S. mainland, but American Eagle has a daily service from Puerto Rico (see p. 340) to Dominica's Melville Hall Airport, in the north of the island (1 hour from Roseau). Local carriers, LIAT, Cardinal, and Air Guadeloupe, provide services from regional transportation hubs including Antigua (see p. 346), Sint Maarten (see p. 345), and the French Antilles. Many smaller

planes use Canefield Airport, just outside Roseau, a convenient option for most hotels.

Dominica can also be reached by scheduled high-speed ferry services from Guadeloupe (1 hour 45 minutes) and Martinique (1 hour 30 minutes); contact L'Express des Îles in Roseau, Tel 767/448-2181. The crossing can be rough.

Entry requirements
U.S. visitors require a valid passport, or proof of citizenship together with a photo ID, and a return or ongoing ticket. Departure tax is US$12.

Festivals & events
February–March Carnival (Mon. & Tues. before Lent)
June–July Domfesta (week-long celebration of island culture)
October Creole Week (end Oct.)
November Independence Day (Nov. 3); World Zouk-Cadence Festival
Other holidays include 1st Mon. in Aug. and Community Day of Service (Nov. 4).

GETTING AROUND
Car rental
Avis, Tel 767/448-2481; Budget, Tel 767/449-2080; Auto Trade Ltd., Tel 767/448-3425; and Valley Rent-A-Car, Tel 767/448-3233. Drivers will need a temporary visitor's permit (US$12) in addition to their valid overseas license. Driving is on the left.

Public transportation
Irregular but frequent minibus services cover all the major destinations around the island from Roseau. Taxis are readily available from the airports and Roseau by day, or make an arrangement with your hotel. Reserve a taxi in advance for evening excursions. Government rates apply and there is usually a two-person minimum for trips from Melville Hall Airport.

PRACTICAL ADVICE
Emergencies
Police, fire, and emergencies: Tel

999. Princess Margaret Hospital in Roseau, Tel 767/448-2231, and Portsmouth Hospital, Tel 767/445-5237, are the island's main medical facilities. Serious medical emergencies are dis-patched to Puerto Rico. Hotels can assist in locating a duty doctor.

Telephones
The area code is 767.

Tourist information
Roseau: Dominica Division of Tourism at the National Development Corporation, Commonwealth of Dominica, Tel 767/448-2045, fax 767/448-5840. There are information offices at the airports and Old Market Square in Roseau.

U.S. office
New York: Dominica Tourist Office, 10 E. 21st St., NY 10010, Tel 212/475-7542, fax 212/475-9728, e-mail: DominicaNY@MSN.com.

GRENADA, CARRIACOU, & PETIT MARTINIQUE

PLANNING YOUR TRIP
Arrival/departure
American Airlines flies daily from Puerto Rico (see p. 340) to Grenada's Point Salines Airport, in the south of the island. BWIA flies several times a week direct from New York and Miami to Grenada with LIAT from regional gateways such as Antigua (see p. 346), Barbados (see p. 351), and St. Lucia (see below). Lauriston Airport on Carriacou is served by daily island-hopper flights from Grenada and St. Vincent by Airlines of Carriacou.

Ferry service from Grenada takes 3 hours (Tues.–Wed., Fri.–Sun.); express catamaran services cut the trip to 90 minutes (Mon.–Tues., Thurs.–Sun.), and continue on to Petit Martinique (Mon.–Tues., Thurs.–Fri., & Sun.). Petit Martinique can also be reached by water-taxi from Windward, on the northeast coast of Carriacou.

Entry requirements
U.S. visitors require a valid passport, or proof of citizenship together with a photo ID, and a return or ongoing ticket. Departure tax from Grenada is US$15; from Lauriston Airport on Carriacou US$4.

Festivals & events
February–March Carnival (Carriacou, held before beginning of Lent); week-long St. Patrick's Day celebration (Sauteurs, Grenada)
May–June Grenada's Spice Island Jazz Festival; Fisherman's Birthday (Feast of St. Peter) in Gouyave (end June)
July–August Carriacou Regatta; Rainbow City Festival (Grenville); Grenada Carnival (St. George's)

Other holidays include Independence Day (Feb. 7), Corpus Christi (June), Emancipation Day (1st Mon. & Tues. in Aug.), and Thanksgiving Day (Oct. 25).

GETTING AROUND
Car rental
Budget, Tel 473/444-2277; Dollar, Tel 473/444-4786; and Avis agents—Spice Island Rentals—Tel 473/440-3936, operate in Grenada. For rentals in Carriacou, contact Martin Bullen, Tel 473/443-7204, or John Gabriel, Tel 473/443-7454. Drivers will require a temporary local driver's permit (US$10) in addition to a valid overseas license. Driving is on the left.

Public transportation
Private minibuses (dollar buses) cover virtually every corner of Grenada and Carriacou on an unscheduled though frequent basis from early morning until early evening. Visitors can flag them down and be squeezed in by the "put-man" who also collects the money. Rap hard on the roof to get off. Taxis are available from the airport and main taxi stand on The Carenage in St. George's, by the ferry dock in Hillsborough, or make arrangements with your hotel. Always agree the price in advance.
For inter-island ferry information, see Arrival/departure.

PRACTICAL ADVICE
Emergencies
Police and fire: Tel 911. Ambulance, St. George's: Tel 434, Grenville: Tel 724, Carriacou: Tel 774. St. George's Hospital in Grenada, Tel 473/440-2051, can cope with most sicknesses, though serious medical emergencies may be transferred to Puerto Rico. Hotels can contact the duty doctor. There is also a private U.S.-managed Grenada School of Medicine, Tel 473/444-4271, at True Blue, in the south of the island but it doesn't deal with emergencies.

Telephones
The area code for Grenada, Carriacou, and Petit Martinique is 473.

Tourist information
Grenada: Grenada Board of Tourism, Burns Point, St. George's, Tel 473/440-2279, fax 473/440-6637, e-mail: gbt@caribsurf.com, www.grenada.org.
There is also an information kiosk at the cruise ship dock on the Carenage in St. George's.
Carriacou: Main St., Hillsborough, Tel 473/443-7948.

U.S. office
New York: Grenada Board of Tourism-U.S.A, 800 2nd Ave., NY 10017, Tel 212/687-9554 or 800/927-9554, fax 212/573-9731.

ST. LUCIA

PLANNING YOUR TRIP
Arrival/departure
Hewanorra Airport on the south of the island is St. Lucia's chief gateway for international jet flights, served by direct services from the United States with Air Jamaica (from New York), BWIA (from Miami and New York), American Airlines (from Puerto Rico), and charter flights during the winter high season. It is a 90-minute transfer to hotels in the north of the island. George Charles Airport can only accept smaller planes, including American Eagle's daily services from Puerto Rico, and frequent LIAT and Helenair services from local transportation hubs such as Antigua (see p. 346) and Barbados (see p. 351).
High-speed ferry services link St. Lucia with Martinique (1 hour 20 minutes); for information contact Caribbean Express, Tel 758/452-2211.

Entry requirements
U.S. citizens require a valid passport and return or onward ticket. Departure tax is US$15.

Festivals & events
February–March Carnival
May St. Lucia Jazz Festival (Pigeon Island & Castries)
September–October St. Lucia Billfishing Tournament (all welcome); Jounen Kweyol Entenasyonnal (International Creole Day); Creole cultural events (Oct. 28)
December Atlantic Rally for Cruisers (Rodney Bay Marina)

Other holidays include Independence Day (Feb. 22), Corpus Christi (June), Emancipation Day (1st Mon. in Aug.), Thanksgiving Day (Oct. 4), and National Day (Dec. 13).

GETTING AROUND
Car rental
Avis, Tel 758/451-6976; Budget, Tel 758/452-0233; National, Tel 758/453-0085; and Hertz agents Sun-Fun Car Rentals, Tel 758/452-0680. A temporary visitor's permit (US$12) is required plus a valid overseas license. Driving is on the left.

Public transportation
Frequent and inexpensive private minibus services cover the route between Castries, Rodney Bay, and the north until about 10 p.m. (later on Fri. for visitors to the Gros Islet jump-up, or party). Less frequent services to Soufrière and the south depart from Bridge St.

Taxi rates are fixed by the government; always agree the fare in advance.

PRACTICAL ADVICE
Emergencies
Police, fire, and ambulance: Tel 911. St. Lucia's main hospitals are the Victoria Hospital in Castries, Tel 758/453-7059, and St. Jude's in Vieux Fort, Tel 758/454-6041. All hotels have a resident or on-call doctor.

Telephones
The area code is 758.

Tourist information
Castries: St. Lucia Tourist Board, Pointe Seraphine Cruise Ship Complex, Tel 758/452-4094, fax 758/453-1121, e-mail: slutour@candw.lc, www:st-lucia.com.lc.

U.S. office
New York: St. Lucia Tourist Board, 820 2nd Ave., 9th Floor, NY 10017, Tel 212/867-2950 or 800/456-3984, fax 212/867-2795.

ST. VINCENT & THE GRENADINES

PLANNING YOUR TRIP
Arrival/departure
Although there are no direct flights to St. Vincent and the Grenadines from the U.S. mainland, American Eagle operates a daily service from Puerto Rico (see p. 340), and there are easy connections from the neighboring islands of Barbados, Grenada, Carriacou, and St. Lucia, as well as Martinique and Trinidad. St. Vincent's E.T. Joshua Airport, outside Kingstown, is a main transportation hub for small island-hopper flights to the Grenadine islands. These can also be reached by scheduled boat services originating from Kingstown.

Entry requirements
U.S. citizens require a valid passport or proof of citizenship and a return or onward ticket. Departure tax is US$8.

Festivals & events
March–April Bequia Easter Regatta
June–July Carnival or Vincy Mas (Kingstown, St. Vincent)
December Nine Mornings marks the nine-day run-up to Christmas with arts and crafts exhibits, parades, carol singers, and night-time jump-ups.

Other holidays include St. Vincent and the Grenadines Day (Jan. 22), Caricom Day (July 5), Emancipation Day (Aug. 2), and Independence Day (Oct. 27).

GETTING AROUND
Car rental
On St. Vincent, Ben's Auto Rental, Tel 784/456-2907 or 718/953-3304 (U.S.), fax 784/457-2686, will pick up from the airport, and Unico Auto Rentals, Tel 784/456-5744, fax 784/456-5745, offers free airport or hotel delivery. You can find rental cars on the Grenadines, too. Driving is on the left.

Public transportation
Private minibuses (known as dollar buses) ply the south coast route between Kingstown and Villa/Calliaqua throughout the day, less frequently in the evening. To hail a bus anywhere along the route, point down at the road; to get off, rap on the roof or shout "driver, stop" over the music. There are services to Layou and the west coast from the waterfront depot in Kingstown. Taxis are available from the airport, downtown Kingstown, and through hotels. Fares are fixed by the government.

PRACTICAL ADVICE
Emergencies
Police: Tel 784/457-1211. St. Vincent's main medical facility is the Kingstown General Hospital, Tel 784/456-1185. Medical emergencies can be airlifted to Barbados or Puerto Rico. Hotels will can contact a duty doctor.

Telephones
The area code for St. Vincent and the Grenadines is 784.

Tourist information
Kingstown St. Vincent and the Grenadines Tourist Office, Bay St., Tel 784/457-1502, fax 784/456-2610, e-mail: tourism@caribsurf.com, www.stvincentandgrenadines.com

U.S. office
New York: 801 2nd Ave., 21st Floor, NY 10017, Tel 212/687-4981 or 800/729-1726, fax 212/949-5946, e-mail svgtory@aol.com.

BARBADOS

PLANNING YOUR TRIP
Arrival/departure
Barbados has good air connections with North America. American Airlines and BWIA both fly direct daily from New York and Miami; American also provides daily services from Puerto Rico. Air Jamaica has a daily direct flight from New York, and services from their Jamaican hub at Montego Bay. LIAT and other local airlines provide a comprehensive network of inter-Caribbean links with the Leeward and Windward Islands, the French Antilles, Sint Maarten, and Trinidad & Tobago.

Entry requirements
U.S. visitors require a valid passport or proof of citizenship and photo ID, plus a return or ongoing ticket. Departure tax is US$12.50.

Festivals & events
July–August Barbados sugar harvest
October–November National Independence Festival of Creative Arts in the month running up to Independence Day (Nov. 30)

Other holidays include New Year's Day, Errol Barrow Day (Jan. 21), Good Friday, Easter Monday, Labor Day (May 1), Whit Monday, Kadooment Day (1st Mon. in Aug.), Emancipation Day (July 31), U.N. Day (Oct. 6), Christmas Day, and Boxing Day (Dec. 26).

GETTING AROUND
Car rental
Hertz agents Auto Rentals, Tel 246/428-9085, and local operators including Courtesy Rent-A-Car, Tel 246/431-4160, or 800/303-3806 (U.S.); National, Tel 246/426-0603 or 800/550-6288 (U.S.); and Sunny Isle Motors, Tel 246/435-7979, fax 246/435-9277, can arrange airport and hotel pickup, and drop-off. In addition to a valid overseas license, drivers must purchase a temporary visitor's driving license (US$5). Driving is on the left.

Public transportation
Regular and inexpensive public bus and minibuses serve the coastal regions and Bridgetown from early morning until around midnight. Taxis are not metered, so agree on a price in advance.

PRACTICAL ADVICE
Emergencies
Police: Tel 112. Fire: Tel 113. Ambulance: Tel 115. Queen Elizabeth Hospital, Bridgetown North: Tel 246/436-6450. Hotels can contact a duty doctor.

Telephones
The area code is 246.

Tourist information
Bridgetown: Barbados Tourism Authority, Harbour Rd., Tel 246/427-2623 or 800/744-6244, fax 246/426-4080, www.barbados.org.
There are information kiosks at the airport and cruise ship berth.

U.S. office
New York: Barbados Tourism Authority, 800 2nd Ave., NY 10017, Tel 212/986-6516 or 800/221-9831, fax 212/573-9850.

TRINIDAD & TOBAGO

PLANNING YOUR TRIP
Arrival/departure
There are daily direct flights with American Airlines from Miami, and BWIA from Miami and New York, to Trinidad's Piarco Airport, 30 miles east of Port of Spain. BWIA and LIAT also offer connections from Barbados, Grenada, and St. Lucia. American Eagle has a direct evening service to Crown Point Airport in Tobago from Puerto Rico, but most visitors prefer to fly to Trinidad and make the short hop to Tobago on one of the frequent Air Caribbean air bridge services (25 minutes), which operate up to eight times a day in both directions.

There is also a very inexpensive but slow ferry service between Port of Spain and Scarborough several times a week (5 hours).

Festivals & events
January–March Preparations for the famous Trinidad Carnival
March Phagwa (Hindu New Year)
June Muslim Hosay, a three-day event tied to the Islamic calendar
July Tobago Heritage Festival
August Steelband Week (Trinidad)
September Tobago Festival
October–November Divali (Hindu Festival of Light)
Other holidays include New Year's Day, Eid-ul-fitr (Jan. 20), Good Friday, Easter Monday, Corpus Christi (June), Labour Day (June 19), Emancipation Day (Aug. 1), Independence Day (Aug. 31), Christmas Day, and Boxing Day (Dec. 26).

GETTING AROUND
Car rental
Thrifty, Tel 868/669-0602; local operators Auto Rentals, Tel/fax 868/669-2277, and Singh's Auto Rentals, Tel 868/664-5417, fax 868/664-3860. All three companies also have offices on Tobago: Thrifty, Tel 868/639-8507; Auto Rentals, Tel 868/639-0644; Singh's, Tel 868/639-0191.

U.S. and Canadian driver's licenses are valid on the islands. Driving is on the left. Gas stations are sparse, so fill up before setting off.

Public transportation
Inexpensive public buses cover most destinations on Trinidad, Tel 868-623-7872, from the main depot at South Quay in Port of Spain. Tickets have to be purchased in advance.

Private minibuses, known as maxi-taxis, and shared taxis are a faster option and also depart from South Quay. The maxis are color coded by destination: yellow stripes for Port of Spain area; red for the east; green for the south. Taxis are readily available from the airport (fixed fares to Port of Spain and other popular destinations), taxi stands in town, and Port of Spain hotels. Share taxis can also be found at taxi stands.

Tobago has public and private bus systems. Public buses depart from Gardenside Road, Scarborough, for Crown Point and other destinations. Maxi taxis (minibuses with a blue stripe) are often a better option and can be flagged down anywhere along the roadside.

Taxis await arrivals at the airport and hover around some of the busier hotels, or can be called by the front desk. There are fixed fares from the airport to hotels.

PRACTICAL ADVICE
Emergencies
Police: Tel 999. Fire and ambulance: Tel 990. Hospitals: Tel 868/623-2951. In Tobago, minor casualties are handled by Scarborough Hospital, Tel 868/639-2551; emergencies may be airlifted to Trinidad.
Hotels can help contact a duty doctor.

Telephones
The area code for Trinidad and Tobago is 868.

Tourist information
Port of Spain: Tourist and Industrial Development Company (TIDCO), 10–14 Philipps St., Tel 868/623-6022 or 888/595-4TNT (U.S.), fax 868/623-3848, www.tidco.co.tt.

HOTELS & RESTAURANTS

Accommodations in the Caribbean are generally very expensive, although cheaper options are available, and prices drop dramatically in low season, sometimes by almost 50 percent, although you will be taking more chances with the weather. All-inclusive resorts can offer good value for money, although it is very easy to stay within the resort and not take the opportunity to explore the island.

The standard of food is high, and there is a huge variety of styles, from street vendors selling jerk chicken to top-class French cuisine. Restaurants are run more informally here than elsewhere, so seating arrangements and closing times are flexible. Call ahead to check. For details of AAA ratings see p. 369.

PRICES

HOTELS
An indication of the cost of a double room without breakfast is given by $ signs.

$$$$$	Over $280
$$$$	$200–$280
$$$	$120–$200
$$	$80–$120
$	Under $80

RESTAURANTS
An indication of the cost of a three-course dinner without drinks is given by $ signs.

$$$$$	Over $80
$$$$	$50–$80
$$$	$35–$50
$$	$20–$35
$	Under $20

JAMAICA

KINGSTON

SOMETHING SPECIAL

🏨 STRAWBERRY HILL

Perched 3,000 feet (900 m) above Kingston in the Blue Mountains with fabulous views over the city, Strawberry Hill is an award-winning property owned by Island Records magnate Chris Blackwell. All villas have private verandas, kitchens, hand-crafted plantation-style furniture, four-poster mahogany beds with mosquito nets, and thick-louvered windows. The hotel also features a well-equipped Aveda spa.

$$$$$
IRISH TOWN
TEL 876/944-8400 or 800/OUTPOST
FAX 876/944 8408
E-MAIL strawberry@toj.com
🛏 12 villas 🏊 🅰 All major cards

🏨 FOUR SEASONS HOTEL

$$
18 RUTHVEN RD.
TEL 876/929-7655
FAX 876/929-5964
E-MAIL info@hotel
www.fourseasonsja.com
Within walking distance of the uptown business/entertain-ment areas, the hotel has a section that was converted from an Edwardian house, and a new annex that surrounds one of Kingston's best hotel pools. The hotel has had the same hospitable management for the last 30 years.
🛏 76 🅰 🏊 🅰 All major cards

🍴 STRAWBERRY HILL

$$$$
IRISH TOWN
TEL 876/944-8400
High up in the Blue Mountains, the hotel's excellent restaurant specializes in "new Jamaican cuisine" with dishes such as dasheen and sweet potato gnocchi, yellowtail snapper with lemon butter sauce, and mouth-watering desserts. Salads, soups, and pasta are popular lunchtime choices, and the hotel is known for its Jamaican brunch.
🅰 All major cards

🍴 EL DORADO

$$–$$$
TERRA NOVA HOTEL,
17 WATERLOO RD.
TEL 876/926-2211
Popular restaurant with an interesting menu of inter-national and local dishes, particularly good seafood and soups. Reservations required for dinner.
🅰 🅰 All major cards

🍴 THE GROG SHOPPE

$$
DEVON HOUSE
TEL 876/929-7029
The bar is housed in the former stables of Devon House and has a pleasant, shady courtyard with a light lunchtime menu, which includes soups, salads, quiche, and sandwiches.
🕐 Closed Sun. 🅰 All major cards

🍴 TERRACE CAFÉ

$
WYNDHAM KINGSTON HOTEL, KNUTSFORD BLVD.
TEL 876/926-5430
Recommended for its breakfast buffet of Jamaican specialties, and sandwiches and salads at lunchtime. Poolside barbecue with live entertainment on Wednesdays.
🅰 🏊 🅰 All major cards

MANDEVILLE

🏨 MANDEVILLE HOTEL

$
4 HOTEL ST.
TEL 876/962-2460
FAX 876/962-0700
A venerable institution, tucked away on a quiet street off Mandeville's main square. The hotel has been in operation since the 19th century.
🛏 65 🅰 🏊 🅰 All major cards

HOTELS & RESTAURANTS

MONTEGO BAY

🏨 ROUND HILL HOTEL & VILLAS
$$$$$
NORTH COAST HWY.
TEL 876/972-2159 or 800/237-3237
FAX 876/956-7505
E-MAIL roundhill@cwjamaica.com
One of Jamaica's finest resorts —if not the Caribbean's— Round Hill is perched on a promontory 10 miles (16 km) west of Mo'Bay. The superb setting was once part of a sugar plantation, Round Hill Estate. Opened in 1953 as a hide-away for celebrities, the resort still welcomes many famous guests. The villas are privately owned and display many personal touches; all have kitchens where housekeepers prepare your breakfast, and many have pools. The service is impeccable.
🛏 36 plus 27 villas 🏊 📺
🞢 All major cards

🏨 HALF MOON GOLF, TENNIS, & BEACH CLUB
$$$$–$$$$$
TEL 876/953-2211 or 800/626-0592
FAX 876/953-2731
E-MAIL hmoondat@infochan.com
Seven miles (12 km) east of Mo'Bay, the colonial-style resort is set on over 400 acres (162 ha). There are nine bars and restaurants, an 18-hole Robert Trent Jones-designed golf course, 13 tennis courts, and almost every other type of recreational activity imaginable, including horseback riding, croquet, and a full range of water sports.
🛏 239 plus 277 suites 🞢
🏊 📺 🞢 All major cards

🍴 ROUND HILL HOTEL & VILLAS
$$$
TEL 876/952 5150
The Georgian-style colonial dining pavilion has a lovely setting overlooking the bay, with a bar lined with photographs of celebrities who have stayed here. Imaginative cuisine is prepared by the hotel's executive chef, Jean-Pierre Blouin. Jamaican buffets served Monday and Friday.
🞢 All major cards

🍴 MARGUERITAVILLE
$$
GLOUCESTER AVE.
TEL 876/952-4777
Wild and wacky bar with big-screen television, a 110-foot (33-m) waterslide into the ocean, a wide range of cocktails, and American and Jamaican food. Part of the same establishment is the Marguerites Restaurant next door, which has a pleasant ambience and fine sea views and specializes in seafood, pastas, and steaks.
🞢 🞢 All major cards

NEGRIL

🏨 THE CAVES
Perched above the honeycomb cliffs of Negril's West End, this beautiful property features hand-crafted thatched and wood cottages nestled in tropical gardens. A series of steps lead down to sundecks and hidden grottoes at sea level. All rooms have CD players and king- or queen-size beds, and there's an Aveda spa treatment center.
$$$$$
LIGHTHOUSE RD., WEST END
TEL 876/957-0270 or 800/OUTPOST
FAX 876/957-4930
E-MAIL thecaves@toj.com
🛏 12 cottages 🏊
🞢 All major cards

🏨 GRAND LIDO NEGRIL
$$$$
NORMAN MANLEY BLVD.
TEL 876/957-4010 or 800/GO-SUPER
FAX 876/957-4317
Situated at the western end of Bloody Bay, Grand Lido is one of the more upscale of Negril's all-inclusives with rooms equipped to a high standard, gourmet dining in a variety of restaurants, 24-hour room service, and unlimited watersports. The resort also features a clothes-optional beach, bar, and pool and daily sunset cruises aboard the magnificent M.V. Ziem, Princess Grace's honeymoon yacht.
🛏 216 rooms, 16 suites 🞢
🞢 🏊 📺 🞢 All major cards

🏨 NEGRIL CABINS RESORT
$$$
NORMAN MANLEY BLVD.
TEL 876/957-4350 or 800/382-3444
FAX 876/957-4381
E-MAIL negrilcabins@toj.com
Attractive resort at the northern end of Negril, with natural wood cabins on stilts scattered among 10 acres (4 ha) of palm trees and tropical vegetation. Just a few minutes' walk away from Bloody Bay.
🛏 80, 2 suites 🏊 📺
🞢 All major cards

🏨 ROCKHOUSE HOTEL
$$$
WEST END RD.
TEL/FAX 876/957-4373
E-MAIL info@rockhousehotel.com
The resort's thatched-roof, octagonal beehive huts overlook Pristine Cove on the West End's rocky foreshore. Connected by wooden walkways, the huts have four-poster beds and ceiling fans. There is a stunning pool on the shore.
🛏 14 cottages 🏊

HOTELS & RESTAURANTS

LA VENDOME
$$–$$$
CHARELA INN, NEGRIL BEACH
TEL 876/957-4277
Spicy Jamaican cuisine with a French twist, a choice of either the à la carte menu or a five-course table d'hôte. Good selection of imported French wines. Folklore shows Thursday and Saturday.
🕐 Closed L daily 🖸 All major cards

RICK'S CAFÉ
$$
WEST END RD.
TEL 876/957-4335
A Negril institution, somewhat swamped at dusk by hundreds of sunset-watchers crowding the bar, but the terrace restaurant is also very popular. Specialties include seafood pasta dishes, broiled lobster, and enticing desserts. The fresh fruit daiquiris are also winners.
🖸 All major cards

CHICKEN LAVISH
$
WEST END RD.
TEL 876/957-4410
Honest local cooking, with specialties that include curried goat, steaks, pork chops, and fresh-caught fish.
🖸 All major cards

PICKLED PARROT
$
WEST END RD.
TEL 876/957-4864
Cliffside restaurant with great sunset views and a waterslide into the water below. Mexican, Jamaican, and American food is served in generous portions at very reasonable prices.
🖸 All major cards

OCHO RIOS

ALMOND TREE
$$
HIBISCUS LODGE HOTEL
TEL 876/974-2813
Popular restaurant with an extensive à la carte menu

SOMETHING SPECIAL

JAMAICA INN
Undoubtedly one of Jamaica's top properties, the hotel exudes a sense of civilized elegance. Its rooms are impeccably furnished, each with a private balustraded balcony overlooking the sea complete with wing chairs, writing desk, and sofa. The hotel has one of the best beaches in Ocho Rios, with excellent swimming in its sheltered cove.
$$$$$
NORTH COAST HWY.,
TEL 876/974-2514 or
800/837-4608
FAX 876/974-2449
E-MAIL jaminn@infochan.com
🛈 45 🖸 ⛱ 🖸 All major cards

featuring Jamaican specialties as well as seafood and steaks. At night dinner is served by candlelight on a terrace overlooking the sea.
🖸 All major cards

EVITA'S
$–$$
EDEN BOWER RD.
TEL 876/974-2333
Set on the hillside above town, this cheerful Italian-owned restaurant serves authentic homemade pasta, salads, soups, and a wide range of desserts in an elegant setting overlooking the bay.
🖸 All major cards

PORT ANTONIO

BLUE LAGOON VILLAS
$$$$$
RTE. 4
TEL 876/993-8491
FAX 876/993-8492
E-MAIL austria@toj.com
Probably the most photographed in Jamaica, these wonderful villas are perched

on the water's edge adjacent to the Blue Lagoon itself. Weekly rates include a rental car and maid service, butler and chef.
🛈 6 villas 🖸 🖸 All major cards

DRAGON BAY
$$$$–$$$$$
TEL 876/993-8751
FAX 876/993-3284
E-MAIL dragonb@toj.vom
Overlooking a spectacular bay adjacent to the Blue Lagoon, Dragon Bay is set on 55 acres (22 ha) of woodland, lawns, and gardens. This superb hotel has its own sheltered beach and is within easy reach of the area's tourist attractions. A central building houses the reception, fitness center, English-style pub, and resort shop. The British colonial-style villas have the suites on the top floors and the rooms below. Suites feature a king-size bedroom, lounge with TV, refrigerator, kettle, coffeemaker, and hair dryer.
🛈 107 🖸 ⛱ 🖸 🖸 All major cards

TRIDENT VILLAS & HOTEL
$$$$
ANCHOVY
TEL 876/993-2602 or
800/633-3284
FAX 876/993-2590
Long-established hotel spread across 14 acres (6 ha) of the shoreline, with rooms and villas furnished in antique style.
🛈 27 rooms, 12 suites, 14 villas 🖸 ⛱ 🖸 All major cards

THE PAVILION
$$–$$$
DRAGON BAY BEACH RESORT
TEL 876/993-8514
Top-notch restaurant in one of the area's finest hotels, nouvelle cuisine with a Jamaican touch and daily themed menus.
🕐 Closed L daily 🖸 All major cards

🖸 Non-smoking 🖸 Air-conditioning ⛱ Indoor/⛱ Outdoor swimming pool 🖸 Health club 🖸 Credit cards **KEY**

HOTELS & RESTAURANTS

🍴 BLUE LAGOON
$–$$
FAIRY HILL
TEL 876/993-8491
This famous waterfront bar has a spectacular setting on the Blue Lagoon itself and serves top-quality jerk chicken, pork, and fish, as well as crayfish and pizzas. A beautiful spot for either lunch or dinner. Live music weekends.
🗺 All major cards

SOUTH COAST

🏨 JAKE'S
$$
TREASURE BEACH, CALABASH BAY, ST. ELIZABETH
TEL/FAX 876/965-0552 or 800/OUTPOST
E-MAIL jake's@toj.com
Superb collection of cottages designed in an eclectic mix of Jamaican, Mexican, and Catalan styles. Simplicity is the key: Cooled by sea breezes and ceiling fans instead of air-conditioning, the cottages have private outdoor showers, no phones or television (CD players are provided).
🛏 10 cottages 🏖 🗺 All major cards

🍴 JAKE'S
$
TREASURE BEACH, CALABASH BAY, ST. ELIZABETH
TEL 876/965-0635
Well-prepared and reasonably priced dishes including local staples such as Escovitch fish, rice'n'peas, and saltfish'n'ackee.
🗺 All major cards

CAYMAN ISLANDS

CAYMAN BRAC

🏨 BRAC REEF RESORT
$$
WEST END
TEL 345/948-1323 or 800/327-3835
FAX 345/323-8827
www.braclittle.com
This beach resort has recently been renovated, and all rooms feature TV, fans, and balcony or patio. The hotel has a good beach and a full service on-site dive shop.
🛏 40 🔘 🏖 🗺 All major cards

🏨 DIVI TIARA BEACH RESORT
$$
WEST END
TEL 345/948-1553 or 800/367-3484
FAX 345/948-1316
E-MAIL divtiara@candw.ky
This property is primarily a diving hotel, with Peter Hughes' Dive Tiara on-site. The hotel has a pool and a shallow beach..
🛏 70 🔘 🏖 🗺 All major cards

🏨 WALTON'S MANGO MANOR
$
STAKE BAY
TEL 345/948-0518
FAX 345/948-0518
E-MAIL waltons@candw.ky
Quaint little bed-and-breakfast in an old house with five spotlessly clean rooms.
🛏 5 🔘 🚫 🗺 All major cards

GRAND CAYMAN

🏨 GRAND CAYMAN MARRIOTT BEACH RESORT
$$$$$
WEST BAY ROAD, SEVEN MILE BEACH
TEL 345/949-0088 or 800/333-3333
FAX 345/949-0288
Deluxe oceanfront resort with a full range of facilities (including diving and water sports). The beach, however, is very popular and can get crowded.
🛏 315 rooms, 4 suites 🔄 🔘 🏖 🗺 All major cards

🏨 HYATT REGENCY GRAND CAYMAN
$$$$$
WEST BAY ROAD, SEVEN MILE BEACH
TEL 345/949-1234 or 800/233-1234
FAX 345/949-8528
Set amid a lush landscape of tropical foliage, the hotel is built in British colonial style and adjoins the Britannia Golf and Beach Resort.
🛏 236 rooms, 55 villas 🔘 🔄 🏖 🗺 All major cards

SOMETHING SPECIAL

🏨 CARIBBEAN CLUB
One of the last remaining original properties on Seven Mile Beach, in a superb position on an uncrowded section of the beach. Each villa has a fully equipped kitchen, living room, and either one or two bedrooms with bathroom.
$$$$$
WEST BAY ROAD, SEVEN MILE BEACH
TEL 345/947-4099 or 800/327-8777
FAX 345/945-4443
E-MAIL reservations@caribclub.com
🛏 18 🔘 🗺 All major cards

🏨 WESTIN CASUARINA RESORT
$$$$$
WEST BAY ROAD, SEVEN MILE BEACH
TEL 345/945-3800 or 800/228-3000
FAX 345/949-5825
One of the smarter resorts along Seven Mile Beach, with rooms equipped with TV, minibar, and marble bathroom. Round-the-clock room service. Two swimming pools, swim-up pool bar, and floodlit tennis.
🛏 340 🔄 🔘 🏖 📺 🗺 All major cards

🏨 SUNSET HOUSE
$$$
S. CHURCH ST., GEORGE TOWN
TEL 345/949-7111 or 800/854-4767

KEY   🏨 Hotel   🍴 Restaurant   🛏 No. of bedrooms   🅿 Parking   🔄 Closed   🔄 Elevator

FAX 345/949-7101
E-MAIL sunseths@candw.ky
A popular budget choice for dedicated divers, Sunset House has a fully equipped dive school, underwater photo school, and good shore diving. Deluxe rooms have ocean views.
🛈 75 ❄ 🏊 🖻 All major cards

LIGHTHOUSE RESTAURANT
$$$$
BREAKERS
TEL 345/947-2047
A Cayman landmark for the last 30 years, this never was a real lighthouse. The very popular restaurant has a terrace overlooking the seashore on the south side of the island. Specialties include seafood salads, pasta, fish, and mixed seafood grills. Excellent, if a bit high-priced.
🖻 All major cards

CRACKED CONCH
$$$
WEST BAY
TEL 345/975-5217
A long-standing institution, the Cracked Conch specializes in local cuisine (including conch steak, fritters, and chowder), as well as grills, pasta, and chicken dishes. Very popular for its Sunday Caribbean brunch. Pleasant bar overlooking the ironshore.
🖻 All major cards

LANTANAS
$$$
CARIBBEAN CLUB, SEVEN MILE BEACH
TEL 345975-5595
Austrian-born chef Fred Schrock has devised a menu that combines the best of the Caribbean with influences from the Southwest. Typical dishes include jerked pork with black beans; rice, plantain and mango salsa; and reef shark with red bell pepper sauce. Generous portions.
🕐 Closed L daily ❄ 🖻 All major cards

RISTORANTE PAPPAGALLO
$$$
CONCH POINT RD.
TEL 345/949-1119
Atmospheric restaurant housed in a large thatched building overlooking a natural lagoon. One of Grand Cayman's top restaurants, it specializes in northern Italian cuisine and seafood.
🕐 Closed L daily 🖻 All major cards

LONE STAR BAR & GRILL
$$
WEST BAY RD.
TEL 345/945-5175
Steaks, BBQ ribs, and Tex-Mex cuisine in a lively atmosphere, this popular watering hole caters for local divemasters after hours.
🖻 All major cards

LITTLE CAYMAN

LITTLE CAYMAN BEACH RESORT
$$$$
BLOSSOM VILLAGE
TEL 345/948-1033 or 800/327-3835
FAX 345/323-8827
E-MAIL bestdiving@aol.com
Modern resort with good facilities, set out around a small pool. All rooms have color TVs, balconies, and ceiling fans. Fully equipped dive center.
🛈 40 ❄ 🏊 💪 🖻 All major cards

PIRATE'S POINT RESORT
$$$
PRESTON BAY
TEL 345/948-1010
FAX 345/948-1011
One of the island's older resorts, with chalet accommodations set on a small beach. The resort has a reputation for gourmet cooking. Two scheduled boat dives daily.
🛈 10 ❄ 🏊 🖻 All major cards

SOUTHERN CROSS CLUB
$$$
SOUTH HOLE SOUND
TEL 345/948-1099 or 800/899-2582
FAX 345/948-1098
E-MAIL scc@candw.ky
Chalets are spaced out across a white sandy beach around a central dining/bar area. Recently refurbished to a very high standard, with a cheerful tropical decor. Small pool and sundeck. Fully equipped dive center.
🛈 19 chalets ❄ 🏊 🖻 All major cards

PARADISE VILLAS
$$
SOUTH HOLE SOUND
TEL 345/948-0001
FAX 345/948-0002
E-MAIL iggy@candyw.ky
Spacious villas on the water's edge, well kept and with fully equipped kitchens. Paradise Divers is just across the road.
🛈 12 villas ❄ 🏊 🖻 All major cards

HOTELS & RESTAURANTS

🍴 HUNGRY IGUANA
$$
SOUTH HOLE SOUND
TEL 345/948-0007
Next door to the airport and Paradise Villas, the restaurant is a popular meeting place with ocean views. Local and international cuisine.
🃏 All major cards

TURKS & CAICOS

GRAND TURK

🏨 ISLAND HOUSE
$$
COCKBURN TOWN
TEL 649/946-1519
FAX 649/946-2646
E-MAIL islandhouse@
GrandTurk.net
A few minutes outside of town, overlooking North Creek, this newly refurbished complex features spacious and well-equipped suites.
🛏 5 🔒 🏊 🃏 All major cards

🏨 SALT RAKER INN
$$
DUKE ST.
TEL 649/946-2260
FAX 649/946-2817
E-MAIL sraker@caribsurf.com
Just down the road from the Turks Head, this charming old inn (once a Bermudian ship-wright's home) has a hospitable atmosphere. The best rooms are those on the first floor, with balconies over-looking the sea.
🛏 13 🔒 🃏 All major cards

🏨 TURKS HEAD HOTEL
$$
DUKE ST.,COCKBURN TOWN
TEL 649/946-2466
FAX 649/946-2825
E-MAIL tophotel@grand-turk.com
Long-established hotel in one of the most charming parts of the town. Recently renovated to a high standard.

🛏 7 rooms, 1 apt. 🔒
🃏 All major cards

🍴 CALICO JACK'S
$$–$$$
DUKE ST., COCKBURN TOWN
TEL 649/946-2466
Recently revamped, the Turks Head Hotel's restaurant is popular for its lunchtime dishes such as cracked conch and steamed grouper, while in the evenings the wide-ranging menu includes dishes such as Thai-style chicken and salmon with lemon dill sauce.
🃏 All major cards

🍴 THE SECRET GARDEN
$$
SALT RAKER INN
TEL 649/946-2260
Tucked away in a leafy courtyard at the back of the hotel, this pleasant restaurant is good value for basic Caribbean or American meals. There is a popular weekly barbecue, featuring resident singer/guitarist Mitch Rollings.
🃏 All major cards

NORTH CAICOS

🏨 PROSPECT OF WHITBY
$$$
WHITBY
TEL 649/946-7119
On a superb beach, this long-established hotel has good facilities (pool, water sports, scuba diving), excellent food, and the island's best quality rooms. This Italian-managed hotel is largely contracted to Club Vacanze, but guests from elsewhere are welcome.
🛏 28 rooms, 4 suites 🔒
🏊 🃏 All major cards

🏨 PELICAN BEACH HOTEL
$$
WHITBY
TEL 649/946-7112
FAX 649/946-7139
This property was the first locally owned hotel on the island and has a friendly, laid-back atmosphere. Rooms are

showing their age but charming nonetheless.
🛏 14 🔒 🃏 All major cards

MIDDLE CAICOS

🏨 BLUE HORIZON RESORT
$$$–$$$$
CONCH BAR, MIDDLE CAICOS
TEL 649/946-6141
FAX 649/946-6139
E-MAIL bhresort@caribsurf.com
Large or small studios on the beach. Fishing trips can be arranged.
🛏 4 🃏 All major cards

PROVIDENCIALES

🏨 COMFORT SUITES
$$$
TEL 649/946-888 or 800/992-2015
FAX 639/946-5444
E-MAIL comfort@caribsurf.com
This complex of suites is set back from the beach, but features all the amenities of the Comfort Suites chain.
🛏 100 🔒 🏊 📺 🃏 All major cards

🏨 EREBUS INN
$$$
TURTLE COVE
TEL 649/946-4240 or 800/323-5655
FAX 649/946-4704
Atmospheric and very quiet little inn perched on the hilltop above Turtle Cove. Rooms in the main block were recently renovated (avoid the old villas). Good restaurant with superb views.
🛏 27 🔒 🏊 📺 🃏 All major cards

🏨 OCEAN CLUB
$$$
GRACE BAY RD.
TEL 649/946-5880 or 800/457-8787
FAX 649/946-5845
E-MAIL oceanclb@caribsurf.com
Well-designed and efficiently managed condominium complex on Grace Bay. The fully equipped and tastefully

furnished studios and suites are set in a lush garden with two small pools. Excellent restaurant (see below).

① 83 🚫 🌊 🏋️
🗒 All major cards

🏨 TURTLE COVE INN
$$
GRACE BAY RD.,
TURTLE COVE
TEL 649/946-4203 or
800/887-0477
FAX 649/946-4141
E-MAIL tcinn@caribsurf.com
Conveniently located on Turtle Cove, within walking distance of several restaurants, shops, and dive facilities. Small pool, lively poolside grill and bar, gourmet restaurant. Comfortable and good value, although some rooms need renovating.

① 30 🚫 🌊 🗒 All major cards

SOMETHING SPECIAL

🍴 ANACAONA
Rivaling the Gecko Grille for the island's best dining, this gourmet restaurant has a romantic setting on the beachfront beneath a circular thatched roof. Dress code elegant, no children under 12. Live music some evenings.

$$$
GRACE BAY CLUB
TEL 649/946-5050
🗒 All major cards

🍴 GECKO GRILLE
$$$
OCEAN CLUB, GRACE BAY
TEL 649/946-5885
One of the island's best restaurants with a reputation for innovative cuisine. Specialties include "ocean escargot" (tender young conch from the island's farm, in a garlicky herb butter), blackened wahoo salad, and pasta dishes. The restaurant has an attractive courtyard;

live music Wednesday and Sunday evenings.

🕐 Closed L & Mon. 🗒 All major cards

🍴 THE TERRACE
$$–$$$
TURTLE COVE INN,
TURTLE COVE
TEL 649/946-4763
On the upper floor of the Turtle Cove Inn, with a terrace overlooking the gardens. Specialties include creative conch dishes and seafood.

🕐 Closed Sun. 🗒 All major cards

🍴 COCO BISTRO
$$
GRACE BAY RD.
TEL 649/946-5369
Housed in a Moorish/Spanish-style hacienda set in a coconut grove, the Coco Bistro specializes in eclectic Mediterranean cuisine that includes Spanish-style tapas, Moroccan tajine dishes and couscous, and classics such as paella and moussaka. Excellent homemade desserts, including crepes, crème brûlée, and coconut tart.

🕐 Closed L daily & June–Oct. 🗒 All major cards

🍴 GILLEY'S AT LEEWARD
$$
LEEWARD MARINA
TEL 649/946-5094
Overlooking the Leeward Channel, Gilley's is well known for its fresh local seafood and extensive wine list. Good soups and salads at lunchtime.
🗒 All major cards

🍴 THE TIKI HUT CABANA BAR & GRILL
$–$$
TURTLE COVE INN
TEL 649/941-5341
A very popular post-dive gathering place that is good value for salads, sandwiches, pasta, and pizza. Open from 7 a.m. for breakfasts. Lively in the evenings.
🗒 All major cards

DOMINICAN REPUBLIC

CABARETE

🏨 CASA LAGUNA
$$
TEL 809/571-0725
FAX 809/571-0704
One of the best hotels in Cabarete, across the road from the beach. It has comfortable, modern studios set around the central pool and garden.

① 48 🚫 🌊 🗒 All major cards

🏨 CARIBE SURF
$
TEL 809/571-0788
FAX 809/571-3346
At the east end of the beach, this Swiss-managed hostelry is clean and well kept with comfortable rooms at reasonable prices.

① 30 🚫 🗒 All major cards

CENTRAL HIGHLANDS

🏨 PINAR DORADO
$
JARABACOA
TEL 809/574-2820
FAX 809/687-7012
Twenty minutes from the town center, pleasant hotel.

① 43 🚫 🌊 🗒 All major cards

🏨 RANCHO BAIGUATE
$
JARABACOA
TEL 809/574-6890
FAX 809/574-4940
E-MAIL rancho.baiguate@codetel.net.do
The country's only dedicated adventure sports center, set on extensive grounds bordered by the Baiguate and Jimenoa Rivers just outside Jarabacoa. Activities include trekking, mountain biking, quad-biking, canyoning, paragliding, rafting, plus expeditions to Pico Duarte. The center has a large pool, restaurant, and bar.

🚫 Non-smoking 🚫 Air-conditioning 🌊 Indoor/🌊 Outdoor swimming pool 🏋️ Health club 🗒 Credit cards **KEY**

Accommodations are clean and simple, and will appeal to those seeking peace and quiet after a full day's activities in the mountains.

🛈 121 ⬌ 🅰 All major cards

SANTO DOMINGO

🏨 HOTEL SANTO DOMINGO
$$–$$$
AVE. INDEPENDENCIA & AVE. ABRAHAM LINCOLN
TEL 809/221-1511 or 800/877-3643
FAX 809/535-4050
E-MAIL hotel.stodgo@codetel.com.do
In a prime location overlooking the sea, the hotel is decorated in a colonial style and has a palm-filled courtyard. Facilities include business center, beauty salon, massage/sauna facility, tennis, casino, bars, disco.

🛈 220 ⬌ 🅲 🅰 All major cards

🏨 RAMADA RENAISSANCE JARAGUA HOTEL
$$–$$$
367 AVE. GEORGE WASHINGTON
TEL 809/221-2222
FAX 809/686-0528
On the Malecon, this well-managed hotel has a casino, tennis facilities, a free-form swimming pool, meetings facilities, and five restaurants.

🛈 300 ⬌ 🅲 🅰 🅆 All major cards

🏨 BARCELO GRAN HOTEL LINA
$$
AVES. MAXIMO GOMEZ & 27 DE FEBRERO
TEL 809/563-5000
FAX 809/686-5521
Very comfortable five-star hotel with well-equipped rooms and efficient service. It has a great swimming pool, and there's also a casino.

🛈 214 ⬌ 🅲 🅰 🅆 All major cards

🍴 VESUVIO I
$$$$$
521 AVE. GEORGE WASHINGTON
TEL 809/221-1954
Considered to be one of the city's top restaurants, the Vesuvio specializes in gourmet international and Caribbean dishes, and home-made pasta.

🅰 All major cards

🍴 CANTABRICO
$$$
54 AVE. INDEPENDENCIA
TEL 809/687-5101
Formal restaurant with a wood-panel dining room well-known for its fish and seafood as well as Segovian suckling pig and other meat dishes.

🅰 All major cards

🍴 MESON DE LA CAVA
$$$
1 AVE. MIRADOR DEL SUR
TEL 809/533-3818
A good-natured place, set in a natural cave 50 feet (15 m) below ground and reached via a spiral staircase. Renowned for its steaks and seafood. Live music and dancing in the evening.

🅰 All major cards

🍴 PALACIO DE JADE
$$$
CALLE JOSE MARIA HEREDIA
TEL 809/686-3226
With an exterior that resembles an Oriental palace, the Jade Palace sets the tone for memorable Pekingese and Cantonese food. Specialties include Peking duck, shrimp with black-bean sauce, and shredded chicken on lettuce. The lunchtime dim sum menu is popular with the local business crowd.

🅲 🅰 All major cards

🍴 SCHEREZADE
$$–$$$
AVE. ROBERTO PASTORIZA 226, ENSANCHE NACHO
TEL 809/227-2323
Located in an ancient Moorish building, this atmospheric restaurant specializes in Mediterranean and Middle Eastern food, plus fish and seafood.

🅰 All major cards

🍴 EL CONUCO
$–$$
152 CALLE CASIMRO DE MOYA
TEL 809/6686-0129
Highly atmospheric restaurant with an entryway and rustic thatch roof reflecting its country theme. The food is excellent, and at lunchtime there is a popular buffet. When the waiters and waitresses are done serving they perform a song-and-dance routine.

🅰 All major cards

EAST OF SANTO DOMINGO

🏨 CASA DE CAMPO
$$$$$
LA ROMANA
TEL 809/523-3333 or 800/877-3643
FAX 809/523-8548
E-MAIL casadecampo@codetel.net.do
The only hotel complex in the region with its own international airport (with daily American Airlines 727 service from Miami), Casa de Campo claims to be the Caribbean's most complete resort. Accommodations comprise luxury villas and spacious rooms, all equipped to a high standard. Its four golf courses are world famous, and it also features a shooting center, polo stables, its own beach and marina, nine restaurants, and 13 tennis courts.

🛈 150 plus 150 villas 🅲 🅰 🅆 All major cards

🏨 IBEROSTAR PUNTA CANA
$$$
PLAYA BAVARO, HIGUEY
TEL 809/221-6500
FAX 809/221-7030
E-MAIL iberostar@iberostar.com
Spacious and comfortable all-inclusive resort on a good

stretch of Punta Cana's beach. Diving, water sports.
[1] 750 🔲 ⓢ 🏊 🚫 All major cards

🏨 PUNTA CANA BEACH RESORT
$$
PUNTA CANA, HIGUEY
TEL 809/221-2262
FAX 809/687-8745
An eco-friendly resort right on the beach. Five restaurants, five bars. Dive center, water sports, horseback riding.
[1] 400 🔲 ⓢ 🏊 🚫 All major cards

WEST OF SANTO DOMINGO

🏨 CASA BONITA
$
BAHORUCO, BARAHONA
TEL 809/696-0215
FAX 809/223-0548
Charming little country inn located on one of the most unspoiled stretches of coastline, set in the hills with terrific views over the rain forest and sea. Restaurant/bar.
[1] 18 ⓢ some 🏊 🚫 All major cards

NORTH COAST

PLAYA DORADA

🏨 JACK TAR VILLAGE
$$$
TEL 809/320-3800
FAX 809/320-4161
E-MAIL isenior@allegro resorts.com
One of numerous all-inclusive resorts in the town, the Jack Tar Village is one of the better known ones and has a casino, two pools, four restaurants, and most water sports. All rooms have balconies. Very popular among tennis players.
[1] 291 ⓢ 🏊 🏋 🚫 All major cards

🏨 OCCIDENTAL FLAM-ENCO BEACH RESORT
$$$
TEL 809/320-5084
FAX 809/320-6319

Well-managed hotel, within the Playa Dorada complex. The decor is Spanish in style. Two pools, water sports, tennis, and an extensive activities program.
[1] 582 ⓢ 🏊 🚫 All major cards

🏨 PLAYA NACO GOLF & TENNIS RESPORT
$$$
TEL 809/320-6226
FAX 809/320-6225
All-inclusive beachfront property. Large pool, pool bar, activities, sports, nighttime entertainment, disco, five bars, three restaurants.
[1] 420 ⓢ 🏊 🚫 All major cards

PUERTA PLATA

🍴 DE ARMANDO
$$$
CALLE SEPARACION
TEL 809/586-3418
The town's top restaurant, in an old house that has been refitted with sophisticated decor. There is sometimes a live band.
🕐 Closed L 🚫 All major cards

SANTIAGO

🍴 PEZ DORADO
$
43 CALLE DEL SOL, PARQUE COLON
TEL 809/582-2518
Fish, fish, and oriental cuisine are the staples of this long-standing and well-regarded restaurant in the center of the city.

SOSUA

🏨 LTI SOL DE PLATA RESORT
$$$
CARRETERA SOSUA-CABARETE
TEL 809/320-3600
FAX 809/571-3389
Midway between Sosua and Cabarete, the hotel is set on extensive grounds and has its

own excellent beach. The enormous central pool is surrounded by a free-form saltwater pool and a kid's pool. Tennis, water sports, miniature golf, six restaurants, and three courtesy cars.
[1] 474 plus 29 villas 🚫 All major cards

🍴 PUNTILLA DE PIERFORGIO
$$-$$$
1 CALLE LA PUNTILLA
TEL 809/571-2215
In a wonderful location on the cliff tops of Sosua, with terraces overlooking the sea, this Italian restaurant is renowned for its pasta and seafood.
🚫 All major cards

🍴 GUAJIRO'S CARIBBEAN CAFÉ
$$-$$$
CALLE PEDRO CLIASANDE, EL BATEY
TEL 809/571-2161
Atmospheric restaurant crammed with nautical paraphernalia, features unusual dishes such as green plantain soup, and the delicious *pollo a la merengue*, chicken in a sweet and spicy sauce. Popular on the regularly scheduled Latin jazz nights.
🚫 All major cards

PUERTO RICO

CENTRAL HIGHLANDS

🏨 HOTEL CASA GRANDE
$
RTE. 612, KM 0.3, UTUADO
TEL 787/894-3939 or 888/343-2272
FAX 787/894-3900
Set high up in the mountains of the Cordillera Central, with stunning views across an unspoiled valley, this peaceful, small hotel has rooms equipped with balcony and hammock. Once a coffee plantation, the house is surrounded by 107 acres (43 ha). There are several hiking

HOTELS & RESTAURANTS

PRICES

HOTELS

An indication of the cost of a double room without breakfast is given by $ signs.

$$$$$	Over $280
$$$$	$200–$280
$$$	$120–$200
$$	$80–$120
$	Under $80

RESTAURANTS

An indication of the cost of a three-course dinner without drinks is given by $ signs.

$$$$$	Over $80
$$$$	$50–$80
$$$	$35–$50
$$	$20–$35.
$	Under $20

---

trails in the surrounding hills. It also has its own restaurant, Jungle Jane's.

① 20 🛋 🅰 All major cards

LAS CROABAS

🏨 EL CONQUISTADOR RESORT & COUNTRY CLUB

$$$$$

AVE. EL CONQUISTADOR
TEL 787/863-1000
FAX 787/863-6586

This enormous complex occupies a commanding position on the cliff tops above the point where the Atlantic and Caribbean meet offshore. The resort comprises four separate hotels, each with a different style, one of which is located on the marina at the base of the cliff; the main hotel is linked to the marina by an automatic cable car. There is no beach here, but the hotel boasts it's own offshore island, with a regular shuttle service from the marina. There is also an 18-hole Arthur Hills' championship golf course, and the resort has 10 restaurants, five pools, and seven tennis courts. The immaculate rooms

all have VCRs and music systems.

① 910 🔁 🅱 🛋 🗦
🅰 All major cards

DORADO

🏨 HYATT CERROMAR BEACH

$$$$

DORADO BEACH
TEL 787/796-1234
FAX 787/796-4647

This large resort is situated on one of the north coast's best beaches and features the world's longest freshwater "riverpool," which winds for 1,776 feet through the hotel grounds and is a fun attraction for families. The hotel also has a windsurfing and water-sports center, scuba diving, two 18-hole championship golf courses, a spa and fitness center, Camp Hyatt for the children, tennis, and five restaurants and bars.

① 506 🅱 🔁 🛋 🗦
🅰 All major cards

GUANICA

🏨 COPAMARINA BEACH RESORT

$$$–$$$$

KM 6.5, RTE. 333, CANA GORDA
TEL 787/821-0505 or
800/468-4553
FAX 787/821-0070

On 16 acres of lush gardens at the water's edge, this resort offers a full range of facilities including water sports, diving, tennis, mountain biking, and ecotours in the neighboring Guanica Biosphere Reserve. The hotel has two pools, a fitness center, and a resident masseuse. The comfortable rooms are decorated in bright tropical colors and equipped with all amenities. The restaurant is excellent.

① 106 🅱 🛋 🗦 🅰 All major cards

MAUNABO

🍴 LOS BOHIOS

$$–$$$

PLAYA Y FARO
TEL 787/861-2545

In a lovely location on the outskirts of Maunabo, with views of the mountains and the ocean. Good seafood, steaks, and local dishes. Very popular on weekends with locals.

🅰 All major cards

PONCE

🏨 HOLIDAY INN

$$–$$$

PLAYA PONCE
TEL 787/259-7676

Efficiently managed and pleasant hotel just outside of Ponce, with views of the city and the ocean from its hilltop position. The comfortable rooms all have balconies and cable TV. The casino and nightclub are popular with locals on the weekends.

① 116 🅱 🅱 🛋
🅰 All major cards

SOMETHING SPECIAL

🍴 WILO'S COASTAL CUISINE

Wilo Benet, owner of San Juan's Pikayo restaurant, has recently opened his second outlet at the Copamarina Beach Resort, and his regulars will not be disappointed. Traditional entrees such as *asopa de langosta* and whole fried snapper with *mojo* are among the choices for any evening's dinner, but unexpected delights, such as pork chops with sweet spiced rum, also accent the typical menu.

$$$

COPAMARINA BEACH RESORT, RTE. 333, KM 6.5, CANA GORDA
TEL 787/821-0505
🕒 Closed L 🅰 All major cards

🍴 PITO'S SEAFOOD
$$$
LAS CUCHARAS
TEL 787/841-4977
With a large terrace overlooking the ocean just outside Ponce, Pito's is a great place for a long, indulgent lunch. Specialties include plantain stuffed with shrimp and lobster, stuffed clams, grilled mahimahi, and red snapper in Creole sauce.
🗝 All major cards

RINCON

SOMETHING SPECIAL

🏨 HORNED DORSET PRIMAVERA

Undoubtedly the island's most chic and exclusive hotel, this Mediterranean-style resort is impeccably run and caters to a discerning clientele seeking absolute tranquility and relaxation—there are no TVs, radios, or telephones (or children under 12) in the hotel. The rooms, furnished in antiques, are immaculate. Set on its own beach, the hotel has won numerous awards. It is also a member of the prestigious Relais & Château group and has a superb restaurant.
$$$$$
APARTADO 1132
TEL 787/823-4030 or 800/633-1857
FAX 787/823-5580
🛏 30 🈂 🏊 🗝 All major cards

🍴 HORNED DORSET PRIMAVERA
$$$$$
APARTADO 1132
TEL 787/823-4030
One of the island's top restaurants outside of the capital, the Horned Dorset's sophisticated setting and imaginative cuisine have won it many admirers in foodie circles. French food with

Caribbean accents, the repertoire includes dishes such as shrimp and fennel bisque, grilled tuna with mango salad, seared breast of duck with caramelized pineapple, and grilled marlin with fresh herbs and lemon.
🕐 Closed L 🗝 All major cards

RIO GRANDE

🏨 WESTIN RIO MAR BEACH
$$$$-$$$$$
6000 RIO MAR BLVD.
TEL 787/888-6000 or 800/WESTIN-1
FAX 787/888-6600
Well-run property on its own beach, 19 miles to the east of San Juan's airport and handy for El Yunque National Park. The hotel's impressive range of facilities includes spa and fitness center, 13 tennis courts, 10 restaurants, casino, shops, a full range of water sports, and 2 swimming pools. The 481-acre complex also includes two world-class golf courses (the River Course and the Ocean Course).
🛏 600 🈂 🈂 🏊 🗝 All major cards

🍴 PALIO AT THE WESTIN RIO MAR
$$$$
6000 RIO MAR BLVD.
TEL 787/888-6000
The resort's top restaurant offers a wonderfully tempting array of dishes styled with Italian flair. Specialties include fish baked in a banana leaf, with tomatoes, fresh peppers, and onions.
🗝 All major cards

SAN JUAN

🏨 HOTEL EL CONVENTO
$$$-$$$$$
100 CRISTO STREET, OLD SAN JUAN
TEL 787/723-9020 or 800/468-2779
FAX 787/721-2877
E-MAIL elconvento@aol.com

This small, deluxe hotel occupies the top floors of a historic building (once a convent) in the heart of the old town; the inner courtyard features cafés, restaurants, galleries, and shops. Each of the well-appointed rooms has its own distinctive character and all have views over San Juan and the sea. Shops, business services, and casino.
🛏 53 rooms, 6 suites 🈂 🈂 🏊 🗝 All major cards

🏨 WYNDHAM OLD SAN JUAN
$$$
100 BRAMBAUGH, OLD SAN JUAN
TEL 787/721-5100 or 800-WYNDHAM
FAX 787/721-1111
Located in the heart of the old city on the newly renovated waterfront and overlooking the cruise ship piers, this comfortable hotel is run with the customary attention to detail and service of the Wyndham hotels. Meeting rooms, business servies, and casino.
🛏 200, 40 suites 🈂 🈂 🏊 🗝 All major cards

🏨 GALLERY INN
$$-$$$$$
NORZAGORAY 204, OLD SAN JUAN
TEL 787/722-1808
FAX 787/724-7360
E-MAIL reservations@ thegalleryinn.com
Charming and idiosyncratic hostelry in an old rambling building, stuffed full of artworks and curiosities, with great views from its vantage point atop the old city.
🛏 13 rooms, 10 suites 🈂 🗝 All major cards

🍴 AJILLI MOJILLI
$$$$
1052 ASHFORD AVE., CONDADO
TEL 787/725-9195
This is a very popular restaurant (reservations

recommended) specializing in local Puerto Rican cuisine. Most people start with their excellent assorted fritters (pumpkin, white yam and cheese, plantain, chicken, and corn) followed by skewered pork, chicken, beef, or swordfish served with their richly flavored trademark Ajilli-Mojilli sauce.
🕐 Closed L. Sat.–Sun.
⊗ All major cards

SOMETHING SPECIAL

🍴 CHEF MARISOLL
Chef Marisoll Hernandez is one of the country's most celebrated chefs (she has her own TV show) and deservedly so, since the food in her tastefully decorated courtyard restaurant is wonderful. Innovative without being fussy, her contemporary cuisine includes dishes such as tortilla filled with cheddar and gruyère, tuna steak with a honey soy sauce, and fillet of grouper with a creole sauce. Reservations required.
$$$$
202 DEL CRISTO ST.
OLD SAN JUAN
TEL 787/725-7454
FAX 787/725-2946
🕐 Closed Mon. & L Sun.
⊗ All major cards

🍴 PIKAYO
$$$$
1 CALLE JOFFRE, CONDADO
TEL 787/721-6194
Chef Wilo Benet is one of the rising stars in the island's culinary world, and his restaurant is one of the most celebrated in the city. His perfectionist attitude to the presentation of food and the combining of flavors ensures a steady stream of repeat customers to this stylish, contemporarily styled restaurant.
🕐 Closed L & D Sun.–Mon.
⊗ All major cards

🍴 RAMIRO'S
$$$$
1106 MAGDALENA AVE., CONDADO
787/721-9056
One of the city's top restaurants, Ramiro's delivers creative Castilian cuisine from the kitchen of renowned chef Luis Ramiro.
🕐 Closed L Sun. ⊗ All major cards

🍴 IL PERUGINO
$$$
1005 CRISTO ST., OLD SAN JUAN
TEL 787/722-5481
Set in a beautifully restored house in the old city, this intimate restaurant has won many awards for its excellent Italian cuisine. Specialties include *pasta a la vongole*, *carpaccio*, rack of lamb, and marinated salmon. Extensive wine list.
🕐 Closed L ⊗ All major cards

🍴 AMADEUS
$$–$$$
106 CALLE SAN SEBASTIAN, OLD SAN JUAN
TEL 787/722-8635
This relaxed and charming restaurant attracts a trendy crowd drawn to its nouvelle Caribbean menu, which includes chicken breast stuffed with escargots and mushrooms, fresh salads, and plantain mousse with shrimp.
🕐 Closed L daily & D Mon.
⊗ All major cards

YABUCOA

🏨 PALMAS DE LUCIA
$
RTE. 901, SECTOR PLAYA LUCIA
TEL 787/ 893-4423 or 800/981-7575
FAX 787/893-00291
This small, friendly hotel is part of the government-run parador scheme. Near the beach and handy for the start of the Ruta Panoramica.
ⓘ 25 ⊙ ⊠ ⊗ All major cards

ST. CROIX

🏨 BUCCANEER HOTEL
$$$$
GALLOWS BAY
TEL 787/773-2100 or 800/255-3881
FAX 787/778-8215
Luxurious family-run resort with secluded beaches, water sports, golf, tennis, kids' club, and eco packages. Spacious accommodations (all with private balconies) in the attractive hilltop main building or nearer the beach, also family villas and deluxe suites.
ⓘ 150 🅿 ⊟ ⊙ ⊠ ⊽ ⊗ All major cards

🏨 SUNTERRA CARAMBOLA BEACH RESORT
$$$$
KINGSHILL
TEL 787/778-3800 or 888/316-9648
FAX 787/778-1682
Elegant former Rockresort spread across 28 beachfront acres (12 ha) with a Trent Jones-designed golf course and excellent sports facilities. Generous suite-style rooms with Mexican tiles in the showers, screened porches, and fully equipped kitchenettes.
ⓘ 151 🅿 ⊙ ⊠ ⊽ ⊗ All major cards

🏨 HIBISCUS BEACH HOTEL
$$$
4131 LA GRANDE PRINCESSE
TEL 787/773-4042 or 800/442-0121
FAX 787/773-7668
Small, relaxing resort arranged in two-story blocks with gingerbread decoration near a lovely beach 2 miles (3 km) west of Christiansted. Well-equipped rooms all with balcony or patio; hammocks under the palm trees.

🛏 37 🅿 ❄ ≋ 🔲All major cards

🏨 HILTY HOUSE INN
$$
GALLOWS BAY
TEL 787/773-2594
FAX 787/773-2594
Charming hilltop B&B with a Mediterranean feel, a glut of dazzling hand-painted Florentine tiles, and four simple but pretty bedrooms, plus two cottages with kitchens. Stylish wood-beamed living area in the shell of an 18th-century rum factory opening onto a garden pool deck.
🛏 6 🅿 ≋ 🔲All major cards

🏨 WAVES AT CANE BAY
$$
CANE BAY
TEL 787/778-1805 or
800/545-0603
FAX 787/778-4945
There are 11 airy and comfortable housekeeping studios and a villa on the waterfront a couple of minute's walk from the beach. Low-key and friendly; good snorkeling and diving; on-site dive shop.
🛏 11 studios, 1 villa 🅿 ❄ some ≋ 🔲All major cards

🍴 TOP HAT
$$$$
52 COMPANY ST.,
CHRISTIANSTED
TEL 787/773-2346
Attractive setting in a restored gingerbread town house. A genuine Danish restaurant, where you can sample homemade sausages and meatballs as well as filet mignon and other upscale international favorites.
🕐 Closed L & Sun.–Mon. 🔲All major cards

🍴 BLUE MOON
$$$
17 STRAND ST., FREDERIKSTED
TEL 787/772-2222
Bistro-cum-jazz spot (live music Fri. night and Sun. brunch) facing the waterfront with a garden patio and eclectic menu, which may include Cajun shrimp, Luna Pie (cheese and vegetable phyllo pastry parcel), and hot, hot hot Creole chicken.
🕐 Closed L Sat. & Mon., D Sun.–Mon. 🔲All major cards

🍴 INDIES
$$$
55-56 COMPANY ST.,
CHRISTIANSTED
TEL 787/773-2026
Charming courtyard setting with 19th-century brick arches and potted plants. Stylish and delicious California-Caribbean menu: grilled vegetable antipasto; citrus, walnut, and heart of palm salad; blackened fish; spice-rubbed duck with pineapple chutney.
🕐 Closed L Sat–Sun. 🔲All major cards

🍴 LE ST. TROPEZ
$$$
67 KING ST., FREDERIKSTED
TEL 787/772-3000
Pretty French restaurant in an old gingerbread house opening onto a leafy courtyard patio. Salade Niçoise and croque monsieur (toasted cheese sandwiches) at lunch; homemade pâtés, frog's legs, and lobster for dinner.
🕐 Closed all Sun., & L Sat. 🔲All major cards

🍴 WAHOO WILLY'S
$$
HOTEL CARAVELLE, 44A
QUEEN CROSS ST.,
CHRISTIANSTED
TEL 787/773-6585
Harborfront views, outdoor tables, and a long menu of burgers, salads, and pizzas from the wood-fired oven. In the evening, there is even more to choose from, including fresh lobster, daily fish specials, and steaks. Open for breakfast.
🔲All major cards

🍴 DOWIES
$
111 MARKET ST.,
FREDERIKSTED
TEL 787/772-0845
Heads wrapped in Creole checkered scarves, sisters Anna Doward and Daphne Davies cook up local specialties such as red pea soup and an award-winning fish pudding made with seasoned bluefish. Traditional Crucian breakfasts served Fri.-Sat.
🕐 Closed Mon. 🔲All major cards

ST. JOHN

SOMETHING SPECIAL

🏨 CANEEL BAY RESORT
Classic Laurance Rockefeller-built luxury resort on a stunning 170-acre (68 ha) peninsula site with seven beaches. Rooms in two-story blocks or stone-walled cottages strung along the shore (no phone, TV, or air-conditioning); tennis, water sports, children's activities.
$$$$$
CANEEL BAY
TEL 340/776-6111 or
800/928-8889
FAX 340/693-8280
🛏 166 🅿 ≋ 🎾 🔲All major cards

🏨 GALLOWS POINT SUITE RESORT
$$$$$
CRUZ BAY
TEL 340/776-6434 or
800/323-7229
FAX 340/776-6520
E-MAIL gallows@islands.vi
Very comfortable rental suites (individually decorated) in two-story units amid gardens, five minutes' walk from Cruz Bay town. Swimming and snorkeling from the shore.
🛏 51 🅿 ❄ ≋ 🔲All major cards

🏨 MAHO BAY CAMPS
$$
MAHO BAY
TEL 787/776-6226 or
800/392-9004
FAX 340/776-6504
E-MAIL mahony@maho.org
Screened tent-style cottages grafted onto the steep forested hillside above Maho Bay in the national park. Communal bathhouses, basic cooking facilities, and eco-conscious ethos. Also more luxurious solar-powered Harmony Studios constructed from recycled materials.
🛏 114 🅿 🐾 All major cards

🍴 ASOLARE
$$$$
NORTH SHORE RD.
TEL 340/779-4747
Gorgeous views overlooking Cruz Bay and St. Thomas, and a dynamic fusion of Asian and Pacific Rim cuisine make this one of St. John's hottest dining experiences. There are a few classical French dishes among the Thai beef salads and specialty seafood dishes. Reservations advised.
🕐 Closed L 🐾 All major cards

🍴 CHATEAU BORDEAUX
$$$$
CENTERLINE RD.,
BORDEAUX MOUNTAIN
TEL 340/776-6611
Cozy and romantic small dining room with a terrace overlooking the surrounding hills. An eclectic international menu equally at home with shrimp green curry and roast rack of lamb or wild game. Lighter fare such as fish sandwiches and burgers at lunch.
🐾 All major cards

🍴 FISH TRAP
$$$
RAINTREE INN, CRUZ BAY
TEL 340/693-9994
Locals recommend this casual al fresco restaurant for its fresh fish specialties, grilled

steaks, pasta dishes, and diet-breaking homemade desserts.
🕐 Closed Mon. 🐾 All major cards

🍴 MORGAN'S MANGO
$$
CRUZ BAY
TEL 340/693-8141
Lively dinner spot and bar with a lamp-lit wooden deck opposite the national park dock. International influences range from the Caribbean and South America to Asia; also a long cocktail menu and live music on Thursdays.
🕐 Closed L 🐾 All major cards

ST. THOMAS

🏨 BOLONGO BAY BEACH CLUB & VILLAS
$$$
7150 BOLONGO BAY
TEL 340/775-1800 or
800/524-4746
FAX 340/775-3208
Lively family-run beach resort property offering extensive water sports facilities, tennis, beach volleyball, and basketball courts.
🛏 85 🅿 🐾 ☀ 🛗
🐾 All major cards

🏨 HOTEL 1829
$$
GOVERNMENT HILL,
CHARLOTTE AMALIE
TEL 340/776-1829 OR
800/524-2002
FAX 340/776-4313
A national historic site, the atmospheric inn is furnished with antiques, painted tiles, and Tiffany glass. The rooms vary considerably in size (the best are in the original building). Splendid bar; tiny courtyard pool.
🛏 14 ☀ 🐾 All major cards

🏨 RITZ-CARLTON
$$$$$
6900 GREAT BAY
TEL 340/775-3333 or
800/241-3333
FAX 340/775-4444

Sybaritic luxury in elegant faux-Italianate surroundings with gardens and tinkling fountains. All the balconied rooms have sea views. Excellent facilities include fine dining, tennis, boat trips, water sports, and a beach.
🛏 152 🅿 🐾 ☀ 🛗
🐾 All major cards

🏨 SECRET HARBOUR BEACH RESORT
$$$$
6250 ESTATE NAZARETH
TEL 340/775-6550 or
800/524-2550
FAX 340/775-1501
E-MAIL shb.vi@worldnet.att.net
Spacious studios and one- and two-bedroom housekeeping condos with tropical decor in a AAA 3-diamond property. Palm-lined beach, water sports center, tennis.
🛏 60 🅿 🐾 ☀ 🛗 🐾 All major cards

🍴 OLD STONE FARM HOUSE
$$$$$
MAHOGANY RUN GOLF COURSE
TEL 340/777-6277
Fine dining amid the 200-year-old brick arches and wooden beams of a former sugar estate building. Sample a light garden vegetable streudel, Caribbean crab cakes, flash grilled tuna, or pan-seared potato-crusted pork loin with Calvados brandy sauce.
🕐 Closed L & all Mon. 🐾 All major cards

🍴 HERVÉ
$$$$
GOVERNMENT HILL,
CHARLOTTE AMALIE
TEL 340/777-9703
Panoramic views over the harbor and a stylish French-American menu with a Caribbean twist. Lunches such as salade Niçoise and crepes, and dinner favorites including pistachio-crusted brie, moules marinière, steaks, seafood, and crème brûlée. Reservations recommended.

⏱ Closed Sun. L 🃏 All major cards

🍴 ZORBA'S
$$$
GOVERNMENT HILL,
CHARLOTTE AMALIE
TEL 340/776-0444
Entertaining Greek restaurant serving all the usual suspects from tasty appetizer dips and fall-off-the-bone lamb to fresh seafood dishes and (rare for the Caribbean) vegetarian and macrobiotic platters.
⏱ L Sun. 🃏 All major cards

🍴 CUZZINS' CARIBBEAN RESTAURANT & BAR
$$
7 BACK ST.,
CHARLOTTE AMALIE
TEL 340/777-4711
Delicious local cooking in an attractive downtown brick dining room decorated with carnival props and local art. Mutton stew, curried chicken, shrimp creole, and a host of tasty local side dishes.
⏱ Closed all Sun. & D Tues
🃏 All major cards

🍴 VICTOR'S NEW HIDEOUT
$$
103 SUBMARINE BASE
(OFF RTE. SR30W)
TEL 340/776-9379
Good views from this hilltop hideout close to the airport. Caribbean curries and specialty lobster Montserrat with fruits as well as seafood and a few continental dishes.
⏱ Closed L Sun. 🃏 All major cards

BRITISH VIRGIN ISLANDS

ANEGADA

🏨 ANEGADA REEF HOTEL
$$$$
SETTING POINT
TEL 284/495-8002
FAX 284/495-9362
Total peace and quiet in simple but charming rooms

(oceanfront or garden); rates include three meals a day. Fishing and diving from the hotel boat; jeep rentals.
🛏 20 🅿 💲 🃏 All major cards

TORTOLA

🏨 LONG BAY BEACH RESORT & VILLAS
$$$$$
LONG BAY,
ROAD TOWN
TEL 284/495-4252 or
800/729-9599
FAX 284/495-4677
E-MAIL res@longbay@idestin.com
Very comfortable and thoughtfully equipped rooms, studios, and one- to three-bedroom villas on the hillside, and waterfront cabanas on the beach. All boast generous decks. Pool rooms (recommended for families); tennis.
🛏 72 🅿 💲 🏊 🃏 All major cards

🏨 SUGAR MILL HOTEL
$$$$$
APPLE BAY, ROAD TOWN
TEL 284/495-4355 or
800/462-8834
FAX 284/495-4696
E-MAIL sugarmill@caribsurf.com
Quiet hideaway attached to a notable restaurant. There are comfortable modern rooms and family suites, a two-bedroom villa, and two simple rooms in a wooden cottage set in rampant garden foliage.
🛏 21 🅿 💲 some 🏊
🃏 All major cards

🏨 LIGHTHOUSE VILLAS
$$
CANE GARDEN BAY
TEL 284/494-5482
FAX 284/495-9101
E-MAIL bvilighthouse@caribsurf.com
Spacious, bright efficiencies, crisp blue and white decor, and balconies overlooking the glorious bay. A minute's walk down to the beach.
🛏 6 🅿 💲 🃏 All major cards

🍴 MRS. SCATLIFFE'S
Reservations are a must for Mrs. Una Scatliffe's West Indian restaurant, which she operates out of her own home. The veranda serves as the dining room, and the four-course set menu features traditional soups, home-baked bread, pot roasts, and fruit and vegetables from the garden.
$$$
CARROT BAY
TEL 284/495-4556
🃏 All major cards

🍴 BRANDYWINE BAY
$$$$
BRANDYWINE BAY
TEL 284/495-2301
Tortola's most elegant dining room with a terrace overlooking the Sir Francis Drake Channel. Florentine specialties grilled over charcoal, homemade pastas and sauces flavored with fresh garden herbs, plenty of Italian wines on the wine list, and superb attention to detail.
⏱ Closed L, Mon., & Aug.–Oct. 🃏 All major cards

🍴 SUGAR MILL
$$$
APPLE BAY
TEL 284/495-4355
Lovely setting in the former boiling house of an old sugar mill decorated with Haitian paintings. Cookbook writers Jinx and Jefferson Morgan offer a small but delicious daily menu: Caribbean sweet potato soup with gingered shrimp, tropical game hen with orange curry butter, and fresh garden vegetables.
🃏 All major cards

🍴 PUSSER'S LANDING
$$
SOPER'S HOLE MARINA,
WEST END
TEL 284/495-4554

🅂 Non-smoking 🅰 Air-conditioning 🄸 Indoor/🄾 Outdoor swimming pool 🆃 Health club 🃏 Credit cards   **KEY**

English-style pub grub at lunchtime replaced by a more refined and international menu in the evening, although beef Wellington still lurks among the Maryland crab cakes and pasta dishes. The decor and diners have a nautical air.
All major cards

🍴 QUITO'S GAZEBO
$–$$
CANE GARDEN BAY
TEL 284/495-4837
Bar/restaurant with a covered deck overhanging the beach. Burgers and sandwiches, fettucine alfredo, or grilled kingfish followed by home-made brownies or pecan pie. Quito himself leads the live music on Fri. & Sat. nights.
All major cards

VIRGIN GORDA

🏨 BITTER END YACHT CLUB
$$$$$
NORTH SOUND
TEL 284/494-2746 or
800/872-2392
FAX 284/494-4756
Friendly yacht club ambience, excellent sailing school, and a three-million-dollar selection of windsurfers, dinghies, and yachts. Hillside villas (good for families) or romantic thatched huts on stilts with wooden decks and hammocks.
95 All major cards

🏨 LITTLE DIX BAY
$$$$$
LITTLE DIX BAY
TEL 284/495-5555 or
800/928-3000
FAX 284/495-5661
Sister to Caneel Bay on St. John (USVI), casually elegant Little Dix bears the inimitable Rockefeller stamp. Hexagonal and stilted rooms catch the breeze, though a/c (and phone) is an option here. Hiking, tennis, water sports, boat trips, children's program.
98 All major cards

🏨 LEVERICK BAY RESORT & MARINA
$$$
LEVERICK BAY
TEL 284/495-7421 or
800/848-7081
FAX 284/495-7367
E-MAIL leverick@caribsurf.com
Brightly painted villas with sea views and amazingly afford-able rates for hotel rooms and one- and two-bedroom suites with kitchen. Tennis, spa, water sports, and dive shop; activity packages.
16 All major cards

🍴 OLDE YARD INN
$$$
THE VALLEY
TEL 284/495-5544
Start with the chef's special pasta or garlicky escargots, followed by chargrilled lamb chops or Caribbean lobster, and homemade desserts. A light lunch at the poolside Sip & Dip Grill ($) includes free swimming for nonresidents. Also serves breakfast.
All major cards

🍴 PUSSER'S LEVERICK BAY
$$
LEVERICK BAY
TEL 284/495-7369
Lunchtime specials from barbecued pork to flying fish sandwiches served on the dockside, while dinner is upstairs in an open-sided gallery. Stir fry, seared tuna, jumbo shrimp on coconut rice, sticky desserts, and specialty coffees.
All major cards

NETHERLANDS ANTILLES & ARUBA

ARUBA

🏨 HYATT REGENCY RESORT & CASINO
$$$$$
J.E. IRAUSQUIN BLVD. 85,
PALM BEACH
TEL 297/861234 or 800/233-1234
FAX 297/865478

Luxurious resort complex on 12 acres (5 ha) of beachfront. Attractive, well-equipped rooms and suites; spectacular pool area, tennis, golf, water sports, and Camp Hyatt offering kids' activities.
360 All major cards

🏨 PLAYA LINDA BEACH RESORT
$$$$$
J.E. IRAUSQUIN BLVD.,
PALM BEACH
TEL 297/861000 or 800/333-3333
FAX 297/863479
Fully equipped one- and two-bedroom condos with balconies in a smart beachfront development. Tennis, water sports, shopping, and pool featuring a waterfall.
194 All major cards

🏨 AMSTERDAM MANOR BEACH RESORT
$$$
J.E. IRAUSQUIN BLVD.,
EAGLE BEACH
TEL 297/871492 or 800/932-6509
E-MAIL ambrmg@mail.setarnet.aw
Pretty Dutch colonial-style all-suite resort. Studios and two-bedroom apartments with kitchens and sea views across from the beach. On-site mini market; water sports nearby.
72 All major cards

🍴 PAPIAMENTO
$$$$
WASHINGTON 61,
ORANJESTAD
TEL 297/864544
Utterly charming family restaurant set in the gardens of a 150-year-old manor house. The Ellis parents occupy the front of the house, while the three children cook award-winning seafood, steaks, and special healthy and vegetarian dishes.
Closed L & Sun. All major cards

KEY 🏨 Hotel 🍴 Restaurant ① No. of bedrooms 🅿 Parking ⊕ Closed ⊟ Elevator

HOTELS & RESTAURANTS

🍴 BOONOONOONOOS
$$$
WILHELMINASTRAAT 18A,
ORANJESTAD
TEL 297/831888
Stylish Caribbean food served up in a brightly painted old Aruban mansion. The name means "extraordinary" in Jamaican, and that goes for the jerk ribs and generous Carib combo taster platter of 11 different island dishes.
🕐 Closed L Sun. 🔕 All major cards

🍴 GASPARITO
$$$
GASPARITO 3, PALM BEACH
TEL 297/867044
Combination restaurant and Aruban art gallery specializing in local cuisine and international dishes. Try barracuda-stuffed ravioli, shrimp in coconut milk and brandy, or a typical *stoba* (stew).
🕐 Closed L & all Sun. 🔕 All major cards

🍴 BRISAS DEL MAR
$$
SAVANETA 222, SAVANETA
TEL 297/847718
Small and casual open-air seafood restaurant run out of a waterfront fisherman's hut. The daily catch might include lobster or baby shark, plus a selection of local side dishes.
🕐 Mon. 🔕 All major cards

BONAIRE

🏨 HARBOUR VILLAGE BEACH RESORT
$$$$
KAYA GOBERNADOR N. DEBROT 72, PLAYA PABAO
TEL 5997/7500 or 800/424-0004
FAX 5997/7507
E-MAIL harbourvil@aol.com
Bonaire's top hotel boasts a palm-fringed beach and attractive rooms or housekeeping condos in Mediterranean-style villas. Also tennis, diving, a full-service marina, and shopping.
🛏 64 🅿 🔆 🏊 🔕 All major cards

🏨 CAPTAIN DON'S HABITAT
$$$
KAYA GOBERNADOR N. DEBROT 85, PLAYA PABAO
TEL 5997/8290 or 800/327-6709
FAX 5997/8240
E-MAIL maduro@netpoint.com
Captain Don is Bonaire's dive supremo, and his Habitat offers casual, comfortable suites, villas, and two-bedroom cottages, plus diving, water sports, a minuscule beach, and Captain Don's weekly dive chats on Tuesdays.
🛏 93 🅿 🔆 🏊 🔕 All major cards

🏨 SAND DOLLAR CONDOMINIUM RESORT
$$$
KAYA GOBERNADOR N. DEBROT 79, PLAYA PABAO
TEL 5997/8738 or 800/288-4773
FAX 5997/8760
Studio, one-, two-, and three-bedroom individually furnished apartments with full kitchens and balconies overlooking the waterfront. Top-rated dive operation, tennis, grocery store, and high season kids' activities program.
🛏 130 🅿 🔆 🏊 🔕 All major cards

🏨 DIVI FLAMINGO BEACH RESORT
$$
J.A. ABRAHAM BLVD 40, PLAYA PARIBA
TEL 5997/8285 or 800/367-3484
FAX 5997/8238
Simple rooms (in a former prisoner-of-war camp!), but a friendly atmosphere, tennis, a casino, and enter-tainment. Dive programs include special facilities for the disabled.
🛏 145 🅿 🔆 🏊 🔕 All major cards

🍴 RENDEZ-VOUS RESTAURANT & GRILLROOM
$$$
KAYA L. D. GERHARTS 3, KRALENDIJK PLAYA
TEL 5997/8454

ACCOMMODATIONS
1-diamond accommodations are usually small, with simple but adequate furnishings and facilities.
2-diamond accommodations are generally small to medium size. They usually have TVs and phones in all rooms, and at least half will have private bath or shower.
3-diamond accommodations are usually medium size, with spacious rooms. They normally have reception service as well as more formal restaurant and bar facilities. All rooms should have private bath or shower.
4-diamond hotels are larger and more spacious. All rooms have private bathrooms, and most hotels offer private suites as well. There is often a choice of restaurants. High standards of comfort and cuisine are expected.
5-diamond accommodations denote luxury establishments offering the highest international standards in facilities, service, and cuisine.

European and local dishes, such as *keshi yena* (melted Gouda cheese stuffed with chicken, fish, or savory ground beef and raisins), feature on the restaurant menu, while the more casual grillroom (D only) specializes in steaks, chicken, fresh fish cooked to order, and a salad bar.
🕐 Closed Sun. 🔕 All major cards

🍴 RICHARD'S WATERFRONT
$$$
J.A. ABRAHAM BLVD. 60, PLAYA PARIBA
TEL 5997/5263
Romantic waterfront setting and a relaxed welcome from Bostonian owner, Richard Beaty. Daily blackboard menus

feature plenty of fresh local seafood, filet mignon, and signature chicken Benito with chopped spinach and Dutch cheese.
⊕ Closed L & all Mon.
✪ All major cards

🍽 CHIBI CHIBI
$$
J.A. ABRAHAM BLVD. 40, PLAYA PARIBA
TEL 5997/8285
The Divi Flamingo Beach Resort's charming open-air restaurant perched on stilts above the sea. Steaks and seafood are menu staples, and reef fish spotting in the floodlit water is a favorite pastime.
✪ All major cards

🍽 ZEEZICHT BONAIRE
$$
KAYA J. N. E. CRAANE 12, KRALENDIJK PLAYA
TEL 5997/8438
Overlooking the downtown waterfront, Zeezicht kicks off the day with an American breakfast, moves on to grilled fish and conch sandwiches for lunch, and produces a flavorful international dinner menu with a few Indonesian specialties.
✪ All major cards

CURAÇAO

🏨 SONESTA BEACH RESORT & CASINO
$$$$$
PISCADERA BAAI
TEL 5999/736-8800 or 800/SONESTA
FAX 5999/462-7502
E-MAIL soncura@ibm.net
Elegant AAA 4-diamond resort with a contemporary colonial-style motif. Very comfortable accommodations with balconies set in land-scaped gardens. Excellent water sports facilities, tennis, complimentary kids' program, full casino.
🛏 248 🅿 🔲 🏊 🎦
✪ All major cards

🏨 PRINCESS BEACH RESORT & CASINO
$$$$
DR. MARTIN LUTHER KING BLVD. 8, CORNELISBAY
TEL 5999/736-7888 or 800/992-2015
FAX 5999/461-4131
E-MAIL pbrbonet@cur.net
Big, busy, family-friendly resort. Spacious rooms in low blocks bordering the beach. Tennis, dive center, entertainment.
🛏 341 🅿 🔲 🏊 🎦
✪ All major cards

🏨 AVILA BEACH HOTEL
$$-$$$$
PENSTRAAT 130–134, WILLEMSTAD
TEL 5999/461-4377
FAX 5999/461-1493
E-MAIL info@avilahotel.com
Charming historic hotel in an old governor's residence with landscaped gardens on the waterfront. Smaller rooms ($$) in the main house, others in modern buildings and the lovely wood-built Blues Wing. Tennis; fine dining.
🛏 110 🅿 🔲 ✪ All major cards

🍽 BISTRO LE CLOCHARD
Cozy dining room in the former fortress jail with a waterfront terrace. Delectable Swiss cuisine includes fondues, beef and shrimp cooked on a heated stone slab brought to the table, and rich chocolate desserts.
$$$$
RIFFORT, WILLEMSTAD
TEL 5999/462-5666
⊕ Closed L Sat.
✪ All major cards

🏨 ALL WEST APART-MENTS & DIVING
$
BANDA ABAO, WESTPUNT
TEL 5999/461-2310
FAX 5999/461-2315
E-MAIL allwest@cura.net

Simple, bright, and attractive studios and apartments (sleep four) with kitchenettes, balconies/terraces, and sea views. Quiet location; dive packages and PADI courses.
🛏 7 🅿 ✪ All major cards

🍽 LA PERGOLA
$$$$
WATERFORT ARCHES, WILLEMSTAD
TEL 5999/461-3482
Cozy dining room tucked into the brick arches of the old waterfort in Willemstad's miniature restaurant row. Tables on the terrace and a northern Italian menu featuring pasta and risotto dishes, veal, and snapper fillets cooked in Pinot Grigio.
⊕ Closed Sun. ✪ All major cards

🍽 FROETS
$$
KORAAL SPECHTWEG 11, CORNELISBAY (OPPOSITE PRINCESS BEACH)
TEL 5999/465-7565
A tropical garden setting with tables arranged on wooden decking around a pond. Eclectic menu featuring the likes of mackerel and shrimp salad with crab wontons, and churrasco steak with baked plantain and chimi churi.
⊕ Closed L Mon. ✪ All major cards

🍽 JAANCHIE'S
$
WESTPUNT
TEL 5999/864-0126
Great spot for a lazy lunch. Outdoor tables shaded by greenery. Seafood and local dishes such as goat stew, or iguana for the adventurous.
⊕ Closed D ✪ All major cards

SABA

🏨 WILLARD'S OF SABA
$$$$
BOOBY HILL
TEL 5994/62498
FAX 5994/62482

E-MAIL willard@sintmaarten.net
A small, upscale retreat boasting a fabulous setting in the hills south of Windwardside. Accommodations in the main building and bright, spacious bungalows. Cliff-top jacuzzi, tennis. No children under 14.
🛈 7 🅿 🏊 🕼 All major cards

🏨 CAPTAIN'S QUARTERS
$$
WINDWARDSIDE
TEL 5994/62201 or 800/446-3010
FAX 5994/62377
E-MAIL SabaCQ@megatropic.com
Charming old inn with a handful of rooms and others in newer blocks, all with four-poster beds and pleasantly decorated with local artwork. Library, gardens, good food, and lovely views.
🛈 12 🅿 🏊 🕼 All major cards

🍽 SCOUT'S PLACE
$$$
WINDWARDSIDE
TEL 5994/62268
Scout's Place is a country inn and local institution just above the village. The lively bar is a popular hangout, there is snack shop for takeout and ice creams, and the veranda restaurant serves plenty of fresh seafood and local dishes.
🕼 All major cards

🍽 BRIGADOON
$$
WINDWARDSIDE
TEL 5994/62205
The dining area is hemmed in by trellises, and the menu is long on seafood. Try the local bouillabaisse-style fish soup, Creole shrimp, or fresh lobster.
🚫 Closed L 🕼 All major cards

SINT EUSTATIUS

🏨 LA MAISON SUR LA PLAGE
$
ZEELANDIA BAY
TEL 5993/82256 or 800/692-4106
FAX 5993/82202

Great location on the east coast with views over the bay and across to the Quill. Very quiet accommodations in simple cottages; good French restaurant in the main house, plus books, backgammon, and a bar.
🛈 10 🅿 🕼 All major cards

🍽 TALK OF THE TOWN
$–$$
ORANJESTAD
TEL 5993/82236
Family-run hotel with a popular dining room. The menu extends from American and oriental dishes through to the specialty Creole lobster stew (order in advance).
🕼 All major cards

SINT MAARTEN

🏨 CUPECOY BEACH CLUB
$$$
CUPECOY BEACH
TEL 5995/52086 or 800/955-9008
FAX 215/572-7731
Privately owned condos offering rooms, suites, and two- to three-bedroom units in a Mediterranean-style complex on the cliffs above a lovely beach. Some rentals; close to restaurants and activities.
🛈 126 🅿 🕼 🏊 🕼 All major cards

🏨 DIVI LITTLE BAY BEACH RESORT
$$$
LITTLE BAY, PHILIPSBURG
TEL 5995/22333 or 800/367-3484
FAX 5996/23911
An appealing jumble of red roofs, whitewashed buildings, and palm trees balanced on a narrow peninsula just outside Philipsburg. Bright rooms and suites with floral fabrics and wooden latticework. Water sports, tennis.
🛈 118 🅿 🕼 🏊 🕼 All major cards

🏨 PASANGGRAHAN ROYAL INN
$$
FRONT ST., PHILIPSBURG
TEL 5995/23588 or 800/223-9815
FAX 5995/22885
Historic inn in a 19th-century former governor's residence on the bayfront. Town center location, but quiet, stylishly refurbished rooms with pretty fabrics, colonial-style furnishings, and balconies.
🕼 🕼 All major cards

🍽 ANTOINE'S
$$$
103 FRONT ST., PHILIPSBURG
TEL 5995/22964
Pretty blue and white terrace dining room with a view across the bay. Classical French menu featuring chilled vichyssoise, scallops Nantaise, veal Dijonnaise, Montmorency duck with cherry brandy, plus a few Italian pasta dishes and an occasional dash of Creole.
🚫 Closed Sun. low-season
🕼 All major cards

🍽 SEAFOOD GALLERY
$$
BOBBY'S MARINA, PHILIPSBURG
TEL 5995/23253
A wooden pub-style establishment with nautical trimmings right on the water. The lunchtime menu diversifies into burgers, sandwiches, and salads, while the evening menu is long on serious seafood from a well-stocked raw bar to garlicky butterflied shrimp and lobster.
🚫 Sun. 🕼 All major cards

🍽 WAJANG DOLL
$$
137 FRONT ST. PHILIPSBURG
TEL 5995/22687
Traditional Indonesian fare from the Dutch East Indies served up in a charming old-time cottage. Wildly generous set-price 14- or 19-dish *rijsttafel* feasts, or go à la carte with *nasi goreng Jawa* (rice

HOTELS & RESTAURANTS

platter with shrimp, pork satay, egg, and spicy red pepper sambal).
🕒 Closed Sun. & L 💳 All major cards

🍴 KANGAROO COURT CAFFE
$
HENDRIK GEVANGENISTEEG
TEL 5995/24278
Tucked down the side of the courthouse, this is a great place for breakfast, coffee and pastries, light lunches (deli sandwiches, pasta, salads), or a refreshing afternoon iced tea in the leafy courtyard shaded by Indian almond trees.
🕒 Closed D Sun.

ST. MARTIN

🏨 CAPTAIN OLIVER'S
$$$$
OYSTER POND
TEL 5995/87 40 25
FAX 5995/87 40 84
E-MAIL captoli@virtualacces.net
Comfortable efficiency bungalows decorated in pastel shades and set on landscaped grounds beside a lagoon. The complex includes a marina, dive shop, and bar frequented by yachting types. Water taxi service to Dawn Beach.
🛏 32 🅿 📶 🏖 💳 All major cards

🏨 HÉVÉA
$$
163 BLVD. DE GRAND CASE, GRAND CASE
TEL 5995/87 56 85
FAX 5995/87 83 88
Small and charming Creole inn just across from the beach. A choice of rooms, studios, and apartments (some with a/c); the nicest have colonial-style mahogany beds draped with mosquito nets.
🛏 8 📶 💳 All major cards

🍴 FISH POT
$$$$
82 BLVD. DE GRAND CASE, GRAND CASE
TEL 5995/87 50 88
Arguably the highlight of

Grand Case's beach-facing restaurant row. Lantern-lit terrace dining, rather formal service, and classic French-Caribbean dishes such as *bouillabaisse des caraïbes* and duck breast cooked in aged rum flavored with paprika, plus a thoughtful selection of vegetarian options.
🕒 Closed L 💳 All major cards

SOMETHING SPECIAL

🏨 LA SAMANNA
Gorgeous super-luxurious enclave with a Moorish-Mediterranean theme set in tropical gardens above the beach. Elegant accommodations in rooms, suites, and villas. Gourmet restaurant, superb service, tennis, and water sports.
$$$$$
BAIE LONGUE
TEL 590/87 64 00 or
800/854-2252
FAX 5995/87 87 86
🛏 82 🅿 📶 🏖 💳
💳 All major cards

🍴 MAISON SUR LA PORT
$$$
RUE DE LA REPUBLIQUE, MARIGOT
TEL 5995/87 56 38
Extravagant gingerbread decorations frame waterfront views and the value-for-money three-course dinner menu might include ravioli stuffed with smoked salmon in a basil sauce, three pepper steak, and crème brûlée. Also à la carte choices and a lunch menu.
🕒 Closed L Sun. 💳 All major cards

🍴 LA RHUMERIE
$$$
RTE. DE COLOMBIER
TEL 5995/87 56 98
A charming country restaurant in the Colombier Valley. Traditional French

cooking and specialty Creole dishes such as Antillean-style conch and Creole crayfish stew. Round off the meal with a tropically flavored rum laced with coconut, passionfruit, or cashew.
🕒 Closed L Thurs. 💳 All major cards

🍴 BAR DE LA MER
$$
BLVD. DE FRANCE, MARIGOT
TEL 5995/87 81 79
A busy sidewalk brasserie near the waterfront serving reliable old favorites such as steak-frites, battered calamari, salads, pizzas, pastas, and barbecued freshwater shrimp the size of small lobsters.
💳 All major cards

🍴 SHANTY TOWN
$
BLVD. DE GRAND CASE, GRAND CASE
This handful of open-air barbecue kitchens overlooks the beach between the two piers. Ribs, chicken, shrimp kebabs, stuffed crab backs, and *accra* (Creole fish cakes) served up with macaroni salad and coleslaw.
🕒 Closed D 💳 All major cards

LEEWARD ISLANDS

ANGUILLA

🏨 CAP JULUCA
$$$$$
MAUNDAY'S BAY
TEL 264/497-6666 or
888/858-5822
FAX 264/497-6617
Gorgeous Moorish-style oasis set on a curving white-sand beach surrounded by lush gardens. Huge rooms decorated in restful beige and white, monumental double tubs in the suites, a tented restaurant, babysitting, and top-notch sports facilities.
🛏 98 rooms, 18 villas
🅿 📶 🏖 💳
💳 All major cards

MALLIOUHANA
$$$$$
MEAD'S BAY
TEL 264/497-6111 or
800/835-0796
FAX 264/497-6011
One of the Caribbean's very finest establishments. Chic Mediterranean-monastic-meets-Asian colonial amid Haitian art and vanilla-scented candles. Guest rooms range from a beach villa to suites or huge and lovely marble-tiled rooms. Excellent facilities, kids' programs, gourmet dining (see Malliouhana, below).
🛏 56 rooms & suites, I villa
🅿 ⑤ 🏊 🦺
🅜 All major cards

ANGUILLA GREAT HOUSE
$$$$
RENDEZVOUS BAY
TEL 264/497-6061 or
800/583-9247
FAX 264/497-6019
E-MAIL flemingw@zemu.
candw.com.ai
Friendly, unpretentious spot on a fabulous beach. Simple, spacious gingerbread cottages with tin roofs, shutters, and mahogany furnishings. Beach bar and restaurant; Thursday barbecues with entertainment.
🛏 27 🅿 ⑤ Some 🏊
🅜 All major cards

BLANCHARD'S
$$$$$
MEAD'S BAY
TEL 264/497-6100
Candle-lit tropical elegance on Mead's Bay. Melinda Blanchard's cuisine incorporates New American and Asian flavors with specialties such as lemon-glazed lobster dumplings and Japanese-inspired tuna fillet. Award-winning wine list. Reservations advised.
🕐 Closed L & all Sun. 🅜 All major cards

MALLIOUHANA
$$$$$
MALLIOUHANA HOTEL,
MEAD'S BAY
TEL 264/497-6111

Great position perched on bluff above the beach. Parisian chef Michel Rostang oversees a gourmet French-Caribbean menu featuring the likes of warm duck foie gras, crayfish risotto, and Sisteron lamb. Long wine list.
🅜 All major cards

MANGO'S SEASIDE GRILL
$$$$
BARNES BAY
TEL 264/497-6479
Casual beachfront setting with a canvas awning over the wooden deck and back wall adorned with tropical murals. Homemade bread, "famous" Barnes Bay lobster cakes, sesame-crusted snapper fillet marinated in soy, mouthwatering cakes and pies (coconut cheesecake to die for), and extensive wine list.
🕐 Closed L & Tues. 🅜 All major cards

RIPPLES
$$
SANDY GROUND
TEL 264/497-3380
A great place to hang out with a cozy indoor dining room and tables on the veranda (reserve ahead). The broad-ranging menu features grilled fish, Thai salads, pasta, crispy coconut chicken, and the like. The bar gets buzzy in the evening.
🅜 All major cards

ANTIGUA

CURTAIN BLUFF
$$$$$
MORRIS BAY
TEL 268/462-8400 or
888/289-9898
FAX 268/462-8409
Antigua's most famous and elegant hotel perched on a steep bluff winding down to the beach. Excellent all-inclusive sports facilities and gourmet dining (jackets for gents after 7 p.m.).
🛏 63 🅿 🏊 🦺 🅜 All major cards

GALLEY BAY
$$$$$
FIVE ISLANDS VILLAGE
TEL 268/462-0302 or
800/345-0356
FAX 268/462-4551
Tranquil all-inclusive beach resort with a distinctive Polynesian accent. Very comfortable rooms and cute little Gauguin Cottages with thatched roofs. Gorgeous gardens, and non-motorized water sports.
🛏 61 🅿 ⑤ 🏊 🦺
🅜 All major cards

HAWKSBILL BEACH RESORT
$$$$$
FIVE ISLANDS
TEL 268/462-0301
FAX 268/462-1515
E-MAIL hawksbill@candw.ag
Bright and comfy rooms and cottage-style accommodations strung out along the shore (access to four beaches including one "clothing optional"). Deluxe club cottages for romantics; beach cottages with connecting doors for families. Water sports, tennis, kids' activities.
🛏 99 🅿 🏊 🅜 All major cards

▦ SIBONEY BEACH CLUB
$$$$
DICKENSON BAY
TEL 268/462-0806
FAX 268/462-3356
E-MAIL siboney@candw.ag
Delightful small property at the quiet end of Antigua's busiest beach. Twelve one-bed suites with kitchenettes and balconies overlooking tropical gardens. The restaurant is a big plus (see Coconut Grove, below). Water sports nearby.
ⓘ 12 🅿 🅢 🏊 🅢 All major cards

▦ ADMIRAL'S INN
$$
ENGLISH HARBOUR
TEL 268/460-1027
FAX 268/460-1534
E-MAIL admirals@candw.ag
Charming historic inn and waterfront garden in Nelson's Dockyard. Simple rooms with antique furnishings in both the main building and an annex (rather dark). Free transportation to the beach.
ⓘ 13 🅿 🅢 Some 🅢 All major cards

🍴 ALBERTO'S
$$$$
WILLOUGHBY BAY
TEL 268/460-3007
Pretty Italian restaurant and local hideaway from the tourist hoards northeast of English Harbour, with decking and lots of greenery. Creamy salmon ravioli, osso bucco, veal dishes, and an ebullient patron.
⏁ Closed L & all Mon. 🅢 All major cards

🍴 CHEZ PASCAL
$$$$
GALLEY BAY HILL,
FIVE ISLANDS
TEL 268/462-3232
Sympathetic French hosts and traditional French cooking served on the pool terrace or in a long, low-ceilinged dining room. Escargots in basil butter, rich seafood vol au vents, rack of lamb with

Provençal herbs, and melt-in-the-mouth tarte tatin.
🅢 All major cards

SOMETHING SPECIAL

🍴 JULIAN'S
Cozy dining room in a restored colonial house with a courtyard for alfresco dining. Classical-modern cuisine with local touches such as butternut soup, snapper ceviche, roulade of pork, and roasted plantain. Beautiful presentation, long wine list, reservations advised.
$$$$
CHURCH ST. & CORN ALLEY, ST. JOHN'S
TEL 268/462-4766
⏁ Closed all Mon. & L.
🅢 All major cards

🍴 COCONUT GROVE
$$$$
SIBONEY BEACH CLUB,
DICKENSON BAY
TEL 268/462-1538
Romantic lantern-lit beach-front setting with smoochy music. Offerings inlcude fresh lobster crêpe, shrimp in beer batter dusted with coconut shavings, Jamaican jerk chicken with banana-guava marmalade. Good wine and brandy list.
🅢 All major cards

🍴 LE CAP HORN
$$$
FALMOUTH HARBOUR
TEL 268/460-1194
Popular and unpretentious French-Argentinean restaurant with a pleasant veranda and a mixed menu that includes generous churrasco steaks, wood-fired thin-crust pizzas, and salads.
🅢 All major cards

🍴 PIZZAS IN PARADISE
$$
REDCLIFFE QUAY, ST. JOHN'S
TEL 268/462-2621

A handy refueling stop in an old brick warehouse smack dab in the middle of the shopping district. Pizzas, sub sandwiches, salads, espressos, capuccinos, and cold drinks.
⏁ Closed Sun. 🅢 All major cards

BARBUDA

▦ K CLUB
$$$$$
SPANISH WELLS POINT
TEL 268/460-0300
FAX 268/460-0305
Italian fashion designer Krizia's exclusive and stratospherically expensive Caribbean hideaway. Spacious and beautifully decorated villas and cottages. All-inclusive rates include water sports, sportfishing, tennis, nine holes of golf, and gourmet Italian meals in the main house.
ⓘ 39 🏊 🅢 All major cards

ST. KITTS

▦ GOLDEN LEMON INN & VILLAS
$$$$$
DIEPPE BAY
TEL 869/465-7260 or
800/633-7411
FAX 869/465-4019
E-MAIL Artmart@Caribsurf.com
Lovingly restored and antique-filled 17th-century great house facing a strip of volcanic sand beach. Six "Old World" rooms in the house and 18 very comfy and chic one- and two-bedroom modern villas with private plunge pools.
ⓘ 24 🅿 🏊 🅢 All major cards

▦ OTTLEY'S PLANTATION INN
$$$$$
OTTLEY'S
TEL 869/465-7234 or
800/729-0709
FAX 869/465-4760
E-MAIL ottleys@caribsurf.com
Splendid 18th-century plantation great house set in lawned gardens surrounded

---

by cane fields. Huge, pretty rooms in the main house with its antique furnishings and breezy verandas, plus one- or two-bedroom cottages on the grounds. Shuttle to the beach. AAA four diamonds.

ⓘ 17 P S ≋ S All major cards

🏨 HORIZONS VILLA RESORT
$$$–$$$$$
FRIGATE BAY
TEL 869/465-0584 or
800/830-9069
FAX 869/465-0785
E-MAIL horizons@caribsurf.com
Well-maintained condo complex with additional hotel rooms ($$$) perched on the hill above the coast. Light and spacious one- to four-bedroom apartments and villas with full kitchen and terrace. Dive packages, tennis, free greens fees for golf nearby.

ⓘ P S ≋ S All major cards

🏨 SUN 'N SAND BEACH RESORT
$$$–$$$$$
FRIGATE BAY
TEL 869/465-8037 or
800/223-6510
FAX 869/465-6745
Medium-size resort complex on the Atlantic side of the island offering deluxe rooms, studio apartments, and two-bedroom cottages on the beachfront. Tennis, children's pool, grocery, babysitting; golf nearby.

ⓘ 16 rooms, 32 studios, 18 2-bedroom cottages P ≋ S All major cards

🍽 RAWLINS PLANTATION INN
$$$$ (Lunch $$)
MOUNT PLEASANT
TEL 869/465-6221
Elegant plantation inn (with 10 rooms $$$$$) serving a superb West Indian buffet lunch—curries, fish dishes, herb-flavored rice, and homemade chutneys—and

set four-course dinners. Reservations advised.

S All major cards

🍽 PATIO
$$$$
FRIGATE BAY BEACH
TEL 869/465-8666
Lantern-lit dining on the namesake patio or inside a private home edged by pretty gardens. Caribbean specialties such as pepper pot stew, fresh seafood, and a few more classical dishes. Compliment-ary wine and liqueurs.

🕐 Closed all Sun. & L S All major cards

🍽 MANGO'S
$$$
INDEPENDENCE SQUARE, BASSETERRE
TEL 869/465-4049
Delightful courtyard setting beneath a spreading mango tree. Bistro menu featuring goat's cheese salads, grills, Thai shrimp curry, chicken enchiladas, pasta, cheesecakes, and tropical fruit ice creams. Live music Fri. nights.

S All major cards

🍽 BALLAHOO
$$
THE CIRCUS, BASSETERRE
TEL 869/465-4197
Popular downtown meeting place. Tuna melt subs, sand-wiches, and burgers for lunch, hot chili shrimp, mahi-mahi steaks with basil-mustard butter, chicken, pasta, and veg-etarian options in the evening.

🕐 Closed Sun. S All major cards

NEVIS

🏨 FOUR SEASONS RESORT
$$$$$
PINNEY'S BEACH
TEL 869/469-1111 or
800/332-3442
FAX 869/469-1112
Terrific position on Nevis's main beach for this sprawling AAA five-diamond property. Large rooms and suites with

oversize bathrooms and private patios by the water-front or the golf course. Sports packages, excellent children's facilities, polished service.

ⓘ 196 P S ≋ ♥ S All major cards

🏨 MONTPELIER PLANTATION INN
$$$$$
FIG TREE
TEL 869/469-3462 or
800/223-9832
FAX 869/469-2932
E-MAIL montpinn@caribsurf.com
Glorious old stone plantation house on a former sugar estate. Airy, elegant rooms in cottages and meals served in the main building English country house-style. Tennis, beach shuttle.

ⓘ 17 P ≋ S All major cards

🏨 HERMITAGE
Enchanting plantation inn with rooms in quaint gingerbread cottages dotted about the flower-filled gardens of the oldest wooden house in the Caribbean (circa 1680–1740). Romantic four-posters, hammocks on the veranda, horseback riding, peace and quiet.

$$$$$
GINGERLAND
TEL 869/469-3477 or
800/682-4025
FAX 869/469-2481
E-MAIL nevherm@caribsurf.com

ⓘ 14 P ≋ S All major cards

🏨 OUALIE BEACH HOTEL
$$$$
OUALIE BEACH
TEL 869/469-9735 or
800/682-5431
FAX 869/469-9176
E-MAIL oualie@caribsurf.com
Small and informal beachfront property with well-priced

HOTELS & RESTAURANTS

rooms and studios in wooden cottages with screened porches overlooking the beach. Diving and windsurfing packages; other sports by arrangement.

🛏 22 🅿 💲 🚫 All major cards

🍽 MISS JUNE'S
$$$$$
JONES BAY
TEL 869/469-5330
A local institution, Miss June Meister cooks a grand Caribbean-Asian-European buffet in her home about three times a week (reservations essential). Guests meet for cocktails at 7:30, before being unleashed on the two dozen gourmet dishes. All drinks included.
🕐 Call ahead for schedule
🚫 All major cards

🍽 UNELLA'S BY THE SEA
$
CHARLESTOWN
TEL 869/469-5574
A breezy upstairs terrace by the ferry dock and a budget menu offering fish burgers with tartar sauce, crabmeat-shrimp-salad stuffed pita pockets, beef stir fry, chicken and fries, and local dishes.
🕐 Closed L Sun. 🚫 All major cards

FRENCH ANTILLES

GUADELOUPE

🏨 LE HAMAK
$$$$$
ST. FRANÇOIS, GRANDE-TERRE
TEL 590/88 59 99 or
800/633-7411
FAX 590/88 41 92
Luxurious and stylish oasis with accommodations in chic bungalows scattered about lush gardens. Private patios with hammocks; small man-made beach; attentive service.
🛏 54 🅿 💲 🚫 All major cards

🏨 LE JARDIN MALANGA
$$$$$
TROIS RIVIÈRES, BASSE-TERRE
TEL 590/92 67 57 or
800/322-2223
FAX 590/92 67 58
E-MAIL malanga@leaderhotels.gp
Fabulous hillside setting with views off to the Îles des Saintes from the pool deck of this low-key hideaway. Minimalist chic rooms in a 1920s plantation house or two elegant wooden cottages.
🛏 5 🅿 💲 🚫 All major cards

🏨 LA TOUBANA
$$$$
STE.-ANNE
TEL 590/88 25 78 or
800/322-2223
FAX 590/88 38 90
Lovely sea views and quaint one- and two-bedroom cottages (toubanas) with kitchenettes on the hill leading down to a small beach cove with water sports. Tennis; some evening entertainment.
💲 32 🅿 🚫 All major cards

🏨 AUBERGE LES PETITS SAINTS
$$
TERRE-DE-HAUT, LES SAINTES
TEL 590/99 50 99 or
800/322-2223
FAX 590/99 54 51
Pretty Creole home overflowing with antiques and kitsch collectibles amassed by the two delightfully eccentric artist owners. Ten comfortable rooms five minutes from the town center; good restaurant.
🛏 10 🚫 All major cards

🏨 RELAIS DU MOULIN
$$
CHÂTEAUBRUN, GRANDE-TERRE
TEL 590/88 23 96 or
800/742-4276
FAX 590/88 03 93
Charming, family-friendly, small resort laid out around an old windmill east of Ste.-Anne. Garden bungalows with

kitchenettes 10 minutes' walk from the beach; tennis, horseback riding, bicycles.
🛏 40 🅿 💲 🚫 All major cards

🍽 AUBERGE DE LA VIEILLE TOUR
$$$$
AUBERGE DE LA VIEILLE TOUR, GOSIER
TEL 590/84 23 23
Elegant hotel dining room with sea views (reserve a window seat) and a classic French-Creole menu. Crayfish tartare, fresh fish with lobster butter, beef Creole, and magnificent desserts.
🚫 All major cards

🍽 IGUANE CAFÉ
$$$
RTE. DE LA POINTE DES CHÂTEAUX, ST.-FRANÇOIS
TEL 590/88 61 37
Bright and funky café on the beach road serving a creative menu strong on local ingredients. Marble of foie gras and lobster with dark rum and shellfish aspic, crispy saffron conch and christophine gratin, five-spice fish.
🕐 Closed L Mon.–Sat., D Sun., & Tues. mid-Sept.–mid-Oct. 🚫 All major cards

🍽 LES OISEAUX
$$$
ANSE DES ROCHERS (COAST RD. W OF ST.-FRANÇOIS)
TEL 590/88 56 92
Cliff-top country restaurant with a stone-walled dining room and pretty terrace framed by arches and greenery. Snails, conch marinière, and seafood "fondue" cooked in aromatic oils at the table.
🕐 Closed L (summer only) & Sun. 🚫 All major cards

🍽 LE VIEUX PORT
$$
ST.-FRANÇOIS
TEL 590/88 46 60
Tiny wooden house facing the seafront with a minuscule veranda and cozy atmosphere.

Soupe de poissons, crayfish with ginger and coconut, curried fish and fresh pineapple in flaky pastry, menu langouste (lobster) for two ($$$$).
🃏 All major cards

🍽 LE KARACOLI
$-$$$
GRANDE ANSE, BASSE-TERRE
TEL 590/28 41 17
Very popular beach restaurant offering value-for-money fixed price menus and slightly more expensive à la carte options. Classic Creole cuisine with plenty of seafood including conch, scallops, stuffed crab, and lobster.
🕐 Closed D   🃏 All major cards

MARTINIQUE

┌─────────────────────┐
│   **SOMETHING**   │
│   **SPECIAL**   │
└─────────────────────┘

🏨 HABITATION LAGRANGE
Lovely 1850s Creole plantation house in a remote forest clearing. Elegant antique furnishings and large rooms in the main house; smaller versions in garden outbuildings around the pool (30 minutes from the beach). Tennis, good food, and charming hosts; a romantic hideaway.
$$$$$
LE MARIGOT
TEL 596/53 60 60 or
800/633-7411
FAX 596/53 50 58
ℹ 18 P ❄ ≋   🃏 All major cards

🏨 MANOIR DE BEAUREGARD
$$$
CHEMIN DES SALINES,
STE.-ANNE
TEL 596/76 73 40
FAX 596/76 93 24
Stylish 18th-century manor house with marble floors, wooden beams, and open, stone archways. A few lovely

rooms with traditional Creole furnishings in the house and simpler accommodations in the garden.
ℹ 11 P ❄ ≋   🃏 All major cards

🏨 SOFITEL BAKOUA
$$$
POINTE DU BOUT, TROIS ILETS
TEL 596/66 02 02 or
800/763-4835
FAX 596/66 00 41
Attractive and well-equipped resort set on a bluff above a private beach. Comfortably appointed rooms with views. Tennis, water sports, helpful tour desk, golf nearby.
ℹ 139 P ❄ ≋   🃏 All major cards

🏨 LEYRITZ PLANTATION
$$
BASSE-POINTE
TEL 596/78 53 92
FAX 596/78 92 44
This old sugar estate is a busy tourist attraction by day, but peaceful retreat by late afternoon. Comfy and antique-filled accommodations in the plantation house, slave quarters, and stone cottages around the grounds. Tennis; 30 minutes from the beach.
ℹ 67 P ❄ ≋   🃏 All major cards

🏨 DIAMANT LES BAINS
$
BOURG DU DIAMANT
TEL 596/76 40 14 or
800/823-2002
FAX 596/76 27 00
Small and welcoming family-run hotel on the beach with bright and simple rooms in the main building and garden bungalows. Diving, water sports, tennis, and horseback riding nearby.
ℹ 24 P ❄ ≋   🃏 All major cards

🍽 LA FONTANE
$$$$$
RUE DE BALATA, LA FONTANE
TEL 596/64 28 70
Gourmet French-Creole restaurant in the hills above

Fort-de-France. Formal dining room in a beautiful old Creole house and terrace tables. Try noisettes of lamb and mushrooms with mango sauce or a lobster ragout with basil.
🕐 Closed Sun.–Mon.   🃏 All major cards

🍽 AU POISSON D'OR
$$
ANSE MITAN, TROIS ILETS
TEL 596/66 01 80
Popular Creole restaurant on the Pointe du Bout road. Lots of bamboo, greenery, and waitresses in traditional costume. Specialties include lime-marinated conch, spicy shark, and grilled lobster Creole.
🕐 Closed all Mon., L (low season only), & July   🃏 All major cards

🍽 LE FROMAGER
$$
QUARTIER ST. JAMES,
MORNE ABEL
TEL 596/78 19 07
Fabulous views over St. Pierre from the veranda of this Creole dining room on the Fond St. Denis road. Notable specialties include *feroce* (avocado, saltfish, and ferociously hot peppers), crayfish colombo (curry), and *blanc mangé* (coconut custard).
🕐 Closed D & Oct.   🃏 All major cards

🍽 LA DUNETTE
$
HOTEL LA DUNETTE,
STE.-ANNE
TEL 596/76 73 90
Seaside views in the heart of the village and a largely seafood menu featuring local delicacies such as smoked fish, snapper stuffed with sea urchins in a curry sauce, and killer chocolate gâteau.
🕐 Closed mid-June to mid-July   🃏 All major cards

🍽 LE MARIE SAINTE
$
160 RUE VICTOR HUGO, FORT-DE-FRANCE
TEL 596/63 82 24

Useful family-style downtown pit-stop serving good and filling Creole food. Tasty *accras* (fish balls), chicken fricassee, banana fritters (beignets).
🕐 Closed D & Sun. 🚫 All major cards

ST.-BARTHÉLEMY

🏨 EDEN ROCK
$$$$$
ST. JEAN
TEL 590/27 72 94 or
800/322-2223
FAX 590/27 88 37
St. Barts' first hotel has a prime spot on the rocks above the beach. Romantic rooms with canopy beds, antiques, and eclectic artwork in the house and one-bedroom beach cottages. Pleasant outdoor bar and gym; intimate atmosphere.
🅿 🛗 ⛱ 🎾 🚫 All major cards

🏨 FRANÇOIS PLANTATION
$$$$$
COLOMBIER
TEL 590/29 80 22 or
800/207-8071
FAX 590/27 61 26
E-MAIL fplantation@compuserve.com
A dozen clapboard Creole cottages with crisp blue and white decor and old colonial furnishings buried in heavenly hillside gardens. Stunning views; excellent restaurant in the elegant estate house (see La Route des Épices, below).
🛗 12 🅿 🛗 ⛱ 🚫 All major cards

🏨 LE TOINY
$$$$$
ANSE DE TOINY
TEL 590/27 88 88 or
800/932-3222
FAX 590/27 89 30
E-MAIL letoiny@saint-barths.com
Superbly elegant and secluded Relais & Châteaux property, with a dozen spacious and beautifully decorated cottages boasting private pools, kitchenettes, and fitness equipment. Excellent restaurant (see Le Gaïac, below).
🛗 12 🅿 ⛱ 🚫 All major cards

🏨 LES ILETS FLEURIS
$$
HAUTS DE LORIENT
TEL 590/27 64 22
FAX 590/27 69 72
Simple and pretty one-bedroom cottages (some canopy beds for romantics) with kitchenettes perched on a hilltop. Affordable rates include rental car (5 minutes to the beach); sea views add to the price ($$$).
🛗 7 🅿 ⛱ 🚫 All major cards

🍴 LE GAÏAC
$$$$$
LE TOINY, ANSE DE TOINY
TEL 590/27 88 88
Small and chic with sea views, Le Gaïac delivers top-notch French-Caribbean cuisine. Chilled spicy mango soup, foie gras terrine, lamb chops with sweet potato and plantain pie, conch ravioli. Reservations recommended.
🕐 Closed Sept.–Oct. 🚫 All major cards

🍴 LA ROUTE DES ÉPICES
$$$$$
FRANÇOIS PLANTATION, COLOMBIER
TEL 590/29 80 22
Romantic open-sided dining room framed by gardens, light and sophisticated French cook-ing, and delightful service. Lobster spring rolls flavored with mint, slow-cooked roasted guinea fowl, magnificent desserts, and notable wine list.
🕐 Closed L all year; Sun. April, June–Oct., & Nov–mid-Dec. 🚫 All major cards

🍴 EDDY'S
$$$$
RUE DU CENTENAIRE, GUSTAVIA
TEL 590/27 54 17
Balinese teak, bamboo, and an explosion of greenery lend a Southeast Asian note to the decor, further reflected in the French-Caribbean-Asian menu. Fashionable spot for shrimp green curry, Creole colombo, and grilled fish.
🕐 Closed L & all Sun. 🚫 All major cards

🍴 LE SÉLECT
$
RUE DE LA FRANCE, GUSTAVIA
TEL 590/27 86 87
Hip downtown bar with bustling garden patio and pumping reggae, zouk, and live music in the old brick warehouse at night. Cheeseburgers and cocktails are the highlights.
🚫 All major cards

WINDWARD ISLANDS

CARRIACOU

🏨 CARIBBEE INN
$$$$
PROSPECT
TEL 473/443-7380
FAX 473/443-8142
E-MAIL caribbee@cacounet.com
Panoramic cliff-top setting and five stylish, breezy, and romantic suites with four-poster beds (two simpler rooms may be available). Intimate atmosphere; pet macaws in the garden; boat service to Anse La Roche beach.
🛗 7 🚫 All major cards

DOMINICA

🏨 FORT YOUNG
$$$
ROSEAU
TEL 767/448-5000 or
800/223-6510
FAX 767/448-5006
E-MAIL fortyoung@tod.dm
Attractive rooms and spacious suites built around a pool deck nestled in the remains of a historic seafront fortress, plus a smart new block down on the water. Good location, in-house tour desk.
🛗 54 🅿 🛗 ⛱ 🚫 All major cards

PICARD BEACH COTTAGE RESORT
$$
PICARD BEACH, PORTSMOUTH
TEL 767/445-5131 or
800/223-6510
FAX 767/445-5599
Simple rooms in quiet
Creole cottages on one of
Dominica's better black sand
beaches. Private verandas and
kitchenettes; lovely gardens on
an old coconut plantation.
🛏 8 P ⓢ Some ⓢ All
major cards

PETIT COULIBRI GUEST COTTAGES
Superbly tranquil and
beautiful eco-friendly
hideaway with three wood
and stone cottages perched in
a hillside garden 1,000 feet
(300 m) above the sea; also
two simple studios ($).
Cottages have full kitchens,
but wonderful home-cooked
food also available.
$$$$
SOUFRIÈRE
TEL 767/446-3150
FAX 767/449-6603
E-MAIL barnardm@tod.dm
🛏 3 cottages, 2 studios
P 🏊 ⓢ All major
cards

ANCHORAGE HOTEL & DIVE CENTRE
$
CASTLE COMFORT
TEL 767/448-2638
FAX 767/448-5680
E-MAIL anchorage@mail.tod.dm
Spic and span modern units
with a splash of Creole color
and balconies overlooking the
sea just south of Roseau. PADI
dive center and hiking trips;
squash court; helpful and
friendly staff.
🛏 32 ⓢ 🏊 ⓢ All major
cards

DE BOUILLE
$$$
FORT YOUNG HOTEL, ROSEAU
TEL 767/448-5000
The island's smartest
restaurant enclosed by rough-
hewn stone walls decorated
with local art. Baked crab with
parmesan, grilled tuna in a
creamy watercress sauce,
conch Creole served with
ground provisions and fresh
garden vegetables.
ⓢ All major cards

LA ROBE CREOLE
$$$
3 VICTORIA ST., ROSEAU
TEL 767/448-2896
Renowned restaurant in a
cozy old stone town house
promising Dominican specialties such as mountain chicken
(frog's legs) crêpe, lobster and
spicy stuffed land crabs in
season. Waitresses wear the
traditional Madras robe créole.
🔒 Closed Sun. ⓢ All major
cards

PAPILLOTTE WILDERNESS RETREAT
$$
TRAFALGAR VALLEY
TEL 767/448-2287
Neat rain-forest inn (8 simple
rooms, $) with tables on a
leafy terrace hemmed in by
greenery. The unpretentious
menu is packed with favorite
Caribbean staples, seasonal
fruits, and vegetables. Reservations recommended for dinner.
ⓢ All major cards

WORLD OF FOOD
$
48 CORK ST., ROSEAU
TEL 767/448-3286
Open-air dining in the courtyard behind Vena's Guest
House. Filling local dishes
include callaloo soup (like
spinach), fish cakes, chicken
dishes accompanied by great
mounds of rice 'n' peas and
vegetables.
ⓢ All major cards

PRICES

HOTELS
An indication of the cost
of a double room without
breakfast is given by $ signs.
$$$$$	Over $280
$$$$	$200–$280
$$$	$120–$200
$$	$80–$120
$	Under $80

RESTAURANTS
An indication of the cost of a
three course dinner without
drinks is given by $ signs.
$$$$$	Over $80
$$$$	$50–$80
$$$	$35–$50
$$	$20–$35
$	Under 20

GRENADA

CALABASH
$$$$$
L'ANSE AUX EPINES, GRENADA
TEL 473/444-4334 or
800/528-5835
FAX 473/444-5050
Sedate and charming
beachfront hotel with very
comfortable suites (some
with small private pools)
arranged in an arc of two-
story garden cottages. Caring
service includes breakfast
prepared in your suite by
the maid. Tennis and non-
motorized water sports; good
food (see Cicely's, below).
🛏 30 P ⓢ 🏊 🎾
ⓢ All major cards

LASOURCE
$$$$$
PINK GIN BEACH, GRENADA
TEL 473/444-2556 or
800/544-2883
FAX 473/444-2561
Luxurious all-inclusive spa
offering an impressive array of
relaxation treatments, archery,
tennis, golf, water sports, and
scuba diving; plus good food
with healthy options.
🛏 100 P ⓢ 🏊 🎾
ⓢ All major cards

HOTELS & RESTAURANTS

🏨 SPICE ISLAND BEACH RESORT
$$$$$
GRAND ANSE, GRENADA
TEL 473/444-4258
FAX 473/444-4807
E-MAIL spiceisl@caribsurf.com
Attractive all-suite property stretching along Grenada's largest beach. Pastel colors, wicker furnishings, and whirlpool tubs (some units have private pools and exercise facilities). Tennis and non-motorized water sports.
🛏 56 🅿 🔲 🌊 📺
🗝 All major cards

🏨 FLAMBOYANT
$$
GRAND ANSE, GRENADA
TEL 473/444-4247 or
800/322-1753
FAX 473/444-1234
E-MAIL flambo@caribsurf.com
A steep (but mercifully short) hike up from the beach, great views across to St. George's, and a selection of comfy rooms, self-catering units, and one- or two-bedroom suites, all with balconies.
🛏 41 🅿 🔲 Some 🌊
🗝 All major cards

🏨 LA SAGESSE NATURE CENTRE
$
LA SAGESSE, GRENADA
TEL 473/444-6458
FAX 473/444-6458
E-MAIL lsnature@caribsurf.com
An off-the-beaten-track beach hideaway with simple but spacious rooms in a 1920s estate house, a beach cottage, and two low-budget options.
🛏 6 🅿 🗝 All major cards

🍴 CICELY'S
$$$$
CALABASH HOTEL, L'ANSE AUX EPINES, GRENADA
TEL 473/444-4334
Elegant and pretty terrace dining room. Try warm shrimp and callaloo tartlet, barracuda with nutmeg and ginger, and chilled espresso mousse. Reservations recommended.
🗝 All major cards

🍴 COCONUTS' BEACH RESTAURANT
$$$
GRAND ANSE, GRENADA
TEL 473/444-4644
Dine on the sand or inside the old wooden house. French Creole specialties such as conch curry, lobster, or catch of the day in a variety of sauces. (Live music Wed., Fri., Sun.)
🗝 All major cards

🍴 AQUARIUM
$$
TAMARIND BEACH, POINT SALINES, GRENADA
TEL 473/444-1410
Casual, woodsy, open-air beach restaurant. Well-prepared world food from satay or pumpkin and ginger soup to snapper with a coriander-herb crust, oven-baked Cornish hen, New Zealand lamb, and U.S. steaks. Sunday barbecues.
🕐 Closed Mon. 🗝 All major cards

🍴 MORNE FENDUE
$
NEAR SAUTEURS, ST. PATRICK'S DISTRICT, GRENADA
TEL 473/442-9330
This small stone plantation home is renowned for its West Indian lunch buffet. A groaning table of local fish, chicken, meat, rice 'n' peas, and vegetable dishes including the famed pepperpot stew.
🕐 Closed D Sun. 🗝 All major cards

🍴 NUTMEG
$
THE CARENAGE, ST. GEORGE'S, GRENADA
TEL 473/440-2539
Casual local meeting place with harbor views, a lively bar, and a simple menu of soups, sandwiches, roti, and fruit or rum punches with a generous sprinkling of nutmeg.
🕐 Closed B Sun. 🗝 All major cards

ST. LUCIA

🏨 ANSE CHASTANET BEACH HOTEL
$$$$$
SOUFRIÈRE
TEL 758/459-7000 or
800/223-1108
FAX 758/459-7700
Set in a steep-sided beach cove down a bumpy track, this delightful small resort is wonderfully relaxing and a good dive center. Lovely rooms in octagonal gazebos or beachside suites, great views, tennis, attentive service.
🛏 49 🅿 🗝 All major cards

🏨 HUMMINGBIRD BEACH RESORT
$$$
SOUFRIÈRE
TEL 758/459-7232
FAX 758/459-7033
Panoramic hillside location overlooking Soufrière Bay to the Pitons and a handful of simple but appealing units, with four-poster beds and balconies set in tropical gardens leading down to the beach.
🛏 10 🅿 🌊 🗝 All major cards

SOMETHING SPECIAL

🍴 DASHEENE
Fabulous hilltop terrace setting, award-winning Creole-international cuisine, and cicadas and candlelight at night. Chilled Creole seafood in gazpacho, herb-crusted seared lamb chops, scallops braised in coconut and ginger.
$$$$
LADERA RESORT, SOUFRIÈRE
TEL 758/459-7323
🗝 All major cards

🏨 HARMONY MARINA SUITES
$$
RODNEY BAY
TEL 758/452-8756
FAX 758/452-8677

E-MAIL harmony@candw.lc
Small and friendly family-run complex on the water minutes from Reduit Beach. Well-equipped standard suites and deluxe units with four-posters, some kitchenettes. On-site mini-mart, beauty and massage salon.
① 30 P 🔄 ≋ 🅰All major cards

🏨 MARIGOT BEACH CLUB
$$
MARIGOT BAY
TEL 758/451-4974
FAX 758/451-4973
Delightful inn with a selection of comfortable rental studios and two- and three-bedroom villas above Marigot Bay. Tiny beach, water sports, dive shop, sailing packages.
① 22 P ≋ 🅷 🅰All major card

🍴 GREAT HOUSE
$$$$
CAP ESTATE
TEL 758/450-0450
Elegant dining in a re-created plantation great house adorned with chandeliers and spreading tropical flower arrangements. Specialties include seafood casserole, beef tenderloin with wild mushrooms, and iced coconut nougat for dessert.
🕑 Closed L & all Mon.
🅰All major cards

🍴 JIMMIE'S
$$
VIGIE MARINA, CASTRIES
TEL 758/452-5142
Popular bar and terrace dining area in a harborside cove behind Pointe Seraphine. Well-deserved reputation for good local food. Jerk chicken, saltfish and green fig (banana), also steaks, seafood risotto, and curries.
🕑 Closed Sun.
🅰All major cards

🍴 RAIN RESTAURANT
$$
DEREK WALCOTT SQUARE, CASTRIES
TEL 758/452-1515
Downtown institution set in a gingerbread-trimmed town house. Rôtis (meat or vegetable chapati parcels), sandwiches, and burgers at lunch; steamed mussels, pork spare ribs, and Malay chicken and green papaya curry by night. Open for breakfast.
🅰All major cards

🍴 SNOOTY AGOUTI
$$
GROS ISLET
TEL 758/450-0321
Woodsy attic dining room with hanging plants, checkered Madras tablecloths, and a thatched bar. World cuisine runs the gamut from sautéed snails and crab cakes to Greek lamb moussaka. Live music/jazz several nights a week.
🅰All major cards

ST. VINCENT

🏨 GRAND VIEW BEACH HOTEL
$$$$
VILLA POINT
TEL 784/458-4811 or 800/633-7411
FAX 784/457-4174
E-MAIL granview@caribsurf.com
Suitably grand views and very comfortable rooms in a turn-of-the-century plantation house with a bright and airy modern wing on a cliff top promontory. Steps down to the beach, tennis, squash; friendly and helpful staff.
① 19 P 🔄 ≋ 🅷
🅰All major cards

🏨 YOUNG ISLAND
$$$$$
OPPOSITE VILLA
TEL 784/458-4826 or 800/223-1108
FAX 784/457-4567
E-MAIL youngisland@caribsurf.com
A private island resort with pretty wood and stone cottages enfolded in tropical greenery. Patios and sea views, some small swimming pools. Tennis, water sports, yachting excursions.
① 30 P ≋ 🅰All major cards

🍴 FRENCH RESTAURANT
$$$
VILLA
TEL 784/458-4972
With French owners and a mouth-watering seafood menu including a whole page of lobster dishes, plus warm goat's cheese salad, Burgundy snails, and fillet of beef with bearnaise sauce, this restaurant has a waterfront setting facing Young Island.
🕑 Closed Sun. 🅰All major cards

🍴 LIME 'N' PUB
$$
VILLA
TEL 784/458-4227
Jolly pub with a terrace, dining room, and bar decorated with fishing nets and colored lights. Huge choice of British-style pub grub, sandwiches, and burgers, plus a more formal dinner menu offering plenty of seafood.
🅰All major cards

BEQUIA

🏨 FRIENDSHIP BAY BEACH RESORT
$$$
FRIENDSHIP BAY
TEL 784/458-3222 or 800/223-1108
FAX 784/458-3840
E-MAIL labambas@caribsurf.com
Casual and friendly small resort with cute rooms and beach cottages featuring hand-painted decorations and ocean views. Tennis, sailing, water sports, dive packages.
① 28 🅰All major cards

🍴 GINGERBREAD
$–$$
PORT ELIZABETH
TEL 784/458-3800
Three dining options in one.

HOTELS & RESTAURANTS

The daytime Gingerbread Café does a great line in coffees, juices, and homemade cakes. Fresh seafood kebabs and chicken end up on the Gingerbread BBQ at lunch. Or there is the Gingerbread Restaurant, with bay views from the veranda and a lunch menu of pasta, salads, omelets. Callaloo and shrimp soup and curries in the evening.
🏊 All major cards

MAYREAU

🏨 SALT WHISTLE BAY CLUB
$$$$$
SALT WHISTLE BAY
TEL 784/458-8444 or
800/999-7256
FAX 784/458-8944
Barefoot island escape with a handful of simple but appealing stone cottages set amid tropical gardens by a fabulous beach. Hammocks, windsurfers, snorkeling, dive packages.
ⓘ 10 🏊 All major cards

MUSTIQUE

🏨 COTTON HOUSE HOTEL
$$$$$
TEL 784/456-4777 or
800/525-4800
FAX 784/456-5887
Luxurious rooms, suites, and cottages amid the gardens of an old sugar estate. Guests gather in the coral stone main building. All-inclusive rates cover meals, drinks, tennis, and some water sports.
ⓘ 20 ⚊ 🏊 All major cards

🏨 MUSTIQUE VILLA RENTALS
$$$$$
TEL 784/458-4621
FAX 784/456-4564; U.S. 212/696-4566 or 800/225-4255
There are about 50 sumptuous two- to seven-bedroom villa rentals on the island. All come with cook and maid.
ⓘ 50 villas 🏊 All major cards

🏨 ALMOND BEACH VILLAGE
$$$$$
HEYWOODS, ST. PETER
TEL 246/422-4900 or
800/425-6663
FAX 246/422-1581
E-MAIL vacation@iag.net
Large and attractively arranged all-inclusive property on a fine beach. Wide range of accommodations and facilities ranging from golf, water sports, tennis, and squash to well-designed children's programs.
ⓘ 288 P 🔆 🏊 📺 🏊 All major cards

🏨 COBBLERS COVE
$$$$$
SPEIGHTSTOWN, ST. PETER
TEL 246/422-2291 or
800/890-6060
FAX 246/422-1460
E-MAIL cobblers@caribsurf.com
Small and elegant Relais & Châteaux all-suite hotel. Lovely accommodations with balcony or terrace overlooking the tropical gardens, plus two fabulous luxury suites. Tennis, water sports, notable restaurant.
ⓘ 40 P 🔆 🏊 🏊 All major cards

🏨 SANDY LANE
$$$$$
PAYNE'S BAY, ST. JAMES
TEL 246/432-1311 or
800/233-3800
FAX 246/432-2954
Barbados' most famous and glamorous hotel is undergoing a massive redevelopment and scheduled to reopen sometime in the year 2000. Sybaritic luxury assured.
ⓘ 120 P 🔆 🏊 📺 🏊 All major cards

🏨 CORAL REEF CLUB
$$$$
HOLETOWN, ST. JAMES
TEL 246/422-2372 or
800/525-4800
FAX 246/422-1776
E-MAIL coral@caribnet.net
Gracious family-owned operation with a faithful clientele. Accommodations in attractive and thoughtfully appointed garden cottages and more luxurious suites. Lovely grounds, tennis, water sports, good food.
ⓘ 68 P 🔆 🏊 🏊 All major cards

🏨 CASURINA BEACH CLUB
$$$
ST. LAWRENCE GAP, CHRIST CHURCH
TEL 246/428-3600 or 800/550-6288 ext. 2210
FAX 246/428-1970
E-MAIL Casbeach@bajan.com
Mediterranean-style beachfront apartment hotel on palm-shaded grounds. Studios and one- and two-bedroom apartments with kitchens. Tennis, water sports, children's play area, activities, tours, entertainment.
ⓘ 158 P 🔆 🏊 🏊 All major cards

🏨 WOODVILLE BEACH HOTEL
$$
HASTINGS, CHRIST CHURCH
TEL 246/435-6694
FAX 435-9211
E-MAIL wdville@caribsurf.com
Large and comfortable studios, and one- and two-bedroom units with kitchenettes on the waterfront a couple of minutes' walk from Rockley Beach. Friendly family management.
ⓘ 49 P 🔆 Some 🏊 🏊 All major cards

🍴 BAGATELLE GREAT HOUSE
$$$$$
HWY. 2A, ST. THOMAS
TEL 246/421-6767
Gracious dining in a 17th-century coral stone plantation house. Light lunches and French-Caribbean specialties at dinner including Caribbean lobster, roast duck, and smoked dorado with fennel

and green peppercorns.
🕐 Closed L Sat.–Sun. 🚭All major cards

🍴 CARAMBOLA
$$$$$
DERRICKS, ST. JAMES
TEL 246/432-0832
Fabulous cliff top terrace setting (try for a moonlit night) and a dashing French-Asian-Caribbean menu. Gingered scallops in coconut-white wine sauce, spicy pork tenderloin, fresh Caribbean lobster. Reservations advised.
🕐 Closed L & all Sun. 🚭All major cards

🍴 THE CLIFF
$$$$$
DERRICKS, ST. JAMES
TEL 246/432-1922
A brace of theatrically lit terraces carved into the limestone sea cliffs and a glittering clientele poised to sample some of the finest cuisine in the region. Creative combinations such as lightly char-grilled tuna with coriander cream sauce; short but impressive wine list. Reservations.
🕐 Closed L 🚭All major cards

🍴 PISCES
$$$
ST. LAWRENCE GAP,
CHRIST CHURCH
TEL 246/435-6564
Pretty split-level dining room with trellises, clambering plants, and terra-cotta lanterns on the water's edge. Seafood specialties include shrimp and tomato stuffed snapper in a parsley-lime sauce or pasta and chicken.
🕐 Closed L 🚭All major cards

🍴 RAGAMUFFINS
$$$
1ST ST., HOLETOWN,
ST. JAMES
TEL 246/432-1295
Jaunty green and blue chattel house with a lively bar and cozy-casual atmosphere. West

Indian curries, blackened shrimp, grilled kingfish, T-bone steaks, and vegetarian options, plus delicious cocktails.
🕐 Closed L 🚭All major cards

🍴 WATERFRONT CAFÉ
$$
THE CAREENAGE,
BRIDGETOWN
TEL 246/427-0093
Handy downtown café on the south bank of The Careenage. Broad-ranging menu from Bajan fishcakes, smoked flying fish, and salads to jerk pork and pasta. Music from steel pan to Latin or jazz nightly.
🕐 Closed Sun. 🚭All major cards

🍴 ATLANTIS HOTEL
$
BATHSHEBA, ST. JOSEPH
TEL 246/433-9445
The set-price menu at the Atlantis Hotel is a lunchtime institution on the tourist circuit, and Sunday's West Indian buffet brunch (reservations) is a veritable feast. Cliff-top terrace and dining room.
🕐 Closed D Sun. 🚭All major cards

TRINIDAD & TOBAGO

TRINIDAD

🏨 ASA WRIGHT NATURE CENTRE
$$$$
ARIMA
TEL 868/667-4655 or
800/426-7781
FAX 868/667-4540
Simple lodgings at the famous rain forest nature center (see p. 325). Double and twin rooms with screened verandas in garden cottages, or two large rooms in the main building. All meals included; field trips extra.
🛏 25 🅿 🚭All major cards

🏨 MARACAS BAY
$$$
MARACAS BAY
TEL 868/669-1914
FAX 868/623-1444
A rare beach hotel on Trinidad's most famous strip of sand. Standard but spick-and-span motel-style rooms with two queen beds and balcony or patio overlooking the bay. Interconnecting rooms useful for families.
🛏 50 🅿 🚭 🚭All major cards

🏨 TRINIDAD HILTON
$$$
LADY YOUNG RD.,
PORT OF SPAIN
TEL 868/624-3211 or
800/445-8667
FAX 868/624-4485
E-MAIL hiltonpos@wow.net
A reliable international option on Queen's Park Savannah, the Hilton makes up for its somewhat bland profile with polished service and good facilities. Well-appointed rooms, tennis, restaurants, and entertainment.
🛏 394 🅿 🚭 🏊 🏋
🚭All major cards

🏨 KAPOK
$
16–18 COTTON HILL, ST. CLAIR,
PORT OF SPAIN
TEL 868/622-5765 or
800/74-CHARMS
FAX 868/622-9677
E-MAIL stay@kapok.co.tt
Pleasant businessmen's hotel on the northwest corner of Queen's Park Savannah. Comfortable rooms with tropical fabrics and wicker furnishings; good restaurant.
🛏 95 🅿 🚭 🏊 🏋
🚭All major cards

🍴 CHATEAU DE POISSON
$$$
38 ARIAPITA AVE. (AT CORNELIO), WOODBROOK,
PORT OF SPAIN
TEL 868/622-6087
Fine seafood restaurant in a lovely old gingerbread house.

🚭 Non-smoking 🚭 Air-conditioning 🏊 Indoor/🏊 Outdoor swimming pool 🏋 Health club 🚭 Credit cards   **KEY**

Specialties include lobster Thermidor, spicy crab, or the combination Neptune's platter with lobster, shrimp, and fish cooked with walnuts and white wine.
🕐 Closed Sun. 🅢 All major cards

🍴 SOLIMAR
$$$
6 NOOK AVE., ST. ANN'S, PORT OF SPAIN
TEL 868/624-6267
Pretty veranda setting with meandering greenery and a tasty international menu. Duck breast with couscous, crab ragout, spicy beef with lemon grass, swordfish gravlax with a saffron-mustard dressing. Reservations recommended.
🕐 Closed L & Sun.; & Mon. March–Nov. 🅢 All major cards

🍴 MONSOON
$
72 TRAGARETE RD., PORT OF SPAIN
TEL 868/628-7684
One of the best (and busiest) Indian eateries in town. A good place to sample chicken, prawn, or spiced conch rotis (generously stuffed unleavened bread parcels), curries, or more exotic offerings. Notable Wednesday night buffet.
🕐 Closed Sun. 🅢 All major cards

🍴 VENI MANGÉ
$
67A ARIAPITA AVE., WOODBROOK, PORT OF SPAIN
TEL 868/624-4597
Funky lunch spot run by local chat show hostess Allyson Hennessy and her sister Roses. Nouvelle Caribbean dining adds up to great soups, creative seafood, and vegetarian options such as black-eyed pea croquettes.
🕐 Closed D Thurs.–Tues., & Sat.–Sun. all day 🅢 All major cards

TOBAGO

🏨 COCO REEF RESORT
$$$$
COCONUT BAY
TEL 868/639-8571 or 800/221-1294
FAX 868/639-8574
Contemporary plantation-style elegance with a grand foyer opening onto a man-made beachfront lagoon. Rooms, suites, and villas with terra-cotta tiles and white wicker furnishings. Tennis, water sports, spa, golf nearby.
🛏 135 🅿 🔲 🏊 🛗
🅢 All major cards

SOMETHING SPECIAL

🏨 FOOTPRINTS ECO RESORT
Hammocks and solar-heated jacuzzis for latter-day Robinson Crusoes. Rooms, suites, and two-bedroom villas built of teak and recycled hardwoods, thatched, and perched on stilts like treehouses. Hiking, snorkeling, organic produce in the restaurant.
$$
CULLODEN BAY
TEL 868/660-0118 or 800/814-1396
FAX 868/660-0027
E-MAIL footprints@ trinidad.net
🛏 9 🅿 🔲 🏊
🅢 All major cards

🏨 KARIWAK VILLAGE
$$
CROWN POINT
TEL 868/639-8442
FAX 868/639-8441
E-MAIL kariwak@tstt.net.tt
A "holistic haven and hotel," Kariwak nurtures guests with yoga, relaxation sessions, massage, and healthy food. Accommodations in garden rooms or pool cabanas a 10-minute walk from the beach. Daily shuttle to Pigeon Point.
🛏 24 🅿 🔲 🏊 🅢 All major cards

🍴 ELEVEN DEGREES NORTH
$$$
STORE BAY RD., CROWN POINT
TEL 868/639-0996
Local art on the walls and Caribbean-Cajun-Mexican cuisine. Lots of fresh fish, the seafood enchiladas are a house specialty, plus grills and sinful desserts. Live music some evenings.
🕐 Closed L daily & Sun.–Mon. 🅢 All major cards

🍴 SHIRVAN WATERMILL
$$$
MOUNT PLEASANT
TEL 868/639-0000
Pretty circular pavilion framed by tropical plants by an old stone mill. Fish salad with tomato vinaigrette, seafood crêpe, grilled freshwater crayfish, char-broiled lamb with rosemary sauce.
🕐 L 🅢 All major cards

🍴 KARIWAK VILLAGE
$$
KARIWAK VILLAGE, CROWN POINT
TEL 868/639-8442
Al fresco dining in a nest of palm-thatched tiki huts. Home-cooking flavored with garden herbs. Seafood soup with cumin and basil, green fig (banana) salad with chives and parsley, scrumptious nutmeg ice cream. Buffet and band Friday and Saturday.
🅢 All major cards

🍴 OLD DONKEY CART
$$
73 BARCOLET ST., SCARBOROUGH
TEL 868/639-3551
Set in the charming garden of a century-old colonial home. Menu highlights include a squid and shrimp platter with coconut-garlic sauce, rib eye steak, and crêpes Suzette. European wines a specialty. Nine studio-apartments ($$).
🅢 All major cards

SHOPPING

JAMAICA

Jamaica offers something for everyone, from hand-rolled cigars to elaborate wood carvings or duty-free goods. The most popular buys from roadside stalls and crafts markets are wood carvings, T-shirts, hammocks, shell craft, straw hats, bamboo items, and alabaster sculptures.

High-quality souvenirs are also available through the government-sponsored **Things Jamaican** shops (in Kingston, Montego Bay airport, downtown Montego Bay, and elsewhere). Bargaining over the price (or "haggling") is the norm—never pay the first asking price. Avoid items made using "tortoiseshell" (from the endangered hawksbill turtle), black coral, or crocodile skins: Importing these into the United States is illegal.

Jamaica has a strong tradition of fine art, spanning many different contemporary forms. In Kingston try the **Bolivar Gallery** (1D Grove Rd., Tel 876/926-8799), the **Contemporary Art Center** (1 Liguance Ave., Tel 876/927-9958), the **Grosvenor Gallery** (1 Grosvenor Terrace, Tel 876/924-6684), or the **Chelsea Galleries** (12 Chelsea Ave., Tel 876/929-0045).

On the north coast, some of the major galleries include the **Sun Art Gallery** (Half Moon Shopping Village, Montego Bay, Tel 876/953-3455), **Harmony Hall Art Gallery** (Tower Isle, Ocho Rios, Tel 876/975-4222), or the **Bougainvillea Gallery** (West End, Negril, Tel 876/957-4109).

Duty-free or "in bond" shops carry items such as silverware, crystal, china, watches, jewelry, linens, and perfumes. Savings can be made, but check the purchase price at home before leaving. All goods must be paid for in U.S. currency; you will need your travel documents (airline/cruise ticket and identification). Alcohol and tobacco purchases are

delivered to airports/cruise ship piers before you leave.

Other things to look out for in Jamaica include red-hot reggae tapes or CDs; the famous Blue Mountain coffee; bodycare accessories such as lotions, soaps, and essential oils from the Blue Mountain Aromatics range; and rum-based liqueurs.

CAYMAN ISLANDS

On duty-free Grand Cayman discounts of between 20–50 percent on U.S. prices are promised, particularly on items such as linen, leather goods, designer clothes, crystal, porcelain, perfumes, watches, and camera equipment. Most shops are in Georgetown, but several malls have sprung up on the West Bay Road, including the **Westshore Center, Galleria Plaza, Coconut Place,** and **Cayman Falls Shopping Center.** In Georgetown itself, the **Anchorage Shopping Center, Duty Free Center,** and **Kirk Freeport Center** are some of the main outlets. (To avoid the cruise ship crowds, go on Fridays and Saturdays.) Grand Cayman also has some excellent diving equipment shops with a good range of the latest gear.

Local arts and crafts are worth seeking out in galleries such as **Pure Art** (S. Church St., Tel 345/949-9133) and **Island Art** (Treasure Island Resort, Tel 345/945-2606). Sea-salvaged coins from Spanish or Dutch treasure ships can be bought at **Artifacts** (Harbour Dr., Tel 345/949-2442), and similar numismatic items are also available at **24 K-Mon Jewelers** (several locations including Cayman Falls, Tel 345/945-7000).

For an unusual underwater souvenir, take home a stunning print by world famous underwater photographer Cathy Church (Sunset House, Tel 345/949-7415, and Coconut Place, Tel 345/945-5650).

The islands' biggest selling export item is rum cake. Made from a recipe reputedly over

100 years old, this cake features as its chief ingredient five-year-old Tortuga Gold rum. Buy it at any one of 14 outlets of the **Tortuga Rum Company** (Tel 800/444-0625, www.caribplace.com/foods/tortuga.htm).

TURKS & CAICOS ISLANDS

Most of the shops here are in small malls along the Leeward Highway on Providenciales, such as **Ports of Call, Arch Plaza, Central Square, Market Place,** and **Caicos Cafe Plaza.**

With no sales tax on the islands, you can buy duty-free goods such as jewelry, watches, perfumes, crystal, cameras, cigars, and liquor. Duty-free outlets include **Royal Jewels** (several locations), the **Gold Smith** (Central Sq.), **KoKo Tok** (Caicos Cafe Plaza), and **Carib West** (downtown, liquor and tobacco products only).

One of the island's best-known galleries, the **Bamboo Gallery** (Market Place), features paintings by local and Haitian artists, as well as beaded jewelry, wooden masks, ceramics, and soapstone and granite sculpture.

Other craft and art outlets include the **Pirate's Chest** (Ports of Call), the **Tourist Shoppe** (Central Sq.), and **Maison Creole** (next to Ports of Call). Good places to look for tropical clothing and swimwear include **Shalimar** (Central Square), **Island Sportique,** and the **Tattooed Parrot** (both at Ports of Call).

DOMINICAN REPUBLIC

Duty-free goods are available at outlets such as **Centro de Los Héroes** and **Las Ataranzas** in Santo Domingo, and your purchases will be delivered to the airport departure gate. One of the main shopping streets in Santo Domingo is **Calle el Conde,** now pedestrianized. Most major resorts have shops selling summer attire, T-shirts, and swimwear. Crafts can be found in the main

SHOPPING

markets in every town (the biggest is the **Mercado Model** on Ave. esquina Santomé in Santo Domingo), although the products tend to be production-line straw hats, wooden boxes, and animal sculptures. Naive Haitian art is also on sale almost everywhere. The Dominican Republic is a major producer of reasonably priced rum and cigars.

PUERTO RICO

Puerto Rico is not a duty-free island but has no sales tax (except on jewelry), and there is no duty on items taken back into the U.S., so you can find good prices on china, crystal, fashions, and crafts. All purchases are in US$. Old San Juan offers a huge variety of shops, especially for jewelry, leather, and clothes. (Retailers here include Tommy Hilfiger, Coach, Polo/Ralph Lauren, and London Fog.) There are also some fine art galleries.

Condado is known for its exclusive boutiques and fashion designer shops such as Louis Vuitton, Cartier, Mercier, Jacardi, La Favorita, and Oggetti.

In the heart of the San Juan metropolitan area is **Plaza Las Americas,** the largest shopping center in the Caribbean, with over 190 stores. **Sears** and **J.C. Penney** are the mall's anchor stores, and both are more upscale than their mainland counterparts. Other retailers here include Armani Exchange, Banana Republic, Gap, and Caché.

Popular souvenirs include *santos* (small carved figures of the saints), carnival masks, and *mundillo*, an intricate handmade bobbin lace. Fine hammocks are also still made here, and, of course, Puerto Rico is a major producer of rum and cigars.

U.S. VIRGIN ISLANDS

ST. CROIX

Downtown **Christiansted** offers the best shopping on the island, centered on Strand, King,

and Company Streets, and King's Alley Walk. The walk offers boutiques and galleries, craft stalls selling coconut shell carvings, and jewelry stores. The **Caribbean Bracelet Company** specializes in Cruzan Hook bracelets: You wear the hook facing your heart if it is taken, away from the heart if you are available.

On Strand Street, **Folk Art Traders** is packed with Caribbean arts and crafts, hand-painted local pottery, costume dolls, amber and coin jewelry, and Carib basketware from the Windward Islands.

Frederiksted's main shopping district is clustered around the cruise ship pier, where local artist Joffre George sells his colorful paintings and prints at **Island We Be.**

You can watch artists at work in the St. Croix LEAP woodwork studio on Mahogany Road (Rte. 76), north of Frederiksted, and buy carvings made from island hardwoods. The **Whim Museum** gift shop has a good range of local crafts, condiments, books, and maps.

ST. JOHN

Shopping in St. John is a low-key event. There are a couple of small boutiques and jewelers in **Wharfside Village,** close to the ferry dock. For a greater selection, head to **Mongoose Junction** (North Shore Rd.), a two-story open-air complex in the local plantation house style. **R. I. Patton Goldsmithing** sell Rudy and Irene's island-inspired designs in 14- to 18-carat gold and sterling silver, as well as authenticated antique Spanish coins set in rings and pendants. **Big Planet Adventurer Outfitters** can outfit hikers and offers colorful swimwear and resortwear for all ages. **Fabric Mill** specializes in table and bed linens, batik, and hand-painted cotton T-shirts and sweaters in fabulous aquamarines and sunset oranges by local designer Sloop Jones.

ST. THOMAS

U.S. visitors can take advantage of a $1,200 duty-free allowance on returning home, and a further $1,000 worth of purchases at 5 percent duty. Any items actually made in the USVI do not count toward the duty-free exemption. Popular buys are fine crystal and china, electronics, jewelry, and perfume, sold in large stores on Dronningens Gade/Main Street and the Havensight Mall in Charlotte Amalie. A slew of boutiques is tucked in the narrow alleys leading down to the Waterfront Highway. In Hibiscus Alley, **Local Colour** does a fun line in pretty Jams World uncrushable sundresses and other cotton prints, straw hats, hand-painted T-shirts, and silver jewelry.

On Trompeter Gade, **Mini Mouse House** is a terrific toy store full of tricks, jokes, and educational games. For great swimwear, **Just Add Water,** in Royal Dane Mall, stocks a huge range of Jantzen, Mossimi, the Solar tan-thru range, and hip Black Flys sunglasses. For great Caribbean crafts and souvenirs, check out **Down Island Traders** on Post Office Alley.

Outside Charlotte Amalie, **Tillet Gardens** is an artisans' enclave with galleries, craft studios, a restaurant, and pet iguanas basking in the shade. At American Yacht Harbor in Red Hook, **Color of Joy** carries souvenirs, crafts, and hand-painted garments by Sloop Jones of St. John.

BRITISH VIRGIN ISLANDS

TORTOLA

Road Town's top souvenir stop has to be the **Sunny Caribbee Spice Co.** on Main Street. This is condiment city, piled high with exotic fruit teas and liqueurs, preserves made from guava, papaya, and passionfruit, tamarind chutney, jerk seasonings, love potions, and hangover cures. The art gallery next door showcases Caribbean paintings, affordable prints, Haitian voodoo flags, and pottery. You can purchase Pusser's rum and yachting-style casualwear at **Pusser's Company Store;** or T-shirts and other small souvenirs at the colorful pastel-painted stalls behind the waterfront.

Shopaholics will also find assorted boutiques and souvenir outlets at the **Soper's Hole Marina** in the West End.

NETHERLANDS ANTILLES & ARUBA

ARUBA

Duty-free bargain hunters will find most of the big stores in the **Wharfside Mall** and **Seaport Mall Marketplace,** also along the main street, Caya G.F. Croes. China, linens, electronic goods, perfumes, and designer clothes are all good buys at around 20–30 percent below U.S. prices, and U.S. visitors can enjoy a $600 duty-free exemption when they return home.

Jewelry is a popular buy, and **Gandelmen Jewelers** outlets around town stock precious and semi-precious jewelry items, designer watches, Montblanc pens, Baccarat crystal, china, and leather accessories.

For arts and crafts, check out the **Bon Bini Festival** at Fort Zoutman every Tuesday evening, and Thursday evening's Watapana **"One Cool Festival"** market in front of the Parliament building (May–Oct.).

CURAÇAO

Willemstad offers good deals on perfume, jewelry, china, cameras, and electronic goods. The major stores and boutiques are crowded into the Punda district around Breedestraat. On the Otrabanda side, by the cruise terminal, is **Arawak Crafts Products,** which has a ceramics factory producing

anything from cute miniature town houses and *landhuizen* to dinner sets with cactus motifs and Delft blue tiles.

Just across the street is **Kas Di Alma Blou** (the Blue House), which showcases local artwork, photographs, and a few antique maps and prints.

SABA

Mary Gertrude Johnson introduced the art of drawn threadwork, or Saban lace, to the island in the 1870s. Taught by convent nuns in Caracas, Venezuela, she passed on her knowledge and founded a cottage industry, which still survives today. Intricately embroidered linen tableware is sold in several **Windwardside** craft shops. Another local specialty is Saba Spice, a 75.5-proof rum flavored with cinnamon, cloves, nutmeg, orange peel, and brown sugar.

SINT MAARTEN/ ST.- MARTIN

Both Dutch and French sides of the island offer duty-free shopping and deals worth 25–50 percent on perfumes, electronic goods, jewelry, china, crystal, linen, and fashions.

Philipburg's **Front Street** shopping district boasts the widest array of goods, and two interesting specialist shops. The **Dutch Delft Blue Gallery** imports blue and white Delftware, and also rare green and Japanese Imari-style Delft designs from Holland.

Greenwith Galleries (20 Front St.) has etchings by island-born Roland Richardson, photographs by Sarah Muenden, and vibrant prints of local scenes by the Lynn family among others.

Marigot is the island's fashion capital. The small mall by the marina is brimful with boutiques selling designer fashions; or for the high priests of the fashion scene, including Dior, Gaultier, Gallino and Lacroix, brave the glacial

assistants and faux Roman ruins décor of **Act III** (3 rue du Général de Gaulle).

Tucked away in an unmarked alley near the entrance to the marina is an outpost of **Hédiard,** the famous Parisian delicatessen, well-stocked with foie gras, fine wines, caviar, and confits. Around the dock, **Gingerbread Mahogany** is one of the best Haitian art galleries in the Caribbean.

LEEWARD ISLANDS

ANGUILLA

Black-belt shopaholics may suffer withdrawal symptoms on Anguilla. However, it does offer a couple of interesting arts and crafts outlets. The **Savannah Gallery** in The Valley specializes in Haitian paintings, tin carvings, and fabulous sequined voodoo flags. Also works by local photographer Suzy Doyle Webster and artist Jo Ann Hill Saunders.

On the main road west of The Valley, look for **Cheddie's Carving Studio,** where Cheddie Richardson exhibits his driftwood sculptures and limited edition bronzes.

ANTIGUA

Downtown **St. John's** is Antigua's chief shopping district. **Heritage Quay** is packed with duty-free stores selling jewelry, designer fashions, perfumes, and gifts. On **Redcliffe Quay, BASE** is well known for cool, understated women's fashions; Hans Smit sells his innovative and temptingly affordable jewelry at **Goldsmitty;** and **Kate Design,** in a shady square marked by signs off the main drag, is a showcase for St. Kitts-based artist Kate Spencer's limited edition prints, greeting cards, table mats, and T-shirts, as well as a small line of stunning printed silk scarves and shirts.

Outside St. John's, **Harmony Hall** on the east coast is a great place to check out local arts and crafts (see pp. 54–55). Also tiny **Seahorse Studios Art Gallery and Gift Shop** at Falmouth Harbour, which overflows with prints, pottery, and hand-painted batik items.

ST. KITTS

The **Caribelle Batik factory** at Old Road Town is a favorite stop on the St. Kitts shopping trail; also the **Plantation Picture House,** painter Kate Spencer's gallery-cum-studio at the Rawlins Plantation Inn in Mount Pleasant. **Island Hopper,** on The Circus in downtown Basseterre, stocks colorful beachwear and souvenirs. Down Bank Street, Kate Spencer strikes again with **Kate Design,** and a collection of prints and greeting cards of local scenes, as well as lovely printed silks.

On Independence Square at the **Spencer Cameron Gallery** you'll find both originals and prints, from Gloria Lynn's market ladies and Donald Dahlke's fishwives to Rosie Cameron Smith's carnival dancers and tropical fruits.

Glass Island (4–5 Princes St.) is chock-full of fused glass plates, picture frames, Christmas tree decorations, and colored glass earrings with silver fittings.

NEVIS

Charlestown's restored waterfront district boasts a few small boutiques and souvenir outlets, as does the Cotton Ginnery building nearby. **Island Hopper,** on Main Street, carries Caribelle Batik's bright, casual clothing from St. Kitts. Its big Hawaiian-style shirts, blouses, wraparound skirts, and beachwear are adorned with prints of hibiscus flowers, vervet monkeys, and other local devices.
St. Kitts artist Kate Spencer's watercolor prints, silk scarves, and Caribbean-style table accessories are on sale at **Kate Design** (near the junction with Government Road).

Stamp collectors can capture a little local color at the **Nevis Philatelic Bureau,** in the alley between the ferry berth and Main Street.

FRENCH
ANTILLES

GUADELOUPE

Shopping is not a high priority in Guadeloupe, though French luxury goods at mainland prices can be tempting. Some **Pointe-à-Pitre** stores offer an extra 20 percent discount on purchases made with a credit card or traveler's checks.

The capital's main shopping streets are **rue Frébault, rue Schoelcher,** and **rue de Noziers,** and there are small, upscale boutiques in the **Centre St.-John Perse** mall by the cruise-ship terminal.

Rum is available from supermarkets, the airport duty-free, or the Musée du Rhum in Bellevue. In St. François, **Artisans Caraïbes,** avenue de l'Europe, specializes in Caribbean arts and crafts; and costume dolls dressed in bright Madras cotton can be found at **Mariposa,** Galerie du Port.

MARTINIQUE

Fort-de-France is the style capital of the French Antilles, offering French luxury goods from designer fashions and perfumes to china and glass at prices lower than in mainland France. Some stores give an additional 20 percent discount for purchases made with U.S. traveler's checks (always ask).

The best selection of boutiques is found along **rue Victor Hugo** and the grid of streets between **rue de la République** and **rue de la Liberté. Cadet Daniel** (72 rue Antoine Siger) is an excellent hunting ground for Baccarat crystal, Limoges porcelain, and jewelry including the *chaîne forçat,* a gold "slave chain" necklace that puts the

finishing touch to traditional Creole costume. Madras cotton traditional costumes and frilly white shirts are sold at market stalls in most towns.

Martiniquan rum is among the Caribbean's finest, and the island's basketware, pottery, shell art and patchwork can be found at the **Centre des Métiers d'Art,** rue Ernest Deproge.

ST.- BARTHÈLEMY

St. Barts' duty-free status is a good excuse to indulge in some seriously upscale retail therapy. Cartier, Gucci, and Hermès all maintain outposts in **Gustavia,** alongside duty-free emporiums such as **Carat,** on rue de la République, **Little Switzerland,** on rue de la France, and **Oro de Sol** at Le Carré d'Or, quai de la République. French perfumes and cosmetics, jewelry, watches, and crystal are all popular buys.

Wine buffs can check out the selection at **Cellier du Gouverneur,** quai de la République.

For the best French and Italian designer fashions, try **Stéphane Bernard,** rue de la République. **Villa Créole mall** in St. Jean has more boutiques, and **La Boutique Made** in St.-Bart carries souvenir T-shirts, paintings, and handcrafted works of art produced on the island.

WINDWARD ISLANDS

DOMINICA

The island's Carib craftsmen are famous for their basketware made from larouma reeds. The intricate designs are fashioned in a combination of natural, brown, and black, and can be bought from roadside stalls in **Carib Territory,** or from one of Roseau's many crafts shops such as **Tropicrafts,** on the corner of Queen Mary Street and Turkey Lane.

Hand-painted souvenirs from clothing to picture frames adorned with parrot, butterfly, and tropical flower motifs can be found at the **Rainforest Shop** (17 Old St.). **Caribana** (31 Cork St.) exhibits Dominica's leading artists in the **Iris Dangleben Gallery**. Names to look out for include Darius David and Arnold Toulon (painters) and Carl Winston (woodcarver). U.S. expatriate artist Loye Barnard operates a small gallery at **Petit Coulibri Guest Cottages,** 2 miles (3 km) inland from Soufrière.

GRENADA & CARRIACOU

Spices are a great buy on Grenada. Mixed baskets of nutmeg, cinnamon, cloves, and bay rum leaves make great gifts for cooks, or as souvenir potpourri.

Carenage boasts several small galleries and craft shops. On Young Street, check out **Yellow Poui Art Galleries** for local art, photography, crafts, and antique map prints. In the **Art Fabrik** boutique you can see the batik process in the factory.

On **Carriacou,** buyers and visitors are welcome at Mr. Canute Calliste's tiny studio in the village of L'Esterre. One of the Caribbean's most famous artists, Calliste's jaunty naive-style island scenes and folklore-related works are sold and exhibited worldwide. The local tourist office will check whether he is home.

ST. LUCIA

The waterfront **Castries craft market,** and the vendors' market across the street, offer T-shirts, hand-woven straw goods, local pottery, and woodcarvings.

Another mini magnet for shoppers is the attractive open-air mall at **Pointe Seraphine.** Among the duty-free stores and boutiques, **St. Lucia Fine Art** sells antique prints of Caribbean flora and fauna and works by contemporary local artists including Llewellyn Xavier (studio visits by arrangement with the gallery). Local cottage industries include **Bagshaw Studios,** which sells their colorful hand-printed clothing and tableware in Pointe Seraphine, and from a factory shop at La Toc, just outside Castries.

On Morne Fortune, **Eudovic's Studio** specializes in woodcarvings. **Made In St. Lucia** showcases island products in the Gablewoods Mall (on the road to Rodney Bay), where **Sunshine Books** features West Indian literature and works by St. Lucian Nobel Prize winner Derek Walcott.

At Victoria in the south, the **Livity Art Studio** is crammed with local earthenware pottery, woodcarvings, and shell jewelry; also the **Arts and Crafts Development Centre** at La Fargue Choiseul (see p. 281).

ST. VINCENT & THE GRENADINES

There is duty-free shopping at the new cruise berth in Kingstown, and a selection of Caribbean crafts, spices, and souvenirs can be found at **Noah's Arkade** on Bay Street. The **Artisans Local Art Craft** store on the second floor of the Bonadie Building, Bay Street, offers a selection of craft items fashioned from straw, banana leaves, and coconuts, and hand-painted and tie-dye clothing.

On Bequia, there is an outpost of **Noah's Arkade** at the Frangipani Hotel. The **waterfront craft market** sells beachwraps, T-shirts, and bead jewelry, or check out the souvenir offerings, bright beachwear, cards, prints, and small selection of sterling silver jewelry at **Local Color.**

Bridgetown is a duty-free port offering savings of up to 30–50 percent off European and U.S. retail prices. The best of the tax-free action is on Broad Street, where the **Cave Shepherd, Harrisons department stores,** and the **Da Costas Mall** offer the widest selection of jewelry and watches, cameras, electronic goods, china, crystal, perfumes, and cosmetics. To make a duty-free purchase, take the immigration slip issued on arrival in Barbados; most stores will deliver to the airport or hotel.

For Caribbean crafts and island fashions, check out the colorful **Chattel Village** shopping complexes in Holetown and St. Lawrence Gap. Holetown also boasts the **Da Costas Mall West,** and **Daphne's Sea Shell Studio** (2nd St.), a popular stop for shell art and other souvenir items.

On the south coast, shoppers head for **Hastings Plaza** and the **Quayside Centre** in Rockley. The **Best of Barbados** boutiques around the island are a good source of quality local crafts and gifts.

The lower end of **Frederick Street** in downtown Port of Spain resembles a hectic international bazaar. Indian sari shops and boutiques spill out onto the sidewalk, street vendors hawk jewelry, leather goods, and the latest calypso, soca, and chutney tapes and CDs, and **Selection House,** on the corner of Woodford Square, stocks souvenirs and kitsch from costume dolls and mini steel pans to crafts and beachwear.

For a more upscale shopping experience, take a trip to the **Ellerslie Court shopping center** in Maraval, and the **Market,** a mall with boutiques, galleries and craft shops attached to the Normandie Hotel on Nook Avenue, St. Ann.

Tobago is somewhat limited on the shopping front. The miniature shopping village at **Store Bay** offers a colorful array of batik and tie-dye beachwear, T-shirts, straw hats, bead jewelry, pottery, and other island crafts. The **Art Gallery**, at Lowlands (on the Crown Point to Scarborough road), sells works by local artists.

ILLUSTRATIONS CREDITS

Cover (tl), (br), (spine), Pictor International, London; (tr), James Davis Travel Photography; (bl), Image Bank.

1, Corbis/Stephen Frink. 2/3, Corbis/Amos Nachoum. 4, Tony Stone Images. 9, Catherine Karnow. 11, Corbis/ Amos Nachoum. 12/3, Catherine Karnow. 14, Catherine Karnow. 15, Catherine Karnow. 17, Adam Woolfitt. 18, Black River Productions Ltd/ Mitch Epstein. 19, Catherine Karnow. 20/1, David Harvey/NGS Image Collection. 23, Image Bank. 27, World Pictures. 28, Robert Harding Picture Library. 29, AA Photo Library/J Wyand. 30/1, World Pictures. 31, AA Photo Library/J Wyand. 32/3, AA Photo Library/J Wyand. 33, AA Photo Library/J Wyand. 34/5, AA Photo Library/J Wyand. 35, AA Photo Library/J Wyand. 36, Robert Harding Picture Library. 37, AA Photo Library/R Wyand. 38, AA Photo Library/R Victor. 39, World Pictures. 40/1, World Pictures. 42, Pictures Colour Library. 43, AA Photo Library/J Wyand. 44, AA Photo Library/J Wyand. 45, AA Photo Library/J Wyand. 46/7, Images Colour Library. 47, World Pictures. 48, AA Photo Library/J Wyand. 49, AA Photo Library/R Victor. 50/1, Nick Hanna. 53(t), Rex Features Ltd. 53(c), World Pictures. 53(b), AA Photo Library/P Baker. 54, Nick Hanna. 54/5, Pictures Colour Library. 55, AA Photo Library/J Wyand. 56/7, Dr. Nicholas J Saunders. 57, AA Photo Library/J Wyand. 58, AA Photo Library/R Victor. 59(t), AA Photo Library/J Wyand. 59(c), AA Photo Library/J Wyand. 59(b), AA Photo Library/J Wyand. 60, Images Colour Library. 61, AA Photo Library/J Wyand. 62, Nick Hanna. 62/3, Nick Hanna. 64, AA Photo Library/J Wyand. 65, Corbis/Stephen Frink. 68/9, Robert Harding Picture Library. 69, Planet Earth/Kurt Amsler. 70, Nick Hanna. 70/1, Jeff Rotman/BBC Natural History Unit. 72/3, Catherine Karnow. 74, Jürgen Freund/BBC Natural History Unit. 75, Jeff Foott/BBC Natural History Unit. 79, Corbis/Bob Krist. 81, Nick Hanna. 82/3, Nick Hanna. 83, Nick Hanna. 84, Travel Ink/Nigel Bowen-Morris. 88/9, Nick Hanna. 89, Bruce Coleman Collection. 86/7, Bruce Coleman Collection. 90/1, Nick Hanna. 91, Nick Hanna. 92/3, Pete Bennett/Bennett Worldwide Productions. 93(t), Ardea,

London/R & V Taylor. 93(b), Jürgen Freund/BBC Natural History Unit. 94, Corbis/Galen Rowell. 95, World Pictures. 98, Nick Hanna. 99, Nick Hanna. 100, Pictor International, London. 101, Pictor International, London. 102(t), Robert Harding Picture Library. 102(b), Pictor International, London. 103, Image Bank. 104, Nick Hanna. 105, Rosine Mazin/ DIAF. 106, Nick Hanna. 107, Yyan Travert/DIAF. 108/9, Black River Productions Ltd/Mitch Epstein. 110/1, Pictor International, London. 111, Pictures Colour Library. 112, Pictures Colour Library. 113(t), World Pictures. 113(b), World Pictures. 114, Yyan Travert/DIAF. 115, World Pictures. 117, Corbis/Adam Woolfitt. 118, Nick Hanna. 119, Gerry Ellis/BBC Natural History Unit. 120/1, Nick Hanna. 121, Amber Museum, 122, Pictor International, London. 123, Nick Hanna. 124, Gerry Ellis/ BBC Natural History Unit. 125, World Pictures. 128, AA Photo Library/D Lyons. 129, World Pictures. 130, AA Photo Library/D Lyons. 131, AA Photo Library/D Lyons. 132, Nick Hanna. 134, Bruce Coleman Collection. 134/5, Pictures Colour Library. 137, Corbis/Neil Rabinowitz. 138, Nick Hanna. 138/9, World Pictures. 140, Museo de Arte, Ponce/Bridgeman Art Library. 141, World Pictures. 142(t), Nick Hanna. 142(b), Nick Hanna. 143, Nick Hanna. 144/5, David Boyer/NGS Image Collection. 145, Pictures Colour Library. 146/7, David Parker/Science Photo Library. 147, Corbis/Roger Ressmeyer. 148, Bruce Coleman Collection. 149, Image Bank. 152/3, Corbis/Amos Nachoum. 153, AA Photo Library/P Baker. 154, World Pictures. 155, World Pictures. 156(t), World Pictures. 156(b), AA Photo Library/P Baker. 157, Pictures Colour Library. 159, Pictures Colour Library. 161(t), AA Photo Library/D Lyons. 161(c), AA Photo Library/D Lyons. 161(b), Pictures Colour Library. 162/3, Pictures Colour Library. 163, AA Photo Library/P Baker. 164/5, Pictures Colour Library. 166, Pictures Colour Library. 167, Pictures Colour Library. 168, Pictures Colour Library. 169, Pictures Colour Library. 170/1, Image Bank. 171, World Pictures. 172/3, Image Bank. 173, Emma Stanford. 174/5, Image Bank. 175, Image Bank. 177, Image Bank. 181(t), Robert Harding Picture Library. 181(b), Pictures Colour Library. 182, AA Photo Library/P

Baker. 183, Pictures Colour Library. 185, Black River Productions Ltd/Mitch Epstein. 186, Image Bank. 186/7, Gerry Ellis/BBC Natural History Unit. 188, Travel Ink/Abbie Enock. 188/9, Planet Earth/Norbert Wu. 190, Robert Harding Picture Library. 191, Image Bank. 192/3, Black River Productions Ltd/Mitch Epstein. 194, Corbis/ Stephen Frick. 194/5, Black River Productions Ltd/Mitch Epstein. 196, Lawson Wood. 197, Pictor International, London. 198, World Pictures. 200/1, Pictures Colour Library. 201, World Pictures. 202, Pictures Colour Library. 203, Catherine Karnow. 204, Catherine Karnow. 206, Image Bank. 207, Image Bank. 208, Pictures Colour Library. 209, World Pictures. 210, AA Photo Library/P Baker. 211, Images Colour Library. 212, Robert Harding Picture Library. 214/5, World Pictures. 216/7, Catherine Karnow. 218, Pictures Colour Library. 219, Pictures Colour Library. 220/1, Catherine Karnow. 222, Catherine Karnow. 223, Catherine Karnow. 224, Travel Ink/Abbie Enock. 224/5, Catherine Karnow. 226/7, John Miller. 228, Robert Harding Picture Library. 229, Pictor International, London. 231, Image Bank. 232, Tony Stone Images. 234, Black River Productions Ltd/Mitch Epstein. 236, World Pictures. 237, Pictures Colour Library. 238/9, Image Bank. 239, Pictor International, London. 241, World Pictures. 242, Corbis/Marc Garanger. 244(t), AA Photo Library/P Baker. 244(b), AA Photo Library/P Baker. 245, AA Photo Library/P Baker. 246/7, Image Bank. 248, E. T. Archive. 249(t), E. T. Archive. 249(b), E. T. Archive. 250/1, Robert Harding Picture Library. 251, Emma Stanford. 252/3, Robert Harding Picture Library. 254, Pictures Colour Library. 255, Catherine Karnow. 257, World Pictures. 258, Robert Harding Picture Library. 259, World Pictures. 261(t), AA Photo Library/Malcolm Birkitt. 261(c), AA Photo Library/P Baker. 261(b), AA Photo Library/P Baker. 262, World Pictures. 263, Pictures Colour Library. 265, Michael Melford/NGS Image Collection. 266, Michael Melford/NGS Image Collection. 269, Michael Melford/NGS Image Collection. 271, Pictor International, London. 272/3, World Pictures. 273, Michael Melford/NGS Image Collection. 274, Robert Harding Picture Library. 276, Bruce Coleman Collection. 276/7, Joel Sartoren/NGS Image

Collection. 278/9, AA Photo Library/P Baker. 279, Joel Sartoren/NGS Image Collection. 281, Black River Productions Ltd/Mitch Epstein. 282, Catherine Karnow. 283, World Pictures. 284, Pictures Colour Library. 285, Robert Harding Picture Library. 286, AA Photo Library/P Baker. 287, AA Photo Library/P Baker. 288, Catherine Karnow. 288/9, Catherine Karnow. 290(t), Catherine Karnow. 290(b), Catherine Karnow. 291, Catherine Karnow. 292, John Miller. 293, Catherine Karnow. 294, World Pictures. 295, Catherine Karnow. 297, Nick Hanna. 298/9, Black River Productions Ltd/Mitch Epstein. 301, World Pictures. 304, World Pictures. 304/5, Pictures Colour Library. 306, Tony Stone Images. 306/7, World Pictures. 309(t), Black River Productions Ltd/Mitch Epstein. 309(b), E. T. Archive. 310, Sunbury House. 311, Robert Harding Picture Library. 312(t), AA Photo Library/ P Baker. 312(b), Catherine Karnow. 313(t), Robert Harding Picture Library. 313(b), AA Photo Library/ R Victor. 314, World Pictures. 314/5, Images Colour Library. 317, Allsport UK Ltd/ Shaun Botteril. 320, David Harvey/NGS Image Collection. 321, Tony Stone Images. 322, Allsport UK Ltd/Clive Mason. 323(t), Allsport UK Ltd/Clive Mason. 323(b), Catherine Karnow. 324/5, Catherine Karnow. 325, Catherine Karnow. 326, Catherine Karnow. 326/7, Tony Stone Images. 328, David Harvey/NGS Image Collection. 329, Robert Harding Picture Library. 331, AA Photo Library/P Baker. 332, Images Colour Library. 332.3, World Pictures. 334, AA Photo Library/P Baker. 335, Images Colour Library.

Published by the National Geographic Society
John M. Fahey, Jr., *President and Chief Executive Officer*
Gilbert M. Grosvenor, *Chairman of the Board*
Nina D. Hoffman, *Senior Vice President*
William R. Gray, *Vice President and Director, Book Division*
David Griffin, *Design Director*
Elizabeth L. Newhouse, *Director of Travel Publishing*
Barbara A. Noe, *Associate Editor*
Caroline Hickey, *Senior Researcher*
Carl Mehler, *Director of Maps*
Joseph F. Ochlak, *Map Coordinator*
Carolinda E. Averitt, Carol Bittig Lutyk, Lise Sajewski, *Editorial Consultants*
Gary Colbert, *Production Director*
Ric Wain, *Production Project Manager*
DeShelle Downey, *Staff Assistant*

Edited and designed by AA Publishing (a trading name of Automobile Association Developments Limited, whose registered office is Norfolk House, Priestley Road, Basingstoke, Hampshire, England RG24 9NY. Registered number: 1878835).
Betty Sheldrick, *Project Manager*
David Austin, *Senior Art Editor*
Amy Jenkins, Ian Morgan, Rebecca Snelling, *Editors*
Phil Barfoot, *Designer*
Simon Mumford, *Senior Cartographic Editor*
Helen Beever, Dawn Cameron, *Cartographers*
Richard Firth, *Production Director*
Steve Gilchrist, *Prepress Production Controller*
Carol Walker, *Picture Research*
Area maps drawn by Chris Orr Associates, Southampton, England
Cutaway illustrations drawn by Maltings Partnership, Derby, England

Library of Congress Cataloging-in-Publication Data
Hannah, Nick.
    The National Geographic traveler. The Caribbean / Nick Hannah & Emma Stanford.
        p.   cm.
    Includes index.
    ISBN 0-7922-7434-2
    1. West Indies—Guidebooks. 2. West Indies—Description and travel.
    3. Caribbean Area—Guidebooks.
    I. Stanford, Emma. II. Title. III. Title: Caribbean.
    F1613.H36 1999
    917.2904'52—dc21   99-44267
                                       CIP

Printed and bound by R.R. Donnelley & Sons, Willard, Ohio.
Color separations by Leo Reprographic Ltd., Hong Kong
Cover separations by L.C. Repro, Aldermaston, U.K.
Cover printed by Miken Inc., Cheektowage, New York.

Visit the society's Web site at http://www.nationalgeographic.com

THE NATIONAL
GEOGRAPHIC TRAVELER

A Century of Travel Expertise in Every Guide

- **Australia** ISBN: 0-7922-7431-8
- **Canada** ISBN: 0-7922-7427-X
- **The Caribbean** ISBN: 0-7922-7434-2
- **Florida** ISBN: 0-7922-7432-6
- **France** ISBN: 0-7922-7426-1
- **Great Britain** ISBN: 0-7922-7425-3
- **London** ISBN: 0-7922-7428-8
- **Miami and the Keys** ISBN: 0-7922-7433-4
- **New York** ISBN: 0-7922-7430-X
- **Paris** ISBN: 0-7922-7429-6
- **Sydney** ISBN: 0-7922-7435-0